There Are Two
Errors In the
the Title of
This Book

There Are Two Errors In the the Title of This Book

a sourcebook of philosophical puzzles, problems, and paradoxes

REVISED AND EXPANDED

Robert M. Martin

broadview press

National Library of Canada Cataloguing in Publication Data

Martin, Robert M.
  There are two errors in the the title of this book: a sourcebook of philosophical puzzles, problems, and paradoxes

Revised and expanded
Includes bibliographical references.
ISBN 1-55111-493-3

  1. Paradoxes. 2. Semantics (Philosophy) 3. Reasoning. I. Title.

BC199.P2M37 2002   165   C2001-904188-8

Broadview Press Ltd. is an independent, international publishing house, incorporated in 1985.

North America:
P.O. Box 1243, Peterborough, Ontario, Canada K9J 7H5
3576 California Road, Orchard Park, NY 14127
Tel: (705) 743-8990; Fax: (705) 743-8353
E-mail: customerservice@broadviewpress.com

United Kingdom and Europe:
NBN Plymbridge.
Estover Road, Plymouth pl6 7py, UK
Tel: 44(0) 1752 202301; Fax: 44 (0) 1752 202331
Fax order line: 44 (0) 1752 202333
Cust. service: cservs@nbnplymbridge.com
Orders: orders@nbnplymbridge.com

Australia & New Zealand
UNIREPS University of New South Wales, Sydney, NSW 2052
Tel: 61 2 9664099; Fax: 61 2 9664520
E-mail: infopress@unsw.edu.au

www.broadviewpress.com

Broadview Press gratefully acknowledges the financial support of the Book Publishing Industry Development Program, Ministry of Canadian Heritage, Government of Canada.

PRINTED IN CANADA

CONTENTS

ACKNOWLEDGEMENTS

The items in this book have three sources:

(1) Some were invented by me
(2) Others were thought up by other philosophers
(3) Some are part of the folklore of the philosophy profession, or of the general tradition of jokes, puzzles, and aphorisms.

I have tried to footnote those in the second category to give their inventor or promulgator credit. But sometimes the philosophical ideas wind up in the third category: they are passed from person to person, and their origin becomes obscure. There are lots of little quotations in here that I've bumped into in various places (especially on the Internet), where they've been given only partial attribution or none at all. It's often impossible, or not worth the enormous effort even if possible, to track down their sources. So I will be forgiven, I hope, for sometimes omitting crediting footnote.

For their ideas and encouragement I offer my grateful thanks to Shelagh Ross, Joan Mahoney, Charles Anderson, Ted Cohen, Mark Phillips, David C. Selley, Sheldon Wein, Sharon Kaye, Michael Hymers, Victoria McGeer, Duncan MacIntosh, Roland Puccetti, Richmond Campbell, Ed Mares, Nathan Brett, and Terry Tomkow; also to George J. Martin, and to the participants in the Sunday Forum, Heritage Village, Southbury, Connecticut; and also to numerous readers of the first edition who wrote me comments, corrections, arguments, and appreciation.

These days it seems that publishers consider for publication only those manuscripts that are almost exactly like dozens of books already selling well. Don LePan, president of Broadview Press, is an exception to this rule. I offer him my gratitude for his courage in publishing this odd work, for his helpfulness while it was in preparation, and for his persuasiveness in getting me to prepare a second, enlarged edition.

ABOUT THIS BOOK

Question: What do you get when you cross the
Godfather with a philosopher?
Answer: An offer you can't understand.

"An ounce of pretension is worth a pound of ma-
nure." — Anonymous

Philosophical writing is always ponderous, pompous, tedious, technical, obscure, and grimly serious, right? Wrong.

Actually, philosophy is fun. It's interesting. It answers question you've always wondered about and raises questions you've never thought of. It tickles your imagination and your funny-bone, and expands your mind. This book is designed to prove all that to you.

Philosophy starts when something goes wrong. Sometimes perfectly ordinary things seem inexplicable when you start to think about them. Sometimes perfectly reasonable assumptions lead, by perfectly acceptable reasoning, to bizarre and unbelievable conclusions. Sometimes ordinary ideas are put together in a new way, and something surprising emerges.

"The point of philosophy is to start with something so simple as to seem not worth stating, and
to end with something so paradoxical that no one
will believe it." — Bertrand Russell[1]

So this book is full of puzzles—that's where philosophy begins. But that's not where it ends. Some students get the mistaken and discouraging idea that the subject contains only unanswerable questions, and wonder what the point is. This idea is wrong. We'll look at the beginnings, at least, of some very good, surprising, interesting answers.

You'll notice that some paragraphs in this book
are written in this contrasting type style. In these
parts answers are given to questions just raised.
When you see a passage in this type style coming up, that's a good place to stop reading for a
while, and to try to figure out answers yourself.

---

[1] "The Philosophy of Logical Atomism" in Russell's *Logic and Knowledge* (London: George Allen & Unwin Ltd., 1956).

Then when you read these passages, you can
see whether your answers match what's given.
Don't worry if, from time to time, you come up
with a different answer from the one given.
Sometimes there are many ways to answer a
question, and the one given is just one of these.
Try to see why the answer given is plausible. Is
it better than yours?

Some solutions philosophers have proposed are much too complicated to be included in here, of course. You'll notice, from time to time,
sections labeled **FOR FURTHER READING**, which tell you where to
look for further discussion of the issues.

In many cases philosophical debate still rages about questions that
have been around a long time. That's what makes the introductory study
of philosophy different from the introduction to many other subjects,
where you learn only what's settled and uncontroversial. And that's one
reason why some people enjoy philosophy more than these other subjects: you can join in the debate right from the start.

Philosophers love to fool around with ideas. A
good deal of chatter around any university philosophy department consists of jokes, anecdotes,
and silly intellectual play. Often, however, these
bits of fluff have a real philosophical purpose.
(Well, *sometimes* they do.) In this book you'll
occasionally come across a passage written in this
type-style; this indicates a fluffy bit. Don't ignore
it! It's usually not merely for fun. Even when it
seems silly or irrelevant, there's something philosophically important about it—something deeper
that it illustrates, which merits thought.

"Wittgenstein once said that a serious and good
philosophical work could be written that would
consist entirely of *jokes* [without being facetious].
Another time he said that a philosophical treatise
might contain nothing but questions [without an-
swers]." —Norman Malcolm[2]

---

[2] *Ludwig Wittgenstein: A Memoir* (Oxford: Oxford University Press, 1984), pp. 27–
28.

CHAPTER I

DIFFERENCES THAT MAKE NO DIFFERENCE:

The Practical Meaning of Questions and Answers

1. WILLIAM JAMES AND THE SQUIRREL

Around the beginning of the twentieth century, the American pragmatist philosopher William James described this puzzle:

> Some years ago, being with a camping party in the mountains, I returned from a solitary ramble to find every one engaged in a ferocious metaphysical dispute. The *corpus* of the dispute was a squirrel — a live squirrel supposed to be clinging to one side of a tree-trunk; while over against the tree's opposite side a human being was imagined to stand. This human witness tries to get sight of the squirrel by moving rapidly round the tree, but no matter how fast he goes, the squirrel moves as fast in the opposite direction,[1] and always keeps the tree between himself and the man, so that never a glimpse of him is caught. The resultant metaphysical problem now is this: *Does the man go round the squirrel or not?*... Every one had taken sides, and was obstinate.

Who is right? The important point here is not who is right, but what James says about this problem:

> "Which party is right," I said, "depends on what you *practically mean* by 'going round' the squirrel. If you mean passing from the north of him to the east, then to the south, then to the west, and then to the north of him again, obviously the man does go

---

[1] We know what James meant, but it might have been clearer if he had said that the squirrel and the human both move in the *same* direction — that is, looking from the top, both move (for example) clockwise.

round him.... But if on the contrary you mean being first in front of him, then on the right of him, then behind him, then on his left, and finally in front again, it is quite as obvious that the man fails to go round him, for by the compensating movements the squirrel makes, he keeps his belly turned towards the man all the time."

The *practical meaning* of a belief has to do with how that belief interacts with the interests and actions of the person who believes it. Exactly what practical difference would it make to you if you believed that or its opposite?

This sort of way of dealing with questions has become extremely influential in contemporary philosophy. It gives us a methodology for dealing with some questions that seemed unanswerable, by anchoring them in the real world. But it also apparently gives us a reason to discard other questions as meaningless.

The influence of this style has not always been beneficial. Spend some time in a bar where undergraduate philosophy majors hang out, and you might hear a good deal of pompous but useless philosophizing to the following effect: "But what do you really *mean* by 'God'/'justice'/'good'/ 'freedom' [etc., etc.]?" It's easy to see why bystanders get the idea that philosophy has abandoned what they take to be its historical mission— The Search For Wisdom—and is now a trivial search for definitions. And why they think that philosophers would save a lot of time and talk merely by consulting a good dictionary.

But this sort of quibble over words is far from what James—or contemporary philosophers—really do. James's example is misleading: it's merely a trivial verbal dispute that's easily made to disappear as soon as the ambiguous senses of a phrase are revealed. But when real philosophical disputes are solved (or made to go away) it is rarely this simple a matter.

When James calls the squirrel argument a "metaphysical problem," he's being ironic. There are traditional metaphysical problems in philosophy that are not so trivial; and getting clear on exactly what is "practically meant" is often a very subtle matter. But James may be right in thinking that this sort of methodology can help with real philosophical problems.

Consider, for example, the dispute over the justice of capital punishment. Philosophers might want first to try to answer the question, "What's really involved in *justice*?" This question asks about the "practical meaning" of 'justice,' and it's an important and difficult question, not solvable merely by looking the word up in a dictionary. We want to know, for example, what tests we should use to judge whether some policy is just or not; so when a dictionary tells us that 'justice' means "Moral rightness; equity. Honour; fairness. Fair handling; due reward or treatment,"[2] that's not much help.

The Unanswerable

- What's the opposite of a duck?
- What does Thursday weigh?
- What was Snow White's father's name?
- What time is it right now on the moon?
- How many angels can dance on the head of a pin?

I'll bet you can't answer these questions. Why can't you? The reason is not that there's some information you lack. There's something wrong with each question: they're *empty* questions.

> The problem about what time it is on the moon arises again for the earth's North and South Poles, where all the time zones come together in a point. But, strictly speaking, there is a way of answering these questions—or was. For the purposes of clear communication about time with astronauts walking around on the moon, or scientists camped at the Poles, they stipulated time zones for those locations. Maybe now that everyone has left both places, the questions have relapsed into emptiness again—now that there's no "practical meaning" for one answer rather than another.
>
> Do you feel that these stipulations, being entirely arbitrary, didn't provide real answers to questions about what time it was? Remember that there's a good deal that's arbitrary about ordinary earthly time zones. In fact, the whole system that assigns a number on the clock to the current time is arbitrary, isn't it?

Something or Nothing?

"The first question which should rightly be asked," wrote G.W.F. Leibniz in 1719, is "Why is there something rather than nothing?"[3] By the midtwentieth century, this question apparently hadn't been answered yet; in

---

2 *The American Heritage Dictionary of the English Language* (New York: American Heritage, 1969), p. 711.

3 G.W. Leibniz, "The Principles of Nature and of Grace, Based on Reason" (1714), in *Leibniz Selections*, ed. Philip P. Wiener, The Modern Student's Library (New York: Charles Scribner's Sons, 1951), p. 527.

1953, Martin Heidegger called it the fundamental question of meta-physics.[4]

What could even count as an answer to the question raised by Leibniz and Heidegger? Maybe nothing. Maybe it's a phony question, and the reason it's so hard to answer is not that it's far too deep, but rather that it's far too shallow.

> Sidney Morgenbesser, a contemporary philosopher known for his witty one-liners, is reported to have proposed this reply to Heidegger: "If there were nothing, you'd still complain."

SOME QUESTIONS TO THINK ABOUT: Why are these questions unanswerable? Is it the same reason in each case? Is it that there's nothing "practically meant" by these questions?

Some philosophers have thought that some traditional philosophical questions lack "practical meaning," and they conclude that they're phony questions nobody should waste time thinking about. Medieval philosophers devoted a lot of time to thinking about angels and other non-existents — see below: **Angels and Superman** in Chapter XII, and **Two Places are Better Than One** in Chapter XIII. But perhaps you shouldn't be too quick in dismissing their problem as a phony one before you've studied in depth what they wrote; perhaps there was some upshot to this question for them.

FOR FURTHER READING: The James quote is from "What Pragmatism Means" in *Essays in Pragmatism* (New York: Hafner, 1948), p. 141. The "ordinary language" philosophers, for example J. L. Austin and Gilbert Ryle, often provide subtle, interesting, and surprising analyses of what is "practically meant." Just about any of the many works by Austin or Ryle provides a good example of this methodology in action. A particularly good example is Austin's article, "A Plea For Excuses" (originally published as "The Presidential Address to the Aristotelian Society, 1956," in *Proceedings of the Aristotelian Society, 1956-1957*, Vol. LVII). The article appears in many anthologies, including J. L. Austin, *Philosophical Papers* (Oxford: Clarendon Press, 1961) and V. C. Chappell, ed., *Ordinary Language* (Englewood Cliffs, NJ: Prentice-Hall, 1964). Chappell's book also contains an article on Ordinary Language Philosophy by Ryle. A. J. Ayer is a good example of a philosopher who rejects

---

[4] Martin Heidegger, *An Introduction to Metaphysics*, (1953) (New Haven: Yale University Press, 1959), pp. 7–8.

many traditional philosophical problems as meaningless. See his *Language, Truth, and Logic* (Oxford: Oxford University Press, 1946.)

2. WHEN EVERYTHING GETS BIGGER

Could you tell if, one day, everything in the universe suddenly doubled in size?[5]

> Your shoes would suddenly get twice as big, but they would continue to fit your feet, which would also have doubled in size. You would suddenly become ten or twelve feet tall, but your clothes, your room, and your car would also double. Yardsticks would become twice as long. The corner store would be twice as far away, but walking there would take the same time because your legs would be twice as long. Everything would be twice as far away, but you would double in size, so they would look the same distance away as before. There would be no *practical* effect of this change at all. Applying James's method to this case would tell us that there's no practical difference between the idea that everything doubles in size and the idea that everything stays the same. So a dispute about whether everything has just doubled or not is perhaps really no dispute at all. (Is this right?)

Proponents of the "relational" theory of space say that there is no such thing as the absolute size of anything: we ascertain something's size by comparing it to other things. So we shouldn't say that this mass doubling might or might not happen: we should rather say that it makes no sense even to contemplate it.

A similar point can be made about the supposition that everything suddenly speeds up to be twice as fast as it used to be. Or that everything suddenly moves three feet to the left.

The Right-Handed Universe

Let's apply this sort of approach to another sort of case. Imagine that the universe contained nothing at all except one *right* hand. Now, imagine

---

5 This puzzle is due to the French mathematician and physicist Jules Henri Poincaré.

that the universe contained nothing at all except one *left* hand. Are you imagining two *different* universes?

> All the relations between points in the first universe would be exactly the same as in the second universe. The "relational" theory of space tells us that there is no absolute "handedness" of anything. There wouldn't be any difference between these universes.

But the great nineteenth-century German philosopher Immanuel Kant argued that *is* a difference between a universe containing only one right hand and a universe containing only one left hand; so the relational theory of space must be wrong. But the relationist can reply that Kant is wrong: there is no difference between these universes.

3. MILDRED'S PECULIAR SENSATIONS

Look around until you see something green. While you're looking at that green thing, you are having a particular kind of visual experience. Call that kind of experience a GE (for "Green Experience"). We think that others also get GEs when they look at green things, but suppose that your friend Mildred doesn't. I don't mean that Mildred is blind or colour-blind. I mean that her experiences are systematically different from yours. When she looks at something green, she has the experience you get when you look at something yellow—a YE. Her experiences, we imagine, are systematically transposed, as given by the following table:

Object is:	Red	Orange	Yellow	Green	Blue	Violet
You get:	RE	OE	YE	GE	BE	VE
She gets:	VE	BE	GE	YE	OE	RE

So whenever Mildred looks at a red thing, she gets a VE (a Violet Experience); whenever she looks at a blue thing, she gets an OE (an Orange Experience); and so on.[6]

Blind or colour-blind people sometimes act differently from people with normal vision; but Mildred doesn't. She has no trouble identifying

---

[6] This example occurs widely in the philosophical literature, and is called the "inverted spectrum."

green things. You ask her what colour the leaves of that tree are, and she unhesitatingly and correctly replies "green." She has, of course, learned to associate the word 'green' with her YE, just as you have learned to associate the word 'green' with your GE. She can, at a glance, tell correctly which are the limes and which are the lemons in a pile of mixed citrus fruit. The lemons are the ones that give her a GE when she looks at them, and the limes give her a YE. Just like you, she drives through green lights, and prepares to stop when the light turns yellow. In fact, all her behaviour is just like yours. Could you tell that there's something different about her experiences? Could she? Could anyone?

> It seems that we are imagining a difference here that makes no difference. Perhaps there really is no difference. What we're imagining here seems in no way distinguishable from the supposition that her experiences were exactly the same as yours.
>
> Some philosophers react to the proposal that Mildred has inverted-spectrum sensations by claiming that this proposal is impossible. What is *meant* by 'a Green Experience' is nothing but the sensation one usually gets when looking at something green, so whatever Mildred gets when looking at limes is by definition a GE. It can't be anything else.

Another Inversion in Mildred

Now try to imagine that Mildred has "inverted experiences" of this sort: Whenever you step on her toe, she feels pleasure. Whenever she is cold and tired and lies down in her nice warm bed, she feels pain. But she behaves just like the rest of us: when you step on her toe, she groans and pushes you off. She hurries eagerly to get into bed after a cold and hectic day. The only difference is in her inward sensations. She peculiarly tries to avoid pleasures, and seeks pain. Is this shown to be nonsense by the same sorts of considerations we raised when considering her inverted spectrum of visual sensations?

SOME QUESTIONS TO THINK ABOUT: If you think that it's impossible for Mildred to have inverted sensations, does this show that all that matters, when we try to determine what sensations someone has, is what they say, how they act, and what features of the external world they're interacting with? Suppose *you* were in Mildred's place. Would *you* be convinced that you actually felt pain when someone stepped on your toe?

4. A WORLD OF FAKE ANTIQUES

Philosophers have often imagined things that everyone knows aren't true, and challenged us to prove—or indeed to give any reason at all to think— that they're not true. One example is the Five-Minute Hypothesis (invented by Bertrand Russell[7] in 1921). Here's how this goes:

Imagine that the entire universe was created exactly five minutes ago, complete with all sorts of "signs" of a non-existent past. The soles of your shoes came into existence five minutes ago worn down, looking like they had been walked on for months. That stuff in the bowl in the back of your refrigerator came into existence covered with green fuzzy mould, just as if it had been left there for weeks. You were created five minutes ago complete with all sorts of fake memories of a past that never happened.

We can't prove that the Five-Minute Hypothesis is false by uncovering evidence around us of what happened more than five minutes ago. Finding a newspaper dated yesterday, for example, won't prove anything, because the Hypothesis explains this and all such "evidence" of a past: all those things are fake antiques.

When we compare the Five-Minute Hypothesis with our ordinary way of thinking, the score is tied when we measure their relative ability to explain the way things seem now. Both the hypothesis that I really have been wearing those shoes for months, as I seem to remember, and the Five-Minute Hypothesis explain why the soles of my shoes are worn. We can say: both hypotheses are consistent with all the evidence.

But consistency with all the evidence is not the only criterion we have for the truth of an explanatory hypothesis. Notice that the Five-Minute Hypothesis involves all sorts of unexplained coincidences. The shoes I pseudo-remember wearing are in fact now worn down, so there is a coincidental coherence between this pseudo-memory and the current state of the shoes. Similarly, the other pair, which I pseudo-remember leaving in the back of my closet permanently just after I bought them, are now, by coincidence, not worn down. Today's newspaper and the radio news both coincidentally report that the same thing happened yesterday. There are innumerable unexplained coincidences such as this involved in

---

[7] *The Analysis of Mind* (New York: Macmillan, 1921), pp. 159–160.

the Five-Minute Hypothesis. A hypothesis full of such unexplained coincidences is a bad one.

But why can't the Five-Minutist reply that a fiendishly clever demon has arranged all these coincidences to fool us?

One way of dealing with the Five-Minute Hypothesis is to treat it as another instance of a "difference" that makes no difference. But we can't resist thinking that it would be a *big* difference if this hypothesis were true.

> The age of the universe was the subject of investigation by the Reverend James Ussher, Archbishop of Armagh. Ussher's *Annals of the Ancient and New Testaments*, a scholarly book published in 1650, reported the results of some careful calculations based on scripture: the universe was created in 4004 BC. This date was accepted by the Church of England as authoritative, and was printed in the margins of their Authorized Version of the Bible. More detailed computations by Doctor John Lightfoot, Vice-Chancellor of the University of Cambridge, made the matter more precise: the Creation took place on October 23, 4004 BC, at 9 a.m. (Lightfoot didn't specify in which time zone it was 9 a.m.)
>
> As science progressed, evidence accumulated that some rocks were millions of years old. How could this be squared with the official view that nothing was more than six thousand years old? The answer given was analogous to the Five-Minute Hypothesis: In 4004 BC, the world was created complete with rocks that *seemed* much older. They were fake antiques.

5. THE BRAIN IN THE VAT

Here's another example, similar to the Five-Minute Hypothesis. Imagine that you are actually a brain in a vat. That is, a mad scientist removed your brain at birth, and installed it in a vat full of nutritive solution to keep it alive. Your brain has been connected by wires to a computer that feeds in incredibly complicated electrical impulses; as a result you have all those experiences that you take to be sensations originating in the external world, but that are in fact all delusions. Like the Five-Minute Hypothesis, this hypothesis is consistent with all your current experience. Do you have any reason at all to think that you are not such a brain in a vat?

> A possible answer to this question depends on the account of what is involved in thinking about something that we will discuss in the item called **Thinking About Vienna** in Chapter XII. If that account is correct, then the

only way for a thought to be *about* something is for it to be connected in the right sort of way to that thing. Now suppose that you really are a brain in a vat. All of your experiences, then, would have come from the wires planted in your brain. None of your thoughts would be connected in the right sort of way with the sky, or breakfast, or Vienna, so none of your thoughts would be about any of these things. Neither would your thoughts have the right sorts of connection with your brain, or with the vat it was in; so you wouldn't be able to have thoughts about your brain or its vat. (It's an interesting question whether you'd be able to have thoughts about anything at all.) So if you were in fact a brain in a vat, you couldn't believe that you were a brain in a vat, and you couldn't believe that you weren't.

SOME QUESTIONS TO THINK ABOUT: If this line of reasoning is right, what does it show? Perhaps it shows that the belief that one is a brain in a vat can't be true. If you were a brain in a vat you couldn't believe it.

But does that show that you're not a brain in a vat? Well, if you were, you couldn't believe you were. But it's still possible that you actually are a brain in a vat. If you were, then your beliefs would be about who-knows-what; but never mind. Have we actually proven that you're not a brain in a vat? Can we prove it? If not, then why do you think you aren't?

FOR FURTHER READING: The brain-in-the-vat example, and a version of the answer to this puzzle we have considered, are found in Hilary Putnam's *Reason, Truth and History* (Cambridge: Cambridge University Press, 1981).

6. IT'S PRACTICALLY TRUE

William James's position is that questions about whose answers we seem to disagree are answered (or made to disappear) when we consider the "practical meaning" of what is being argued about. He thought that the real significance of the dispute whether X is true or false was what difference believing X would make to anyone's life. If there is no difference, then the dispute is empty. But where there is a difference, James argued that the test for whether X was true or false involved the evaluation of the practical results of believing X—whether people who believed X would be better off in coping with their surroundings than people who didn't. If they were better off, then there are grounds for believing X. What James has here is a theory of truth: X is true when believing X makes people better off.

Is this theory correct?

> Sometimes this theory gives results that look right. Suppose, for example, that Archibald believes that the Number 4 bus stops on this corner, and Millicent believes it doesn't. It's easy to imagine that the person who is correct is also the person who will be better off when she or he wants to catch the Number 4 bus.

But James had more controversial uses of his theory in mind. In his book *The Varieties of Religious Experience*,[8] he described what he took to be the typical psychological effects of religious conversion and belief. These effects, he claimed, were beneficial for the believer. Since the practical implications of religious belief are beneficial, it follows from his theory of truth that religious beliefs are true.

> To preach scepticism to us as a duty until 'sufficient evidence' for religion be found, is tantamount therefore to telling us, when in presence of the religious hypothesis, that to yield to our fear of its being error is wiser and better than to yield to our hope that it may be true. It is not intellect against all passions, then; it is only intellect with one passion laying down its law. And by what, forsooth, is the supreme wisdom of this passion warranted?
> —William James[9]

SOME QUESTIONS TO THINK ABOUT: James's defense of religious belief is, of course, open to debate. For one thing, we could question his claims about the beneficial effects of religious belief. But more importantly, we might wonder whether the fact that a belief is good for people is all there is to a belief's being true. Couldn't some beliefs be good for people even though false? Couldn't some beliefs be bad for people, even though true?

---

[8] New York: Longmans, Green, 1902.
[9] *The Will to Believe* (New York: Longmans, Green, 1897).

William James used to preach the 'will to believe.' For my part, I should wish to preach the 'will to doubt.' What is wanted is not the will to believe but the will to find out, which is the exact opposite.—Bertrand Russell[10]

> "The average man does not get pleasure out of an idea because he thinks it is true; he thinks it is true because he gets pleasure out of it."—H. L. Mencken.

Suppose that a historian discovers what people ate for breakfast in Ancient Rome. It's hard to see how this belief could have any beneficial effect on us. The historian's belief is, then, true but useless. Is James's theory of truth mistaken?

FOR FURTHER READING: Pascal's Wager, examined in Chapter II, is another argument for religious belief based on the benefits of that belief. In Chapter VII we'll take another critical look at the idea that the benefits of believing something are grounds for thinking it's true.

7. INTO THE MAINSTREAM OF PHILOSOPHY

In this chapter, as in all the following ones, there is what seems to be a rather random and disorganized bunch of musings; but there is method in this madness. The items in each chapter are (for the most part) connected to one of the major fields of academic philosophical study.

At the end of each chapter, then, is an item titled INTO THE MAIN-STREAM OF PHILOSOPHY. In these items I'll describe, in very brief outline, the general area of mainstream philosophical study relevant to the chapter at hand, occasionally mentioning the conventional names philosophers use to refer to their major areas of concern and their major positions on these areas. I'll pull together some of the musings into the chapter, to show you a bit about how they are connected.

You've already seen some notes on where you might go to do further reading on the particular problems and positions discussed. In the INTO THE MAINSTREAM items I'll often suggest how to find readings on the general issues raised in the chapter.

A good place to start reading philosophy is in any of the scores of major introductory philosophy anthologies widely available in university bookstores. The articles in anthologies are by a wide variety of phi-

---

[10] *Sceptical Essays* (London: George Allen & Unwin, 1928).

losophers, and are usually grouped by subject matter; you'll find contiguous articles arguing for different positions on the same question. Most anthologies contain articles that are on the one hand important, deep, and revealing, while at the same time understandable to someone not yet immersed in the field.

Well, then, about this first chapter:

We had a glance at James's views. His position, influential not only among American philosophers, is called *pragmatism*. It goes some way to answering questions about *meaning*—by telling us what the meaning of a question or of a declarative sentence is. It is also the germ of a theory of truth, holding that what it is for a sentence to be true is for it to be (putting things roughly) useful. The core of his position is that the meaning or truth of anything is to be determined by its connections with real-life experience. This position has had a rather radical effect in some areas. What are we to make of the (supposedly) meaningful—perhaps sometimes even true— things that are said in religion, for example, where talk about God and angels seems quite disconnected from everyday mundane reality? How are we to understand scientific theory? You can't ever experience an electron; so how can you talk about one? (Perhaps, on James's criterion, talk about electrons is "really" just talk about the sort of things we can interact with: light bulbs, electric meters, and so on.) How can historians talk about a past they can't interact with? How (if at all) can psychologists discover anything about the minds of other people, locked privately inside them?

Pragmatism has affinities with another view, popularized originally by a group of Viennese philosophers who came to England and America around the time of World War II: the Vienna Circle. Their view, called *Logical Positivism*, emphasized the necessity of sense-experience and practical testability in evaluating the truth, and understanding the meaning, of any statement. Like James's, this view tended at first to have a destructive, or at least a radically re-evaluative effect, on many areas of talk and enquiry.

Philosophy since it began has struggled with "sceptical questions": How do we know that we're not brains in a vat? How about the Five-Minute Hypothesis? What makes us think that there is an external world at all? (Maybe it's all hallucination!) How can you prove that anything is right or wrong? Pragmatism and Logical Positivism are both sometimes inclined to see these questions as meaningless: that since their answer would make no difference in our experience, there's something wrong with the question. Not everyone has found this answer satisfying.

CHAPTER II

GOD

The Philosophy of Religion

1. THE PRACTICAL MEANING OF RELIGIOUS TALK

Murgatroyd and Millicent come across a patch of land containing flowers and weeds. The following discussion ensues:

> *Murgatroyd*: A gardener must tend this plot.
> *Millicent*: I don't think so. Look, it's full of weeds.
> *Murgatroyd*: The gardener must like those weeds. They are nice, aren't they?
> *Millicent*: Those weeds grow around here all by themselves; anyway, I've talked to people who live around here, and nobody told me anything about seeing any gardener at work.
> *Murgatroyd*: Well, the gardener must have been here when everyone was asleep.

They take turns watching, day and night, but no gardener is seen. Murgatroyd explains this fact by supposing that the gardener must be invisible. They set up an electric alarm system sensitive to heat, and patrol with bloodhounds, but there's no reaction from either. Murgatroyd is still not convinced.

> *Murgatroyd*: The gardener is not only invisible, but undetectable to the alarm system, and without odour the bloodhounds could smell.
> *Millicent*: I'm getting fed up with your argument. Your gardener is supposed to be invisible and completely undetectable to anyone, and is supposed to have planted things the way they would have grown anyway. What makes him different from no gardener at all?

The analogy here is to arguments about God's existence. Believers often admit that there's a natural scientific explanation of the way things are. They also admit that God is undetectable by all the ordinary detection methods.

The question we might ask here is this: How is the assertion that such an undetectable God exists any different from the assertion that there isn't any God? Here's one possible answer:

> There's no real difference in beliefs or expectations about the real world in the religious believer and in the disbeliever. There's just a difference in how they feel about things. If so, then maybe there's no question about who is right and who is wrong.

SOME QUESTIONS TO THINK ABOUT: If this response to the Invisible Gardener story is right, then religions don't say things that should be judged true or false. What they say is more like poetry: the expression of feelings and attitudes. If you are a religious person, consider whether this squares with your view of religious "truths."

The response given above to the argument between Millicent and Murgatroyd is like William James's response to the squirrel debate. Do you see the similarity?

FOR FURTHER READING: The Parable of the Invisible Gardener, and the response to the question we've considered, are both found in John Wisdom's article "Gods" in *Proceedings of the Aristotelian Society*, 1944-45, reprinted in *Logic and Language*, ed. Antony Flew (Garden City, NY: Anchor Books, 1965) and elsewhere. For a three-way discussion of these issues, see Antony Flew, R. M. Hare, and Basil Mitchell, "Theology and Falsification," in *New Essays in Philosophical Theology*, ed. Antony Flew and Alasdair MacIntyre (New York: Macmillan, 1955).

Industrial Prayer

It's sometimes claimed that prayer doesn't work—I mean, that it doesn't increase the probability of getting what you prayed for. George Santayana puts it this way:

> No chapter in theology is more unhappy than that in which a material efficacy is assigned to prayer. In the first place the facts contradict that notion that curses can bring evil or blessings can cure; and it is not observed that the most orthodox and hard-praying army wins the most battles.[1]

---

[1] *Reason In Religion* (*The Life of Reason*, vol. 3) (New York: Collier Books, 1962), pp. 32–33.

If prayer really "attracted superhuman forces to our aid by giving them a signal without which they would not have been able to reach us," says Santayana, then

> There would be nothing in it more impossible than in ordinary telepathy; prayer would then be an art like conversation, and the exact personages and interests would be discoverable to which we might appeal. A celestial diplomacy might then be established not very unlike primitive religions. Religion would have reverted to industry and science.[2]

But, of course, religion is not just another industry. You can tell that by contrasting churches with factories. The latter are utilitarian places, single-mindedly directed toward creation of a product; their décor pays no attention to beauty—it's the rare factory that has stained-glass windows or gothic arches—or to uplifting effect on the people inside. They don't characteristically have organ music; factory workers rarely sing songs together.

So what is prayer for? According to Santayana, prayer is a soliloquy, not a conversational request. In rational prayer, he says,

> The soul may be said to accomplish three things important to its welfare: it withdraws within itself and defines its good, it accommodates itself to destiny, and it grows like the ideal which it conceives.[3]

SOME QUESTIONS TO THINK ABOUT: Santayana's views on religion are fairly radical ones, and seem quite mistaken to many people—mistaken about what religion is actually taken to be by the religious, and about how it ought to be taken. You probably have seen the TV evangelists who promise you that prayer will cure your diseases or get you a raise in salary—those prayers, that is, that the evangelist will perform if you send him a donation. A large number of people send these TV evangelists money; surely they believe in the material efficacy of prayer. And many more religious people distrust the TV evangelists, but believe in the material efficacy of prayer anyway. It seems, then, that Santayana is wrong anyway about how religious practice is thought of by many religious people. If a very large proportion of religious people think that prayer has material effect, how can Santayana claim that its "real" function is something else?

---

[2] Santayana, pp. 33–34.
[3] Ibid, p. 34.

But the more important question is whether Santayana's interpretation of religion is meaningful to you. Maybe you'd prefer the more conventional and conservative religious view of prayer. Or maybe you agree with him that prayer has no material effect, but disagree with him when he claims that it has some other valid function in the rational life.

> A mountain climber slips over a precipice and clings to a rope over a thousand-foot drop. In fear and despair, he looks to the heavens and cries, "Is there anyone up there who can help me?" A voice from above booms, "You will be saved if you show your faith by letting go of the rope." The man looks down, then up, and shouts, "Is there anyone *else* up there who can help me?"[4]

One Hell of a Rainstorm

It says in the Bible that during the Flood, "all the high hills that were under the whole heaven were covered." The mathematician John Allen Paulos has made some calculations. He figures that in order to cover every mountain, there must have been ten to twenty thousand feet of water on the earth's surface, about half a billion cubic miles of water. It rained forty days and forty nights. To produce a flood of that size in those 960 hours, it must have rained, on average, fifteen feet of water per hour. A really heavy and destructive rainstorm in our day can put several inches of water on the ground per hour. But fifteen feet of water in an hour, Paulos remarks, is enough to sink an aircraft carrier. How did Noah's little wooden ark, loaded with thousands of animals, stay afloat?[5]

> Maybe you want to reply that this is just another one of those religious miracles we're not supposed to be able to understand. Or maybe you think that what's said in the Bible is not supposed to be taken literally like this. Perhaps someone who "believes in the Bible" need not have beliefs in different *facts* from someone who doesn't. But maybe you just think that a good deal of what it says in the Bible ain't necessarily so.

---

[4] Told by Steven Pinker, *How the Mind Works* (New York: W. W. Norton, 1997), p. 550.
[5] *Innumeracy: Mathematical Illiteracy and Its Consequences* (New York: Vintage Books, 1990), pp. 16–17.

A QUESTION TO THINK ABOUT: Suppose you agree that the difference between believers in the Bible and non-believers *isn't* a matter of believing different facts. Then what is the difference?

Faith

Seen as a way of finding out what's true, religious faith is pretty peculiar, when you get right down to it. For one thing, faith isn't believing because of good evidence—it's believing when there isn't any evidence, or even evidence to the contrary. Is this a good idea?

Ordinarily, coming-to-believe something is unintentional—it just happens to us. In the section called "Believe or I'll Shoot!" in Chapter VII, we wonder if it's even possible to start believing something on purpose. But this is what faith is supposed to be. And if it is possible, doesn't this raise the undesirable prospect that we're believing something because we want it to be true, not because it is true?

> "Faith may be defined briefly as an illogical belief in the occurrence of the improbable."—H. L. Mencken

> "A man full of faith is simply one who has lost (or never had) the capacity for clear and realistic thought. He is not a mere ass; he is actually ill. Worse, he is incurable."—H. L. Mencken

> "'Faith' means not wanting to know what is true."—Friedrich Neitzsche[6]

> "Faith is believing what you know ain't so."—"A schoolboy" quoted by Mark Twain.

> "Trust in Allah, but tie your camel."—Arab proverb[7]

2. GOD'S DIFFICULTIES

Most religions believe that God is omnipotent. This means that God can do anything He wants to do. Could God create a stone too heavy for Him to lift?

---

[6] *The Antichrist.*

[7] The proverb and the Mark Twain quote are both cited by Robert Byrne in *1,911 Best Things Anybody Ever Said* (New York: Fawcett Columbine, 1988), pp. 138, 139.

Let's suppose He can. Then, if He did, He'd have created a stone too heavy for Him to lift. Since He couldn't
lift it, He wouldn't be omnipotent. So let's suppose He
can't. But then there is something God can't do, so He
isn't omnipotent. Either way, omnipotence is impossible.
Maybe omnipotence makes no sense.

The suggestion here is that major religions must be mistaken in thinking that there is an omnipotent God, because omnipotence is logically
impossible.

God Made Me Do It

The doctrine of God's omnipotence raises similar problems when connected with the idea that we have free will. Does the fact (if it is a fact) that
we are free mean that our decisions can't be controlled by outside influences? If so, then there's another limitation on God's power. As in the
unliftable stone example, we can put this problem in the form of a
dilemma:[8] If God *can* create a person whose actions He can't control, then
this person's actions would be a limit to His power: He wouldn't be omnipotent. If He *can't* create such a person, then that's a limit to His power:
He wouldn't be omnipotent. Either way, omnipotence is impossible.

God the Counterfeiter

Another thing God can't do is make a genuine ten dollar bill. God could,
presumably, make an atom-for-atom duplicate of a genuine ten dollar bill
that would fool everyone, but that bill would be counterfeit. Only bills
produced by the government mint are genuine. God could, of course, make
the mint produce a genuine bill, but He couldn't make one directly.

Here's another limit to God's omnipotence. The familiar poem says
that "Only God can make a tree," but perhaps God can't make a tree. According to some biologists, what it takes for something to count as an oak
tree, for example, is that it has to have come from another oak tree. Suppose you manufactured something out of chemicals that looked and
worked exactly like an oak tree, that even dropped acorns in the fall that
grew into things just like it. What you made wouldn't be an oak tree, since

---

8 In the very beginning of Chapter V I'll talk about what *dilemmas* are.

it didn't come from an oak tree. Your inability to make an oak tree isn't the result of your lack of ability in biochemistry. No matter how accurate a look-alike you made out of chemicals, it wouldn't *count* as an oak tree, since oak trees are, *by definition*, what comes from other oak trees. So God, with infinite biochemical abilities, couldn't make an oak tree either.

These two peculiar cases share something in common. What it takes to be a genuine ten dollar bill or an oak tree is not merely a matter of what something is made of, or how its parts are put together, or how it works. In both cases, there has to be a *historical* characteristic present— something true about its *past*.

> Historical characteristics played a role in a newsworthy event of a few years ago. During the riots and looting in Los Angeles, somebody broke into Frederick's of Hollywood, the famous erotic underwear store, and stole Madonna's bra from from their Museum of Famous Underwear. Frederick's posted a huge reward for the return of the famous garment, and a few days later, a bra was brought in by someone claiming the reward. It was exactly the brand, model, and size of the one stolen earlier, but it was a phony: it wasn't the one worn by Madonna. It differed from the genuine article only in a historical characteristic. We can wonder: if all its *present* characteristics were identical with the real one, how did the Frederick's staff know it was a phony?

SOME QUESTIONS TO THINK ABOUT: In order to count as an *antique*, something has to have a historical property: it has to have been made more than a certain number of years ago. Can you think of other categories that require historical properties?

We can distinguish between *intrinsic* and *relational* properties. The former are characteristics of a thing that are true of it in itself; the latter are true of it insofar as it is related to something else, or insofar as something happened at another time or place. Two things might be identical in all their intrinsic properties, and differ only in their relational properties. A genuine ten dollar bill and a really perfect counterfeit are an example of a pair like this. Historical properties are one sort of relational property; another is *ownership*. Imagine that you and I each own brand-new copies of the same book. The books are (almost perfectly) alike in all their intrinsic properties, but they differ in an important relational way: one is owned by me, and the other one isn't. Because they're intrinsically indistinguishable, there might be no way for someone to tell which one is mine and which one is yours just by looking at them—that is, by examining their intrinsic properties. Of course, someone could tell which one was mine if I had written my name in it, but then they would differ in a relevant intrinsic property.

We'll have another look at the relevance of historical properties when we take a look at the philosophy of art (see **The "Mona Lisa" by Schmidlap**, Chapter XVII).

This is another relational property: being the tallest mountain on earth. No matter how much you examined Mt. Everest, no matter how much you knew about its intrinsic properties, you couldn't tell whether it was the tallest mountain on earth unless you know how it was related in size to the other mountains. Can you think of other sorts of relational property?

If you subscribe to a religion including belief in an omnipotent God, what sort of changes would you have to make if you were convinced that God really can't be omnipotent? Would that affect the real substance of your religion in important ways?

But can you think of ways to get around the problems about omnipotence? Here are some suggestions.

> The argument shows that omnipotence is logically impossible. But logical problems don't bother God. God isn't subject to the laws of logic. He can have logically impossible characteristics.

One problem with this answer is that it's impossible for us to understand logically impossible characteristics. For example, suppose that I said to you, "I have a glass here which has this peculiar characteristic: it's filled with water and empty." First you'd suspect that I was playing with words, or telling an obscure joke. But if I assured you that I was speaking literally, you would doubt what I was saying, because the very idea of a glass which is both filled and empty makes no sense at all. It's not as if I was talking about some characteristic that, for some reason, glasses weren't allowed to have; it's that I'm just talking nonsense.

Some religious people cheerfully admit that religious truths surpass all understanding. (The mystery of religious truths is something that some religious people find attractive.) But other people aren't comfortable with the idea of saying, or trying to believe, things that make no sense.

Here's another suggestion for a response:

> Let's agree that if He couldn't create a stone too heavy for Him to lift, He wouldn't be omnipotent. If He could

create this stone *and did*, then there would be a stone around He couldn't lift; so again, He wouldn't be omnipotent. But suppose He *could* create this stone *but didn't*. Where's the problem with His omnipotence now?

We might want to reply to the problem about free will in the same sort of way: that God *could* create an uncontrollable human but *doesn't*. But this reply won't work here: religions usually hold that God *did* in fact create humans with free will.[9]

A Proof That Everything Is Hunky-Dory

Let's assume that God, as conventional religions conceive of Him, really did create the universe. God, of course, wanted to create the best universe He could, and His omnipotence means that He was capable of doing anything He wanted. So it follows that this is the best of all possible universes. (This view has been called "cosmic Toryism," referring to the smug and complacent attitude of certain members of the British Conservative Party.) You're wrong if you think that anything could be any better. Does that make you feel good? You should cheer up.

Now that you know that everything is perfect, you'd better be more careful about changing the way things are. When you walk through the woods, you might move a pebble an inch south, messing up God's perfect creation.

A QUESTION TO THINK ABOUT: It's not obvious to everyone that this is the sort of perfect universe that would be created by a benevolent all-powerful God who had our interests at heart.

> A ship is tossing dangerously in a storm. A passenger rushes to the captain and asks him about the danger. "We are all in God's hands," says the captain. "Oh no! As bad as that!" exclaims the passenger.

> "How can I believe in God when just last week I got my tongue caught in the roller of an electric typewriter?"— Woody Allen[10]

---

[9] A similar problem about God's power is discussed in Chapter XI, in the item called **God Knows What I'll Do.**

[10] "Selections from the Allen Notebooks," in *Without Feathers* (New York: Ballantine, 1986).

"If God lived on earth, people would break his windows." —
Jewish proverb

What explains all the features of our world that seem to go against us?

"Imagine the Creator as a low comedian, and at once the
world becomes explicable." — H. L. Mencken

"Suppose the world was only one of God's jokes, would
you work any the less to make it a good joke, instead of a
bad one?" — George Bernard Shaw

3. HOW THERE GOT TO BE ONLY ONE GOD

The belief that there is only one God who is genuinely perfect — infinite
in power and knowledge — arose a long time ago, and there is little hard
historical evidence about how it came about. Here, however, is one hypothesis.

Today's major monotheistic religions, Judaism, Christianity, and Islam, all have their origins in the Middle East: Judaism developed there
first, then Christianity arose within the Jewish tradition and separated from
it. Later the Muslims (the followers of Islam) branched off from Christianity. Is their common origin in the Middle East just a coincidence? Some
people think not.

Most religions are polytheistic, recognizing the existence of a number
of limited Gods. Polytheists often see one of the gods as the god of their
group, the one who looks specially after their interests. In a sense, poly-
theism reflects and encourages a sort of tolerance and inter-tribe stability. A polytheistic tribe typically accepts the existence not only of their
own special god, but also of the gods of the neighbouring tribes.

In the hostile climate and terrain of the ancient Middle East, however, there must have been little tolerance and stability. The necessities
of life — water, and food plants and animals — were hard to come by. Often these necessities were available only for a short time in one place;
when they ran out, the tribe had to move on. So tribes were nomadic,
constantly on the move. Stability of territory could not develop, and we
can imagine a good deal of inter-tribe conflict and hostility as one tribe
encroached on another.

The constant hostility of these tribes did not encourage tolerant rec-
ognition of the others' gods. We can imagine that their conflict was reflected by religious competitiveness, with each tribe claiming that its god
was bigger, better, stronger than the others'. "My god is stronger than

yours!" says the priest of Tribe A. "Oh yeah? Well, *my* god is stronger than one hundred men!" claims the priest of Tribe B. "*My* god is stronger than one thousand men!" retorts the Tribe A priest. This continues. At last one tribe comes up with a topper that can't be beaten: "*My* god is *infinitely* strong. He knows *everything* and can do *anything He wants*." A god who is literally infinite in all his attributes must be the *only* real god there is. Thus monotheism.

The infinite god that results is a highly abstract entity, not much like the polytheistic gods, who are seen merely as people writ large. The logical problems we have examined regarding God's infinity are faced only by a highly rarefied and abstract monotheistic theology.

On this view, then, monotheism grows out of and encourages hostility to other religious groups, and encroachment on them. History and current events do seem to show an extraordinary amount of intolerance for other religions among the monotheistic religions, and even between the sects within them. Wars are not uncommon in history, of course, but wars based on religious intolerance seem especially prevalent among and between the monotheists. Think of the Crusades, which were religious wars between the Christians and the Muslims; the waves of Christian antisemitism; and the present-day hostility and warfare between Middle Eastern Muslims and Jews. Rival sects of Muslims wage war in Lebanon, and rival sects of Christians in Northern Ireland. The history of Christianity is marked by expansionism, the attempt to convert the rest of the world to its own unique God, often by force when persuasion fails.

Historians and theologians may cringe at this oversimplification of the history of religious thought, but perhaps there is a grain of truth to it. In any case, you might consider whether the notion of a unique and infinite god really does reflect and encourage nasty belligerence and intolerance, as this historical hypothesis indicates.

4. PROVING THE EXISTENCE OF GOD

God as the Tortoise on the Bottom

A commonly heard argument for the existence of God is the following:

> Every natural event in the world has a cause. So something that happened today had a cause that happened earlier, and this other event was itself caused by a still earlier event, and so on back. But there must have been a first cause in this series, or else it wouldn't have gotten started. This first cause is God.

Here is Bertrand Russell's reply to this argument:

> If everything must have a cause, then God must have a cause. If there can be anything without a cause, it may just as well be the world as God, so that there cannot be any validity in that argument. It is exactly of the same nature as the Hindu's view, that the world rested upon an elephant and the elephant rested upon a tortoise; and when they said, "How about the tortoise?" the Indian said, "Suppose we change the subject." The argument is really no better than that.[11]

According to John Allen Paulos,

> The cogency of this reply to the first-cause argument is indicated by Saint Augustine's reaction to a version of it. When he was asked what God was doing before He made the world, he answered, "He was creating a hell for people who ask questions like that."[12]

Well, that's a good laugh at St. Augustine's expense, but it's not exactly what Augustine said. Here's what he said:

> How, then, shall I respond to him who asks, "What was God doing *before* He made heaven and earth?" I do not answer, as a certain one is reported to have done facetiously (shrugging off the force of the question). "He was preparing hell," he said, "for those who pry too deep." It is one thing to see the answer; it is another to laugh at the questioner—and for myself I do not answer these things thus. More willingly would I have answered, "I do not know what I do not know," than cause one who asked a deep question to be ridiculed—and by such tactics gain praise for a worthless answer.

So Paulos has it exactly backward. But what exactly is Augustine's answer?

> Rather, I say that thou, our God, art the Creator of every creature. And if in the term "heaven and earth" every creature is included, I make bold to say further: "Before God made heaven

---

[11] "Why I am Not a Christian," in *Why I am Not a Christian and Other Essays on Religion and Related Subjects* (New York: Simon and Schuster, 1957).

[12] *I Think, Therefore I Laugh* (New York: Columbia University Press, 2000), p. 71.

and earth, He did not make anything at all. For if He did, what did He make unless it were a creature?" I do indeed wish that I knew all that I desire to know to my profit as surely as I know that no creature was made before any creature was made.[13]

Sharon Kaye explains:

> As a matter of fact, it is clear that Augustine was much exercised by the question. He is unable to come up with an answer to it in the Confessions. He indicates, after chastising the jokers, that it is important to be humble in the presence of God's mysteries. (This is a common theme throughout the Confessions.) What he is getting at in that second paragraph, though, seems to me to be this: Well, if "heaven and earth" includes all of creation, then we can be sure that God was not creating before He made heaven and earth. After all, it would be a logical contradiction to create before creation. So, we may not know what God was doing, but at least we can be certain what He was *not* doing. Augustine seems to recognize that his answer is partial and inadequate.
>
> But in *City of God* bk. XII, ch. 15 he comes up with a better answer. He argues that the question is moot because God created time when He created the world. So there was no "before" creation. He writes: "For where there is no creature whose changing movements admit of succession, there cannot be time at all." Russell might still say this constitutes "changing the subject." Maybe, maybe not.
>
> We shouldn't be too hard on Paulos, though, for calling the joke "Augustine's reaction." I have heard it presented as Augustine's many times. And I don't think this is too unfair. One way to read the text is to say that Augustine repeats the joke precisely because he is tempted by this response himself. It would be very like him to use a rhetorical device to avoid answering a question. He did it all the time. In this case, however, he doesn't really want to dismiss the question. He wants an answer, and it takes him some nine years [between *Confessions* and *City of God*] to find it.[14]

---

[13] Augustine, *Confessions*, Chap. 12, Sec. 14.

[14] Her email to me, 3 May 2001. Sharon M. Kaye is co-author (with Paul Thomson) of *On Augustine* (Belmont, CA: Wadsworth, 2001).

Augustine's eventual answer, that there was no before creation because that's when time started, might not seem to be very good to you. But Augustine is in good company when he gives this answer. It's exactly what many contemporary astrophysicists say when asked what was going on before the Big Bang, which they now consider to be the first event that started things off.

> In a more widely known turtle story, Bertrand Russell (or in other versions, some famous scientist) was giving a public lecture in which the facts about the arrangement of the solar system were mentioned. At the end of the lecture, a little old lady at the back of the room got up and said: "What you have told us is rubbish. The world is really a flat plate supported on the back of a giant tortoise."
>
> Russell (or the scientist) gave a superior smile before replying, "What is the tortoise standing on?"
>
> "You're very clever, young man, very clever," said the old lady. "But it's turtles all the way down."[15]

The Miracle on the Expressway

Hugely unlikely events are sometimes seen as miracles by religious believers, and counted as evidence for the existence of God. Russell offered the following facetious argument along those lines, paraphrased here:

> The next time you're on an expressway, take note of the number on the license plate of one car at random. Now calculate the probability of seeing exactly that number: given the thousands of cars with different license-plate numbers that travel on that expressway, the probability of seeing that one is minuscule. A miracle! God must exist.

A QUESTION TO THINK ABOUT: Nobody is fooled by this reasoning, but it's not easy to explain exactly what has gone wrong. Can you?

> Some unusual arguments for God's existence:
>
> "The Bible has been translated into hundreds of different languages, but God's existence is mentioned in *every single translation*! Such widespread testimony would be inexplicable unless He exists." —from a paper written by one of my students.

---

15 A version of the story is told by Stephen W. Hawking in *A Brief History of Time: From the Big Bang to Black Holes* (New York: Bantam Books, 1988).

> "This old world has three times as much water as land but
> with all of its twisting and turning not a drop sloshes off
> into space." — cited as evidence of God's guiding hand in a
> magazine symposium[16]

Another argument for God's existence is the result of some funny business in the logic of self-reference; see the section in Chapter VI called **Another Silly Proof of God's Existence**. See also, in the same chapter, **Oh No!** *More* **Silly Proofs of God's Existence!**.

I Believe in Love

It seems to be good advice to get clear first on what your idea of God is, before you try to present proofs that He exists. Well, when some religiously-minded people think about God, they're inclined to identify him with *love*: "God is love." If this is accepted, then there's surely no problem in establishing the existence of God, because it's clear that love exists.

The problem here is that this "proof" appears to change the subject. If that's all you mean by 'God,' then I think everyone would admit that what you call 'God' exists. But religious people, while often agreeing that there's some sort of close connection between God and love, would deny that love is all there is to God. Then proving his existence gets a little harder.

> Russell used to outrage a lot of conventional people by giv-
> ing lectures advocating sex outside of marriage. During the
> question period after one of those lectures, a woman got up
> in the audience and said, "The trouble with you, Professor
> Russell, is that you don't believe in love." Russell replied:
> "Believe in it, madam! I've seen it done!"

God, Whales, and Wales

> "The probability of life originating from accident is com-
> parable to the probability of the Unabridged Dictionary re-
> sulting from an explosion in a printing factory." — Edwin
> Grant Conklin, Professor of Biology, Princeton University,
> 1903-1933. Conklin was not a Darwinian; he believed in
> what was called theistic evolution. He is perhaps best known
> for his spirited attempt to interpret the Bible in terms of

---

[16] "Why I Believe in God," *Ebony Magazine* (November 1962), p. 96. Quoted by B. C. Nerlich in "Popular Arguments for the Existence of God," in *The Encyclopedia of Philosophy*, ed. Paul Edwards (New York: Macmillan, 1967), p. 409.

modern science, in which he suggested, among other things,
that Jonah could not have resided in the whale's stomach;
he must have been in the laryngeal chamber.

Among the more serious attempts to prove God's existence, one sort of argument frequently proposed says that the way the visible natural world is arranged gives us reason to think that it was designed that way by an intelligent being, on purpose; and this being must be God. The assumption behind this argument is that the visible world wouldn't have gotten to be the way it is all by itself, by ordinary natural processes. (Compare, in this respect, the argument for the Invisible Gardener, considered above.) This familiar argument—usually called the Argument From Design—has convinced many people; on the other hand, it has also received a lot of criticism, mostly on the grounds that there are, at least nowadays, perfectly good scientific ways in which to account for the way the world is arranged. The spectacularly complex adaptations of living things, for example, which used to be taken as conclusive evidence of God's designing hand, are these days thought by most people and just about all scientists to be explainable by evolution.

Here, however, is an unfamiliar and interesting version of the Argument From Design.

Imagine you are taking a train west from London. You doze off for a while, then wake up and look out the window. Adjacent to the tracks you see a field of flowers in bloom, which spell out in different colours, "BRITISH RAIL WELCOME YOU TO WALES." You believe as a result of seeing this that you are entering Wales.

It's reasonable for you to come to this belief, but only if you think that somebody planted the flowers to spell out that message on purpose. But if, by an incredible coincidence, a field of wild flowers just happened by accident to spell out that message, you wouldn't be justified in coming to believe that you were entering Wales. Of course, it's also reasonable for you to think that the flowers were arranged that way on purpose by somebody who wanted to give you the message they spelled. The point here is that we wouldn't be justified in taking things as *signs*, as giving us *information*, if we didn't think that they were arranged that way on purpose by an intelligent designer to communicate something to us.

Now, note that we often find out information from the *natural* world— from features of the world that we know were not designed and arranged by people. For example, the appearance of a particularly shaped hill you recognize out the train window would tell you that you're on the outskirts of a certain town. So it must be that even certain features of the natural world—the ones we justifiably get information from—were made on purpose by an intelligent designer. But they weren't designed by people; they must have been designed by another being, one even more clever and powerful than we are. They must have been designed by God.[17]

SOME QUESTIONS TO THINK ABOUT: I don't think this argument works. If you share my reaction, you might try to figure out exactly where it goes wrong. Perhaps you should think about the principle that only what's designed and put there on purpose can give us information. The train story is intended to convince us that this principle is right; are you convinced? Why/why not?

God and the Perfect Pizza

The Ontological Argument is a comparatively unfamiliar proof of God's existence. It's puzzling: many philosophers are convinced that there's something wrong with it, but it's difficult to say exactly what. Here it is:

'God' means *the perfect being*. That's merely a matter of definition. Now, being perfect includes existing. Non-existence is a defect, after all. If I told you about a pizza that was perfect in every way except for the fact that it happened not to exist, you would take that as a very serious flaw.

Well, because existence is one of the things implied by 'perfection,' and because God is, by definition, perfect, God must exist—by definition. To say that God doesn't exist is to utter something that couldn't possibly be true—just as it couldn't be true, by definition, that somebody's sister is male.

I said that it's difficult for those who think that this argument makes a mistake to explain exactly what that mistake is. But perhaps this will convince you that something has gone wrong: if the argument works, wouldn't it prove the existence of the perfect pizza as well? But that's absurd. So something must be wrong in here.

> Amazingly, Bertrand Russell, known for his highly critical attitude toward religion, at one time thought the Ontological Argument was a good one. He wrote:
>
> "I remember the precise moment, one day in 1894, as I was walking along Trinity Lane, when I saw in a flash (or thought I saw) that the ontological argument is valid. I had gone out to buy a tin of tobacco; on my way back, I sud-

---

[17] I have seen this argument attributed to Antony Flew.

denly threw it up in the air, and exclaimed as I caught it: 'Great Scott, the ontological argument is sound.'"[18]

FOR FURTHER READING: Just about every general introductory philosophy book contains something about the Ontological Argument. But do take a look at the source of the title for this section: *God, the Devil, and the Perfect Pizza: Ten Philosophical Questions*, by T. Govier (Peterborough, ON: Broadview Press, 1989).

> The French Enlightenment philosopher Denis Diderot (1713-1784) paid a visit to the Russian Court at the invitation of the empress; there he freely and enthusiastically expressed his atheist views. The empress was much amused, but some of her councillors suggested that it might be desirable to check these expositions of doctrine. The empress didn't want to ask Diderot to stop saying those things, so she contrived a plot to quiet him. Diderot was informed that a learned mathematician had an algebraic proof of the existence of God; would he like to hear it? Diderot said he would, so the great mathematician Leonhard Euler (1707–1783), who was in on the plot, came to court, and announced gravely to Diderot, "Monsieur, $(a + b^2)/n = x$, therefore God exists. Any answer to that?"
>
> Diderot, who knew absolutely no algebra, was embarrassed and disconcerted, and returned to France at once.[19]

5. WHY BELIEVING IN GOD IS A GOOD BET

Pascal's Wager, named for its inventor, the French philosopher and mathematician Blaise Pascal (1623–1662), is a very peculiar argument in favour of belief in God. Here's how it goes.

Many religions suppose that God punishes non-believers with suffering in Hell after death, and that He rewards believers with bliss in Heaven.

Now, suppose you believed in God. Either God exists or He doesn't. If He does, you'll be granted post-mortem eternal heavenly bliss as a reward for your belief; if He doesn't, you will be wrong, but there's no great harm in this. You would have made a fairly harmless mistake.

---

[18] Bertrand Russell, "My Mental Development," in *The Philosophy of Bertrand Russell*, ed. Paul A. Schilpp (Evanston, IL: Library of Living Philosophers, 1944), p. 10.

[19] The source for this anecdote is Thiebault, "Souvenirs de vingt ans de séjour à Berlin," 1804, reported by James Newman in *The World of Mathematics* (New York: Simon and Schuster, 1956).

But suppose you don't believe in God. Either God exists or He doesn't. If He does, you'll suffer hell-fire and damnation as a punishment for your disbelief. If He doesn't, you'll be right, but there's not a great deal of benefit attached to this.

Here's a table that summarizes the potential benefits and dangers of belief and disbelief, given God's existence or non-existence:

	God exists	God doesn't exist
You believe	You get huge benefit (eternal heaven)	You get tiny harm (you were (mistaken)
You don't believe	You get huge harm (eternal hell)	You get tiny benefit (you were correct)

Should you believe?

> You can see that believing gives a potential huge benefit, at the risk of tiny harm. Non-belief gives a potential huge harm, or else a tiny benefit. Even if you happen to think God's existence is hugely unlikely, it's clearly a very good bet for you to believe anyway.

Compare this argument with James's reasoning discussed above; the similarity is that both argue in favour of belief in God on the grounds that it's potentially good for you.

One thing that makes Pascal's reasoning peculiar is that it argues that it's a good idea for you to believe something on the basis of a cost-benefit analysis. It does not give you the normal sort of reason in favour of believing something—namely, reason to think that it's *true*.

Later on, in the item called **The Power of Positive Thinking** in Chapter VII we'll encounter a related case.

Why Believing in God Is Not a Good Bet

But consider this contrary reasoning of the same type.

There's really very little evidence for the existence of God, and rational people harbour reasonable doubts about it. Surely a just God who values rationality wouldn't punish people for being reasonable. He might even reward them for their careful and independent habits of thought. And He might even punish believers for their credulity—for their sloppiness of mind in going along with the herd, believing what there's so little evidence for.

On the other hand, believing the truth is a good thing, its own reward. If there isn't any God, non-believers were right, and believers wrong. We should all value being right above being wrong.

So the table above is mistaken. Here is the right one:

	God exists	God doesn't exist
You believe	Big punishment (hell) for credulity	You get tiny harm (you were mistaken)
You don't believe	Big reward (heaven) for rationality	You get tiny benefit (you were correct)

Should you believe?

Either way, you're better off being a non-believer.

> "The infliction of cruelty with a good conscience is a delight to moralists—that is why they invented hell."—Bertrand Russell

6. WHAT IF THERE ISN'T ANY GOD?

> "If God is dead, then everything is permitted."—attributed (mistakenly) to Fyodor Dostoyevsky[20]

> "I often think how comforting life must have been for early man because he believed in a powerful, benevolent Creator who looked after all things. Imagine his disappointment when he saw his wife putting on weight. Contemporary man, of course, has no such peace of mind. He finds himself in the midst of a crisis of faith. He is what we fashion-

---

[20] Everyone thinks this quote is found in *The Brothers Karamazov*, but it's not. See http://www.infidels.org/library/modern/features/2000/cortesi1.htm for a long story about this. One of the characters in *The Brothers Karamazov* does, however, say, "If there's no immortality of the soul, then there's no virtue, and everything is lawful."

ably call 'alienated.' He has seen the ravages of war, he has known natural catastrophes, he has been to singles bars. My good friend Jacques Monod spoke often of the randomness of the cosmos. He believed everything in existence occurred by pure chance with the possible exception of his breakfast, which he felt certain was made by his housekeeper." — Woody Allen[21]

7. INTO THE MAINSTREAM OF PHILOSOPHY

Traditional religious truths have been a cornerstone of the intellectual foundation of philosophy through the centuries — as they have been, of course, in every area of life. But philosophers have always wanted to use their tools of rational, logical enquiry on the accepted dogmas of religion, just as they use them on every other area of thought. Religious believers often thought that these truths might be justified by rational considerations, and there is a long history of attempts to provide logical arguments to prove God's existence — and an equally long history of the critical treatment of these arguments. The history of philosophical theology contains many more arguments than I have introduced here, of course, and more serious ones — most of the argument I've presented are silly ones, interesting not because they might actually convince someone, but because of the errors they make. An examination of some of the serious arguments for God's existence, and their criticisms, is a good place to start in the study of philosophy of religion — if not to undermine or create belief, at least to give your intellectual skills a workout. It's also interesting to consider the attempts to reconcile the apparent imperfection of the way things are with God's omnipotence and benevolence. This problem is classically known as the Problem of Evil.

Until recently, it got you into a lot of trouble to question the official views of religion, or even to suggest that they needed some clear-headed sceptical consideration. Wise-guy sceptics like Bertrand Russell got themselves in big trouble within living memory. Within the past fifty years, conventional religious belief has suffered a considerable decline in the intellectual arena, but philosophy of religion is still a very lively area. The classical arguments for God's existence still provoke interesting debate. But an important new trend involves the attempt to understand religious belief and practice in new ways. You can see how the pragmatists and the logical positivists might merely reject talk about God as mean-

---

[21] "My Speech to the Graduates," *Side Effects* (New York: Random House, c.1980).

ingless or false; but you can also see how they (and their contemporary successors) might want to think of religious talk and action as a special and unusual sort of thing. Perhaps "statements" of religious "truths" aren't even meant to have the same sort of meaning, function, and testability as ordinary statements about the visible and mundane. Much contemporary philosophy of religion searches for an account of what might be the real meaning of religion.

> "If only God would give me some clear sign! Like making
> a large deposit in my name at a Swiss bank." — Woody Allen

CHAPTER III

TAKING CHANCES:
Probability Theory

R. A. Sorenson claims to have had a friend who objected to
assigning chores by a random lottery, because that's biased
in favour of lucky people.[1]

"You say it's fifty-fifty, but actually it's the opposite."—
George Raft

1. SOME PROBABLE FACTS

Rosencrantz Flips a Coin

In the beginning of Tom Stoppard's play *Rosencrantz and Guildenstern
are Dead*,[2] Rosencrantz has idly been flipping a coin, and it has come up
heads ninety-two times in a row. He is surprised, and he should be. Runs
of two or three heads in a row are not rare, but runs of ninety-two heads
in a row are rather unlikely. How unlikely? Well, the odds of this happening are exactly one in 4,951,760,157,141,521,099,596,496,896. This
is not an easy number to comprehend.

Imagine you were flipping a coin, one flip per second, trying to get a
sequence of ninety-two heads in a row. Each "sequence" of flips ends
when you get a tail. Half of these sequences would last only one flip—
tails the first time—and thus be one second long. But some of these sequences would last longer, when you were lucky enough to get an initial
run of heads. Your average sequence would be two flips long, and thus
would last only two seconds.

The more sequences you ran, the more likely it would be that larger
runs of heads showed up. For example, a run of ten heads in a row shows

---

[1] In *Blindspots* (Oxford: Clarendon Press, 1988), p. 186.
[2] London: Faber and Faber, 1967.

up about once every five hundred twelve sequences. The probability that you'd get at least one run of ten heads in a row would be greater than fifty per cent if you had more than about three hundred fifty sequences. To make it more likely than not that you'd get a run of ten heads in a row, then, you would have to flip coins for about 700 seconds, that is, about twelve minutes.

How long would you have to flip to make it fifty per cent likely that a run of ninety-two heads would show up? A long time. You'd certainly need help. Suppose you engaged 6.2 billion people—the whole population of the earth—in flipping, day and night, year in, year out, without stop. Then it would be fifty per cent likely that we'd come up with a run of ninety-two heads if we all flipped coins for about 35 billion years. That length of time is about three times the estimated current age of the universe. It's not worth the effort.

> Among the explanations Rosencrantz considers for this unusual event is that it's a spectacular vindication of the principle that each individual coin spun individually is as likely to come down heads as tails and therefore should cause no surprise each individual time it does. This is a philosophical joke, of course.

to be or not to xq

Here's another closely related, somewhat surprising application of probability mathematics. You've probably heard the old saying that if some monkeys were typing at random long enough, one of them would eventually write *Hamlet*. Yes, but this would happen on average once in an *exceedingly* long time. What's interesting is how long.

Well, let's change the story to give them a chance of succeeding in a reasonable length of time. First, we'll give them a smaller task than reproducing all of *Hamlet*. All we'll look for is that one of them produce
    to be or not to be
We'll help them out by disabling the shift-key and all the punctuation and number keys on the typewriters, so all they can type are lower-case letters and the space bar.

And we'll use a *lot* of monkeys. A football field is an ideal place to put a big crowd of monkeys where we can keep an eye on them, to make sure they keep typing and don't get up to any monkey business. American football fields have an area of 5,350 square yards in-bounds, and if we really crowd those monkeys, and keep their little desks really small, we can fit one monkey per square yard. There are about two thousand degree-granting colleges and universities in the United States, and just about every one of them has a football field that we'll take over. (The colleges and universities are sure to agree. Filling their field with randomly typing monkeys is, after all, just as academically relevant as what normally takes place on those fields.)

Okay; now we have over 10,700,000 monkeys typing away at random. We allow them only an hour a day to eat, sleep, go to the bathroom, scratch themselves, or pick fleas off each other. Imagine that they type pretty fast: about two characters per second. So each monkey turns out an eighteen-character string—the length of the target quote—every nine seconds. How long would they have to type to make it more than 50% likely that one of these strings is that line from Hamlet?

The probability of typing the initial 't' from among the twenty-seven keys is 1/27. The probability of typing the eighteen-character string (including spaces) that we're looking for is $(1/27)^{18}$. To make it 50% likely that they'd produce at least one string that said 'to be or not to be' the monkeys would have to produce 40,306,326,253,959,541,280,123,558 strings. That's a lot. Do the arithmetic: at nine seconds a string per monkey, how long would it take 10,700,000 monkeys to do this?

> It would take them a bit over a trillion years, about thirty times as long as it would take to make ninety-two heads 50% probable. Don't hold your breath waiting for this one either.

Another Surprising Sequence

Now suppose that you flipped a coin ninety-two times and got this sequence (which I've generated using a randomizing program on my computer):

TTHTTHHTTTHHTTTHHHTTHTHHTTHHT
HTTHHTTHTTHTTTHHHTHTHHHTHHTTTTH
HTTTTHTTHTHTHHTHTHHHHHTHTHHTTHTH

Would you be surprised?

> Before you answer, note that the probability of throwing exactly this sequence of heads and tails is exactly equal to the probability of throwing ninety-two heads in a row. Every possible string of ninety-two throws is equally sur-

prising! But we have made the same mistake as Russell was joking about in his license-plate "proof" of God's existence (Chapter II, **The Miracle on the Expressway**).

You're On a Roll!

Examine that random sequence of coin-flips in the last item carefully. Do you see that sequence about two-thirds of the way through where it goes TTTTHHTTTT? That's two bunches of four tails within ten flips! Tails is really having a hot streak! What a rally! But the rally fizzles, and Tails goes into a slump. The momentum switches to Heads—about a dozen flips later, Heads gets five in a row. Notice how quickly the momentum usually shifts: several times during this run, TT is followed by HH, or HH by TT.

Does all this talk of streaks and rallies, momentum and slumps, remind you of sportscaster talk? Maybe such things really do exist in sports, but they certainly don't in a random series of coin flips. *None* of these notions is needed to explain what's going on in the random series of flips. It's just random; that's all there is to it. The important thing to remember, however, is that in any long random series, patterns will (just by accident) show up. But these patterns don't need any explanation. (What would need explanation is if they *didn't* show up.)

The next time you're listening to sportscaster prattle, ask yourself whether the "patterns" they're so interested in detecting need all that elaborate explanation they give them, or whether they're just accidental features of a largely random series.

FOR FURTHER READING: For an excellent discussion of the probability of improbable chance events, see Chapter 2 in John Allen Paulos's *Innumeracy: Mathematical Illiteracy and Its Consequences* (New York: Vintage Books, 1990). Paulos convincingly argues, for example, that DiMaggio's streak of hitting safely in fifty-six consecutive games was not all that unlikely. Given the normal range of batting averages of baseball players, and the number of games that have been played, it's not surprising that just by accident some player has had a streak of this size.

Your Extraordinary Ancestors

The following reasoning embodies a similar mistake about probabilities. See if you can discover where the mistake is.

One hundred years ago, life was tougher and medical science less effective, and a larger percentage of the population died in infancy and childhood. Several hundreds of years back, it was quite common for people to die before they reached puberty; and in general the pre-puberty mortality rate increases the further back one looks.

Now consider that large group of people who are your ancestors: your mother and father, your four grandparents, your eight great-grandparents, and so on. Here's an extraordinary—even miraculous—fact about them. Not a *single one* of them died before reaching sexual maturity!

How Many Ancestors Do You Have?

Answering this question depends on how far back we're supposed to go; do those pre-human organisms that evolved into us count as ancestors? It's difficult to date the appearance of humans, not only because we don't know all the facts. Even if we knew all the facts about the history of the evolution of our pre-human primate ancestors into the first humans, it would be a matter of somewhat arbitrary decision where to count the first humans as showing up, along a scale of gradually changing organisms. The Population Reference Bureau in Washington, D.C., you might like to know, now counts the first humans as showing up in about 200,000 BC, and calculates that there have been about 100 billion humans, including the 6.2 billion now alive, on earth ever.

We can, however, make some assumptions and calculations. You had two parents, four grandparents, eight great grandparents, sixteen great-great-grandparents, thirty-two great-great-great-grandparents, and so on. Assume that your human ancestors gave birth to the next generation when they were twenty, on average. One hundred years ago, then, gets us five generations back, to the time of your thirty-two great-great-great-grandparents. Two hundred years ago is ten generations back; then you had 2^{10} = 1,024 ancestors alive. Five hundred years ago, twenty-five generations back, these calculations give you 33,554,432 ancestors. One thousand years ago, there must have been 1,125,899,906,842,624 of them. But this number is *much* larger than the number of humans alive then, which was somewhere around 300 million. It's over ten thousand times the number of humans that have *ever* existed. Something has gone drastically wrong here, but what?

The answer is that some of your ancestors themselves share ancestors. That is to say, at a number of places in your family tree there must have been cases in which married ancestors of yours were at least distantly related. Suppose, for example, that your mother and your father shared a pair of great-great-great-grandparents. This fact alone would cut the number of people in your family tree in half. There must have been a lot of this in everyone's family.

The Miracle of You

If your mother and father had never met, then you would never have been born, right? But *they* would never have existed (nor would you) if *their* parents had never met; and so on back through the number—whatever it is—of your ancestors. An enormous number of fortuitous and improbable meetings and marriages, stretching back into the distant past, were necessary for you to be here today.

Not just that, but each man releases millions of sperms during each ejaculation. Had a different one of your father's sperms fertilized your mother's ovum, a person with a different genetic makeup would have been born—not you, right? So each fertilization of an ovum is the outcome of an enormous lottery. Had any of these been different, in any of your ancestors, you would not be here today.

Now put these two facts together, and calculate how improbable your existence really is. Your being here is so improbable that we can't even conceptualize probabilities that small. It's a miracle! Everyone else's existence is a miracle too! Most of the events in the universe, come to think of it, are also miracles!

This is still another mistake analogous to Russell's "proof" of the existence of God (**The Miracle on the Expressway**, Chapter II).

2. ONE-THIRD OF TWO

Take three cards out of a deck: an ace, a king, and a queen. Shuffle the three, and put them face down on a table. Clearly the probability of picking an ace out of these three at random is 1/3.

But suppose you brush one of the three, at random, off the table; it falls face down on the floor, and you don't turn it over, so you don't know which card fell. Now you pick one of the two remaining cards at random. What is the probability now of picking an ace?

> A surprising number of people either think the probability is 1/2, or can't answer the question. The real answer is 1/3. People are puzzled by the fact that you are picking one card out of *two*.

3. HAPPY BIRTHDAY DEAR YOU-TWO

Suppose there are forty people in a room; how likely is it that two (or more) of them share the same birthday?[3]

> Most people would estimate that it is quite improbable, since there are over nine times as many days in the year as there are people in the room; but in fact, it is about 90 per cent likely—that is, likely enough to be a safe bet.
>
> It's easiest to think about the probability that a certain room contains *no* shared birthdays; the probability of at least one shared birthday is one minus that number.
>
> Imagine a party at which guests show up one at a time. When the host is alone in the room, it's of course impossible that there are two in the room sharing a birthday. The first person enters; her birthday may be on any one of the 365 days of the year, and chances are 364 out of 365 (.9973) that her birthday is different from the host's. When the third arrives, the likelihood that there are still no shared birthdays is this number times the probability that the third guest has a different birthday from either of the first two—363/365. Thus it is about .992 likely that there are no sharers among the three. When the fourth arrives, the probability that there are still no shared birthdays is .992 times 362/365 = .984. At the fifth arrival it is .984 times 361/365: .973.
>
> We continue to multiply by gradually smaller numbers as more people arrive. When there are ten people, the probability there is *no* shared birthday is about 88

---

[3] Another traditional mathematical surprise reported in Paulos's *Innumeracy*, pp. 35–37.

per cent; it falls slightly below 50 per cent when the twenty-third guest arrives; it is slightly below 30 per cent when the thirtieth shows up. When there are forty people in the room, the probability is around 10 per cent that no birthdays are shared, so it is about 90 per cent that there is a shared birthday. If there are fifty guests, the probability of no shared birthdays is a mere 3 per cent.

4. THE TROUBLE WITH TAXIS

Suppose that psychologists have discovered that witnesses to a single-car accident are 80 per cent likely to be able to report the colour of the car correctly. Now, suppose that 95 per cent of the taxis in Moose Jaw are yellow, and the remaining 5 per cent are blue. A taxi dents a light-pole, then speeds away; a witness reports to the police that the taxi was blue. Should the police regard this evidence as trustworthy, and think it likely that a blue taxi was the culprit?

Most people would say that since people are 80 per cent trustworthy at reporting, the police should regard this testimony as fairly (80 per cent) reliable. But this is wrong. In fact, the odds are almost five to one the witness was mistaken, and the taxi was really yellow.

Here's a way to think about this that may make it more plausible. Consider a random bunch of one hundred witnessed taxi accidents in Moose Jaw. Since 95 per cent of the taxis are yellow (and assuming that the colour of the taxi has no bearing on how accident-prone it is), about ninety-five of these accidents will involve yellow taxis, and about five of them blue taxis. Now consider the yellow-taxi accidents and the blue-taxi accidents separately.

Since witnesses are 80 per cent reliable, they will report the colour in the ninety-five yellow-taxi accidents correctly in about seventy-six cases; in the remaining nineteen yellow-taxi accidents they will report falsely that the colour was blue. And they will report the colour in a blue-taxi accident correctly in four of the five cases; in one case, the report will be an incorrect report that it was yellow.

So among these one hundred accidents, there will likely be nineteen cases in which the witness says the taxi was blue and was incorrect; and four cases in which the witness says the taxi was blue and was correct. For a random taxi accident, then, it's more likely that the report of a blue taxi was mistaken. In fact, the probability that it was correct is only four out of twenty-three: 17 per cent.

The mistake in this case arises because most people consider the wrong probability. Eighty per cent is the probability that a witness says "blue" given that the taxi was blue, but the question is about a different probability: that the taxi was blue given that the witness says "blue."[4]

5. DO COINS OBEY THE LAW?

Suppose a coin is flipped five times, and comes up heads every time. What would you guess the next flip will be?

Many people think that it's quite likely that the next flip will be tails—that the coin, in docile obedience to the "law of averages," will try to even out the total. If it's a fair coin, however, the probability the next flip is heads is 1/2. (In fact, the first five flips are evidence that the coin is not fair—that it's a trick coin designed to come up heads—so these flips make it more likely that the next flip will come up heads.)

The mistake is such a common one among gamblers that it even has a name: it's called the Gambler's Fallacy, or the Monte Carlo Fallacy. (Many gamblers at Monte Carlo presumably believe that the longer a number has not come up on a roulette wheel, the more likely it is that it will come up, or that if black has come up on many more than half of the last run of rolls, then it's likely that red will come up on more than half of the next run of rolls.)

The coin mistake is based on a correct premise: that as the number of flips of a fair coin increases, the percentage of heads and tails will tend to grow more equal, closer to 50 per cent each. But the way this will happen is not by the coin's preferring tails for a while: a large number of suc-

---

[4] A similar example is given in *Innumeracy*, pp. 164–165.

ceeding flips will most likely be about half heads and half tails, and adding this large number of heads and tails will tend to wash out, in the grand total, the early preponderance of heads.

A QUESTION TO THINK ABOUT: Here's some incorrect reasoning that argues to the opposite conclusion of the Gambler's Fallacy: if there has just been a run of tails you should bet that the next one will be *tails*.

It's really improbable that a sequence of flips will alternate heads and tails (HTHTHTHT...). What's much more likely is a sequence with streaks of heads—a few heads in a row—and streaks of tails: HHTTTHHTHHHTTT for example. Given this fact, if the last flip was tails, you should bet that the next one is tails.

What's wrong with that reasoning?

(I'm told that real gamblers in real casinos tend to bet in streaks—that is, given a couple of tails, they'd bet on tails. So maybe this is the real "Gambler's Fallacy.")

Why It's Not Certain That You'll Be in a Plane Crash

What are the chances you'll be in a plane crash? In the U.S. there are, on average, about two crashes out of about a million commercial flights per year. For simplicity, let's suppose the chances of a crash are one in a million.

Now let's suppose that you took a million plane trips. (This would be hard to do; it would mean 27 flights a day for 100 years.) Would your chances of being in a plane crash rise to one in one—that is, to certainty? Many people would think so. But this is a mistake about probabilities related to the ones we have already seen. Let's see if I can make clear exactly where the mistake lies.

Let's begin with a simpler case. Imagine a cup containing two jelly beans: one red and one green. Suppose you reach in without looking, and pick one of them out. What is the probability that the one you picked is red? The answer, of course, is 1/2.

Now suppose instead that you make two picks out of the cup: what is the probability of picking a red one now? Well, that depends. I haven't given you enough information about the picking procedure for this question to be answered. Perhaps the procedure is this: you pick one jelly bean out, then holding on to that one (or eating it) you pick a second one—the only one remaining. If that's the procedure, then it's certain that you'll get the red one, because you get both. The probability you have the red one after the first pick is 1/2; after the second pick it's 2/2, or 100 per cent. You just do a simple addition of fractions: 1/2 + 1/2.

But perhaps the procedures is this: you pick one jelly bean out and look at it. Then you replace that jelly bean, shake the cup up, and pick again. Now, it should be clear, it's *not* certain that you'll get the red one on either of the two picks. You might, for instance, get the green both times.

Here's the difference between these procedures. In the first procedure, what you get on the one pick affects the probability of picking a red jelly bean on the next pick. If you do get the red one the first time, for example, the probability of picking a red one the second time is of course zero. If you don't get a red one the first time, that means that the only remaining one is red, so the probability of getting a red one the second time is 100 per cent. But in the second procedure (when you replace the first one), the probability of getting a red bean on any pick is 1/2, and is independent of what happens on any other pick.

Now, the plane-crash problem is like the second jelly bean procedure. That is: the probability of any particular plane crashing is (we assume) one out of one million, and is unaffected by whether or not another plane has crashed earlier. That's why a simple addition of fractions (1/1,000,000 + 1/1,000,000 etc.) doesn't calculate the probability of a plane crash in several trips, and that's why the probability of a crash in one million trips is not 1,000,000 x 1/1,000,000 = 1.

A Frequent Flier Bonus

Well, how *do* you figure out the odds of a crash among one million flights? Let's look first at the simpler jelly bean case, second selection procedure.

When previous picks are replaced, there are four different possibilities for the results of two picks:

PICK 1	PICK 2
R	R
R	G
G	R
G	G

Each of these possibilities is equally probable. Now, among these four ways, one has *no* red jelly beans picked (the last one on the list). That means that the chances of your picking no red jelly beans at all is 1/4; and the chance of your picking the red jelly bean at least once is 1 minus 1/4 = 3/4.

How can we calculate these numbers in general? Note that the chance that any one pick does not get a red jelly bean is 1/2. The chance that the jelly bean picked on the first pick is non-red *and* the jelly bean picked on the second pick is non-red 1/2 X 1/2 = 1/4. So the probability of getting red on at least one pick is 1 minus this: 3/4.

Let's apply this to the airplane case. The chances of *no* crash on any one flight is 999,999/1,000,000. The chances of no crash during a million flights is this number times itself one million times, in other words, this number to the millionth power. In case you don't have the time to work out this arithmetic by hand, I have done it for you on my computer. The probability of no crash during a million flights is .363; so the probability that there will be at least one crash is .627 — about two out of three. So it's more likely than not that at least one of these flights will end in a crash, but at least it's not certain. That's a small frequent flier bonus.

You needn't start worrying about the odds of being in a plane crash getting as high as two out of three, by the way. If you went on ten separate plane trips a day, every day of the year, it would take you 274 years to travel on a million flights.

A QUESTION TO THINK ABOUT: The chances that someone has a bomb in his luggage on any particular flight are small, but they're large enough to make some people worry. The chances that any particular flight is carrying *two* people who have bombs in their luggage are very much smaller. (If the probability that there's one person is $1/n$, then the probability that there are two people is $1/n^2$. Do you see why?)

The reasoning so far is correct, but consider the following. Smedley is quite worried that flights he's on will be destroyed by luggage-bombs. But the chances of there being *two* bombs are so small that he's not concerned about that event. What he does, then, is to carry a bomb in his luggage, designed not to go off, or course. He reasons that in order to be in danger of being killed by a luggage-bomb, someone else must have a bomb on the plane too, but the chances of two bombs on the same plane are so small that he doesn't have to worry. Smedley is making a mistake in his reasoning about probabilities. Can you explain exactly where his mistake is?[5]

---

[5] An old story told again by John Allen Paulos in *Innumeracy*, pp. 33–34.

6. INTO THE MAINSTREAM OF PHILOSOPHY

Philosophers concern themselves with probability in two ways. One of these is the attempt to provide the rules for calculating probabilities. In this we overlap with what's done in mathematics departments. This is a fairly well-developed science, and you can find out its basics in many introductory logic books, to be found in university bookstores. The mathematics of elementary probability theory isn't too complicated, and there are plenty of interesting puzzles even at this level. My chapter has provided a rather unfair sample of the applications of probability theory, in that I have presented a number of cases in which the theory gives results that are unexpected and rather surprising. In ordinary life, we confidently apply probability calculations in all sorts of ordinary ways, with unsurprising results. The academic study of probability rarely conflicts with our ordinary ways of probabilistic thought. Its usual concern is rather to explain our ordinary thought—to provide a systematic and precise theory for it.

The second area of philosophical concern about probability is to explain what it means. Here's a sample question. Suppose a coin is flipped only once, then destroyed. (It's a chocolate coin: you flip it, then eat it.) It comes up heads. Now what does it mean to say that the probability is 50 per cent that the coin comes up heads? A natural way to explain the statement that something is 50 per cent probable is to say that about 50 per cent of a very long series of events will come out that way. But there isn't a very long series of flips of the chocolate coin: there's only one flip. Does it make any sense to talk about probabilities here? A second sort of question is raised indirectly by the Rosencrantz example. Suppose (to make things a little less bizarre) that a coin is flipped five times, and comes up heads each time. We nevertheless want to say that the probability of its coming up heads is only 50 per cent, and that the run we got was fairly unlikely. What does this mean? How can we say that the probability of heads was only 50 per cent, despite the fact that we got 100 per cent? What is probability anyway?

CHAPTER IV

MAKING CHOICES:
Decision Theory

1. SOME DECISION PUZZLES

The Elusive Wine-Bottle

Suppose you have been given the magnificent inheritance of $10 from a late rich uncle. The string attached is that you can invest this money if you like, but you must use the money (or the eventual proceeds from its investment) to buy a bottle of wine. You're glad to have the money, since you love wine and can't afford much. Now, you can buy a mediocre bottle for the $10 right now, but a perfectly safe investment will give you 10 per cent interest per year; so next year at this time you'll have $11. Even counting in inflation and taxes on your investment, let's imagine that the proceeds of your investment will get you a slightly better bottle of wine, so you decide to wait, because you're in no hurry. But next year, you can invest that $11 for another year, yielding $12.10 a year from then, which will buy a still better bottle. So you invest again. Do you see a philosophical paradox arising?

> But every year you face the same choice, and every year you're better off investing than spending. So you never buy the bottle. You not only deprive yourself of the bottle you'd enjoy; you also violate the terms of the will.

A version of this paradox has resulted in a problem for some of my friends. They have wanted to replace their old computers for years, but prices for computers have kept coming down, and they keep thinking (correctly) that they should wait a while to get a better deal. So they never replace their old one.

A QUESTION TO THINK ABOUT: What has gone wrong with the reasoning in these two examples?

The Proof That Many People are Crazy or Stupid

There is a pretty persuasive line of reasoning that argues to the conclusion that anyone who ever buys a lottery ticket or gambles in a casino is either crazy or stupid. (The state-run lottery has been called a "stupidity tax.") This is a distressing conclusion, given the huge number of people we're talking about.

When is a choice rational? Answering that question is a tall order, but some philosophers think that progress toward an answer can be made by thinking in terms of the *expected utility* of an action.

The *utility* of something for you is simply a measure of how much you like it. If you would prefer X to Y, then X has more utility than Y. If you'd trade two Y's for one X, then X has at least twice the utility of Y. In some cases, we might even be able to assign numbers to the utilities someone gives some things. Now we can say that the rational choice among alternatives is the choice that would give that person the greatest utility. If an action has several consequences, its utility is the sum of the utilities of each of the consequences.

But many choices are made when we're not sure what the results will be. Sometimes the outcomes of our action are a complete surprise, pleasant or otherwise. But sometimes we can at least judge the *probabilities* of outcomes of our choices. When we know the probability of an outcome, we can calculate its *expected utility* by multiplying its utility times its probability. Suppose for example, that there's one chance in 1,000 you'll win a lottery, and if you win you'll get $3,000. The expected utility of this outcome is $1/1000 \times \$3,000 = \$3$. There's a probability of $999/1000$ that you'll get nothing. So the expected utility of this outcome is $999/1000 \times \$0 = \$0$. So the total expected utility of all outcomes is $\$3 + \$0 = \$3$. But suppose it costs $1 to buy a ticket. Then the total expected utility of playing this lottery once = $\$3 - \$1 = \$2$. If you buy only one lottery ticket once, you're likely to lose, of course. But if you play many times, you can expect to come out ahead in the long run, by $2 per game played. It's a good idea to play this lottery.

But suppose that lottery costs $5 per ticket. The total expected utility of playing this lottery once is now $\$3 - \$5: -\$2$. This means in the long run you can expect an average loss of $2 per game played. This is not a rational way to make money. Playing this game is like throwing $2 down the toilet each time.

But the games run by lotteries and casinos *all* work like this second lottery. They *all* offer players an average expected loss on each game. The reason is simple: they are all running their gambles to make money; and for them to make money in the long run, players must, on average, lose money.

Now why would anyone play a sucker's game such as this? Here are two possible reasons: (a) They're suffering from a psychological problem that forces them to gamble self-destructively. (b) They don't understand the logic behind expected utility. Putting the matter very bluntly, they're either crazy or stupid.

But before you get too depressed about the mental health and intelligence of the rest of the human race, consider two things people might say to explain why they play lotteries and gamble in casinos.

(1) "It's fun." What this means in terms of our calculations is that we haven't calculated the overall utility of the second lottery correctly, because we haven't added in the enjoyment of playing. Suppose that the fun is worth, in money terms, $3 per game. Even though the average money loss will be $2, the fun-value gain is $3; so everything considered, you'll be ahead, on average, by the equivalent of $1 each game. It still means that you will lose money in the long run, but you will have enough fun playing to make it worth it.

(2) "The five dollars I spend on a ticket means next to nothing to me, but if I won a prize it would be worth a great deal." This again means that we haven't calculated the worth of each game correctly. The calculation multiplies the *utility*—a measure of desirability—times its probability. Now we have merely stuck in dollar figures here. Using these implies that $3,000 has 600 times the value of $5; but this may not be the case. Here, in fact, what the person seems to be saying is that the worth of $3,000 to him or her is *greater* than 600 times the worth of $5. Suppose, then, that we assign (arbitrarily) a utility of 5 units to $5, and a utility of *10,000* units to $3000. This makes the calculations quite different: the average payoff is (1/1000 x 10,000) + (999/1000 x 0) = 10 units. The cost of playing is 5 units, so we're ahead on average 10 - 5 = 5 units each game.

Perhaps this restores your faith in humanity's sanity and intelligence. But then again, there's the matter of the popularity of TV wrestling.

2. THE GENERAL MAKES SOME BAD CHOICES

Two psychologists, A. Tversky and D. Kahneman, conducted a famous series of experiments on people's decision making. Here's one of their results.

First they gave a bunch of people Problem 1:

1. Imagine you are a general surrounded by an overwhelming enemy force which will wipe out everyone in your 600-man army unless you take one of two available escape routes. Your intelligence officers explain that if you take the first route you will save 200 soldiers, whereas if you take the second route the probability is 1/3 that all 600 will make it, but 2/3 that they'll all die. Which route do you take?

Three out of four people choose the first route, since 200 lives can definitely be saved that way, whereas the probability is 2/3 that the second route will result in even more deaths.

Maybe this reasoning is okay and maybe it isn't. Notice that on standard decision theory we could calculate the "expected deaths" for the second route as $(1/3 \times 0) + (2/3 \times 600) = 400$. This is the same as the "expected deaths" for the first route: $(1 \times 400) = 400$. But perhaps (as in the lottery case) something else is going on in here. Maybe people also want to avoid the possibility of everyone dying on the second route.

Anyway, then Tversky and Kahneman gave people Problem 2:

2. Imagine again you're a general faced with a decision between two escape routes. If you take the first one, 400 of your soldiers will die. If you choose the second route, the probability is 1/3 that none of your soldiers will die, and 2/3 that all 600 will die. Which route do you take?

Four out of five people now choose the second route, reasoning that the first route will lead to 400 deaths, while there's at least a probability of 1/3 that everyone will get out okay if they go for the second route.

Can you see what's wrong with the reasoning the majority of people are doing here?

Look carefully at Problems 1 and 2. They describe identical choices! It looks like there isn't any subtle evaluation of alternatives going on here. What's going on here is just a flat-out mistake. People are making irrational decisions, misled by the way the question is phrased.

FOR FURTHER READING: A good summary of some of Tversky and Kahneman's conclusions is found in Chapter 1 of *Judgement Under Uncertainty: Heuristics and Bias,* ed. Daniel Kahneman, Paul Slovic, and Amos Tversky (Cambridge: Cambridge University Press, 1982).

Why We're All Nasty

Here's an interesting speculation that stems from other work of Kahneman and Tversky.

Most things we do many times have a degree of variability in their performance. A baseball player with a batting average of .300 gets a hit 30 per cent of the time; but he might get a hit during four out of five at-bats at one game, and during only one out of five at-bats at another game. Kahneman and Tversky's study looked at the behaviour of student pilots and their instructors. When practising landings, there was the expectable variation in quality: sometimes the student pilots performed a landing that was much smoother than their average and sometimes one that was much rougher than their average.

Now, imagine that a .300 hitter has had a very bad day: no hits for five at-bats. Because his average is better than this, it's likely that the next day will be better. Similarly, a very good day, on which the batter performs way above his average—for example five hits for five at-bats—will likely be followed by a worse performance the next day. This statistical phenomenon is called "reversion to the mean."

Wait a minute! Isn't this the Gambler's Fallacy?

No it isn't. Go back and read **Do Coins Obey the Law?** in Chapter III if you need to be reminded what this fallacy is; and make sure you see why what has just been said is different.)

Don't interrupt! Where was I? Oh yeah.

The pilot trainers observed by the psychologists praised their students for smooth landings, and criticized them harshly for rough ones. Simply because of reversion to the mean, a very bad landing was often followed by a better one; and the instructors mistakenly attributed this to the harsh criticism. Reversion to the mean also meant that a very good landing was often followed by a worse one; and the instructors took this to show that their praise for the good one wasn't of any use—maybe it even made the student performance worse. The instructors concluded that verbal rewards are detrimental to learning, while verbal punishments are beneficial. (This conclusion, claim Kahneman and Tversky, is "contrary to accepted psychological doctrine.")

Now this sort of thing might be generalized to all sorts of areas of human interaction. The mere operation of statistical laws have the result that we're encouraged to punish others, and discouraged from rewarding or praising. Maybe that's why we're all so nasty.[1]

3. A GOOD LOTTERY STRATEGY

In some lotteries you choose your own number to play. If that number comes up, you win the jackpot. If several people have picked that number, then the jackpot is divided among them.

Suppose you can pick any number between 1 and 1000. Would you be tempted to pick 1? How about 1000? Would you think it would be more likely that 437 would win than 1?

> Assuming this is a fair lottery, the chances of 1, 1000, 437, or any other number between 1 and 1000 coming up are all equal: one out of 1000.

Were you tempted to avoid picking 1 or 1000? Many people are, because these numbers don't look "random" to them. They look "special." People think that it would be an unlikely coincidence for one of these "special" numbers to come up; they think that "random" numbers such as 119, 437, 602, and 841 are much more likely to come up in a random draw.

Now, given this mistake many lottery players make, and given the rules of this lottery, there's a good strategy for you to use in choosing a number. Can you see what it is?

> What you want to do is to pick a number which nobody else has picked, so that you would get the whole jackpot,

---

[1] The flight training observations and Kahneman and Tversky's conclusions can be found in their article "On the Psychology of Prediction," *Psychological Review*, v. 80, 1973, pp. 237–251. It's summarized in the book chapter mentioned above.

instead of having to share it. Given that people are less likely to pick "special" numbers like 1, 1000, 500, and 666, you should pick one of these, because it's likely that few other players would pick it. Of course, the strategy of picking a number others will see as "special" doesn't make it more likely that you'll win. Each number stands an equal chance—one out of 1000—of winning. But it does make it more likely that *if* you win, you'll win big, because you won't have to share the jackpot with many others.

Another way of making it likely that there aren't many others who have picked the same number is to pick the number that won the previous lottery. As we've just seen in the coin-flipping case, people often expect that the "law of averages" makes it especially unlikely that a number will repeat. Thus many of them will reason incorrectly that the number that came up last time is now "special" and won't come up again.

4. HOW TO GO HOME A WINNER

Here's a sure-fire way to go home a winner at any gambling game.

For simplicity, let's imagine that you're playing this simple game. You put down a bet and flip a coin. If the coin comes up heads, you collect twice your original bet from the casino; if it comes up tails, you lose your bet.

Bet $1 on the first toss. If you win, you get $2; you're ahead, so go home. If you lose, you're down $1; play again, betting $2 on the next game. You have lost $1 on the first game, and bet $2 on the second, so you have spent $3. If you win on this second game, you get $4, so you're $1 ahead. Go home. If you lose, you're down $3. Bet $4 on the next; now you've spent $7. If you win you get $8, so you're a dollar ahead; go home. If you lose, you're down $7; bet $8 on the next game. And so on.

If you keep losing, you'll have to bet $16, $32, $64, and so on, on succeeding games to make sure you'll come out ahead, all told, if you win. But it's absolutely certain that you'll win if you keep at it: you can't keep throwing tails forever! When you win, go home.

Other gambling games aren't this simple; neither are the odds so fair, as we've seen, when you're playing against a casino. But the general strategy can be widely applied: keep betting enough so that if you win, you'll be ahead all told; and quit when you're ahead. It can't fail to work.

This very old strategy for winning gambling games is called "the Martingale."[2] A website dedicated to winning at roulette gives this information about using the Martingale in that game:

> There are many variations of the Martingale roulette system, and it can be used with other methods. For example, you can use a three-stage Martingale of 10-20-40 combined with betting that the decision before the last one will repeat.... or bet that the FIRST shooter (only) will throw a pass (or don't pass). In this latter one you are betting only one bet on each shooter.[3]

(I don't know what any of that means. I include it in case it makes sense to roulette players.)

Is there a flaw in this reasoning? If not, why doesn't everyone use this strategy, and always go home a winner?

No, there is no flaw in this reasoning. One reason why people don't follow it is that it's difficult to quit while you're ahead. There's a simple psychological explanation for this: the experience of winning is such a strong behaviour-reinforcement that it tends to make people continue to play.

But a more important reason this strategy isn't widespread is that, to carry it out, you would need, in theory, an indefinitely large amount of funds available. Every time you lose in this simple game, you have to double your bet. How long can you keep doing this? If you're lucky, you'll win before you run out of money, but this is not guaranteed. So this is a guaranteed strategy only for people with an indefinitely large bankroll, and there aren't any such people.

In any case, real casinos won't let you play the Martingale. The way they prevent this is by putting an upper limit on the size of bets they permit. After a fairly short string of losses, the Martingale strategy would have you bet an amount larger than the limit imposed by just about any casino.

---

[2] Thanks to Ted Cohen, University of Chicago, for this information.
[3] http://www.roulette-systems.com/martingale-roulette.html

SOME QUESTIONS TO THINK ABOUT: Imagine you had an in-definitely large bankroll, and could keep doubling your bet forever. (How could this be? Well, maybe you're Dictator of Klopstokia, and can order the Klopstokian Mint to print up more money any time you run low.) Would this strategy work then?

Notice that using this strategy you'd be ahead just one dollar when-ever you went home; you might not think this sort of win would be worth it. But how about this: whenever you win, using this strategy, you put your one dollar in a vault, and started playing again, using the same strat-egy. You could do this forever, right?

Those of you who know a little about economics will be able to an-swer this question: Why won't this strategy work even for the Dictator of Klopstokia?

5. GETTING MONTY'S GOAT

The Monty Hall Paradox

Announcer:	And now...the game show that mathematicians argue about...LET'S MAKE A DEAL. Here's your genial host, Monty Hall! [Applause]
Monty:	Hello, good evening, and welcome! Now let's bring up our first contestant. It's... YOU! Come right up here. Now, you know our rules. Here are three doors, numbered 1, 2 and 3. Behind one of these doors is a beautiful new PONTIAC GRAN HORMONISMO!
Audience:	Oooh! Aahh!
Monty:	Behind the other two are WORTHLESS GOATS!
Audience:	[Laughter]
Goats:	Baah!
Monty:	Now, you're going to choose one of these doors. Then I'm going to open one of the other doors with a goat be-hind it, and show you the goat. Then I'll offer you this deal: if you stick with the door you've chosen, you can keep what's behind it, plus $100. If instead you chose the remaining unopened door, you can keep what's be-hind it. Now choose one door.
Audience:	Pick 3! No, 1! 2!
You:	Um, oh well, I guess I'll pick...3.

> *Monty:* Okay. Now our beautiful Charleen will open door number
> 2. Inside that door, as you can see, is a WORTHLESS
> GOAT. You can keep what's behind your door 3 plus
> $100, or you can make a deal and switch for whatever's
> behind door 1. While we take our commercial break, you
> should decide: do you wanna MAKE A DEAL??

While the first commercial is running, you think: I really want that car. I
can stick with door 3 or switch to door 1. There's a car behind one of
them and a goat behind the other. It's random, fifty-fifty, which door hides
the car. But I'll also get one hundred dollars if I stick with door 3. So I'll
stick.

But the first commercial is immediately followed by a second. While
the second commercial is running, you think: It was 1/3 likely that door
3, the one I picked, had the car, and I'd get the goat if I switched. But it
was 2/3 likely that door 3, which I picked, had a goat. If it does, then the
car must be behind door 1 (since I can see that door 2 has a goat). So if I
switch to 1, then I get the car. That means that switching gives me a 2/3
chance of winning the car. Of course, I'll lose the extra one hundred dollars if I switch, but it's worth paying that price for a 2/3 chance of getting
the car. So I'll switch.

Then while third commercial is running, you review both lines of
reasoning. Both look completely correct, but they come to opposite conclusions. What should you do?[4]

> The right answer is given by your second line of reason-
> ing: you should switch. The probability that door 3 has
> the car is 1/3; so the probability that it doesn't—that it's
> behind 1 or 2—is 2/3. After Monty opens one of these,
> which he knows hides a goat, the probability of the other
> hiding a car is now 2/3. This answer is right, but hard to
> believe.

---

[4] Chris Cole, the man who maintains the Internet newsgroup REC.PUZZLES, says
this about the sources of the Monty Hall problem: "The original Monty Hall problem (and solution) appears to be due to Steve Selvin, and appears in *American Statistician*, Feb 1975, V. 29, no. 1, p. 67 under the title 'A Problem in Probability.' It
should be of no surprise to readers of this group that he received several letters con-
testing the accuracy of his solution, so he responded two issues later (*American Statistician*, Aug 1975, V. 29, no. 3, p. 134). However, the principles that underlie the
problem date back at least to the fifties, and probably are timeless."

A version of this problem caused great public controversy a few years ago. In September 1990, Marilyn vos Savant (listed in the *Guinness Book of World Records* for "highest I.Q.") published the puzzle in *Parade* magazine, and answered it with an argument that you should switch. She estimates that she received ten thousand letters, most of which, especially those from mathematicians and scientists, scathingly attacked her reasoning. During July 1991, Monty Hall himself ran a little experiment in his Beverly Hills home to see who was right, and announced that his results show that switching is the right strategy. The case is complicated by the fact that, in the original version published by Ms. vos Savant, it was not clear whether Monty would offer the switch automatically, whether or not the first door picked was in fact the one with the car.

In Which I Try to Convince You That I'm Right

Do you believe that switching is a much better strategy than sticking? A lot of people are really sure that it is not. This item in the first edition of *Two Errors* produced more response from my readers than the whole rest of the book put together, and almost everyone who responded to this item insisted that I'm wrong.

I've tried three strategies for convincing these people that I'm right. The first one, which goes through the probability reasoning above more slowly and carefully, doesn't work at all. My second one was to program a computer simulation of the Monty Hall Game, in which the game is played rapidly thousands of times as you watch. Each time, the placement of the car and the initial choice of door is random; and the "player" switches every time. Sure enough—the "player" wins two-thirds of the time. But maybe some people suspect I've faked things in programming this simulation.

The third strategy invites consideration of a game in which there are instead one hundred doors, only one of which hides the car. As before, you pick one of these; but then Monty opens ninety-eight of the remaining ninety-nine to show that they conceal goats, leaving only one. Should you stick with the door you've picked, or switch to the remaining unopened door? Now I think I can convince you that switching is the best strategy.

Consider this. In this revised game, it's extremely likely—99 per cent likely—that the door you initially picked hides a goat. So it's 99 per cent likely that one of the other doors hides a car. Then this scenario is extremely likely: Monty, who knows where the car is, must open the other ninety-eight goat-doors, leaving the door hiding the car. If you switch, you'll get the car.

If you're convinced to switch in the one-hundred-door example, then you should realize that the three-door case is just like this, except for different probabilities. I'll repeat the reasoning given above, substituting the numbers appropriate for the three-door game: In the original game, it's fairly likely—67 per cent likely—that the door you initially picked hides a goat. So it's 67 per cent likely that one of the other doors hides a car. Then this scenario is extremely likely: Monty, who knows where the car is, must open the goat-door, leaving the door hiding the car. If you switch, you'll get the car.

Convinced?

FOR FURTHER READING: See "Behind Monty Hall's Doors: Puzzle, Debate and Answer?" by John Tierney, *The New York Times*, July 21, 1991.

The Paradox of the Three Prisoners

Okay, now that you're so good at thinking about the Monty Hall paradox, here's another one very much like it.[5] See if you can answer the questions that follow.

Suppose that you and two other members of the Klopstokian Liberation Front, Schmidlap and Blattzburg, have been thrown into jail, and the dictator of Klopstockia has announced that two of the three of you will be executed in the morning. None of you knows who those two will be, and each of you calculates that your own chance of surviving is 1/3. You start a conversation with a guard who is sympathetic to your cause. He refuses to tell you whether it's planned that you'll live or die, but he does tell you that Schmidlap will be one of the two to die.

SOME QUESTIONS TO THINK ABOUT

1. You are of course interested in your chances of surviving the morning. Is what the guard told you good news, bad news, or no news at all in that respect?

2. Blattzburg is willing to change clothes with you, so that everyone will think you are Blattzburg and Blattzburg is you. Would this increase or decrease your chances of surviving, or leave them the same?

---

[5] Adapted from the story reported (created?) by Simon Blackburn in *The Oxford Dictionary of Philosophy* (Oxford: Oxford University Press 1994) p. 377.

6. PARADOXICAL BABIES

Here's another fact about probabilities that seems to almost everyone to be clearly false. What's the probability of conceiving a female baby? a male baby? I don't know what the facts are, and it doesn't make any difference. Let's imagine that among the Klopstokians it's equally probable that a baby will be a girl or a boy: 50 per cent each. In this society births will be half girls.

Now suppose that Klopstokians think females are more valuable to society than males; so they pass a law saying that every couple must have children, but that they must stop after the first girl. If a couple's first baby is a girl, they'll stop there. If it's a boy, they'll have a second baby; if that one's a girl, they'll stop there. If it's a boy, they'll have a third. And so on.

Now here's the question. By how much will this increase the proportion of female births in Klopstokia?

> The right answer is: by nothing at all. In this society, the proportion of female babies will be 50 per cent.

If you found this answer hard to believe, here's one way of thinking about this that may convince you that I'm right.

Imagine that you are an Klopstokian statistician, collecting information on the babies that have been born to each couple after this policy of stop-when-you-get-a-girl began. The first couple you interview had a girl for their first baby, then stopped. So you write down

G

on your list. The second family had a boy, then a girl. So you add BG to your list, making it:

GBG

The third family had two boys, then a girl. So you add BBG to your list:

GBGBBG

And so on, until you have a really long list of B's and G's. What proportion of G's would you anticipate?

Consider just one conception of a baby. Remember that whatever factors determine the gender of the child conceived make it 50 per cent probable that it is a girl. Now you have a very long list of events, but in each individual case on this list, it's 50 per cent probable that it's a G. So, of course, you can anticipate that a very large collection of events of this sort will have very close to 50 per cent G's in it.

After this law had been in force for a generation, Klopstokian families would be unusually constituted. No girl would have a sister. The youngest child in each family would be a girl, and the rest of the children in her family would be boys. Every only-child (that is, every child without siblings) would be a girl. What would not be strange would be the proportion of girls and boys, which would be, as usual, fifty-fifty. Consider how this would work: half the families would have one girl and no boys. A quarter of them would have one of each. All the rest would have two or more boys, but only one girl.

7. VOTING PROBLEMS

Why You Shouldn't Vote

What are the chances that your vote will make a difference in who wins in an election? What I mean by "making a difference" is breaking what otherwise would have been a tie, or creating a tie, in the final total. The chances of this happening are minuscule. You are foolish to think that your vote is even remotely likely to create or break a tie, and thus to affect who wins; so no matter how passionately you care about the outcome of an election, it's a waste of time to vote.

This reasoning, so far, sounds impeccable. But, of course, if this is true in your case, it's true for all the other thousands or millions of voters too. Therefore it doesn't make sense for anyone to vote!

This line of reasoning is sometimes known as the Voter's Paradox.

Fred's Confusing Preferences

Suppose that, when offered a choice between Fritos and Twinkies, Fred always chooses Twinkies. But, when it's a matter of choosing between Twinkies and Slim Jims, Fred will always opt for Slim Jims. However, he will always pass up Slim Jims when offered Fritos instead. Let's summarize his preferences.

Fred prefers Twinkies to Fritos.
Fred prefers Slim Jims to Twinkies.
Fred prefers Fritos to Slim Jims.
Something has gone wrong here. Can you see what?

> Well, for one thing, we'd expect a set of preferences to
> issue in some sort of action when there's a choice. But

> imagine that Fred is presented with one of each junk-food, and allowed to pick one. He might reason like this: "Twinkies! I like them. I'll take them! Whoops, wait a minute. There's Slim Jims—they're better than Twinkies. Gimmie them Slim Jims! Uh oh, I just noticed those Fritos—even better. I'll have them! No, there's Twinkies, which I like even better than Fritos...."

Well, maybe that problem doesn't bother you. After all, indecision isn't such an uncommon thing, or a sign that something has gone badly wrong. But here's a worse problem that Fred will get himself into.

> Suppose that if he has a bag of Fritos, he'd trade them plus five cents for your bag of Twinkies; and he'd trade those Twinkies plus five cents for a bag of Slim Jims; and he'd trade those Slim Jims plus five cents for a bag of Fritos. Acting on his preferences long enough, Fred would lose everything.

So it does appear that there's something badly defective about Fred's set of preferences.

Fred's preference set is irrational. Some philosophers think that it's a general requirement that any set of rational preferences avoid this sort of problem. They think, in other words, that it's a necessary condition for rationality that a set of preferences be transitive: that if someone prefers X to Y, and prefers Y to Z, then that person also prefers X to Z. (Fred prefers Z to X.)

How Not to Choose a Movie

Here's a surprising way in which trying to add up the different preferences of people results in a failure of transitivity. Confusingly, it's also sometimes known as the Voter's Paradox.

When there's a difference of preference among a group of people, taking a vote will always provide a fair solution by giving the majority's preference. Right? Wrong.

Consider the following example. There are three people, Alice, Bertha, and Carl (abbreviate their names A, B, and C). They want to go to the movies together, and there are three movies in town: "One Night of Bliss," "Two Tickets to Timbuktu," and "Three Babies and a Man" (abbreviate their names 1, 2, and 3).

A, B, and **C** discuss the merits of each movie inconclusively. Here are the preferences of each:

A prefers **1** to both the others, and prefers **2** to **3**.

B prefers **2** to both the others, and prefers **3** to **1**.

C prefers **3** to both the others, and prefers **1** to **2**.

They decide to put matters to a vote. First they vote on whether to go to **1** or **2**. **A** votes for **1** (preferring it to any other); **C** really wants to go to **3**, but prefers **1** to **2**; so he also votes for **1**. **B** prefers **2** to **1**, so she votes for **2**. It's 2 to 1 in favour of movie **1**. That's progress, anyway.

Well, because **2** has been ruled out, they decide to compare **1** and **3** in a vote. **A** votes for **1**; **B** votes for **3**; **C** votes for **3**. Disappointingly for **A**, it now appears that **3** is the winner.

But **A** (who likes **3** least) suggests that they test whether **3** is really the best choice, by comparing it to **2**. So they take a vote comparing **3** and **2**. **C** votes for **3**, but **A** and **B** vote for **2**. Well, things are getting confusing, so they make a list of what they have discovered, by these perfectly straightforward votes:

Vote I: **1** is preferable to **2**

Vote II: **3** is preferable to **1**

Vote III: **2** is preferable to **3**

This conversation follows:

A: Look, **Vote I** tells us that **1** is better than **2**, so let's go to **1**.

C: Yeah, that would be okay if it weren't for **Vote II**, which chooses **3** over **1**. **3** is clearly the winner. Let's go there.

B: No, despite the desirability of **3**, **Vote III** clearly shows that the majority of us prefer **2** to **3**. **2** is the grand champion. We go there.

A: I agree that **2** is well-liked. But remember that we decided, by a clear majority in **Vote I**, that **1** is better even than **2**.

C: Yeah, that would be okay if it weren't for **Vote II**, which chooses **3** over **1**. **3** is clearly the winner. Let's go there.

B: No, despite the desirability of **3**, **Vote III** clearly shows that the majority of us prefer **2** to **3**. **2** is the grand champion. We go there.

And so on.

Several things are interesting about the problem A, B, and C have found themselves in. Their problem is to try to use their individual preferences to establish what might be called the Group Will. But those preferences that they try to combine into a Group Will fail to give a good answer, given the two-at-a-time comparative voting method they use. Whatever choice is made, these preferences tell us that another choice is better.

When we try to sum the three people's individual preferences, we get a result that violates the principle of transitivity for a preference set; note that it's a result of the votes we take that:

1 is better than **2** (**Vote I**);
and
2 is better than **3** (**Vote III**);
and by Transitivity it would follow that **1** is better than **3**. BUT:
3 is better than **1**. (**Vote II**)

The Group Will of **A**, **B**, and **C**, as manifested by this group of preferences, is unworkable.

The second interesting fact is that a seemingly straightforward procedure for arriving at the Group Will resulted in this pickle. Each of the three start with individual preferences that are perfectly straightforward and individually workable; their individual preferences violate no rules of rational preference. And the procedure they use to form a Group Will on the basis of their individual preferences also seems perfectly okay; majority vote is, after all, the clearest example we have of an eminently fair and workable way to form a Group Will based on individual preferences. But here it has run aground, badly.

The Group Will is an important concept in the thought of many political philosophers, who thought that the measure of the worth of any political system is not to what extent that system furthered any particular person's will, but to what extent it furthered the Group Will. Problems such as this one lead to wonders about the possibility of understanding the Group Will as some kind of sum of individual wills.

SOME QUESTIONS TO THINK ABOUT: Can you devise a good way for **A**, **B**, and **C** to vote on which movie to go to see? What result would show that a system of voting in this case was fair? Must the score be tied? But then there wouldn't be any decision. What to do?

How to Win at Dice

Here is an example involving probabilities with a similar paradoxical conclusion. This one is a bit more complicated.

Suppose that you're going to play a game with four specially marked six-faced dice. Here's how the four dice, **A**, **B**, **C**, and **D**, have their faces marked:

A:	0	0	4	4	4	4
B:	3	3	3	3	3	3
C:	2	2	2	2	7	7
D:	1	1	1	5	5	5

Each time you play, your opponent chooses one of them, then you choose another. Whoever throws the higher number wins.

It seems plausible to think that these dice are not equally good; some are more likely to win than others. If there's one that's most likely to win, then your opponent should pick that one to throw. If she throws this one all the time, then in the long run, she'll come out the winner. If all the dice are equally good, then the two of you are likely to come out even in the long run. If some dice are tied for best, then she can pick one of the best ones, and the best you can do again is tie. So it seems that your opponent has a strategy that, in the long run, means she's very unlikely to lose. And it seems that the person who has the first choice of the die to throw has the advantage.

But which die is the best one?

> Perhaps you reason: the die with the highest average value on its faces is the best. Here are their average values:
>
> **A**: 2.7
> **B**: 3.0
> **C**: 3.7
> **D**: 3.0
>
> Calculation shows you that **C** has the highest average value, so it must be the one that will beat the others in the long run, right?

Nope. This reasoning is all wrong. Let's compare what is likely to happen given choices by you and by your opponent.

Suppose your opponent chooses **B**. You can beat her (on average) by choosing **A**. Your opponent always throws 3, but 4/6 times on average you throw 4. This means that, on average, 4/6 times you win. In the long run, **A** will win two out of three times. So **A** is better than **B**.

Suppose she chooses **C**. You can beat her (on average) by choosing **B**. 4/6 times **C** throws 2, which is beaten by **B** which always throws 3. So **B** beats **C**, on average, two out of three times. **B** is better than **C**.

What if she chooses **D**? You beat her again by choosing **C**. Comparing **C** and **D** is more complicated. One half of the times, **D** throws 1, so **D** is beaten by **C** which always throws a higher number. The other half of the times, **D** throws 5, which is beaten by **C** two out of six times. This means that half of the time (when **D** throws 1) **C** wins; the other half of the time **C** wins two out of six times. **C** is better than **D**, because **C** beats **D** two out of three times on average.

But if she chooses **A**, you can beat her by taking **D**. Half the time **D** throws 5 and wins. The other half of the throws, **D** wins on average two out of six times. So on the whole **D** beats **A**, again two out of three times.

Summarizing:

A is better than **B**

B is better than **C**

C is better than **D**

D is better than **A**

There is no die that is better than all the rest, or tied for best. Just as in the last example, "better than" is not transitive.

What this means is that if you play this game against an opponent who chooses her die first, you can always choose a die which is likely to beat her. So the first person to choose is at a *disadvantage* in the long run. Perfectly correct reasoning about probability shows that the second person to choose a die can always pick one likely to beat the other one. This correct conclusion is deeply contrary to our feelings about probability and preferability.[6]

This result is exactly similar to the previous example, involving movie choice. Whichever movie you name, I can pick one that two out of three people would prefer.

Rock, Scissors, Paper

Rock, Scissors, Paper is a simpler game with the same structure. You probably know how this works: a different hand-sign stands for each of these three things. Two people produce a hand sign simultaneously. The winner is determined by these rules:

Rock beats **Scissors**

Scissors beats **Paper**

Paper beats **Rock**.

It's a fair game when the two people make their signs simultaneously; but imagine that you get your opponent to go first, and then you produce your sign after you've seen what your opponent does. It's easy to see how you could win every time. The interesting thing here, as in the cases of choosing a movie and the dice game just discussed, is that there isn't anything that's better than the rest.

---

[6] This example is found in *Concepts of Modern Mathematics* by Ian Stewart (Harmondsworth, England: Penguin Books, 1975), pp. 248–250, and in *Innumeracy*, pp. 134–135, where Paulos attributes its invention to the statistician Bradley Efron.

8. INTO THE MAINSTREAM OF PHILOSOPHY

The philosophical topic of this chapter is called decision theory. You can see that to some extent it's an application of probability theory (the topic of the previous chapter) to action in situations of uncertainty. Philosophers share this area of study with economists. As is the case in probability theory, decision theory is mostly an attempt to systematize and clarify the way we all think rationally in everyday situations; and, as in the case of the previous chapter, this one provides a rather unrepresentative sample of its theory, insofar as I have produced cases in which theory conflicts surprisingly and sometimes bizarrely with ordinary expectations. The problem is worse in the case of decision theory, however, in that it seems that a larger number of our ordinary procedures and expectations differ from what theory (so far) counts as rational behaviour. The basic theory of rational decision is currently less adequate and more controversial than the theory of probability.

Unfortunately, most introductory philosophy and logic books ignore decision theory altogether. It's a fascinating and important field, and its beginnings are not hard to grasp. The best books I can recommend for the beginner are: Part Three of Ronald N. Giere's *Understanding Scientific Reasoning,* 3rd ed. (Fort Worth: Holt, Rinehart and Winston, 1991), which sets up the basics in a very clear and friendly fashion; and Richard C. Jeffrey's *The Logic of Decision,* 2nd ed. (Chicago: University of Chicago Press, 1983), which starts you at the beginning, and proceeds in a rather brisk and formal fashion to some fairly advanced topics.

CHAPTER V

LOGIC

Two guys are sitting in a bar.
"What do you do?" asks the first.
"I'm a logician," answers the second.
"What's that?"
"It's someone who does logic."
"What's logic?"
"Well, it's reasoning that gets you to conclusions. Look, I'll give you an example. Do you have an aquarium?"
"Yes, as a matter of fact, I do."
"So then you must like fish and water."
"Well, yes, I do."
"So you must like the beach."
"Yep, I like the beach."
"You take walks on the beach with your girlfriend."
"Yeah, I do that."
"So you must be heterosexual. That's logic!"
After the logician leaves the bar, the first guy starts a conversation with someone else. "That guy I was just talking to—he's a logician."
"What's that?"
"It's someone who does logic."
"What's logic?"
"It's reasoning that gets you to conclusions. I'll give you an example. Do you have an aquarium?"
"Nope."
"So you must be a homosexual."

1. SOME MISTAKES ABOUT LOGICAL WORDS

Dilemmas

The word 'dilemma' is comonly used loosely to mean a problem or predicament. Careful speakers use that word in its strict sense, restricting it to cases in which the predicament arises from a choice between two equally balanced, and equally undesirable, alternatives. In this sense, then, it is a mistake to say that we face the *dilemma* of a growing number of homeless people, since no choice between two alternatives is indicated.

The "horns of a dilemma" are the two undesirable consequences. This picturesque metaphor sees us as being charged by a horned animal: if we dodge one of its dangerous protuberances we are gored by the other.

Logicians use the word to refer to that variety of argument in which certain assumptions are shown to lead logically to one or the other of two unacceptable consequences. A "destructive dilemma" concludes that those assumptions must be wrong. A "constructive dilemma" is a different sort of argument. Here's one:

If it rains, the picnic will be cancelled.

If it doesn't rain, Pete will insist we go to the beach, so the picnic will be cancelled.

It will either rain or not.

Therefore the picnic will be cancelled.

The Exception that Doesn't Prove the Rule

Another interesting English usage that derives from a mistake is the cliché, "The exception proves the rule." What could this mean?

One kind of rule is a generalization about how things are: "All birds fly." Penguins are an exception to this "rule"; but this exception doesn't prove the rule—it disproves it.

Another kind of rule is a statement that tells you what to do: "Drivers must stop at red lights." The fact that ambulances and fire trucks are an exception again *disproves* the rule. (Compare another cliché: "Rules are made to be broken.")

What could "the exception proves the rule" mean? Perhaps there is something reasonable embodied in it. Even though exceptions can never *prove* generalizations or rules for action, nevertheless most of our generalizations and rules *tolerate* exceptions. Most of the general "truths" we believe are true only on the whole. Rules for behaviour usually do admit of justified exceptions.

But the origin of this cliché is an interesting mistake. A central meaning of the word 'prove' was once *test* (whence "the proof of the pudding," and "proof" as the measure of alcohol in drinks: the results of comparing it to "proof spirit"—a mixture of alcohol and water kept as a standard for testing). In this sense, the statement makes perfectly good sense. A proposed exception does put a supposed rule to the test; if it's a genuine exception, the rule *fails* the test. In current English we mostly ignore this old sense of "prove," though the old cliché lives on, now meaning something quite different.

Begging the Question

Another logical term widely misused by careless speakers is 'begging the question.' This is often thought to mean *raising* (or *forcing*) the question. It doesn't. To beg the question is to presuppose the conclusion in one's argument, thus to reason circularly. (Peculiarly, all valid deductive arguments seem to beg the question.)

I imagine that people began using the phrase improperly because "this begs the question" *seems* to mean that this begs us—asks us earnestly, entreats us—to raise and consider the question.

The actual origin of the phrase seems to come from a mistranslation of the Latin phrase the medieval logicians used to refer to an argument that assumes its own conclusion: '*petitio principii.*' This is fairly literally translated as "assuming the starting point." But 'petitio' also means "begging" (whence the English word 'petition').

2. CIRCULAR REASONING

The Divine Circle

Here's an example of circular reasoning. Some neatly dressed people who came to my door once actually used this to try to convince me of the existence of God.

> *Them:* The Bible says that God exists.
> *Me:* But what makes you think that everything in the Bible is true?
> *Them:* Well, it's the word of God.
> *Me:* How do you know that?
> *Them:* It says so right there in the Bible.
> *Me:* Sorry, I have something else to do right now.

The Marvellous Suspension Bridge

My seventh-grade civics teacher one day decided to take time off from telling us about the major agricultural and industrial products of every country in the world to describe that wonder of modern engineering, the suspension bridge. The following dialogue ensued:

> *Mr. V.:* The engineering problem is to hold the roadway up in the air. It's held up by a lot of vertical cables attached on top to those big curving horizontal cables.
>
> *Us:* What holds up those big curving horizontal cables?
>
> *Mr. V.:* They're held up by those big vertical steel posts.
>
> *Us:* What holds them up?
>
> *Mr. V.:* They're attached to the roadway.
>
> *Us:* Yeah, but what holds up the roadway?
>
> *Mr. V.:* I already told you. They're held up by those vertical cables.
>
> *Us:* And what holds up those vertical cables?
>
> *Mr. V.:* How many times do I have to go through this? The big curving horizontal cables hold them up.

Mr. V.'s reasoning is circular, but it's not exactly what logicians call "circular reasoning," which is the mistake of using what you're trying to prove in the course of trying to prove it.

Anyway, after a few trips around the bridge, Mr. V. finally saw the circularity problem. "Well," he concluded, "those big vertical steel posts go down below the roadway, and they're embedded in great big cement blocks that float on the surface of the water."

3. THE ILLOGIC OF ENGLISH

"Or" Confusions

The "logic" of the English language is a mess.

A simple example of this is provided by the logical word 'or.' That word is sometimes used to connect two sentences to make a third; for example, we can connect 'Bernadette is in the pub' and 'Bernadette is in class' to make 'Bernadette is in the pub *or* Bernadette is in class.' This sentence is true if Bernadette is in class, not in the pub; and it's true if she's in the pub and not in class. But what if the class is being held in the pub, and *both* parts are true?

But consider this sentence: 'It's raining or it's Tuesday.' Again we can see that that sentence is true on a rainy Thursday, and on a sunny Tuesday; and that it's false on a sunny Thursday. But how about on a rainy Tuesday?

You might be tempted to say that the sentence is false on a rainy Tuesday. 'Or,' it seems, means *one or the other,*

> *but not both.* But it's not completely clear that 'or' always means this. Suppose somebody served you coffee, and told you, "You can have sugar or cream." This sentence seems to imply that it's possible that you have sugar *and* cream. 'Sugar or cream' here means *either one or the other only, or both.*

Logicians distinguish between the *exclusive* and the *inclusive* senses of 'or.' The first allows the truth of one of the two sentences connected by 'or' but not the truth of both. The second allows one of them to be true, *and* it allows both of them to be true.

It's sometimes not clear which sense 'or' has; so English is in this way logically ambiguous. It's important that legal documents be unambiguous, so in Legal English one sometimes uses the awkward term 'and/or,' to make it clear that the inclusive sense is what's meant. It's possible that other languages do not share this ambiguity. In Latin, there are two words for 'or': '*aut*' and '*vel*.' I have heard it claimed that the first expresses the exclusive 'or,' and the second the inclusive. I'm not sure if this is true. I have consulted several fat Latin dictionaries that attempt to explain the several ways in which these two words have different senses. None gives exactly this difference, expressed in clear logical ways, though several rather ambiguously suggest it.

"The" Confusions

This is another example of the logical messiness of English.

What is the logic of phrases of the form 'The x...'? Under what conditions would 'The tallest mountain in the world is Mt. Everest' be true?

> This sentence is true providing that there's exactly one tallest mountain (that is, that two or more aren't tied for tallest), and it's Mt. Everest. Here the word 'the' tells us that we're talking about exactly one thing.

But what does 'The lion is a dangerous beast' mean? Under what conditions would it be true?

> This sentence does not mean that exactly one lion is dangerous. It means that *all* lions are dangerous. This is not the result of the fact that we're talking about lions,

not mountains. 'The lion chasing Irving is a dangerous beast' refers to exactly one lion, not to all of them.

What does 'In a zoo, the lion is a dangerous beast' mean?

It's ambiguous. It might mean that the speaker has a particular zoo in mind, and that this zoo contains exactly one lion, and that that lion is dangerous. Or the speaker might mean that all lions in any zoo are dangerous.

This is one of very many reasons why non-English speakers have so much trouble learning English.

The Messy Counterfactual

Verdi was Italian and Bizet was French. They were not countrymen. But what if they were countrymen? Which of these sentences is true:
- If Verdi and Bizet were countrymen, then Bizet would have been Italian.
- If Verdi and Bizet were countrymen, then Verdi would have been French.[1]

Notice that they can't *both* be true, because then the Italian Bizet and the French Verdi would *not* have been countrymen. Can they both be false? Is there some third country they both would have belonged to? Or if exactly one of them is true, which one?

We don't really know how to answer these questions.
How about these two:
- If Julius Caesar were commander in Korea, he would have used the A-bomb.
- If Julius Caesar were commander in Korea, he would have used catapults.[2]

Each of these seems reasonable to say. Both of them can't be true: if Caesar had used the A-bomb, he surely wouldn't have had much need for catapults.

---

[1] This example is Kripke's.
[2] This example is Quine's. A catapult, in case you didn't know, was a mechanism for hurling big things, used as a weapon in ancient times.

Sentences of the form "If A were the case, then B would be the case" are known by logicians as *counterfactuals*. To determine whether a counterfactual is true, we imagine a "possible world" like the real one, except that A is true; the counterfactual is true provided that B would be true in that possible world.

Counterfactuals are hard to evaluate for truth when it's not clear exactly what changes we should assume in the possible world we imagine. We know that Caesar used the most powerful weapons available to him. In the imaginary possible world we imagine, he is commander in Korea. But should we think of that possible world as one in which only the weapons that Caesar really had were available to him? Or as one in which the weapons that really were available during the Korean War were available to Caesar? You can see from these examples that counterfactuals are not very well behaved logically.

FOR FURTHER READING: A well-known work on the logic of counterfactuals is David Lewis, *Counterfactuals* (Oxford: Blackwell, 1973).

4. THE UNSPOKEN IMPLICATION

It Never Turns Blue Either

Years ago (so the story goes) a company that sold canned tuna increased its sales tremendously when it began using the advertising slogan "it never turns black in the can." Millions of consumers chose that brand, visualizing the blackened fishy mess they might encounter if they opened a can of a competing brand. The slogan was misleading: *no* brand of tuna *ever* turned black in the can. But what it *said* was actually *true*. How can a statement lead you to believe something it doesn't actually say?

It's tempting to think that all that's really meant by a statement has to do with what would make it true. But we often say statements intending to communicate more than what's literally implied. Imagine I look at my watch and say to you "It's one o'clock." What I intend to communicate is more than merely what time it is: I also want to let you know that it's time for you to go. Perhaps it's a good idea to think about the meaning of statements as more than merely what facts make them true or false: we should also think about what they're actually used to communicate, given certain contexts.

FOR FURTHER READING: John R. Searle's book *Speech Acts* (Cambridge: Cambridge University Press, 1969) is a far-ranging treatment of meaning considered with regard to the *uses* we make of language.

Making Chopped-Liver of Language

A good deal of Jewish humour depends on playing around with language—with what is literally stated vs. what might be meant. Here's an example:

> "Marvin, close the window, it's cold outside."
> "Mph."
> "Marvin, close the window! It's cold outside!"
> "Urmph."
> "Marvin, CLOSE THE WINDOW!! It's COLD outside!!"
> "Oh, okay. There. So now it's warm outside?"

This next example needs some background explanation. The Hebrew word *eretz* means "land" (as in "land of Israel") though that doesn't have any bearing on the story. "Gimel" is a letter of the Hebrew alphabet, roughly corresponding to "G." The word '*eretz*' is not spelled with a gimel. The bit of Jewish humour involving these terms is, like the preceding one, a dialogue; but this one isn't exactly a joke. It's a bit of almost-sense:

> "Why should '*eretz*' be spelled with a gimel?"
> "A gimel? It isn't."
> "Why shouldn't '*eretz*' be spelled with a gimel?"
> "Why *should* 'eretz' be spelled with a gimel?"
> "That's what I'm asking you—Why should 'eretz' be spelled with a gimel?"

Is this funny or witty or at least interesting, or just a bit of unintelligible nonsense? Some people I've tried it on react with puzzlement—not because there's some sort of deep puzzle here, but because they just don't see the point. But Ted Cohen, who reports this joke with evident relish, says that the philosopher Stanley Cavell "who has a deep appreciation of the wonder of this dialogue...tells me that he has seen important philosophers transfixed by the exchange." Go figure.

FOR FURTHER READING: My source for the *"eretz"* dialogue and that report about Cavell is Ted Cohen's book *Jokes: Philosophical Thoughts on Joking Matters* (Chicago: University of Chicago Press, 1999), pp. 66–67.

Cohen thinks that the Jewish fascination with tricks of logic and language comes from their tradition of debate and disagreement without any final authority—there is no Jewish Pope. (Cohen speculates that this is why there are so few Jesuit standup comics.) I'll say more about Cohen on humour in Chapter XVII.

> "In my own household, where a taste for verbal play pre-
> vails, it is a rare day that does not see the utterance of at
> least a dozen patent absurdities before breakfast." —Stephen
> Stich[3]

Has the Present King of France Stopped Robbing Banks?

Related matters arise in connection with a famous debate about philosophy of language. Consider the sentence

The present king of France is bald.

Given that there is no king of France at the moment, is this sentence true or false? Bertrand Russell argued that this sentence strictly implies that there is at present a king of France, so the sentence is false. (But then, the sentence

The present king of France is hairy.

is also false.) P. F. Strawson, however, argued that the first sentence does not strictly imply that there is a present king of France: it merely *presupposes* it. Because what the sentence presupposes is false, we wouldn't say either that the sentence is true or that it's false. This seems likely: perhaps you'd agree that we couldn't sensibly say that it's true or false. But the idea that some meaningful sentences are neither true nor false is a surprising one that goes against our normal inclinations about the way we think about language, and also against powerful theoretical motivations in the philosophical theory of meaning to think that all meaningful declarative sentences are either true or false.

A better known example of a related phenomenon is the following. Suppose the prosecuting attorney, while cross-examining the accused man,

---

[3] *The Fragmentation of Reason* (Cambridge, MA: MIT Press, 1990), p. 31. Stich's remark pays tribute to a famous passage from *Through the Looking Glass*—see the item called **I JUST CAN'T BELIEVE THAT** in Chapter VII below.

asks him: "True or false: You have now stopped robbing banks?" Suppose the man has never robbed a bank. Can you see why he would have trouble answering this question?

> If he answers "True" the implication is that he used to rob banks, but he doesn't now. If he answers "False" the implication is that he used to rob banks and he still does. If he's never robbed a bank, the the statement "He has now stopped robbing banks" seems strangely to be neither true nor false.

FOR FURTHER READING: Russell's views on the present King of France were presented in his *Introduction to Mathematical Philosophy* (London: George Allen and Unwin, 1919), pp. 167–180. P. F. Strawson's reply is in his article "On Referring" in *Essays in Conceptual Analysis*, Anthony Flew, ed. (London: Macmillan and Company, 1956), pp. 21–52.

5. MUCH ADO ABOUT NOTHING

Over the years, logicians have concocted a bunch of puzzles involving the negative words "nothing," "nobody," and so on. Here are some of these cases:

- "What did you put into that closet?
  "I put nothing in there."
  "Really? You put *that* in there? It looks empty to me!"
- Hamburger is better than nothing.
  Nothing is better than steak.
  Therefore hamburger is better than steak.
- No cat has two tails.
  Every cat has one more tail than no cat.
  Therefore every cat has three tails.
- The sun and the nearest star, Alpha Centauri, are separated by empty space.
  Empty space is nothing.
  Therefore nothing separates the sun and Alpha Centuri.
  If nothing separates two things, they're right next to each other.
  Therefore the sun and Alpha Centauri are right next to each other.

These examples fool nobody. ("Really? He's fooled by them?") What's of interest here is what these mistakes show about the language. In grammar class I was taught to chant, "A noun is a name of a person, place, or thing." But clearly the noun 'nothing' is not the name of a person or place or thing. Some of the blunders in these examples seem to result from mistakenly treating it as the name of a thing.

SOME QUESTIONS TO THINK ABOUT: How, after all, do ordinary nouns work? Nouns aren't always names. 'Unicorn' isn't the name of anything. (Even proper names aren't always names: "Santa Claus" doesn't name anything either.)

And exactly what is the difference in the way these negative nouns work?

> "Take some more tea," the March Hare said to Alice, very earnestly.
>
> "I've had nothing yet," Alice replied in an offended tone, "so I can't take more."
>
> "You mean you can't take *less*," said the Hatter: "it's very easy to take *more* than nothing." —Lewis Carroll, *Alice's Adventures in Wonderland*

6. INTO THE MAINSTREAM OF PHILOSOPHY

Logic is the attempt to provide a theory of what makes a good argument good. Two factors can make an argument bad: if the assumptions it starts from are false, or if it reasons from these assumptions in the wrong way. In general, it's not a matter of logic whether or not the assumptions of an argument are true or false; more precisely, then, logic is the theory of how to reason from assumptions in the right way.

Much of the work of logicians concentrates on systematizing and making precise—discovering the rules of—the perfectly ordinary, uncontroversial, unsurprising reasoning of the sort we do every day. But the surprise here is that our everyday reasoning is interestingly complex—often easy to do, but hard to explain systematically.

There are two sorts of logic you'll come across. Sometimes logicians do informal logic: "informal" here doesn't mean "casual"—it means that they talk through their ideas in ordinary English. The contrast is with formal logic, often called "symbolic logic," which resembles technical science or mathematics: it uses special symbols (which are, however, carefully defined in English!). In this area, logic merges with some of what mathematicians study (though people with mathophobia need not fear the elementary parts of formal logic).

Here's a tiny and elementary bit of symbolic logic. Let's use the symbol 'v' to mean (inclusive) *or* (see **THE ILLOGIC OF ENGLISH**, above). Then the logic formula 'A v B' stands for the sentence we get when we connect the two sentences symbolized by 'A' and 'B' with 'or.' The symbol '~' stands for 'not.' '~(A v B) negates the whole sentence 'A v B'—the parentheses show that the '~' negates the whole sentence, rather than just the 'A.' In the sentence '~A v B,' just the A is negated. Now consider these two sentences, '~(A v B)' and '~A v B.' Suppose that the truth value of A is TRUE (i.e., that 'A' is true) and that the truth value of 'B' is also TRUE. Can you see why the truth value of '~(A v B)' is FALSE, but the truth value of '~A v B' is TRUE? Let '&' stand for 'and.' Can you see why whatever the truth values of 'A' and 'B' are, the truth values of '~(A v B)' and '~A & ~B' are the same?

There are scores of textbooks in symbolic logic widely available. There is some difference in the symbols they use, but any of them can provide you with an idea of how one begins in symbolic logic.

CHAPTER VI

MORE LOGIC:
Surprises and Paradoxes

1. IMPOSSIBLE SURPRISES

The Surprise Quiz that Never Happens

Your logic teacher announces, "There will be a surprise quiz given during one of the next three class-meetings." That annoying "A" student in your class requests that your teacher define 'surprise.' The teacher obliges: "A surprise quiz is a quiz whose date you can't figure out in advance. You won't know it's coming until I actually give it to you."

After a moment's thought, the student announces that it can be proven that such a quiz is impossible. Here's the proof:

> Will the quiz be given during the third meeting of class? If it were, then the quiz wouldn't have taken place during either of the first two classes. At the end of the second class, we'd know that the quiz must happen during the third class, so we would be able to figure out the date of the quiz in advance. So a quiz during the third class wouldn't be a surprise. Therefore, the surprise quiz can't happen during the third class.
>
> So will it happen during the second? We already know that it can't happen during the third class. At the quizless end of the first class, we'd be able to figure out that there must be a quiz during the second class. Thus a quiz during the second class wouldn't be a surprise. So it follows that the quiz couldn't take place during the second class either.
>
> The only remaining possibility is the first class; but we know this, so that wouldn't be a surprise either. It follows that a surprise quiz is impossible.

Obviously this conclusion is mistaken; a surprise quiz is, of course, possible.

A QUESTION TO THINK ABOUT: What has gone wrong in the apparently impeccable reasoning that has led to this conclusion? (I don't think you'll come up with a good answer to this—it's a surprisingly difficult question, on which there had been a good deal of philosophical controversy.)

FOR FURTHER READING: The famous logician and philosopher W. V. O. Quine presents what he thinks has gone wrong in this reasoning in his article "On a Supposed Antinomy," printed in his collection of articles, *The Ways of Paradox and Other Essays* (New York: Random House, 1966); this is a slightly amended version of his article "On a So-Called Paradox" in *Mind* (Vol. 62, January 1953).

The Surprising Meatloaf

The last example purports to show the impossibility of a surprise; this one the necessity of a surprise.

Every year on her husband Marvin's birthday, Irene rushed home from the philosophy class she taught to cook him a dinner with a surprising menu. One year it was a Chinese banquet in which each dish had an interesting name. Here's the menu:
- Hairy Melon Soup
- Jade Trees Hidden in the Dragon Tongue
- Grandmother Pockmark's Bean Curd
- Ants Climb a Tree
- Red Around Two Flowers
- Drunken Chicken
- Strange-Taste Chicken
- Peking Dust

Another year it was "Flambé Dinner" in which each dish was served on fire. On a third occasion, an appalling concoction appeared; the surprise was that all the ingredients rhymed (ham, clam, jam, yam, Spam, and lamb).

But one year, Marvin sat down to a birthday dinner of leftover meatloaf, mashed potatoes, and canned peas.

Marvin was a little upset, and thought he ought to say something. "Every year you made me a surprising birthday dinner. I was expecting something unusual, but this one is very ordinary."

Irene replied, "Yeah, you found this menu quite a surprise, didn't you?"

It's not easy being married to a philosopher.

Why All Numbers are Interesting

This case is similar to both of the preceding ones.

Let's define an "interesting number" as a positive integer with some special property. Some numbers are interesting because of their arithmetical properties. 1 is the smallest prime. 2 is the smallest even number. Other numbers are mentioned in some fact we know about. 3 is the number of bears Goldilocks met in the woods. 4 is the number of the day in July on which the U.S. celebrates its national holiday. 5 is the number of fingers on one hand.

After a little thought, you can discover a reason why 6, 7, 8, 9, and 10 are interesting numbers. Perhaps special properties can be discovered for each number into the thousands. What is the first number you come to which is uninteresting? Well, suppose you think it is 2,504. But you are wrong: that number does have some special property: it's the smallest uninteresting number. Well, let's consider the next number, 2,505. But if that's the smallest uninteresting number, then that one has a special property, so that one is interesting too. But this line of reasoning can be continued for each succeeding number. Therefore there are no uninteresting numbers.

2. WHY EVERYBODY IS POOR

A sorites argument is a string of sub-arguments each of which applies the same line of reasoning to the conclusion of the one before. Here's an example that reaches an obviously false conclusion at the end of the string. Its premises are:

    (1) A person who has only one dollar is poor.

    (2) For every number n, if a person who has n dollars is poor, then a person who has $n+1$ dollars is poor.

The first (surely true) conclusion drawn from these premises is

    (3) A person who has only two dollars is poor.

This conclusion plus premise (2) yields

    (4) A person who has only three dollars is poor.

This plus premise (2) yields

    (5) A person who has only four dollars is poor.

And so on. Continuing to reason this way, we eventually get to

    (1,000,001) A person who has only a million dollars is poor.

What has gone wrong?

An argument that reaches a false conclusion either has one or more false assumptions from which it starts, or reasons badly from them. (Some really bad arguments both have false assumptions and reason badly from them.) The reasoning here is fine, so we should reconsider those assumptions.

Premise (1) is unquestionably true; premise (2) must be the culprit. But note that for premise (2) to be false, there must be some number *n* such that a person who has *n* dollars is poor, but a person who has *n*+1 dollars is not poor. What number is that? I'll bet you can't tell me. Is it that there is such a number but you don't know exactly what it is? Surely not. No amount of investigation will tell you what *n* is, for you'll never be satisfied in saying that giving one dollar to someone who has $*n* will turn that person from poor to non-poor.

A QUESTION TO THINK ABOUT: The answer above isn't right. What is the right answer? Here's a suggestion for how to think about the problem: maybe there is a range of numbers where it is unclear whether the person with that number of dollars is poor or not.

'*Sorites*' (pronounced SO-RIGHT-EEZ) is the Greek word for "heap." The standard version of this puzzle in ancient times went this way: Take away one grain of sand from a heap of sand of any size, and you still have a heap. Now, suppose you have a large heap from which you remove one grain; application of this principle tells you that you still have a heap. Repeat this procedure; you still have a heap. Repeat it over and over again, and you'll eventually get one grain of sand: but the principle tells you that this is still a heap.

3. PARADOXES OF SELF-REFERENCE

The Non-Existent Barber

An old and famous puzzle (popularized by Bertrand Russell) invites us to imagine a village in which there is a male barber who shaves all and only those men in the village who don't shave themselves. Does this barber shave himself?

Suppose he doesn't. Because he lives in the village and shaves every man in the village who doesn't shave himself, then he does shave himself.

Suppose he does. Because he lives in the village and doesn't shave any man who shaves himself, then he doesn't shave himself.

So if he does, he doesn't. And if he doesn't, he does.

Something has gone badly wrong here. Can you figure out what?

There couldn't be a village containing such a barber. It's logically impossible for such a barber to exist, for he would have to do the impossible: shave himself and *not* shave himself. The story told to set up this paradox thus describes a situation that is self-contradictory. The story must be false.

The Trouble with Adjectives

The barber puzzle is one of a large number of *paradoxes of self-reference*—problems that arise when we try to apply something to itself. Here's another, known as *Grelling's Paradox.*

A *homological* adjective is one that is true of itself. 'Short' is a homological adjective, because the word 'short' is short. 'Polysyllabic' is also homological, because the word is polysyllabic. A *heterological* adjective is not true of itself. 'Misspelled' is heterological, because the word isn't misspelled. So is 'German.'

Now consider the adjective 'heterological': is it homological or heterological?

Either it is heterological or homological. Let's consider these possibilities one at a time.

(1) If that adjective is homological, it applies to itself. What the word 'heterological' applies to is heterological. So if that adjective is homological, then it's heterological. This contradiction proves that it's not homological.

(2) If that adjective is heterological, it doesn't apply to itself. What the word 'heterological' doesn't apply to isn't heterological. So if that adjective is heterological, it's not heterological. This contradiction proves that it's not heterological.

We solved the Barber Paradox by deciding that the story that set up the problem must be false. Do you think that Grelling's paradox might be solved in the same sort of way?

> Grelling's paradox can't be easily solved by rejecting the story that set it up. This story consists merely in the definitions of 'homological' and 'heterological.' To reject this story is to think that sometimes the notions of *true of* and *not true of* don't make sense—when neither is applicable. This is quite a radical conclusion, since these notions are basic to our understanding of what adjectives are all about.

The Troublesome Statement in the Box

A similar crisis in our ways of thought is brought about by consideration of the paradox of self-reference engendered by the following statement:

> The statement in the box is false.

Is that statement true or false?

> If that statement is false, then it's true. If it's true then it's false. The statement in the box can't be either true or false.

So this paradox leads us to question our basic assumption that every statement is either true or false. Philosophers and logicians worry about this conclusion.

A QUESTION TO THINK ABOUT: Is there a third category—neither true nor false—which is necessary to classify statements?

Another Silly Proof of God's Existence

Here come more boxed statements:

> 1. God exists
> 2. Both of these sentences are false.

Consider Sentence 2 first. Is it true or false? Suppose it's true. What it says is that it (and the other one) are false, so it couldn't be true. It must be false. Okay, now if it's false that *both* of those sentences are false, then at least one of them is true. We've already shown that Sentence 2 is false, so it must be that Sentence 1 is true. Voila! We've just proven God's existence, right?

Well, whatever you think about God, you're right to think that something funny has gone on in this proof. It's another example in which good sense flies out the window when self-reference walks in the door.

Self-Referential Jokes

Numerous witticisms — many of them not terribly hilarious, some of them only half-witticisms — depend on self-reference. The title of this book is one (but more on the the title later in Chapter VIII). Here are some more:

> The two rules for success are: 1. Never tell them everything you know.

> There are three kinds of people in the world: those who can count, and those who cannot.

> How long is the answer to this question? Ten letters.

On Being a Member of Yourself

The Russell Paradox involves the notion of a *set*, which we can think of simply as a collection of things. Now, it seems obvious that for any characteristic you can think of, there is a set of things that have that characteristic. Of course, there are some characteristics that apply to nothing at all, such as the characteristic of being the largest number, or of being a unicorn. But these are counted as corresponding to the *empty* set.

Now consider the characteristic: *is a member of itself.* Some sets have this characteristic. For example, the set of sets that have more than three members is itself a set with more than three members, so it is a member of itself. Similarly, some sets have the characteristic: *is not a member of itself.* For example, the set of dog-biscuits is not a member of itself, since the set itself is not a dog-biscuit.

But what about the set of all sets that are not members of themselves? Is that set a member of itself?

Suppose this set is a member of itself. But since it is
the set of things which are *not* members of themselves,

87

it should then be one of these things—something not a member of itself.

Suppose then that this set is *not* a member of itself, that is, that it is not among the set of things which are not members of themselves. But if it isn't in this set, then it must be among the things which *are* members of themselves.

Thus we have found a characteristic that doesn't correspond to a set. Like the Grelling paradox, this one leads us to question something very basic: in this case, the assumption that for every characteristic there is a set consisting of those things (if any) that have that characteristic. The notions of sets and characteristics are very basic ones, especially in the theory of the foundations of mathematics.

Gottlob Frege, the German founder of mathematical logic, published a hugely important work called *Grundgesetze der Arithmetik* [*The Basic Laws of Arithmetic*], in which he attempted to establish the foundations of mathematics in the laws of logic. Just as the second volume of this work was about to be printed in 1903, Frege received a letter from Bertrand Russell, in which Russell informed him about the problem about self-reference we have just discussed. "Arithmetic totters," Frege is said to have written in answer. An appendix that he added to the volume opens with the words: "A scientist can hardly encounter anything more undesirable than to have the foundation collapse just as the work is finished. I was put in this position by a letter from Bertrand Russell..."

Here's why Frege said that "arithmetic totters" because of the Russell Paradox. Roughly speaking, Frege argued that the basic concepts of arithmetic (for example, the concept of a number) could be defined in terms of sets and the logical principles involved with them. But Russell's Paradox reveals a basic contradiction in the notion of a set. The set Russell considers both is and isn't a member of itself. If the notions of set and set-membership are contradictory, then this can hardly provide a secure foundation for arithmetic.

FOR FURTHER READING: Quine tells the Russell-Frege story in "The Ways of Paradox." This article also discusses the implication of the barber paradox, and other paradoxes of self-attribution. It's a serious and complex work of philosophy and logic. If, on the other hand, you'd like to read something much lighter and more amusing about a variety of these paradoxes, look at *I Think, Therefore I Laugh: The Flip Side of Philosophy* by John Allen Paulos (New York: Columbia University Press, 2000).

Paulos gives versions of some of the classical logical paradoxes I discuss, and some others.

This is Not the Title of This Item

There are a number of other statements which give peculiar results when applied to themselves. After reading each one, see if you can figure out what's peculiar about it.

- I am lying.

  If whoever says this is telling the truth, then she is lying. So she can't be telling the truth. But if that person is lying when she says "I am lying," then she is telling the truth. So she can't be lying. What this person says can neither be true nor false.

This is a genuine paradox, very similar to the statement-in-the-box example, above. What we have here is a version of the ancient Liar Paradox, discovered in the fourth century BC by the Greek philosopher Eubulides. The classical Liar Paradox is a bit different. Here it is.

- Epimenides of Crete says "All Cretans are liars."

  If we take a liar to be someone who *always* utters falsehoods, then if Epimenides' statement is true, all statements by a Cretan are false. But since Epimenides is a Cretan himself, his statement must be false. Thus if what he said were true, then it would be false. So it can't be a true statement. Could it be false? To say that it's false is not to say that Cretans *always* tell the truth—it's merely to say that they *sometimes* do. But this is consistent with the falsity of this statement by a Cretan. We have just proven that the Epimenides' statement must be false. The neither-true-nor-false problem does not arise.

Another peculiar result arises from the statement

- All universal claims are false.

You might hear this statement made by people who hold the view that universal claims (statements about *every one* of a kind of thing) are to be distrusted.

But it can't be true. It is, itself, a universal claim, and if all universal claims were false, *it* would have to be false too. There is, however, no contradictory implication from the supposition that it's false. Again, there is no paradox. The statement is false, and we have proven it.

- No knowledge is possible.

This one is highly unlikely to be true, of course, but logically speaking, no contradiction arises from assuming either that it's true or that it's false. Someone would, however, get into trouble if she claimed that she *knows* that it's true.

- Nothing at all exists

This one is clearly false. We can prove that it's false without having to prove that any of the ordinary things we think exist really do exist. Suppose that statement were true. Then nothing would exist—not even that statement. If that statement doesn't exist, then what is it that we just assumed was false?

- THERE ARE TWO ERRORS IN THE
  THE TITLE OF THIS BOOK

If you have read the back cover of this book, you will already have considered whether what this title says is true.

The first error (involving the repetition of 'THE') is hard to see, but once you've noticed it, you have no trouble seeing that it is an error. (See p. 136 for further discussion of this error.)

But a paradox arises when you think about whether there is a second error. You think: there's only one error in the title (the repeated 'THE'). So what it says (that there are two errors) is false. Wait a minute—*that's* the second error. So there are two errors in the title after all. But then what the title says is correct. But if what the title says is correct, then what it says is not an error, so it only contains one error (the repetition). But if it only contains one error, then what it says is wrong, so it contains two errors....

Is the title true or false? Either answer leads to a contradiction. The source of this paradox is again self-reference: the title talks about itself.

The paradoxical structure here is exactly the same as what we encountered earlier in "I am lying" and in the statement in the box. Again, it seems, we are forced into the position that some apparently meaningful statements are neither true nor false.

Lawyers are Like That

This traditional puzzle concerns the ancient Greek Protagoras (c. 480–411 BC—the same person who turns up in one of Plato's dialogues). Protagoras taught law, and had this generous contract with Euathlus, one of his students: Euathlus is to pay Protagoras for his education if he wins his first case; if he doesn't win, he doesn't have to pay.

Having just graduated, Euathlus sues Protagoras for free tuition. Euathlus gloatingly tells Protagoras: If I win this case, I get free tuition, since that's what I'm suing for. This is my first case, so if I lose, I don't have to pay tuition—that's what the contract says. So either way I won't have to pay.

Protagoras replies: If you win, you'll have to pay me, because that's what our contract says. If you lose your suit for free tuition, the court will order you to pay tuition, so you'll have to pay me. Either way, you'll have to pay.

A QUESTION TO THINK ABOUT: Do you think either of the two is right? Suppose you were the judge hearing this case in court. What would you do?

FOR FURTHER READING: Some paradoxes of self-reference are interestingly discussed in Douglas R. Hofstadter and Daniel Dennett, *The Mind's I* (New York: Basic Books, 1981).

> One of Groucho Marx's most famous remarks was that he wouldn't want to be a member of any club that had such low standards that it would admit *him*.

4. OH NO! *MORE* SILLY PROOFS OF GOD'S EXISTENCE!

It's obvious that the two "proofs" I'm going to give you make mistakes in logic. The reason I'm including them is that the mistakes are interesting ones. The "proofs" tell us nothing about the Divine, but they do tell us about logic.

The Proof with the Bonus

To understand this proof you'll need to have a little background knowledge about modern logic.

One of the basic sorts of statement used in systems of logic is the "conditional statement"—a statement of the form "If P then Q." Examples:

If it's Tuesday, then we have logic class.

If it's below freezing, then the car won't start.

As they understand the conditional statement, contemporary logicians take the negation—the denial—of a conditional statement to be equivalent to the affirmation of the first part—the "P" part—and the denial of the second part—the "Q" part. So for example, if we deny "If it's Tuesday then we have logic class," then this is equivalent to saying that it *is* Tuesday, but we *don't* have logic class.

Those of you who have done a little bit of modern symbolic logic will recognize that these two sentences are provably equivalent: $\sim(P \supset Q)$ and $(P \ \& \sim Q)$.

Okay, now consider the conditional statement: "If God exists, then there is unnecessary pain and suffering." We can symbolize this statement as $(G \supset U)$. Believers and unbelievers alike would take this to be a false statement. The existence of God would mean that there's a reason for pain and suffering—it would (somehow) be part of God's plan, all for the best, not unnecessary at all. So everyone must admit that the denial of this conditional statement is true; we can safely take $\sim(G \supset U)$ as the premise of an argument. But this is equivalent to saying $(G \ \& \sim U)$. So what immediately logically follows from this is that God exists. Q.E.D.!

And, by the way, as an additional bonus, notice that another thing that follows from this is that there is no unnecessary pain and suffering.[1]

Of course there's a mistake in here. The mistake arises because modern logic assigns that sort of logical behaviour to the conditional, but this does not reflect what we take the "logic" of "If...then" statements in English to be. So when everyone admits the denial of that "If...then" statement about God, nobody is thinking of an "If...then" construction which behaves like the logicians' conditional.

---

[1] This "proof" was shown to me long ago by C. L. Stevenson, the philosopher who was the central figure in emotivist ethics. I think he invented it. At the time, he was interested in the paradoxes of material implication.

We shouldn't conclude from this, by the way, that there's something wrong with modern logic. Modern logicians are very well aware that the "If...then" statement they use as the basis of elementary symbolic logic is an extremely oversimplified version of what we mean when we use conditional statements in ordinary language. The question of what we really do mean turns out to be quite a difficult one, and there has been a good deal of productive attention paid by modern logic to answering that question.

God Knows that He Exists

Everyone agrees that this next "proof" of God's existence also makes a mistake, but the mistake here turns out to be a subtle one, one that's a good deal harder to pinpoint. I've gotten several intelligent and logically expert philosophers stumped by this one.

This "proof" might be a bit hard to follow if you don't have a background in elementary logic, but give it a try anyway. Here it is:

As we've already seen in Chapter II, God is classically assumed to be *omniscient*—all knowing. That means that He knows all truths: if some proposition is true, He believes it, and if He believes it, it's true. In other words,

(1) For all propositions **P**: **P** is true if and only if God believes **P**.

But that way of putting it seems to assume that God exists, so let's put that in a way that believers and atheists alike would accept:

(2) For all propositions **P**: **P** is true if and only if: (If God existed, then God would believe **P**).

So everyone can accept (2) as a true premise. It follows (we might want to say) merely from the definition of 'God.'

Now, since (2) is true for every proposition, it's true in particular for the proposition 'God exists.' Substituting 'God exists' for **P** in (2) yields

(3) 'God exists' is true if and only if: (If God existed, He would believe 'God exists.')

Or, to say the same thing more briefly:

(4) God exists if and only if (if God existed, He would believe that He existed).

This follows logically from (2), the premise everyone agrees on.

Now consider the proposition in the parentheses inside (4). It is:

(5) If God existed, He would believe that He existed.

93

Again, (5) does not assert the existence of God; but it does follow from the "definitional" assumption that God (if He existed) would be omniscient. So (5) is uncontroversially true.

But if any sentence 'X if and only if Y' is true, and Y is true, then it follows that X is true. So from (4) and (5), it follows that

(6) God exists.

Okay, what's wrong with that? The answer, "Nothing's wrong with that— God really does exist!" is not a good answer. Everyone agrees that there must be something funny in this "proof" which seems to get something out of nothing. But what is it?

5. PROVING THAT 1 = 2

A familiar arithmetical paradox is a "proof" that $2 = 1$. Here is one version of it:[2]

1. Whatever x is, it's obvious that:	$x = x$
2. Square both sides:	$x^2 = x^2$
3. Subtract x^2 from both sides:	$x^2 - x^2 = x^2 - x^2$
4. Factor both sides:	$x(x - x) = (x + x)(x - x)$
5. Divide both sides by (x - x):	$x = (x + x)$
6. Divide both sides by x:	$1 = (1 + 1)$
7. So:	$1 = 2$

Where is the mistake?

> The mistake here is in step 5, where we divide by (x - x), which is 0. Division by 0 isn't allowed.

Quine uses a version of this "proof" and the Barber Paradox to distinguish between kinds of paradox. The "proof" that $1 = 2$ uses incorrect reasoning that purports to show that something that is really false is true. Quine calls examples of this sort of reasoning "falsidical" paradoxes. A "veridical" paradox, by contrast, uses correct reasoning. When it comes up with an apparently false conclusion, we must conclude either that the conclusion is true after all, or that one of the assumptions made in the course of the reasoning was incorrect. In the Barber Paradox, the incorrect assumption is that there exists—or even could exist—such a town with such a barber.

---

[2] Thanks to Ted Cohen, who suggested this version of the paradox to me in a letter.

FOR FURTHER READING: William Poundstone, in *The Labyrinths of Reason* (New York: Doubleday, 1988), gives another version of the "proof." This book contains interesting discussions of paradoxes.

6. ZENO'S PARADOXES

The Speedy Tortoise

The paradox of Achilles and the tortoise was invented by the ancient Greek philosopher Zeno of Elea (c. 490 BC–?).

Achilles, we imagine, is a very fast runner; suppose he runs one hundred times as fast as a tortoise. But if the tortoise gets any head start at all in a race, Achilles can't catch up with him. Here's why. Imagine that the tortoise is given a head start of one hundred metres. Achilles and the tortoise start running simultaneously; but by the time Achilles has travelled the one hundred metres to where the tortoise has started, the tortoise has run another metre. To catch up with him again, Achilles runs that additional metre, but by the time he gets there, the tortoise has advanced a hundredth of a metre (one centimetre). And by the time Achilles has gone that additional centimetre, the tortoise has gone a very little bit further. And so on. In general, we can see that whenever Achilles has caught up to where the tortoise was, the tortoise has gone further, and is still ahead. So Achilles never catches up to the tortoise.

A QUESTION TO THINK ABOUT: This reasoning clearly reaches a false conclusion. Where has it gone wrong?

The Arrow that Never Reaches the Target

Another of Zeno's famous paradoxes is this one:

An arrow is shot at a target. Suppose it takes one second to go half the distance to the target. It still has to travel the remaining half the distance. In another half-second it travels half the remaining way. But this still leaves some distance to go. In 1/4 of a second it has covered half the distance still remaining; but there's still a small distance left to go. In a short time it covers half this distance. And so on.

You can see that no matter how many additional trips (of half the remaining distance) we add, the arrow still hasn't reached the target. We seem to have shown that it can never reach the target.

A QUESTION TO THINK ABOUT: Obviously the arrow reaches the target. Assuming it travels at a constant speed, it will hit the target two seconds after it was shot. That's easy to see. What's harder to see is exactly where the reasoning has gone wrong. Any ideas? (Is it the same mistake as made in "The Speedy Tortoise"?)

7. INTO THE MAINSTREAM OF PHILOSOPHY

Here's a hint that may be helpful in thinking about the surprising meatloaf and the smallest uninteresting number. Note that what's surprising about the meatloaf is that it's not a surprise; and what's interesting about the smallest uninteresting number is that it's uninteresting. Both of these descriptions look self-contradictory. Maybe we should rule out this sort of surprise, and this sort of interestingness.

It seems that we can respond to the paradoxes of self-reference in two main sorts of ways. (1) We might try to live with the peculiar results. For example, we might admit that the statement in the box is neither true nor false (or maybe it's *both* true and false!). What would happen if there were statements like this? (2) Patterns of reasoning that get us into trouble when they are applied self-referentially seem to work perfectly well otherwise. Perhaps there's just something illegitimate about self-reference. But even self-reference seems sometimes to be okay; so maybe there are some non-arbitrary restrictions we should make on self-reference to make sure that paradox doesn't result. This is the approach that many logicians have taken.

If you know enough mathematics to understand the notion of the limit of the sum of an infinite series, then maybe you can find a satisfactory way to understand why Achilles really does win the race, and why the arrow really does reach the target. In both cases, an infinite series of decreasing numbers really does add up to a finite number.

The Poundstone work already mentioned is a highly recommended, entertaining and informative book of paradoxes and similar puzzles. Another one is Ronald Smullyan's *What is the Name of This Book?* (Englewood Cliffs, NJ: Prentice-Hall, 1978).

CHAPTER VII

BELIEF, LOGIC, AND INTENTIONS

1. BELIEVING THE IMPLICATIONS

Consider these two statements:

(1) It's Tuesday.

(2) It's raining.

If both of these statements are true, then this statement can't be false:

(3) It's Tuesday and it's raining.

Logicians say that the set of statements consisting of statement (1) and (2) *implies* statement (3). This means that if (1) and (2) were both true, then (3) would have to be true.

Now, suppose you believe that it's Tuesday, and you believe that it's raining. Do you therefore automatically believe that it's Tuesday and it's raining? It's hard to see how someone could believe statements (1) and (2), but not believe (3), the statement that is implied by (1) and (2). It's plausible to think that there's a general principle here:

PRINCIPLE 1: If someone believes all the statements in a set, and if that set implies a further statement S, then that person believes S.

A valid deductive argument is one in which the premises imply the conclusion. It's a peculiarity of valid deductive arguments that they seem not to advance our knowledge significantly. After all, if you already knew that it's Tuesday and that it's raining, wouldn't you *already* know (3)? What use, then, would this argument be? An argument, after all, doesn't establish its premises: it's useful only for someone who already believes the premises, and it's used to convince that person of the truth of the conclusion. But that person would already believe the conclusion.

So valid deductive arguments are all, it seems, useless. But this is a very strange thing to think. Have we made a mistake?

Maybe the mistake here is the idea that we automatically believe all the deductive consequences of what we believe. Maybe Principle 1 is false.

Proving that Archibald is in the Pub

Here is some evidence against Principle 1.

Suppose Archibald, Bernard, and Carlos are identical triplets. You go into the pub and see one of them. Later, I ask you if Archibald was in the pub, and you tell me you don't know; you saw one of the triplets, but you can't tell them apart. I point out to you that we both know the following facts:

(4) At least one of them was in the pub.

(5) Bernard never goes to the pub without Archibald.

(6) Carlos never goes to the pub without another triplet.

You reply, "Okay, but I still don't know if Archibald was in the pub." This is possible, right?

But the set of statements (4), (5), and (6) *implies* statement

(7) Archibald was in the pub.

Can you see why it does?

If you don't see why, consider the following. (Abbreviate the three names 'A,' 'B,' and 'C.') We know by statement (4) that at least one of them was there. There are three possibilities:

(a) It was A you saw.

(b) It was B you saw. But statement (5) tells us that if B was there, A was also there.

(c) It was C you saw. But statement (6) tells us that if C was there, A or B was also there. So either A or B was there. But if B was there, we know by statement (5) that A was also there.

So *whichever* you saw, it follows logically that A was there.

The fact that you believed all the statements in the set {(4), (5), (6)}, but didn't automatically therefore believe (7) shows that it's possible that someone believes everything in a set of statements but not what that set implies. Principle 1 is not always true.

But even though we don't necessarily believe what's implied by our beliefs, it seems clear that we *should*. After all, the truth of a set of statements guarantees the truth of anything they imply.

The same line of reasoning seems to show that anyone who *realised* that a statement was implied by his other beliefs would believe that statement. Seeing that a set implies a statement is seeing that it's impossible that everything in the set be true if the statement were false.

So here are the two plausible principles we have come up with:

PRINCIPLE 2: Everyone should believe what's implied by their beliefs.

PRINCIPLE 3: Everyone does believe what they realise is implied by their beliefs.

But neither of these principles is true either. The reason for this is shown by an example called the Lottery Paradox.

The Lottery Nobody Wins

Suppose there's a lottery with one thousand tickets, one of which, drawn at random, will be the winner. There's a chance of one in one thousand that any particular ticket will win.

Consider ticket number 1: do you think it will win? Well, there's a tiny chance it will win. But if you are reasonable, you will believe it won't win.

Now consider ticket number 2. You also believe ticket 2 won't win. So you have two beliefs:

(1) Ticket number 1 won't win
(2) Ticket number 2 won't win

But of course by the same line of reasoning, you also believe

(3) Ticket number 3 won't win
(4) Ticket number 4 won't win
(5) Ticket number 5 won't win

and so on, up to

(999) Ticket number 999 won't win

and

(1000) Ticket number 1000 won't win.

But the set of 1000 statements (1–1000) implies statement (1001):

(1001) Ticket number 1 won't win and ticket number 2 won't win and ticket number 3 won't win and ticket number 4 won't win and ... and ticket number 999 won't win and ticket number 1000 won't win.

But statement (1001) is false, because this says that *none* of the tickets in the lottery will win, and you know it's false. You *don't* believe (1001), and you shouldn't.

What has gone wrong?

Perhaps both Principle 2 and Principle 3 are wrong.

So maybe we should replace them with:

PRINCIPLE 4: People shouldn't believe everything that's implied by their beliefs.

and

PRINCIPLE 5: People don't believe everything they realize is implied by their beliefs.

Be Careful What You Believe

It may have occurred to you, while thinking about the Lottery Paradox, that perhaps the problem with the reasoning that reaches such a false conclusion occurs at the very beginning, when you believe that ticket number 1 won't win. After all, it might be said, why do you believe this? It's possible that ticket number 1 *will* win. Why believe it won't? So you don't get to the obviously false statement (1001).

What's going on in the Lottery Paradox is, after all, that one of the 1000 statements that you incautiously believed was true was actually false—namely the one that referred to the winning ticket, and said it wouldn't win. Now, you don't know in advance which of the 1000 statements this one is; but you know it's there somewhere. The careful thing to do is to withhold belief from all of them. After all, isn't care in managing our beliefs exactly what the study of logic and philosophy is supposed to teach us?

Yes, but think about the policy advocated here. Is it really a good idea to withhold belief from any statement which *might* turn out false? Think about all those things you now believe:
- Fish generally live under water.
- You drank coffee with breakfast this morning.
- The United States has a larger population than Canada.
- Carl Yastrzemski used to play for the Red Sox.
    etc. etc.

You *might* be mistaken about any of these. Which of your beliefs, come to think of it, is so trustworthy that it is utterly impossible that it be mistaken? Beliefs that are learned from experience (such as the above) are not 100 per cent infallible; and neither are those beliefs that you arrive at using the powers of your mind alone—for example, in arithmetic. Even in arithmetical reasoning, it's possible that you have made a mistake. It turns out that employing this strict a test of believability will rule out *all* beliefs. (Some philosophers have argued that there are a few peculiar beliefs about which it's impossible that the believer is mistaken. Even if they're right, we nevertheless face the undesirable consequence of having to withhold belief from *almost* everything we now believe.)

Thus the policy of accepting beliefs about which we are not 100 per cent certain is not a mistake. Sometimes we'll turn out wrong; but the alternative—withholding belief from anything that is not 100 per cent certain—is worse, because it would mean that we would believe nothing (or extremely little).

The sensible thing to do is to believe some things about which we are not perfectly—100 per cent—certain. Just how likely must something be before it's okay to believe it? The answer to this isn't clear. Maybe the degree of assurance we need changes with circumstances, depending on how important it is to be right, and what sort of disasters would result if one were wrong. In any event, statement (1) in the Lottery Paradox example is 99.9% probable. It seems that that's probable enough to satisfy almost everyone, in almost every circumstance. But so is (2), and (3), and so on. So the Paradox is still there.

Knowing Nothing about Birds

Maybe you now think that even though it's not necessary to restrict our beliefs to those things that are 100 per cent probable, we should arrange our beliefs so that their probability of truth is maximized. This might look like good advice. Nevertheless, suppose you look out the window, and see what you take to be an English sparrow at your bird feeder. You're tempted to believe

(1) There's an English sparrow out there.

Now, you're pretty good at recognizing at least the common birds like the English sparrow. But, of course, there's some possibility you're wrong; other sparrows resemble the English sparrow. If you believed *instead*

(2) There's a sparrow out there.

this would increase the probability you're right. So on the principle that we should maximize the probability of truth of our beliefs, you believe (2) instead of (1). But now consider

(3) There's a bird out there.

This is even more likely to be true than (2); so you should discard (2) and accept (3) instead. But, of course, we can continue this process of reasoning, and replace (3) with

(4) There's some living thing out there.

and replace (4) with

(5) There's some object out there.

and perhaps even replace (5) with the more certain

(6) I seem to see something out there.

This process does increase the probability that your beliefs are correct, but the ones that are more likely to be correct also contain less information. What we are left with is one that's very likely true, but claims almost nothing. Following this strategy for belief-selection would result in very few beliefs indeed, and ones with very little informational content.

A QUESTION TO THINK ABOUT: What *is* the right strategy for choosing what to believe?

The Hobgoblin of Little Minds

A lot of people have inconsistent beliefs. It's fairly easy to come up with examples of this. Here's an example of a sort of inconsistency: a poll determined that 97 per cent of Americans believe that "following your own conscience" is a mark of a strong character, while 92 per cent of Americans believe that "obeying those in positions of authority" is.[1]

But here's an interesting general line of reasoning that shows that all reasonable people have inconsistent beliefs.

Are all your beliefs true? Obviously the answer is no: only an unreasonable egotist would think the contrary. All reasonable people believe this statement:

- At least one of my other beliefs is false.

Now consider the hypothetical list of your belief statements, with this last belief added at the end:

- Fish generally live under water.
- You drank coffee with breakfast this morning.
- The United States has a larger population than Canada.
- Carl Yastrzemski used to play for the Red Sox.
  ...
  ...
- At least one of the other statements on this list is false.

---

[1] Source: Institute for Advanced Studies in Culture, University of Virginia (Charlottesville); cited in *Harper's Magazine*, May 2001, p. 11.

This is not merely a set including at least one false statement. It is an *inconsistent* set: it is *logically impossible* that all the statements in this set are true. To see this, imagine that everything in the list up to the last item is true; but this makes the last one false. It's *logically necessary* that at least one statement on the list is false.

If you are reasonable, then, you have an inconsistent belief set.

FOR FURTHER READING: This paradox (as well as several others in this book) is discussed interestingly and entertainingly in Raymond Smullyan's *What is the Name of This Book?* Sometimes this paradox is called the "Paradox of the Preface": in one version (not Smullyan's) we are to consider a book whose preface contains the usual comment, "There are, no doubt, errors in this book." That comment is logically true: if there are no errors elsewhere, then that statement is an error. It also makes what's said in the book logically inconsistent.

> "The test of a first-rate intelligence is the ability to hold two opposed ideas in the mind at the same time and still retain the ability to function."—F. Scott Fitzgerald

> "Do I contradict myself?
> Very well then I contradict myself,
> (I am large, I contain multitudes.)" —Walt Whitman,
> "Song of Myself" in *Leaves of Grass*

> "Consistency is the hobgoblin of little minds."—a familiar aphorism attributed to Ralph Waldo Emerson[2]

You'll Believe Just Anything

Well, what is wrong with inconsistent beliefs? The obvious answer is that an inconsistent set is one in which it's logically impossible that everything is true. We aim—presumably—at beliefs that are all true; so we should avoid inconsistent sets of beliefs.

But a subtler objection to inconsistent beliefs is that a set of inconsistent statements implies *every* statement. This widely accepted principle of logic may seem peculiar to you, and deserves some justification.

Here's one way of looking at implication that may make that principle seem reasonable. To say that a set of statements {**A**} implies a state-

---

[2] What he actually said (in "Self Reliance," *Essays: First Series* [1841]) was "A foolish consistency is the hobgoblin of little minds, adored by little statesmen and philosophers and divines." "*Philosophers*"? Thanks a lot, Ralph, and same to you. Well, anyway, the inclusion of the word "foolish" changes the meaning somewhat.

ment **B** means that it's logically impossible that all the statements in set {**A**} be true while **B** is false. So, for example, it's logically impossible that all the statements in this set: {'It's raining,' 'It's Tuesday'} are true while 'It's raining and it's Tuesday' is false. So the set {'It's raining,' 'It's Tuesday'} implies 'It's raining and it's Tuesday.' Here's another example: {'If it's raining, then the picnic is cancelled,' 'The picnic is not cancelled'} implies 'It's not raining.' Think about these statements and you'll see why. It's logically impossible that all three of these hold: (1) 'If it's raining, then the picnic is cancelled' is true; *and* (2) 'The picnic is not cancelled' is true; *and* (3) 'It's not raining' is false.

Now a *logically inconsistent* set of statements is a set of statements such that it's logically impossible that every statement in that set be true. A simple example of such a set is {'Today is Monday,' 'Today is not Monday'}. Strangely enough, that set of statements implies 'Fred is wearing pink socks.' To see why this is true, all we have to do is to apply the account of implication just given. It's impossible that all three of these hold: (1) 'Today is Monday' is true; *and* (2) 'Today is not Monday' is true; *and* (3) 'Fred is wearing pink socks' is false. (The reason why this is the case has nothing to do with what colour socks Fred is wearing. The first two conditions suffice to make it impossible that all three hold.)

Similar reasoning can show why the set {'Today is Monday,' 'Today is not Monday'} implies *any statement at all*. And similarly, *any* inconsistent set of statements implies *every* statement.

Now recall the two principles we were considering above:

PRINCIPLE 2: Everyone should believe what's implied by their beliefs.

PRINCIPLE 3: Everyone does believe what they realise is implied by their beliefs.

Bearing in mind that
- All statements are implied by an inconsistent set of statements.
- The statements you believe are an inconsistent set.
- You now know that the set of your beliefs are inconsistent.

these obviously absurd conclusions follow:
- You should believe all statements.
- You do believe all statements.

Something has gone drastically wrong here. We have already seen reasons to question Principles 2 and 3. If we reject these principles, we can also reject their absurd consequences. But perhaps we can also question the principle of logic that every statement is implied by an inconsistent set of statements. However, it's hard to see what should replace this principle. It merely follows from the definition of 'implication.'

A QUESTION TO THINK ABOUT: Can you suggest a better definition that avoids this peculiar result?

2. I JUST CAN'T BELIEVE THAT

There are some things that are true but you don't believe them. But is there anything true that you *couldn't* believe—that it's *impossible* for you to believe? At first glance, you might think that there couldn't be anything like that. Suppose that some sentence S were true, and suppose you didn't believe it. But it doesn't seem that it would be *impossible* for you to believe it. Suppose that you had a very reliable and smart friend, and you believed everything that friend told you. This isn't impossible, right? Now, if your friend told you sentence S, you'd believe it.

We can, however, turn up examples of sentences such that, were they true, it would be impossible for you to believe them. Here's an example of one of them:

_____ is now dead. (Insert your name in the blank.)

This sentence is obviously false. But (I'm sorry to tell you) some day it will be true. When it's true it will be impossible for you to believe it.

Here's another. Suppose you wake up one morning with a bad hangover, badly confused. You think it's Monday, but actually it's Sunday. The true situation at that point is expressed by the sentence:

_____ believes it's Monday, but it's not. (Insert your name)

Your friend might find out that that sentence is true. But consider your own beliefs. Later on, when your head clears, you realize the truth, and you believe this sentence:

I believed (earlier this morning) that it was Monday, but it's not.

But consider the state of affairs earlier that morning. At that point, you believed that it was Monday, and it wasn't. This sentence, if you happened to say it then, would have been true:

I believe it is Monday, but it's not.

Notice, however, that you wouldn't have uttered that sentence, because it's impossible that you believe that what that sentence says is true.

Your reliable friend shows up first thing in the morning, and tells you this:

You believe it's Monday, but it's not.

Could you believe what your friend says?

> Part of what your friend's sentence says is that it's not Monday. But if you believe this part, then you wouldn't believe that it's Monday. But then the other part of your friend's sentence ('You believe it's Monday') would be false, and you'd know it's false.
>
> Or things might work the other way. On hearing your friend's sentence, you first notice the part that says 'You believe it's Monday.' Assuming your friend speaks the truth, you do believe it's Monday, and you believe this part of the sentence. But then you would think that the second part of the sentence is false. You couldn't believe the whole sentence.

> Niels Bohr (1885-1962), the renowned Danish physicist, had a horseshoe over his desk. One day a student asked if he really believed that a horseshoe brought luck. Professor Bohr replied, "I understand that it brings you luck if you believe in it or not."

> "'I can't believe *that*!' said Alice.
> 'Can't you?' the Queen said in a pitying tone. 'Try again: draw a long breath, and shut your eyes.'
> Alice laughed. 'There's no use trying,' she said: 'one *can't* believe impossible things.'
> 'I daresay you haven't had much practise,' said the Queen. 'When I was your age, I always did it for half-an-hour a day. Why sometimes I've believed as many as six impossible things before breakfast.'" —Lewis Carroll, *Through the Looking Glass*

The Queen's "six impossible things" remark has become a favourite of new-age spiritual boys and girls, who put it on their web pages along with other quotations they take to be inspirational. They seem to have interpreted it to mean something like "Dream the impossible dream"—to urge us to think outside the box, to boldly mentally go where no man has gone before, blah blah blah. This is not what the quote means, new-age spiritual boys and girls! Take it off your web pages! Lewis Carroll was a hard-headed logician. He was talking about the possibility of belief in the logically impossible, or maybe about what's logically impossible to believe.

3. DESCARTES' THOUGHT

René Descartes is famous for the quote "I think, therefore I am." What's not quite so widely known is why he said it.

Descartes began his work *Meditations* by noting that some of our ordinary beliefs have turned out to be false. Most of your ordinary beliefs seem obviously true, and you have no reason to think they're false; but even these just *might* be false. Descartes thought that philosophy should begin with beliefs about which it is *impossible* to be mistaken. Are there any beliefs like that?

The first one Descartes turned up was his own belief that he existed. This is not the belief that his body exists: it is the belief that he has mental existence—that he exists as a thinking thing. The famous quote embodies his reasoning to prove that this belief couldn't be mistaken. The supposition that the belief that he exists is mistaken couldn't be true. If he were mistaken in this belief, then he would, anyway, have a mistaken belief; and anything that has a mistaken belief is an existing thinking thing. Anyone who thinks he or she exists must be right.

Descartes' quote has spawned innumerable jokes. Here's one:

Descartes walks into a café and sits down ready to order. A waiter comes up to him and asks, "Do you need a menu?" Descartes replies, "I think not," and he disappears.

Descartes' real death was the result of thoughtlessness, too—on the part of Queen Christina of Sweden. She hired Descartes in 1649 as her personal tutor in mathematics and philosophy. This was good news for the philosophy profession—we're always seeking new kinds of employment.

Question: What words are spoken by PhDs in philosophy at their first jobs?
Answer: "Do you want fries with that?"

The bad news, however, was that the Queen wanted instruction beginning at 5 a.m., and Descartes had a lifetime habit of staying in bed till 11. After only a few months in the cold northern climate, walking to the palace for 5 o'clock every morning, he died. UNIVERSITY ADMINISTRATORS TAKE NOTE: NO EARLY MORNING CLASSES FOR PHILOSOPHERS!

4. SELF-FULFILLING AND SELF-DEFEATING BELIEFS

The Power of Positive Thinking

A self-fulfilling belief is a belief of the following sort: believing it will tend to make it true. An example of this is the belief that you will do well on a test. Generally speaking, if you have this belief, you will go into the test relaxed and confident, and will do better as a result. The opposite belief—that you will do poorly on the test—similarly tends to be self-fulfilling. If you go into the test convinced you'll do poorly, you'll be nervous and unhappy, and this will tend to lower your score.

Another example of a belief that tends to be self-fulfilling is the belief that somebody important to you likes you; it will result in your acting toward that person in a natural and confident way, and this might result in their liking you. Similarly, the opposite belief is self-fulfilling.

Insomniacs are unfortunately quite familiar with the self-fulfilling nature of the belief that you won't be able to get to sleep.

I'm about to give you a suggestion that can change your life enormously for the better! (Wonderful! Didn't you always hope that philosophy had such useful wisdom to offer?) The suggestion is this: if you want something to be true, and if the belief that it is true tends to be self-fulfilling, believe that belief. Thus, go into every test convinced that you'll do well; and you will do well (or, at least, you'll do better than you would have). Believe that people you want to like you do like you, and they will like you (or at least will tend to). The belief that you will succeed in a business will result in your acting in ways that may improve your chances of success. The cultivation of self-fulfilling positive beliefs is essentially the technique for improvement of your life advocated by "positive thinking" training.

The problem here (and in Pascal's Wager, discussed in the section called **WHY BELIEVING IN GOD IS A GOOD BET** in Chapter II) is that for most of us, consideration of the consequences of believing something has no power whatever to make us believe it. What would make us believe something is evidence that it is *true*.

But on closer inspection, it appears that self-fulfilling beliefs are not exactly like Pascal's Wager. Believing a self-fulfilling belief tends to make it true. So it appears that the fact that you believe a self-fulfilling belief *is* some evidence that what you believe is true.

How to Fail at Baseball

Related to the notion of a self-fulfilling belief is the notion of a paradoxical intention. This is involved when it's less likely you can do something if you try to do it.

A good baseball swing is a complex sort of action. You might naturally have a good swing, the first time you pick up a bat; or you might get a good swing from advice and practise. But it's likely that if you are told what's wrong with your swing and what you should be doing, and then you swing while trying to do the right thing, you'll do worse than you ordinarily do when you're not thinking about it.

Trying to go to sleep is another example. Trying to do it may very well tend to prevent you from doing it.

People who think too much are poor at doing things that involve paradoxical intentions. Philosophers, whose business it is to think about things, hope that paradoxical intentions aren't too widespread. (My Philosophy Department's softball team was soundly thrashed by almost every team we played. On the other hand, we did defeat the team from the Registrar's Office where there's no evidence of thought at all.)

The Pursuit of Happiness

Is the pursuit of happiness another example of this phenomenon?

> Some philosophers think that the achievement of happiness also involves paradoxical intentions—that trying to be happy is not the way to achieve happiness. Maybe it even interferes with happiness. It's been suggested that a good strategy for achieving happiness is finding things that matter to you, and working hard to get them. Perhaps this is good advice; but note that someone who is working toward growing a beautiful lawn, or breaking 100 on the golf course, or solving a philosophical problem, has intentions, desires, and aims directed toward gardening, or golf, or philosophy—not toward happiness.

> Thomas Jefferson wrote, in the American Declaration of Independence, that we all have the right to the pursuit of happiness. But if pursuing happiness is a bad way to get it, then this right isn't worth much.

A QUESTION TO THINK ABOUT: Maybe there isn't really any such thing as the pursuit of happiness. We know what it means to pursue skill at golf, or to try to open a jar whose lid is stuck. But what does it mean to try to get happiness?

Fooling Yourself

Descartes thought that you couldn't be wrong about what your own mental states were. Is that right?

> *Reporter:"* Yogi, have you made up your mind yet?"
> *Yogi Berra:* "Not that I know of."

> "I think if you know what you believe, it makes it a lot easier to answer questions. I can't answer your question."— George W. Bush, in response to a question about whether he wished he could take back any of his answers in a televised presidential election debate

Self-deception—if such a thing is possible—would be a particularly interesting example of being mistaken about what you really believe. Positive thinking is, in a sense, a sort of attempted self-deception: the only reason you have to try so hard to have a self-fulfilling belief is that you really believe it's false—or, at least, fear it might be.

Is self-deception possible? Suppose that you need a good night's sleep for some important task the next day, and that you believe you won't be able to go to sleep because you tend to be insomniac. You realise that this belief will tend to keep you awake, because you will worry about not being rested; so you try to believe instead that you'll go to sleep as soon as your head hits the pillow. The only reason you're trying so hard to believe you'll go right to sleep is that you already believe you won't. How can you believe something while you believe the opposite? How can you believe something *because* you believe the opposite? Perhaps self-deception is impossible.

But maybe I've spoken too fast. What is the familiar phenomenon called "wishful thinking" but the sort of self-deceptive process of coming to believe something not because you have evidence for its truth, but because you wish it were true?

Sorry, I'm Not Free Right Now

The attempt to practise self-deception plays a key role in the analysis of the human condition advocated by some existentialists. In their view, a centrally important, universal and necessary human characteristic is *freedom*: there are no causes for your feelings, values, or behaviour, not even your personality (which they regard as a myth). Neither are there objective standards obliging you to do one thing rather than another, provided by God, society, or moral reasoning. Thus you must make yourself up—create your own standards and motives out of nothing—with no cause and no guidance. As a result, you're wholly responsible for everything you do.

Your realization that you are in this state is not a pleasant one: it's terrible to think that nothing pushes or helps or guides you in your self-creation, and that you are totally responsible for yourself. That's why you spend so much of your time trying to give excuses: attempting to pretend to yourself and others that there are real causes or standards, or that you really have a "personality" or a "role" that forces you to be some way. But this is always a mistake, and you know that it's a mistake. How can you actually come to believe you're not free, while you really believe you are?

A QUESTION TO THINK ABOUT: How about it? Is all that true about you? C'mon now, be honest, stop trying to fool yourself.

5. MENTAL IMPOTENCE

Believe or I'll Shoot!

It would be a good idea for you to believe something you want to be true and your belief would help make it true, or if it were helpful to you to believe it.

Suppose someone held a gun at your head, and said, "Believe that the Dodgers will win next year's World Series, or I'll shoot!" You might try to convince this loony that you did believe that the Dodgers will win. But if you didn't already believe the Dodgers will win, his threat wouldn't result in your coming to believe it. You would surely *want* to believe it— it would be very much to your benefit to believe it—but this has no bearing on the matter.

But it seems that we don't have the power to believe what we want to believe. We can't believe things on purpose.

How to Intend to Kick Your Cat

Having somehow escaped the loony in the last example, you walk further down the street and another loony approaches, holds his gun at your head, and says, "Intend to kick your cat tomorrow, or I'll shoot!" Perhaps you are in a different situation now from the one you were in when you encountered the first loony. You can't develop beliefs at will, but maybe you can develop intentions at will.

You love Tabitha and certainly don't want to kick the poor fuzzy defenceless thing. Having no intention to kick her, your first strategy might be deception: you would try to convince this loony that you had just developed the intention he demanded.

But suppose there's no fooling him: he can tell that you're insincere in reporting your intention—it shows on your face.

So you consider this second strategy: you'll develop the intention to kick the cat—what else can you do?—and avoid getting shot. But, you reason, having the intention to do something doesn't mean that you really will do it. After your assailant has gone away, you can certainly change your mind. So your intention to kick Tabitha, you're relieved to see, will be harmless. You can merely get rid of the intention before tomorrow, and thus avoid both being shot and kicking Tabitha.

But the loony is too clever for you. "I can tell," he says, "that what you're trying to do is to develop the intention now to kick your cat, but that you also intend to get rid of that intention after I go away. So what you really intend is not to kick your cat at all!" He points his gun.

You think: I really have to develop the intention to kick Tabitha. If I also intend now to change my mind later, then I don't really intend now to kick Tabitha. So I guess the only thing I can do is to decide now to kick her, without intending to change my mind later.

So you develop two intentions:

(1) to kick Tabitha; and

(2) not to change your mind later about (1).

You tell the loony what you've decided, and he sees that you're sincere. Will that do the trick?

Even if it does, there's a puzzle here. Your intention (2) is really a crazy one. Why not change your mind later? He will, after all, have gone away, and you won't be in any danger. (There's an analogy here with the "Doomsday Machine" example I'll present in Chapter XIV, in an item called **Bombing the Russians.**")

But maybe it won't do the trick. "I'm way ahead of you," says the loony. "What you really are going to do is to change your mind about (2) later. Then at that time you'll be able to change your mind about (1). So to avoid being shot you also need another intention, (3): that you won't change your mind about (2)."

But if this is the case, then to satisfy him, wouldn't you *also* need to have intention (4): not to change your mind about (3)? This line of reasoning continues: maybe you need an infinite number of intentions. Is it possible for anyone to have an infinite number of intentions? Is your assailant demanding the impossible after all?

6. INTO THE MAINSTREAM OF PHILOSOPHY

Some of the problems that arose in the items in this chapter result from the assumption that we must believe everything that's implied by our beliefs. Many philosophers think that this assumption should simply be rejected. But this rejection brings its own problems. For one thing, is it really logically possible that somebody believes that all pigs are sloppy eaters, but fails to believe what's implied by this, that nothing that is a neat eater is a pig? It seems inconceivable that somebody believe one but not the other. Do you think that this is possible?

Again, some philosophers urge us to become reconciled to the position that it's possible to have contradictory beliefs. Thus, for example, someone might believe both that it's Tuesday and that it's not Tuesday, simultaneously. Is this really possible? If someone *said* both of these sentences with a look of deep sincerity, we wouldn't know what that person believed. Try to think of a plausible story that involves someone's having contradictory beliefs. Can you? Maybe this doesn't even make sense.

As in the case of the previous chapter, you'll find useful reading on these matters in the Smullyan and Poundstone books.

Another topic in this chapter is self-defeating and self-fulfilling beliefs, and self-deception. These do not fit neatly into any particular subject-matter area in mainstream philosophy, though there are occasional treatments of these ideas by philosophical writers in various contexts. For those interested in further reading, the best I can do is lamely to suggest you keep your eyes open. In the meantime, I can propose some questions for you to think about.

(1) One way to account for self-deception is to think of the mind as having parts, only some of which are conscious. Thus, for instance, when we have a belief we don't want to have, this gets shoved down into an unconscious area of the mind, and replaced in the consciousness with a preferable one. Perhaps this way of thinking necessitates postulation of a third area, which does the evaluation and the shoving. Students familiar with Freudian psychology will recognize this as a version of Freud's tripartite division of the mind. But is it really necessary to complicate things

to this degree? It really does seem to be an affront to common sense to think of desires or beliefs in someone who sincerely denies they are there. How could anyone know they are there? If what's in our mind is nothing but what we are aware of, then isn't it self-contradictory to talk about parts of our mental life of which we're unaware?

(2) Certain considerations above tended to lead us to talk about beliefs about beliefs, intentions about intentions, desires about desires. These are sometimes called "second-order" beliefs, intentions, and desires, and they are puzzling things. Do they even make sense? Consider this example. Suppose you and all your friends smoke; everyone else wants to stop smoking, but you (unconvinced or unmoved by the threats to your health and bank account) don't. Now suppose that you're a conformist, and want to be like all your friends. You'd like to share their desire to stop smoking, but you don't share it. In other words, you have the first-order desire to keep smoking, but you have the second-order desire not to have this first-order desire. You want to keep smoking, but you want *not* to want to keep smoking. Is this possible? Maybe second-order desires, if genuine, simply collapse into first-order desires. Thus if you genuinely do want to want to stop smoking, then you automatically want to stop smoking. Is this right?

CHAPTER VIII

GOOD AND BAD REASONING

1. THOUGHT-TRAPS FOR THE UNWARY

The Price of a Cork

Here's a question that most people answer wrong. If a bottle and a cork together cost $1.10, and the bottle costs $1.00 more than the cork, then what does the cork cost?

> The answer everyone jumps at is 10¢. If you don't see that this is the wrong answer, notice that if the cork cost 10¢, and the bottle cost $1.00 more than the cork, then the bottle would cost $1.10, so together they would cost $1.20.

This is, of course, an arithmetic puzzle, not a philosophical one. What may be of philosophical interest here is why almost everyone gets the wrong answer. Is there something about the way the puzzle is posed that leads people in the wrong direction? Is there something about our normal strategy in dealing with arithmetical questions that normally works fine, but that leads us astray when we think about this puzzle?

Maybe we get the wrong answer because of a combination of these two factors. We all share certain reasoning strategies. Some of these are learned in school. More are learned in the course of everyday experience, by imitation and suggestion from others, and by trial-and-error. There might even be some inborn problem-solving strategies wired into our brains, and genetically determined. These strategies work pretty well, in general. Most people are able to solve many problems—at least, problems of the sort that we're liable to run into in everyday life. But there are some simple problems that most people answer wrong. Our common strategies are not geared to deal with these problems successfully. A careful examination of a variety of these problems might show us exactly how our common strategies work.

The fact that your problem-solving strategies tend to fail on certain sorts of simple problems does not mean that you're stupid, or that your strategies need fixing. Any problem-solving strategy will be good at some problems and bad at others. Some of them will be much easier to learn and use, given the wiring of our brains and the nature of our environment. It just might be the case that the ones you in fact use achieve just the right combination of high percentage of success and ease of learning and use. But maybe not.

What are our strategies for doing arithmetic? That's a hard question to answer; but whatever they are, they are different from the ones computers use. Computers are much better than we are in multiplying large numbers. They can calculate answers in a tiny fraction of the time it takes humans, and we get wrong answers far more often than they do. But we're much better at figuring out what sort of computations are necessary to solve problems than they are. Imagine that you could get your brain surgically replaced with a computer. You could multiply large numbers much better as a result, but you'd be much worse off at problem-solving in general. The way we work is not so bad.

Splitting Up the Diamonds

The next few items demonstrate other arithmetic traps for the unwary. This one is an old puzzle that confused me and my friends as children.

A will specifies that several diamonds, to be found in a safe-deposit box, are to be distributed to the deceased's three children as follows: 1/2 of them to the eldest, 1/4 of them to the middle, and 1/5 to the youngest. The executor is puzzled about what to do when it turns out that there are nineteen identically-sized diamonds in the box. You can't give out 1/2 or 1/4 or 1/5 of this collection without cutting some diamonds into pieces, and cutting a diamond would ruin its value. What can the executor do?

> The executor hits on this ingenious plan: he borrows another diamond of the same size from a jeweller friend, and adds it to the nineteen, making twenty. He takes 1/2 of the twenty—ten of them—and gives them to the eldest child; then 1/4 of the twenty—five—to the middle, and 1/5 of the twenty—four—to the youngest. He has distributed nineteen diamonds; one remains—the one he borrowed from the jeweller—which he now returns. The eldest child is delighted, reasoning that she was entitled to only 9½ diamonds (one-half of the nineteen) but has

received ten instead; the other two think they have received a similar bonus.

A QUESTION TO THINK ABOUT: Something is peculiar about this
very nifty solution. Do you see what has gone wrong? (Hint: there's something wrong in the terms of the will.)

The Disappearing Dollar

This puzzle is in some ways similar to the one about the diamonds.

Three men, travelling together, check into a hotel and register for a
single room that they will share. The desk clerk tells them that the room
will cost $30, so they each give the clerk a ten-dollar bill and go up to the
room. A few minutes later, the desk clerk notices that he made a mistake:
the room costs only $25. So he gives the bellman a five-dollar bill and
tells him to go up to the room and give the money back to the men.

On the way upstairs, the bellman has these thoughts: To split up the
$5 evenly among the three men would take lots of change, which he
doesn't have, and probably the men don't either. Anyway, $5 can't be
divided by three exactly evenly. The men don't know that they're getting
any refund at all, and they'd be happy to get anything. So if he gave each
man a one-dollar bill, they'd be happy, and he would keep the remaining
$2. He has three one-dollar bills. So the bellman goes to the room and
gives each man a one-dollar bill.

Here's the puzzle. Each man originally put in $10, for a total of $30.
Each man got a refund of $1, meaning that each now paid $9, for a total
of $27. The bellman pocketed $2. $27 + $2 = $29. What happened to the
other dollar?

> The hotel now has $25, and the three men now have
> paid $27 altogether. The bellman's $2 should be added
> to the hotel's $25 or subtracted from the tenants' $27,
> not added to the tenants' $27.

Free Beer

This puzzle has money magically appearing, not disappearing. It's unusual because what looks like faulty reasoning turns out to be correct.

At one time, the Canadian and U.S. dollars were discounted by ten
cents on each side of the border (i.e., a Canadian dollar was worth ninety
U.S. cents in the U.S., and a U.S. dollar was worth ninety Canadian cents

in Canada). A man walks into a bar on the U.S. side of the border, orders ten U.S. cents worth of beer, pays with a U.S. dollar and receives a Canadian dollar in change. He then walks across the border to Canada, orders ten Canadian cents worth of beer, pays with a Canadian dollar and receives a U.S. dollar in change. He continues this throughout the day, and ends up dead drunk with the original dollar in his pocket. Two questions: (1) Who paid for the drinks? (2) When did this happen?

> (1) The man paid for all the drinks. But, you say, he ended up with the same amount of money that he started with! However, as he transported Canadian dollars into Canada and U.S. dollars into the U.S., he performed "economic work" by moving the currency to a location where it was in greater demand (and thus valued higher). The earnings from this work were spent on the drinks. Note that he can only continue to do this until the Canadian bar runs out of U.S. dollars, or the U.S. bar runs out of Canadian dollars, i.e., until he runs out of "work" to do.[1]

> (2) A beer for *ten cents*?? This happened approximately a gazillion years ago.

Nobody Works at All

Another arithmetic mistake:

There are 365 days in the year; but people usually work 8 hours a day; that's one-third of the 24-hour day. So people actually work only the equivalent of one-third of 365 days—that is, about 122 days.

But people usually work only weekdays. This means two days off a week; there are 52 weeks in a year, so there are 104 days off per year. Subtracting this from the 122 days leaves only 18 days.

Suppose, on average, a ten-day vacation. This leaves eight days. But there are at least this many regular holidays in the year. So nobody works at all.[2]

A QUESTION TO THINK ABOUT: Can you explain what's wrong with this reasoning?

---

[1] Thanks to an anonymous contributor to the newsgroup rec.puzzles for this puzzle and answer (1).

[2] A version of this traditional puzzle is in *Innumeracy*, pp. 167–168.

More Math Troubles

Here are a couple of other amusing[3] arithmetical paradoxes:

I. Clearly: 1 yard = 36 inches
    Dividing through by 4:   1/4 yard = 9 inches
    The square root of both sides: 1/2 yard = 3 inches
But that's clearly wrong. Where's the mistake?[4]

II. Consider a large pile of cubical toy blocks. The smallest has a side of exactly $1''$ (so it has a volume of $1^3 = 1$ cubic inch). The next largest has a slightly larger side, and they keep getting gradually larger, up to the largest, which is $3''$ on a side (with a volume of $3^3 = 27$ cubic inches). The average length of side in this pile is 2 inches. The average volume must be $(1 + 27)/2$ cubic inches: 14 cubic inches. So the block in this pile which is of average size must measure 2 inches on a side, and have a volume of 14 cubic inches. That's a pretty peculiar block.[5]

Better Pay or Worse?

There are two groups of workers in a huge office: 100 clerks and 100 accountants. Neither group is restricted to all males or all females. There are 100 males and 100 females altogether. Now suppose that all female clerks make more money than male clerks, and that all female accountants make more than male accountants. So it follows that the average salary of the females in that office is larger than the average salary of males, right? Wrong. Here's a way that the average female salary might be lower than the average male salary:

> **CLERKS:**
> 90 females, each making $25,000.
> 10 males, each making $20,000
> **ACCOUNTANTS:**
> 10 females, making $50,000
> 90 males, each making $45,000
> **TOTAL EMPLOYEES:**
> 100 females; average salary $27,500
> 100 males; average salary $42,500

---

[3] Well, perhaps I exaggerate. Anyway, people who find this sort of thing amusing will find these to be things of the sort that amuse them.

[4] *Innumeracy*, p. 95.

[5] Adapted from an example in *Innumeracy*, p. 169.

His Father's Son

This item is another example of a conceptual trap—but not an arithmetical one.

Raoul is looking at a photograph. You ask him, "Whose photograph is that?" Raoul poetically replies "Brothers and sisters have I none; but this man's father is my father's son." By "this man" Raoul means the man in the photo. Who is that man?

> The answer is that the man in the photo is Raoul's son. Is that the answer you arrived at? If the right answer is not obvious to you, note that the person Raoul calls "my father's son" has to be Raoul himself; and since *that* person (Raoul) is "this man's father," then "this man" has to refer to Raoul's son.

Almost everyone jumps at the answer that the man in the photo must be Raoul. They reason: because Raoul has no brothers or sisters, then the person he calls "my father's son" must be him. So far so good; but people forget that "my father's son" is *the father* of the man in the picture. Perhaps something about the way the riddle is stated makes people forget that, and makes us think about the problem in the wrong way. Do you feel that the problem setup causes confusion, by producing information overload? I couldn't possibly fail not to disagree with you less.

> For a joke based on the "my father's son" confusion, see the section called **The Washington Intelligence Community** in Chapter XIII.

The Card Mistake

Here's an experiment you can run on yourself. A psychologist used this as part of a test of people's reasoning ability.

Examine the following four cards:

$$a \qquad b \qquad c \qquad d$$

Half of each card is masked. Your job is to figure out which of the hidden parts of these cards you *need* to see in order to answer the following question decisively: *Is it true in all cases that if there is a circle on the left there is a circle on the right?* Of course, if you unmasked all the cards, you could answer this question; but it's not necessary to unmask all of them to answer it conclusively. Which are the cards it's necessary to unmask?

> Is your answer that you need to see the masked part on only card a? Or is your answer that you need to see the masked parts on both card a and card c? These are the answers people commonly give, but both of these answers are wrong. The right answer is that you need to see the masked parts on card a and on card d.
>
> Here's help in figuring out why the right answer is right. What would it take for it to be true that all the cards follow the rule? It would have to be the case that any card with an 0 on the left would have to have an 0 on the right. In other words, there could be no card with an 0 on the left and nothing on the right. To test this, we can ignore card b, which doesn't have an 0 on the left. Similarly, card c can be ignored, since whether or not there's an 0 on the left, it can't be the sort of card we are looking for: with an 0 on the left, and nothing on the right. Card d must be unmasked, however, because it might have an 0 on the left. If it does, then that general rule would be shown false. If it doesn't, then the rule can still be true.

But what's important here is not what the right answer is, or why it's right. The point is that in the experiment very few people got the right answer, even when the subjects were a group of university students with high intelligence. (In one group of 128 university students, only five got the right answer. So don't feel bad if you got the wrong answer.) Why did such a large proportion of intelligent people get it wrong?

Consider, by contrast, this puzzle. Imagine you're a bouncer in a bar, and are enforcing the rule "If a person is drinking beer, he must be eighteen or older." Which do you have to check (for beverage or age): A beer-drinker? A coke-drinker? A twenty-five-year-old? A sixteen-year-old? Most people correctly answer that you have to check the beer-drinker's age and the sixteeen-year-old's beverage. The bouncer question has exactly the same logical structure as the card problem. What's the difference that accounts for the fact that people do so much better at the bouncer question?

One theory is that the card problem is posed in an abstract way, as a mere puzzle, and has no bearing on anyone's practical experience; but the bouncer question is much more like a real-world scenario—one we can easily imagine ourselves in.

But the concreteness of the situation is not what makes the difference. Here's an equally concrete puzzle that people find as daunting as the card problem. Suppose you're in that bar again, and you're interested in finding out whether a certain theory of bar-behaviour is right. According to this theory, people follow this rule: "If a person eats hot chili peppers, then he drinks beer." Whom must you check? A chili-eater? Someone who's eating French fries instead? A beer-drinker? A coke-drinker?

So it's not concreteness after all. Any ideas?

> Work of the psychologist Leda Cosmedes shows that people get the answer right when the rule is a contract, an exchange of benefits, of the form, "If you take a benefit, you must meet a requirement." (In our example, beer is the benefit, and being over eighteen is the requirement. But beer and chili peppers do not have a benefit-requirement relationship.) This suggests that our minds are attuned to detecting rule-cheaters, but not to other forms of conditional-testing.

A QUESTION TO THINK ABOUT: What reason do we have for classifying some reasoning as good, and other reasoning as bad? One way of explaining this classification is that it summarizes and systematizes how smart people really reason. When smart people are given the card problem, they come to the "wrong" conclusion. Does this show that their conclusion is not really the wrong one?

FOR FURTHER READING: This experiment, and ones like it, were run by P. Wason and P. Johnson-Laird. It's described and discussed in: Wason, "Reasoning about a Rule," in *Quarterly Journal of Experimental Psychology* 20 (1968), pp. 273–281; Wason and Johnson-Laird, "A Conflict between Selecting and Evaluating Information in an Inferential Task," *British Journal of Psychology* 61 (1970), pp. 509–515; and several articles in Johnson-Laird and Wason, eds., *Thinking* (Cambridge: Cambridge University Press, 1977). You can find accounts of Cosmides' work in L. Cosmides, "The Logic of Social Exchange: Has Natural Selection Shaped How Humans Reason? Studies With the Wason Selection Task," *Cognition*, 31, 187-276. My source for information in this section is a wonderful book that I recommend you read lots of: Stephen Pinker, *How the Mind Works* (New York: W. W. Norton, 1997). Pinker's discussion of the Wason task is on pages 336–338.

2. THE REASONING OF OTHER CULTURES AND PAST CULTURES

Azande Witches

It's amazing what cultures radically different from our own believe about the world, and count as good reasoning.

Consider the thinking of the Azande tribe. The Azandes believe that post-mortem examination of someone's intestines for "witchcraft substance" can show conclusively whether or not that person was a witch. They also believe that witchcraft is strictly inherited—that is, if a parent of yours is a witch, then you *must* inherit this trait. But they refuse to draw the conclusion that people are witches when they are the offspring of someone determined, post-mortem, to have been a witch.

Something is peculiar here, but what? Of course, most of us would object to the Azandes' idea that there are witches and intestinal "witchcraft substance." But that's not the interesting point of this example. It seems, in addition, that they are making an elementary reasoning mistake. They appear to agree to the following premises:

> X's parent is a witch.
> If someone's parent is a witch, then that person is a witch too.

but to refuse to accept the following conclusion:

> X is a witch.

But we shouldn't be too hasty here. Maybe they really do accept that the conclusion follows from these premises, but don't like calling live people witches, and are too polite to agree to the conclusion. Or maybe the anthropologist who translated what the Azandes said got the translation wrong. Or maybe the native informants were joking with the anthropologist, or telling deliberate lies.

FOR FURTHER READING: The philosophical implications of Azande reasoning are discussed by Peter Winch, "Understanding a Primitive Society," *American Philosophical Quarterly*, 1 (1964), pp. 307–324. Winch's position is discussed by Charles Taylor in "Rationality," in Martin Hollis and Steven Lukes, *Rationality and Relativism* (Oxford: Basil Blackwell, 1982), p. 94. This book is a splendid collection of articles about the general questions raised in this item.

Camels in Germany

Here is an excerpt from an interview by the psychologist A. R. Luria with a Kashdan peasant:

Q: (the following syllogism is presented) There are no camels in Germany. The city of B. is in Germany. Are there camels there or not?

A: (subject repeats syllogism exactly)

Q: So, are there camels in Germany?

A: I don't know, I've never seen German villages.

Q: (the syllogism is repeated)

A: Probably there are camels there.

Q: Repeat what I said.

A: There are no camels in Germany, are there camels in B. or not? So probably there are. If it's a large city there should be camels there.

Q: But what do my words suggest?

A: Probably there are. Since there are large cities, then there should be camels.

Q: But if there aren't any in all of Germany?

A: If it's a large city, there will be Kazakhs or Kirghiz [types of camels] there.

We can't jump to the conclusion in this case that the peasant is unable to reason logically. Notice that the peasant doesn't get this bit of reasoning:

There are no camels in Germany.

The city of B. is in Germany.

Therefore there are no camels in B.

but provides this bit of reasoning:

There are camels in large cities.

B. is a large city

Therefore there are camels in B.

Never mind that the second bit of reasoning contains a false premise (the generalization about camels in large cities)—the reasoning on the basis of this premise is correct. So it seems that this peasant is able to understand and use a basic logical syllogism.

What has gone wrong, then?

> Perhaps the peasant's inability to understand the first syllogism is the result of the fact that it is (at least for him) *hypothetical*—he doesn't know, and isn't told, that the premises are true. He's just asked to suppose that they are. It might be the case that, in certain cultures, reason-

ing about (what are thought to be) the facts works fine, but there's an inability to apply it to hypothetical situations.

FOR FURTHER READING: This example and many others are discussed fascinatingly in Don LePan's *The Cognitive Revolution in Western Culture*, Vol. 1: *The Birth of Expectation* (London: Macmillan, 1989). LePan offers the hypothesis that peasants from primitive cultures (as well as children in ours) show deficits in reasoning about hypothetical situations. LePan cites Hallpike, *The Foundations of Primitive Thought* (Oxford: Oxford University Press, 1979) as the source for the Luria interview.

If We Had Three Nostrils, Would There Be Eight Planets?

Here is a sample of what appears to be very bad reasoning from our own culture. Galileo looked through his telescope at Jupiter, and in 1610 published a work in which he claimed to have seen four moons around that planet. But a number of contemporary thinkers were sure that what Galileo saw couldn't have been moons. Seven "planets" (meaning bodies in space: the sun and the moon, Mercury, Venus, Mars, Jupiter and Saturn) were already known, and these additional four would raise the number to eleven; but one contemporary of Galileo argued:

> Just as in the microcosm there are seven "windows" in the head (two nostrils, two eyes, two ears, and a mouth), so in the macrocosm God has placed two beneficent stars (Jupiter, Venus), two maleficent stars (Mars, Saturn), two luminaries (sun and moon), and one indifferent star (Mercury). The seven days of the week follow from these. Finally, since ancient times the alchemists had made each of the seven metals correspond to one of the planets; gold to the sun, silver to the moon, copper to Venus, quicksilver to Mercury, iron to Mars, tin to Jupiter, lead to Saturn.
>
> From these and many other similar phenomena of nature such as the seven metals, etc., which it were tedious to enumerate, we gather that the number of planets is necessarily seven.... Besides, the Jews and other ancient nations as well as modern Europeans, have adopted the division of the week into seven days, and have named them from the seven planets; now if we increase the number of planets, this whole system falls to the ground.... Moreover, the satellites are invisible to the naked eye and therefore can have no influence on the earth, and therefore would be useless, and therefore do not exist.

This is dreadful astronomy, but it does represent respectable mainstream thought of its era.

A Bibliographical Note and Cautionary Tale

I encountered the "seven windows" quote in Charles Taylor's article cited above. Taylor does not give the quote's author, but does cite Sidney Warhaft's book *Francis Bacon: A Selection of His Works* (Toronto: MacMillan of Canada, 1967), p. 17. So in the first edition of *Two Errors*, I attributed the quote to Bacon, remarking on the fact that Bacon was otherwise taken to be a brilliant champion of the new empirical science.

Well, it turns out that the quote is not by Bacon after all; in fact, Warhaft gives it in the introduction to his book, not in the main body of selections from Bacon, attributing it to "a respectable representative of the old school," and citing it as just the kind of thinking that Bacon crusaded *against*. It turns out to have been written by an astronomer named Francesco Sizzi, in his book *Dianoia Astronomica, Optica, Physica* (Florence, 1611).

Oops.

Anyway, there's a moral here for all you junior cadet researchers out there. When you want to cite something a writer got from somewhere else, it's a good idea to look up the source cited to make sure you have it right.

Nobody Could Be *That* Wrong

How could astronomy have been done that poorly? Are you tempted to think that the author of that quote was just stupid? Or that the fault was, more likely, in the primitive scientific methodology accepted at the time, which wrongheadedly and superstitiously relied on analogy and metaphor instead of observation?

But a more sophisticated, popular, and politically acceptable conclusion is the view (loosely called "post-modern") that the thinkers of other times and places, who often seem to us to have been reasoning very poorly and to have gotten things dreadfully wrong, were probably just as smart as we are; the reason they look stupid to us is that they were operating from very different viewpoints from the ones we have. Our counting them as stupid is just our own narrow-minded intolerance—even a form of racism, when applied to non-European cultures. A better way to under-· stand this sort of thought is to see it as successful in achieving aims different from those of our culture's thinkers. Each group has its own aims, procedures, and presuppositions, and the procedures of one group can seem stupid to others. What is really happening is merely that we don't—

perhaps even can't—understand what they're doing. We shouldn't even be making any judgements about who's really smarter than whom, or about which society has the superior methodology.

But this view doesn't seem adequate either. Taken to an extreme, this approach would seem to indicate that *nobody* can be mistaken about the facts or use faulty reasoning. *Whenever* someone disagrees with me, it can always be argued that I merely don't understand what that person is doing. Surely *somewhere* there must be examples of people who believed falsehoods or thought irrationally. Surely we all live in the same world, and some of us are right and others wrong about what this world is like, and about the best way to think about it.

But here's a philosophical argument for the conclusion that it's literally *impossible* for us to find somebody who gets things really badly wrong.

Imagine that an anthropologist claims to have discovered a tribe where mistaken beliefs run rampant. We are told that people in this tribe—we'll call them the Falsoids—believe, for example, that pigs have thick, hard, elongated woody trunks rooted in the ground, that they sometimes grow over twenty metres high, and that they produce lobed leaves which fall off in late autumn, the time when those pigs produce acorns. Now, it's pretty clear to us what has gone wrong here: the anthropologist has simply mistranslated Falsish, the language of the Falsoids. The best explanation is that this anthropologist has merely mistranslated as 'pig' the Falsish word for 'oak tree.'

Or imagine that the anthropologist claims that the Falsoids believe that rain is boiling hot, solid, poisonous, alive, flammable, and blue; that it makes a noise like clucking when disturbed; and that every bit of it ever discovered has been stored for safe-keeping underground. Well, it's clear that something has gone wrong in translation again, though we have no idea what the Falsoids might have meant by whatever the anthropologist heard them say in Falsish.

The point here is that a translation of some other language isn't counted as correct if it translates a great deal of what the speakers of that language say into sentences in our language that we count as badly wrong. The only translation we're willing to count as correct is one in which we count what they're saying as, on the whole, true. Now, since what they say is the main way we have for finding out what they believe, there will be no case in which we claim to know what they believe, *and* that what they believe is badly wrong. If we have no way of translating what they say into largely true sentences, then we'll conclude not that they have things badly wrong, but rather that we don't know what they believe.

Thus we can conclude that it is impossible for us to discover a tribe that we will count as having a very large number of false beliefs.

The same line of reasoning can be used to show that we can't ever discover someone in *our own tribe*—someone who speaks the same language as we do—who has very badly mistaken beliefs. Imagine that someone says to you, in English, "Pigs have thick, hard, elongated woody trunks rooted in the ground. They sometimes grow over twenty metres high, and they produce lobed leaves which fall off in late autumn, the time when those pigs produce acorns." You might be tempted to conclude that this person has badly mistaken beliefs, or that he or she has gone crazy; but in some circumstances the preferred interpretation would be that he or she is speaking English peculiarly—that he or she means *oak trees* by the word 'pigs,' and has true beliefs about oak trees.

FOR FURTHER READING: Winch, in the article cited above, champions the view that cases in which we seem to detect horribly bad reasoning in other groups are probably cases in which we have misunderstood them. The most prominent philosophical advocate of the view that any "translation" of what someone else says is counted wrong if it does not attribute to that person at least some degree of rationality is Donald Davidson. A good place to look for an introduction to Davidson's views, criticism of them, and references to the work of Davidson and others is Chapter 2 of Steven Stich's *The Fragmentation of Reason* (Cambridge, MA: MIT Press, 1990). We'll have more to say about related issues—see **SCIENCE AND "TRADITIONAL KNOWLEDGE"** in the next chapter.

Warning for Tourists: Watch Out for Extreme Politeness

A Canadian who spent some time in India told me that he ran into a peculiar problem there, several times. He'd be walking down a street, and he'd ask someone for directions, say, to a museum. The person he asked would point in the direction the Canadian had been walking. But the museum turned out to be in a different direction altogether.

What was going on here? The places the Canadian was looking for were all well-known to the locals; they couldn't have been mistaken about them so often, or too stupid to be able to give walking directions. Neither did the people he asked seem to be motivated to lie to him; they all appeared quite friendly and eager to help. At last the Canadian arrived at the hypothesis that the people who told him falsely that the place he was looking for was in the direction he was walking were just being extremely polite: they thought it would be rude to tell people (especially foreigners) that they were walking in the wrong direction.

Here's a similar problem, this time involving Americans and Japanese. This one is reported by the humourist Dave Barry. Before he and his wife left for Japan, she phoned a Japanese travel agent to make hotel and plane reservations. Here's Barry's account of what these phone conversations were like:

Beth: ... and then we want to take a plane from Point A to Point B.
Travel Agent: I see. You want to take a plane?
Beth: Yes.
Travel Agent: From Point A?
Beth: Yes.
Travel Agent: To Point B?
Beth: Yes.
Travel Agent: Ah.
Beth: Can we do that?
Travel Agent: Perhaps you would prefer to take a train.
Beth: No, we would prefer to take a plane.
Travel Agent: Ah-hah. You would prefer to take a plane?
Beth: Yes. A plane.
Travel Agent: I see. From Point A?

And so it would go, with arrangement after arrangement.

The problem, they discovered, was not that the Japanese could not communicate. This travel agent, it turned out, was telling her, in Japanese style, that there was no plane from Point A to Point B. Barry summarizes how the Japanese tell you things (of course, with a touch of comic exaggeration) in the following table:

English Statement Made by a Japanese Person	Actual Meaning in American
I see.	No.
Ah.	No.
Ah-hah.	No.
Yes.	No.
That is difficult.	That is completely impossible.
That is very interesting.	That is the stupidest thing I have ever heard.
We will study your proposal.	We will feed your proposal to a goat.[6]

---

[6] *Dave Barry Does Japan* (New York: Fawcett Columbine, 1992), pp. 35–37.

My Canadian acquaintance who got bad directions in India corroborates Barry's point about Japan. He tells me that when studying the Japanese language in preparation for a trip there he of course learned the words for "yes" and "no", but during his stay in Japan, he never heard the word for "no."

It's easy to see how a Westerner might jump to the conclusion that those Indians, who so often give you wrong directions, are stupid or malevolent; or that those Japanese, who never seem to come to grips with the issue, are bad communicators or hopelessly inefficient. The point here is not exactly that it's easy to jump to the wrong conclusion about people in a distant culture. The point is that understanding them is a matter of *interpretation*. If you start out feeling that the foreigners are in some way inferior to your group, you'll interpret what they do as stupidity or malevolence or inefficiency. But if you start out with respect for them, and are prepared to admire their differences from your culture, you'll interpret what they do in a favourable way.

The necessity of *interpretation*, and the fact that so much depends on the attitudes the interpreter comes to the foreign culture with, become clearest when the culture is extremely alien and the evidence about what's going on extremely skimpy. The Canadian I've been talking about is an academic interested in the inhabitants of Mesopotamia almost four thousand years ago. Among the extremely scant evidence we have about them is what are apparently some rules they wrote down divining the future on the basis of signs like eclipses and characteristics of the livers of sacrificed sheep. But the rules are bizarre. Any idiot could see, it would seem, that these predictions were utterly unreliable. But my acquaintance says that he came to this study believing in advance that the ancient Mesopotamians were not idiots—that they observed reality as clearly as we do, and had as much common sense and reasoning ability as us. Given these presuppositions, he's come up with some pretty ingenious interpretations of what they meant by those writings. His interpretations would be quite different from those of a scholar who believed at the outset that ancient people were mired in superstition, couldn't reason very well, and knew very little about the external world.

A QUESTION TO THINK ABOUT: Maybe when it comes to understanding foreign cultures there isn't any truth of the matter at all—it's all just a matter of interpretation. So then the problem with the interpreters who think of other cultures as stupid or malevolent is not that they're making a *factual* mistake. There is no fact to get right or wrong. The problem with them is that they have immoral presuppositions—attitudes that are insulting to the other cultures.

Could this be right?

3. THINKING IN GROOVES

In the puzzles that follow, seeing the solution involves dropping our automatic assumptions, and seeing things from a different angle.

(1) The Boy With Two Fathers

A father and his son are involved in an automobile accident. Both are seriously injured and are rushed to separate hospitals. The son is immediately readied for emergency surgery; at the first sight of him, however, the surgeon says, "I can't operate on this patient—he's my son!" How is what is reported here possible?

> The problem almost everyone sees in this story is, of course, that it is impossible that the surgeon is the boy's father. What makes this story possible, however, is the supposition that the surgeon is the boy's *mother*.

(2) How to Win a Camel Anti-Race

The Sheikh of Al-Cindor orders two of his subjects, Abdul and Jabbar, to participate in a special camel race. The winner will receive a prize of a thousand rials. The finish line is the entrance to the main square of the neighbouring town of Kareem. But what's special about this race is that the winner is the contestant whose camel crosses the finish line *second*.

Abdul and Jabbar get on their camels, and the race begins. They watch each other carefully, each trying to get his camel to move more slowly than the other's, and pretty soon both camels come to a halt. Abdul and Jabbar dismount, sit down in the shade of a palm tree, and try to figure out what to do. At last, they decide to ask the advice of a wise man of their town. The wise man offers them a solution; they jump on the camels, and head off full-speed toward Kareem.

What did the wise man tell them?

> He told them to switch camels.

(3) **Thinking Straight about Roman Numerals**

Here is a number (in Roman Numerals): VI. By the addition of one line, can you make it into a seven? The answer is simple enough—VII. But now suppose you are given the following problem: Here is a number, IX. By the addition of one line, can you make it into a six?

> In front of IX you add the (curvy) line S, making it SIX.

(4) **Reducing Speeding Violations**

The New York State Thruway Authority faced the problem of an excessive number of speed-limit violations. They could have, at great expense, hired more troopers to track down the violators. Can you think of an easier and more effective means of reducing the number of violations?

> They raised the speed limit. (Fortunately, there was no increase in the accident rate.)

(5) **Smashing a Fly**

Often in algebra problems we are asked to imagine bizarre and inexplicable situations, and this is no exception. Imagine two train locomotives facing each other on a single track, 200 miles away from each other. Both locomotives will begin moving toward the other simultaneously at 50 miles per hour, ending in a head-on crash. (They accelerate instantaneously to that speed.) Sitting on the front of one of the locomotives at the beginning is a fly. When the two begin to move, the fly will fly quickly toward the other locomotive; when it reaches it, it will turn around and return to the first locomotive, then turn around again and fly back to the second; it will continue shuttling back and forth until the locomotives crash (when it will get nicely and thoroughly smashed between them). The fly flies at 75 miles per hour. Before the spectacular finale, how far will the fly travel?

I now pause to allow some readers to sigh morosely as memories of high school algebra flood back.

> Bravely, a few readers take out pencil and paper and begin calculation. It's not a very difficult bit of algebra to determine the length of the fly's first trip, from the one locomotive at the start, to the other locomotive moving

toward it. Having calculated this, however, or maybe even before, you realise that there will be an infinite series of shorter and shorter trips for the fly as the locomotives converge. Calculating the sum of an infinite series will defeat all but the most stalwart of amateurs, and at this point almost everyone gives up.

But there's a trick, involving a radically different way of thinking about the problem. In two hours, each loco-motive will travel 100 miles, meeting in the middle of the 200-mile-long track and crashing. The fly is flying all this time. Since the fly goes at 75 miles per hour, it travels 150 miles. That's it!

> It's reported that the great mathematician Von Neumann was given this problem, thought about it for a few seconds, and gave the correct answer. When asked how he did it, he re-plied, "I summed the series."

(6) The Enormous Tiddly-Wink Tournament

Another puzzle with an unobvious easy solution.

The Klopstokian Tiddly-Winks Federation runs a huge national tour-nament each year in which the national champion of Klopstokia is deter-mined. The country is divided into four divisions. In each division, all ranked winkers are paired up, and play each other. The loser of each game drops out of the tournament; the winner goes on to play again. After a sufficient number of games, there's only one winker left in each division; they form two pairs who play, then winners of these games play for the championship. Here is a list of the number of ranked winkers in each division:

NORTH:	57
SOUTH:	83
EAST:	51
WEST:	49
TOTAL:	240

The question is: how many games are played altogether in the tourna-ment?

> If I hadn't led you to suspect that there's a trick easy so-lution, you'd probably do this the hard way:

In the North division, there are 57 winkers. So the first round has 28 games, pairing up 56 of these, and one winker gets a bye. The losers drop out, leaving 28 winners plus the winker who had the bye. So there are 14 games in the next round, plus one bye again. In the following round there are 7 games plus one bye; in the next there are 4, with no byes, and in the next 2, and then 1. This produces a winner of the North Division, after a total of, um, let's see, 28 + 14 + 7 + 4 + 2 + 1 = 56 games. Arrgh, now we have to do the same calculation for all the other divisions.

No! Wait a minute! The number of games in the North division is one less than the number of winkers, and it has to be, because players drop out after losing one game, and to get a winner, 56 out of the 57 have to lose. So there's the easy solution to the problem: There are 240 players in all; 239 of them will have to lose one game each. So that means the tournament will have 239 games in all. Voila!

(7) Notes from the Underground

Here's another puzzle that most people will try to answer the hard way and fail.

Examine this series of numbers; determine the principle here, and supply the next few numbers in the series:

14, 18, 23, 34, 42, 50, 59, 66, 72, 79...

The next few numbers are 86, 96, 103, 110, 116, 125. The principle here is that these are the stops on the north-bound IRT West Side Broadway/7th Avenue subway line in New York City: 14th Street, 18th Street, and so on.

You can be excused for not having seen that answer, because you probably aren't familiar with the New York subway. So you don't merit a "Gotcha!" but my classmates at Columbia University and I did. We were presented with this problem while sitting in a classroom less than one hundred metres from the 116th Street station of the IRT West Side Broadway/7th Avenue subway line. Almost all of us had spent a good proportion of our undergraduate lives riding that subway line through many of those stops, and we were supposed to be a smart bunch of kids. Why didn't any of us get the answer? The reason is, of course, that the question strongly suggested a well-worn conventional sort of solution, and we were all thinking in that groove.

Thinking Outside the Box

The inability most of us have to see the trick in the surgeon story is a good example of a familiar phenomenon: we are prevented from solving a problem because of our automatic assumptions. A lesson that might be drawn is that we should avoid "thinking in grooves"—that we must think creatively, throwing aside our automatic assumptions, to solve problems.

This is advice you may have encountered especially often recently, when it has become fashionable to blame old-fashioned "linear" thought for everything from the failure of the elementary school system to ecological catastrophe to oppression of women and of the Third World.

What these examples have in common is that we come to a problem with certain automatic assumptions. In the surgeon example, our assumption that a surgeon is male is, of course, suspect; but given the (unfortunate) fact that the vast majority of surgeons in our society are male, it's not unjustified. The way the SIX problem is set up, we are led—reasonably—to assume that we are supposed to add a line to the Roman numeral IX to turn it into the Roman numeral VI. And we assume in the Thruway example that the problem is to get people to obey the *current* speed limit. These assumptions aren't *stated* as conditions of the problems, but given the ways the problems are stated and given our background experience, they are reasonable ways of approaching them. But the solution is found only when the assumptions are rejected.

Is rejection of our automatic assumptions in general a good strategy for solving problems? Don't jump to this conclusion too quickly. In these particular cases automatic assumptions do interfere with our solution to the problem; but very frequently the hidden assumptions we bring to all problems are an aid, not a hindrance, to solutions.

To see this, let's return to the surgeon puzzle. There are other—reasonable—assumptions we bring to this story, which also lead to our reaction that the situation is impossible. We think that the father who is injured in the accident and brought to a different hospital cannot be the surgeon who shows up to perform surgery on his son. Why not? Because, it's reasonable to assume, the surgery would have to be performed soon after the accident; and the father was injured and being treated elsewhere. But

the story does not *say* that the father would be in treatment simultaneously with his son; perhaps he recovered so fast that he could travel to
the hospital where his son was, and could resume his work as a surgeon
there in time to be called to his son's case. We assume that this could not
happen, and this assumption is a fairly reasonable one; but the apparent
impossibility of the story disappears if we withdraw this assumption as
well. Another reasonable assumption that works the same way is that what
the surgeon exclaims on seeing the boy is true.

Now generalize this point to all the problems you solve in everyday
life. Suppose, for example, that you have to be at an appointment downtown in a half hour, and you only have a couple of dollars in your pocket,
not enough for taxi fare. You have no car, and walking would take more
than a half hour. The cash machine is nearby, but if you walked there
first, then began to look for a taxi, you'd be late. Well, maybe there's a
solution to your problem, but it probably won't be found if you start by
questioning some very reasonable background assumptions: that a taxi
won't take you there for free, or that a helicopter hasn't suddenly landed
in your backyard just for the purpose of giving you a free lift downtown,
or that you haven't suddenly developed the ability to fly. There are count-
less highly plausible assumptions you don't question, and you're right
not to question them. You'd never solve any problem if you brought all
your assumptions into question. Thinking "in grooves" is almost always
a very good strategy: after all, the world almost always works "in grooves."

FOR FURTHER READING: The SIX and speed-limit example are in
Crazy Talk, Stupid Talk by Neil Postman (1966). The title of Postman's
book tells you what he thinks of some examples of "lateral" thought. "His
Father's Son," "The Boy with Two Fathers" and "Smashing a Fly" are all
in Raymond Smullyan's book, *What is the Name of This Book*. You can
find a huge collection of logical puzzles on the internet, collected by Chris
Cole:

http://www.faqs.org/faqs/puzzles/archive/logic/

I have adapted the camel-race example from one of Cole's puzzles.

The the Title of This Book

If you've already read the back cover of this book, you'll have found the
repeated 'THE' in the title of this book.

What's interesting about this error is that it's so hard to see. I have
asked dozens of people to read the title, and not one of them noticed this

error the first time they read it. Some people found the error after I asked them, several times, to read the title carefully, word-for-word. Some people couldn't find it after this. I had to show the repetition to them: "Look— here's one 'THE' and here's another."

This example shows that we even *see* in grooves. When we read something, we automatically and unconsciously process what we see, making "corrections" in accord with expectations about what sequences normally occur in our reading. Perhaps when you read the title, this "correction" process drops out the second word when it finds a repetition. Or maybe, more generally, there's a process that "corrects" what you seem to read so that it makes sense.

Whatever this process is, it's clear that it has resulted in misperception in this case. But it's also clear that it usually is very advantageous to us. If we had to concentrate on each word in a sentence, our reading would be very slow and laborious. Instead of this, our eyes glance lightly and quickly over the words we read, and this process fills in the blanks and corrects the errors that result from this fast skimming. On the whole, then, this process permits fast and accurate reading. It does, however, produce rare errors, especially in those cases (like the the title of this book) when what we're reading is very unusual.

This is another example in which our automatic strategies for encountering the world, based on expectations of how things usually are, can lead us astray; but, again, the moral is not that we should discard these strategies. They're extremely useful. We'd be much worse off in finding out things without them.

4. INTO THE MAINSTREAM OF PHILOSOPHY

What makes something good reasoning anyway? One way of answering this question is that patterns of good reasoning are patterns that *work* for a person or a community. It's perhaps a consequence of this position that what counts as good reasoning for you, or for your community, depends on your situation: on what sorts of problems you encounter, and on what your needs are. Different communities have different situations, so maybe what's good reasoning in one community is bad in the other.

Here's a plausible example of this. Imagine two tribes, the Alphas and the Betas. Both tribes hunt for wild mushrooms for food. The Alphas use a complicated and laborious test to tell which mushrooms to take home and which to ignore. The Betas use a different, much easier test, and take home a lot of mushrooms the Alphas ignore. The Alphas sometimes leave behind perfectly good mushrooms the Betas would have used. Who is using the right test? Well, suppose that there are poisonous mushrooms in Alphaland, but none in Betaland. The Betas' simple test sometimes results in their taking home and eating mushrooms that taste awful—but the result is just a bad-tasting dish. If the Alphas used the Betas' test, disaster would result when they ate poisonous mushrooms. The Alphas' procedure costs them more effort and results in fewer mushrooms, but it keeps them from being poisoned. The Betas' procedure is easy and collects a much greater number of edible mushrooms, but occasionally it results in a bad-tasting dish. We can see now that *both* mushroom-hunting strategies are correct, given the different situations of the tribes.

Well, it's not difficult to imagine how this parable might be extended to more general reasoning patterns. It might just be the case that the surprisingly different general patterns of reasoning exhibited at other times, and by different cultures, are suitable given the difference in situation.

If you find this line of reasoning attractive, however, you should be careful not to allow it to go too far. It seems clear that there *must* be such a thing as *bad* reasoning. We shouldn't assume that just any old pattern of reasoning must be well-suited to the situation of those who use it. Even the fact that some pattern is widely used, and has stood the test of natural selection of reasoning patterns over the ages, doesn't necessarily make it good. A large number of people now believe in perfectly useless astrology.

Note, further, that we have thinking of a correct strategy of reasoning merely as one that works to satisfy the needs of the reasoners. But it seems possible that occasionally a strategy might result in a whole lot of false beliefs that, by an odd set of coincidences, serve the practical needs of the believers well. Doesn't the fact that a lot of false beliefs result show that something is wrong with this (undoubtedly useful) reasoning strategy? Isn't the test of the correct reasoning strategy *truth*, not *usefulness*? (Recall our consideration of this question in Chapter I.)

Rationality and Relativism, cited above, is a very good place to look for articles on these issues.

CHAPTER IX

LEARNING FROM EXPERIENCE:
Inductive Logic

1. A DEPRESSING SAMPLE

There's a mistake in drawing a conclusion from experience that John Allen Paulos thinks results in unnecessary gloom; once we realise the error, we will cheer right up. Oh good! We need cheering up.

Here's the mistake. You walk around town on a nice summer night and you see a whole lot of cheerful people. They're holding hands, chatting, laughing, eating ice-cream cones, and so on. They're clearly happier, more loving, more successful at life than you are. Isn't that depressing? But can you see what the mistake in reasoning is here?

> Your mistake is that you're not observing a representative sample of humanity. Happy people walk around with each other having fun in public. Sad and depressed people stay home and are invisible to you. So the sample of people you see isn't a fair sample—it's biased, heavily weighted toward the cheerful and successful. Actually the world is full of people who are just as depressed and lonely as you are—who are failures just like you.[1]

Wow, that cheers you up, doesn't it?

> No.

2. INDUCTION BY ENUMERATION

What Pink Socks Tell You about Ravens

A very simple and obvious way we use experience to come to know general truths is called "simple induction" or "induction by enumeration." In this

---

[1] *Innumeracy*, pp. 109–110.

process we look at a lot of "instances" of a general hypothesis. For example, we might confirm the general hypothesis that all bears hibernate in the winter by observing a lot of bears in winter, and finding that each bear we see is hibernating. Induction by enumeration seems quite an obvious and unproblematic way of finding things out; but puzzles about it arise.

To show, by induction, that all ravens are black, we look at a lot of ravens. A single non-black raven will show that this general hypothesis is false, but no single observation will conclusively show the truth of that general hypothesis. As the number of observations of different ravens, all of which turn out black, gets larger, the generalization is more strongly confirmed.

Now the general statement "All ravens are black" is *logically equivalent* to the statement, "All non-black things are non-ravens." They mean the same thing. You can see this by noticing that if one of them is true, the other must also be true; and likewise, if one is false the other must also be false. We can conclude, then, that whatever confirms one of these statements will confirm the other.

Now, to confirm "All non-black things are non-ravens" by simple induction we look at a large number of non-black things, and check whether they are non-ravens. As the number of observations of different non-black things, all of which turn out to be non-ravens, gets larger, the generalization is more strongly confirmed. Suppose you start looking around, and the first thing you see is one of your pink socks. It's non-black, and it's a non-raven. This adds a little confirmation to the generalization "All non-black things are non-ravens." Now you see another non-black thing, this grey thing over here. It's a grey elephant: another non-black thing has turned out to be a non-raven. So we gradually build up confirmation for "All non-black things are non-ravens" by finding a lot of things that aren't black, and seeing that they turn out not to be ravens.

But because whatever confirms that statement also confirms "All ravens are black," finding a pink earthworm or a white tooth confirms "All ravens are black" as well.

But something has gone drastically wrong here. Imagine that you pay some scientists to confirm the hypothesis that all ravens are black, and they run around happily recording what their research has turned up: a green frog, a silver key, a red stop-sign, etc. "You're wasting my research grant!" you scream; but they calmly point out that each of these instances confirms the hypothesis you have been paying them to investigate.

FOR FURTHER READING: The Paradox of the Ravens was invented by Carl Hempel, *Aspects of Scientific Explanation and Other Essays in the Philosophy of Science* (New York: The Free Press, 1945).

Something Even Worse about Pink Socks

Well, you might try to resign yourself to the idea that pink socks *do* confirm that all ravens are black. Here's some reasoning that might make that idea a little more plausible. Imagine a really far-reaching study of non-black things that discovered that not a single thing in the group was a raven. Wouldn't that give us reason to think that all ravens are black? As the group of non-black things observed got larger and larger, the continuing absence of ravens in that group would give us better and better reason to think that all of them were black. Of course, at the beginning of this survey—when all we've examined was one pink sock—we have only the very tiniest evidence that all ravens are black; we need to look a whole lot further to produce substantial evidence for that conclusion. But it's a beginning. It does provide *some* evidence, though only a minuscule bit.

But here's a further problem. Consider the competing hypotheses:

All ravens are green.

All ravens are white.

All ravens are blue with orange polka dots.

[Etc.]

Note that each of these may be restated in an equivalent statement: All non-green things are non-ravens. All non-white things are non-ravens. All non-blue-with-orange-polka-dot things are non-ravens. Etc. And the one pink sock confirms each of these statements to the same (tiny) degree that it confirms the black hypothesis. So if you accept that the sock gives some (tiny) degree of evidence that all ravens are black, you have to accept as well that it gives the same (tiny) degree of evidence for a whole lot of competing incompatible hypotheses: that all ravens are green, etc.

Are you now thoroughly confused? Good. Philosophers are still trying to work out a sensible theory of confirmation.

> The coastline of Nova Scotia was once frequented by pirates, and people occasionally dig for buried pirate treasure. On a local radio program a few years ago I heard an interview with someone who had done a study of attempts to find pirate treasure. He claimed that in most of the cases in which treasure was actually found, it was in a place where treasure-hunters had dug before, rather than in a brand new, previously undug, location. Past diggers simply hadn't dug deep enough. The previous digger had, in fact, often stopped just short of the treasure. If the previous digger had dug a little deeper than he did, he would have found it.
>
> The interviewer asked him what advice he would give to treasure hunters on the basis of this study; producing an interesting application of induction, he lamely suggested that diggers should dig a little deeper than they in fact do.

3. THE INDUCTIVE CIRCLE

How Long Will This Keep Going On?

Past experience is, of course, the basis of our expectations about the future. The fact that all emeralds found in the past have been green leads us to expect that the emeralds we will find in the future will be green, too. This natural thought-process in us is induction by enumeration.

But do we have any reason to trust this habitual and normal thought process? Why does the discovery of a past uniformity give you any good reason to believe anything about the future?

Our natural reply to this question is: "Well, induction by enumeration has very often worked in the past; so that's reason to think that it will continue to work."

But this reasoning assumes what it sets out to prove. Notice that our observation of past successes of induction by enumeration is evidence for its future success, providing that what's observed in the past is evidence about the future. But this is exactly what we're supposed to prove. This is circular reasoning, and unacceptable.

Sometimes this problem is phrased: "Will the future, by and large, resemble the past?" This isn't a very good way of putting the problem, because this question has an obvious answer: "Of course it will, you idiot!" Everyone agrees on this answer. The real problem is to give some reason to think that this answer is correct. Can you solve this problem?

> Here's one way of thinking about it. Induction from past experience is the only way we have of justifying substantive beliefs about the future. It's exactly *what we mean* by justifying such a belief. So when we're asked for justification of the belief that the future will, by and large, resemble the past, the only thing possible to reply would be to give an induction from past experience. So it's *not* a mistake to give past successes in using this belief as a justification for our belief that it will continue to be a valid principle.

FOR FURTHER READING: The problem of justifying induction by enumeration has its classical source in the writings of the eighteenth-century Scottish philosopher David Hume. See Section IV of Hume's *An Inquiry Concerning Human Understanding*. The answer given for your consideration is a version of Nelson Goodman's answer in *Fact, Fiction and Forecast*, 2nd ed. (Indianapolis: Bobbs-Merrill, 1965). See Chapter III, parts 1 and 2.

"The future ain't what it used to be." —Yogi Berra

"Things are more like they are now than they have ever been." —President Gerald Ford[2]

The Inevitability of Scientific Error: Another Circle

Scientific prediction can sometimes be unreliable, because scientists sometimes manipulate their experiments to make the results come out the way they want them to.

I have personal experience of this happening. When I took high school chemistry, I knew how the experiments I did in the laboratory were supposed to turn out, because the chemistry book told me. But because of the impurity of the chemicals and the lousy equipment I was working with, not to mention my shoddy experimental technique, almost nothing turned out the way it was supposed to. So I "adjusted" the experiments in progress, and I "corrected" the results I wrote up afterwards, so that my results were fairly close to what they were supposed to be.

It's known that this sort of outright fraud happens sometimes in real science, too. Scientists often have a lot at stake when they attempt to prove their theories. Renown, promotion, and big research grants sometimes will follow from one experimental result rather than another. Anyway, nobody likes his or her theories to turn out false. The horrible truth is now known: scientists are only human, and sometimes they fiddle things.

This kind of straightforward fraud doesn't happen too often, however. Nobody except loony conspiracy-theorists thinks that science is so fraud-ridden that its results are quite useless.

But there is another argument for the general unreliability of science. This argument points at the fact that there's an unconscious tendency we all have to ignore or discount "bad" data—evidence that goes against what we believe or want to believe. So scientists must sometimes unconsciously massage or misreport experimental results, so that they come out the way the scientists want them to. This raises doubt about the objectivity of any science, even when done by scientists who want to be honest.

But how seriously should we take this? To what extent does this unconscious falsification go on? This is an important question, and it seems we might be able to answer it, to some extent, by doing a scientific study

---

[2] This quote (or its variant "Things have never been more like the way they are today in history") is sometimes attributed instead to Dwight Eisenhower. Attribution to either president is plausible: both are on the long and growing list of presidents known for mysterious utterances (called nowadays "Bushisms").

of the behaviour of scientists. We could, for example, get a group of scientists to test a hypothesis they think is false (or whose falsity would result in promotions, research grants, etc.). Then we could get another group of scientists who think that this same hypothesis is true (or who have some stake in its truth) to do the same experiments. Then we could compare the results reported by these two groups.

We hope, of course, that investigations like this would show that science is, on the whole, pretty reliable, and that unconscious fraud is rare. But those who argue for the widespread unreliability of science use this very hope to cast doubt on the reliability of *our* conclusion. Even if our investigations resulted in the conclusion that this sort of bias is rare, they could claim that this investigation *itself* is untrustworthy, because of *our* biases. You can't show by means of the methods of science that the methods of science are reliable. That would be circular reasoning.

> "EXPERTS LIE, SAY OTHER EXPERTS"—newspaper
> headline in "BIZARRO" cartoon, June 28, 2001

4. THE GRUESOME PROBLEM

Nelson Goodman invented the adjective 'grue' to raise a different problem about induction.

'Grue' is defined as follows:

Something is to be called *grue* if

(a) it's earlier than time T (say time T is January 1, 2050), and the thing is green;

or

(b) it's time T or later, and the thing is blue.

Now, all the emeralds we have seen so far have been green; so induction by enumeration permits us to conclude that all emeralds are green, and thus to predict that emeralds we see during 2050 will be green.

But all the emeralds we have seen so far have been grue as well. (If you don't see why, examine that definition of 'grue' carefully.) So induction by enumeration permits us to conclude that all emeralds are grue, and thus to predict that emeralds we see during 2050 will be grue. But if an emerald is grue in 2050, it follows from the definition above that it is blue then, not green.

So perfectly good reasoning using induction by enumeration leads us to two contrary predictions: that emeralds in 2050 will be green, and that they will be blue. And, of course, because all emeralds so far have also been *grellow*, we can confidently predict that they will also be yellow. And so on.

In short, induction by enumeration yields all sorts of contrary predictions. We can invent an adjective that will allow us to use that principle to predict anything we like. It's useless.

Has something gone wrong with this reasoning?

Some people react to the "grue" problem by claiming that it's illegitimate to predict that things will continue to be grue because the idea of grue is itself illegitimate for prediction purposes, containing, as it does, mention of a particular time. But Goodman replies that it's not necessary to define 'grue' this way. Here's his argument. We can define 'bleen' as follows:

Something is to be called *bleen* if

(a) it's earlier than time T, and the thing is blue;

or

(b) it's time T or later, and the thing is green.

Now suppose that someone took 'grue' and 'bleen' to be basic (as we take 'green' and 'blue' to be basic). Then that person might say that *our* terms 'green' and 'blue' were the peculiar ones, illegitimate in making predictions. For *that* person might claim that 'green' and 'blue' are defined in terms of 'grue' and 'bleen' plus mention of time T. (See if you could construct definitions of 'green' and 'blue' in terms of 'grue' and 'bleen' and time T.) This seems to show that what you count as illegitimate depends on where you start.

If this is right, it's a very startling and important conclusion: it appears to show that our way of thinking and talking about things partly determines what generalizations we take our experiences to establish. That is: if we think/talk one way, we take our experiences to give evidence for a general proposition **G**, but if we think/talk another way, those same experiences will be taken to be evidence for another proposition incompatible with **G**.

FOR FURTHER READING: Goodman introduced "Grue" and its problems in *Fact, Fiction and Forecast*; see Chapter III, part 4.

> Every weekday morning, the CBC radio network used to broadcast a popular three-hour interview program across Canada hosted by a genial man named Peter Gzowski. One morning a few years ago I happened to be home, and the radio was on. Gzowski was interviewing a sociologist who had made a study of academic humour, travelling from campus to campus collecting jokes from the various academic disciplines. Here's approximately how part of that interview went.
>
> "Which discipline has the most jokes?" asked Gzowski.
>
> "Mathematicians have a lot of mathematics jokes," said the sociologist, "but philosophers have far and away more jokes than anyone."

"Tell a philosophy joke," said Gzowski.

"Well, I just heard one the other day but I didn't understand it, and I don't think you will either."

"Doesn't matter—let's hear it anyway."

"Okay. It's a riddle. The question is: What's a *goy*?"

"I dunno. What's a goy?"

"The answer," said the sociologist, "is: Someone is a goy if they're a girl before time T or a boy after."

A couple of seconds of radio silence followed. Then Gzowski said "I don't get it." "Neither do I," said the sociologist. Neither did the vast majority of Canadians listening. But you do.

5. CAUSE AND EFFECT

Cause and Correlation

When we find a correlation between A and B, we often jump to the conclusion that A and B are causally related—that is, that one causes another. For example, if it is found that people who have been exposed for long periods to a certain chemical have much higher than average cancer rates, we may be tempted to conclude that this chemical causes cancer.

But reasoning from correlation to cause is sometimes a mistake. Correlation does not always mean causation. Here are a few examples which show this.

Suppose you have two petunia plants on opposite sides of your garden. The one on the left side starts to bloom, and at just about the same time, the one on the right starts to bloom. The times of their blooming are correlated: you don't get one without the other. But this doesn't mean that the left one's blooming *causes* the right one to bloom.

Smoke and burning are correlated. Whenever there's smoke there's burning. But this doesn't mean that smoke causes burning.

Whenever Seymour drinks too much, his words get slurred, and he bumps into things a lot. Seymour's words getting slurred, and his tendency to bump into things, are perfectly correlated. But the slurring of his words doesn't *cause* him to bump into things.

So it's clear that there's more to cause-and-effect than merely correlation. But what?

> Well, maybe you think that it's the *order* of things that makes a difference. If X and Y are correlated *and* X comes before Y, then X causes Y.

But even this won't do. Another example from your garden will show this. Every year your strawberry plants bear fruit in June, then in July your raspberry plants bear fruit. You never get one without the other, so they are correlated; and the strawberries come before the raspberries. But this doesn't mean that the strawberries cause the raspberries.

Wednesday always follows Tuesday. Does this mean that Tuesday causes Wednesday?

A QUESTION TO THINK ABOUT: Why, exactly, are these examples of correlation not cases of cause? What, in addition to the correlation of **X** and **Y**, do we need to discover to tell that **X** causes **Y**?

The Tickle Defense

We do often conclude that **X** causes **Y** when we find out that **X** and **Y** are correlated and **X** comes before **Y**. This line of reasoning can be mistaken in an interesting way.

Suppose that it was discovered that people who eat a kumquat are one hundred times likelier to get a nosebleed the next day than people who don't. Doesn't this show that eating kumquats causes nosebleeds? No. In fact, this evidence is consistent with kumquats' *preventing* nosebleeds. How could this be?

Imagine this (entirely fictitious) story: Some people are born with a genetic condition such that their liver manufactures an abnormally low amount of vitamin Z on certain days. A deficiency of vitamin Z causes nosebleeds. Kumquats provide a dietary source of small amounts of vitamin Z. At those times when these people suffer vitamin Z deficiency, they (without knowing why) get the desire to eat kumquats. These help a little with that deficiency, but do not completely remedy it, and they tend to get nosebleeds anyway.

This story explains why people who eat kumquats get nosebleeds, but if it's true, then kumquats don't cause nosebleeds—they tend to prevent them.

How could we find this out? Suppose further that a vitamin Z deficiency made your nose tickle the day before the nosebleeds started. Scientists working for the Kumquat Growers' Association could then prove the true story: they could arrange experiments in which people who had a nose-tickle ate kumquats, and others with the tickle ate none. If the second group got more nosebleeds than the first, then this would show that kumquats helped prevent nosebleeds. They could use the "tickle defense" to show that their product was not to blame—that it actually was beneficial.

The serious moral of this imaginary fable is that correlation does not necessarily show cause. One real-life application of this sort of thinking involves the link between smoking and lung cancer. The correlation be-tween the two was known for a long time; but the kumquat story shows, by analogy, that this wasn't sufficient evidence for causal connection. This correlation might be found even if smoking *prevented* lung cancer. Scientists had to rule out any possible "tickle defense," and they did.

To make it clearer why correlation doesn't automatically go with cause, consider these two stories:

1. Smoking causes lung cancer. Does it follow that a higher per-centage of smokers will have lung cancer than do non-smokers? Not necessarily. Imagine this (purely imaginary) scenario. Sup-pose that smokers for some reason tend to get more exercise, and that more exercise tends to reduce the risk of cancer. So it might work out that smokers get a lower incidence of lung cancer.
2. Now think about things the other way around. Suppose that a much higher proportion of smokers have lung cancer than do non-smokers. Does this show that smoking causes lung cancer? Not necessarily. Imagine this (purely imaginary) scenario. Suppose that people who smoke a lot also tend to drink a lot of beer, and that it's the beer-drinking, not the smoking, that raises the risk of cancer.

Here's another case in which the answer isn't so clear. Over the past twenty years, the average childbearing age of women has increased sub-stantially, and so has the rate of breast cancer. It's possible that waiting until later to have children causes a greater likelihood of breast cancer. But the correlation alone doesn't show this.

Can you imagine other hypotheses to explain this correlation?

It might be the case that something else causes women both to tend to bear children later and to tend to have breast cancer. (Imagine that some factor reduces fertil-ity, thus postponing the age of child-bearing on average, and increases the likelihood of breast cancer.) Or breast cancer, in its early stages, might cause them to be less likely to conceive, thus increasing the average age of child-bearing. Or it might just be a coincidence, the re-sult of two separate and unrelated causes.

SOME QUESTIONS TO THINK ABOUT: To show that **X** causes **Y** we have to rule out every other plausible hypothesis that might explain their correlation: for example, that **Y** causes **X**, or that there's some third factor that causes both **X** and **Y**, or that the correlation is just a coincidence. Here are some cases of correlation. Do you think one item in the pair causes the other, or that they're merely correlated? How might scientists find out for sure?

- More pornography available/Increase in sex crimes
- Sluggish economy/Increase in movie attendance
- Small children in the household/Friction between husband and wife

Can Science Explain Anything?

Science, it's often supposed, gives explanations when it provides causes. But there are, as we've seen, philosophical problems with the notion of cause, sufficient to convince Bertrand Russell that "the word 'cause' is so inextricably bound up with misleading associations as to make its complete extrusion from the philosophical vocabulary desirable."[3]

But if cause is philosophically suspect, does that mean that science really provides only description, never explanation? Steven Weinberg, a Nobel-Prize-winning physicist, writes:

> After my remarks [on the successes of particle physics], a faculty colleague (a scientist, but not a particle physicist) commented, "Well, of course, you know science does not really explain things—it just describes them." I had heard this remark before, but now it took me aback, because I had thought that we had been doing a pretty good job of explaining the observed properties of elementary particles and forces, not just describing them....
>
> Ludwig Wittgenstein famously remarked that "at the basis of the whole modern view of the world lies the illusion that the so-called laws of nature are the explanations of natural phenomena." ...
>
> [In] E.M. Forster's novel *Where Angels Fear to Tread* ... Philip is trying to find out why his friend Caroline helped to bring about a marriage between Philip's sister and a young Italian man of whom Philip's family disapproves. After Caroline reports all the conversations she had with Philip's sister, Philip says, "What you have given me is a description, not an explanation." Everyone knows what Philip means by this—in asking for an explanation, he wants to learn Caroline's purposes.

---

[3] B. Russell, "On the Notion of Cause." *Proceedings of the Aristotelian Society* 13 (1913).

There is no purpose revealed in the laws of nature, and not knowing any other way of distinguishing description and explanation, Wittgenstein and my friend had concluded that these laws could not be explanations. Perhaps some of those who say that science describes but does not explain mean also to compare science unfavorably with theology, which they imagine to explain things by reference to some sort of divine purpose, a task declined by science.[4]

At summer camp as a small boy, I was taught this old song:

Tell me why the stars do shine
Tell me why the ivy twines
Tell me why the sky's so blue
And I will tell you just why I love you

Because God made the stars to shine
Because God made the ivy twine
Because God made the sky so blue
Because God made you, that's why I love you.

Later on, however, I ran into this alternative version of the second verse:

Nuclear fusion makes stars to shine,
Tropisms make the ivy twine,
Raleigh scattering make skies so blue,
Testicular hormones are why I love you.[5]

SOME QUESTIONS TO THINK ABOUT: There's a lot more to be said about the notion of cause; most philosophers disagree with Russell, and think that it's something that needs to be explained, not tossed into the trash. But ask yourself this: if the notion of cause really doesn't make sense, then is the only other kind of explanation the one where we give someone's purposes? Then maybe theology can give genuine explanations where science fails. Are you willing to accept that conclusion?

6. SCIENCE AND "TRADITIONAL KNOWLEDGE"

Is it a Boy or a Girl?

Beliefs that are passed from person to person but do not have the blessing of official (Western) science are sometimes now known by the politi-

---

4 "Can Science Explain Everything? Anything?" *New York Review of Books* 48, no. 9 (May 31, 2001).

5 I don't think he made this up, but it's found collected in *Isaac Asimov's Treasury of Humor* (Boston: Houghton Mifflin, 1991).

cally correct term "traditional knowledge." Here are some bits of traditional knowledge concerning ways of telling the gender of a fetus:

- If your baby's heart rate is less than one hundred forty beats per minute, it's a boy; if more, then a girl.
- If you're carrying your baby high, it's a girl; if low, it's a boy.
- If you're having severe morning sickness, it's a girl.
- If the baby is very active, it's a boy.
- If you're looking particularly beautiful, it's a boy.
- If you're craving sweets, it's a girl.
- If you have a V-shaped broken blood vessel in your right eye, it's a girl; if in your left eye, it's a boy.
- If a wedding ring or needle suspended over your belly moves in a strong circular motion, it's a girl; if it moves to and fro like a pendulum, it's a boy.
- If your urine turns bluish yellow when you mix in a bit of Drano, it's a boy; greenish-brown means a girl.[6]

The trouble with this (and much other) traditional knowledge is that it's not knowledge at all. For something to count as knowledge it must have sufficient justification, and there's no real justification for any of the beliefs on this list. Many of them have been shown to be just plain false.

Why is it that they have been so widely believed, then? One reason for the beliefs listed above is that there's roughly a fifty-fifty chance you're right each time you use any of these methods to predict a baby's sex, and people are more likely to remember successes at prediction than failures.

A second reason is that we remember, and make much of, the occasions when scientific results have brought harm.

There are also political reasons why people resist the authority of official (Western) science when it contradicts the views of other cultures: this seems to some people to be imperialistic intolerance, Eurocentricism, racism. (We discussed this already in the previous chapter: see **Nobody Could Be *That* Wrong**.)

Another reason is a sentimental romantic view about the Wisdom of the Noble Indian, or the Noble Farmer or whatever. This sort of view is not new. Very shortly after Columbus returned to Europe with news of the indigenous people he had found there, the Europeans began believing that those people were wise, peaceful "noble savages," even though nobody knew the first thing about them.

---

[6] Ann Douglas, "Boy or Girl?" *Canadian Living Magazine* 25, no. 10 (Oct. 2000), pp. 79–80.

The Wisdom of the Dumbest Yokel

Even some scientists believe in the superior knowledge of the unedu-
cated. Here's a description of the views of Theobald Smith (1859-1934),
a pioneer microbiologist and one of America's greatest scientists:

> Now, though Theobald Smith was born in a city, he liked the smell
> of hay just cut and the brown furrows of fresh-turned fields. There
> was something sage — something as near as you can come to truth
> for him in a farmer's clipped sentences about the crops or the
> weather. Smith was learned in the marvelous shorthand of math-
> ematics; men of the soil don't know that stuff. He was absolutely
> at home among the scopes and tubes and charts of shining labora-
> tories — in short, this young searcher was full of sophisticated wis-
> dom that laughs at common sayings, that often jeers at peasant
> platitudes. But in spite of all of his learning (and this was an arbi-
> trary strange thing about him!) Theobald Smith did not confuse
> fine buildings and complicated apparatus with clear thinking — he
> seemed always to be distrusting what he got out of books or what
> he saw in tubes.... He felt the dumbest yokel to be profoundly right
> when that fellow took his corncob pipe from his maybe unbrushed
> teeth to growl that April showers bring May flowers.[7]

Of course we want to act and talk respectfully about members of our
own culture and of others. But it is not clear that this sort of unquestion-
ing and automatic acceptance of the views of "the dumbest yokel," or of
the traditional beliefs of other cultures, actually shows those people respect. Maybe it would show more respect to them to take their views
seriously and to dispute them when they are false or unjustified.

Well, let's look further into the story of Theobald Smith, to see what
reasonable position about science it might illustrate.

Smith became interested in a disease called Texas fever that was killing beef cattle by the thousands. Texas fever had the scientists stumped,
but

> certain wise old Western cattle growers had a theory — it was just
> what you would call a plain hunch got from smoking their pipes
> over disastrous losses of cows — they had a notion that Texas fe-

---

[7] *Microbe Hunters*, by Paul de Kruif (New York: Harcourt, Brace and Company, c.
1926), p. 251.

ver was caused by an insect living on the cattle and sucking blood; this bug they called a *tick*.[8]

When Smith got on this case, he actually listened to the cattlemen, who—you guessed it—turned out to be right.

It's important to note here that the cattlemen's hunch was just that—a hunch. It took Smith's sophisticated microbiological science to prove them right. So what this story does not show is that the wisdom of the folk is a far superior substitute for all that fancy book-learnin'. But the story also illustrates the genuine valid function of folk-wisdom in knowledge-production. It provides hypotheses—hunches—which sometimes turn out true.

Here's a picture of scientific procedure that shows where folk-wisdom fits in. When faced with a question, a scientist does not jump right into experiments or observations. The question all by itself suggests nothing about what experiments to perform, or where to look. Observations and experiments test hypotheses—hunches about answers to these questions. So first the scientist must accumulate one or more hypotheses to test.

Hypothesis-testing is a systematic methodical process, with well-known rules for procedure. But hypothesis-formation is not like this. It can involve imagination, creativity, guessing—though it's not just wild guessing. Rather it's the reasonable guessing of someone who has had a lot of experience with the matter under investigation. So folk-wisdom is often extremely valuable in hypothesis formation: it doesn't require the background in scientific method needed for the subsequent states of testing, which folk don't have, but it does require thorough practical experience, which folk have in abundance.

Kekule's Dream

Because hypothesis-formation involves creativity and imagination, not systematic method, many important scientific hypotheses have arisen in weird ways. Here's the story of one.

August Kekulé, a nineteenth-century German chemist, was responsible for a major discovery in organic chemistry: the ring-structure of benzene. Here's his account of how he arrived at this hypothesis:

> I was sitting writing at my textbook but the work did not progress;
> my thoughts were elsewhere. I turned my chair to the fire and

---

[8] de Kruif, p. 249.

dozed. Again the atoms were gamboling before my eyes. This time the smaller groups kept modestly in the background. My mental eye ... could now distinguish larger structures of manifold conformation: long rows, sometimes more closely fitted together all twining and twisting in snake-like motion. But look! What was that? One of the snakes had seized hold of its own tail, and the form whirled mockingly before my eyes. As if by a flash of lightning I awoke; and this time I spent the rest of the night in working out the consequences of the hypothesis.

Let us learn to dream, gentlemen, then perhaps we shall find the truth.[9]

7. INTO THE MAINSTREAM OF PHILOSOPHY

The theory of the ways experience leads to general knowledge is the study undertaken in the philosophical fields of inductive logic and philosophy of science. As usual, this book includes puzzles and surprises that arise in this field of study, while a major task of philosophers has been to elucidate and systematize the perfectly ordinary, unparadoxical, and unsurprising kinds of reasoning done all the time. For an excellent, easy-to-follow, but thorough account of the basics in these fields, see Ronald N. Giere's *Understanding Scientific Reasoning,* 3rd ed. (Fort Worth: Holt, Rinehart and Winston, 1991). Another good place to look for further discussion of these and other issues in this chapter is Brian Skyrms' *Choice and Chance.* But even better than any of these books is *Scientific Thinking* by Robert M. Martin (Peterborough, ON: Broadview Press, 1997).

What's the difference between correlation and cause, anyway? People tend to think that there's some sort of *connection* between items that are causally related, but not between items that are merely correlated. But David Hume, in the work cited above, argued in a compelling way that we can observe no such connection. Think about Hume's point. Putting ice into a glass of liquid causes the liquid to become colder. But what do you observe? Nothing but one event followed by the other. You can see no "cause" going on. Try to figure out what exactly does justify the distinction between cause and correlation—if anything!

---

[9] August Kekulé, speech given in the Berlin City Hall, 1890. Translated by O. Theodor Benfey, *Journal of Chemical Education* 35, pp. 21–30.

CHAPTER X

KNOWING WITHOUT EXPERIENCE

1. THE A PRIORI AND DEFINITIONS

Why Your Sisters Are Female

You know that this statement is true:

> Everyone who is somebody's sister is female.

How do you know this?

It's possible that you know this from experience, through induction by enumeration. Perhaps you have observed a large number of people who are somebody's sister, and have noticed that all of them have been female.

But it's unlikely that you have found out the truth of the statement that way. The statement applies to all sisters, past, present, and future. But you have observed only a very small proportion of all those past and present people who are somebody's sister; and you have observed no sisters at all who are yet to be born. It's important that a very large and varied sample of things be observed before one has enough inductive evidence to claim that one knows a generalization.

Of course, you need not rely on your own observations for inductive knowledge of the truth of generalizations. You know, for example, that days are usually warm in the middle of the Sahara Desert even if you have never visited there. You can rely on other people's observations, too.

But it's clear in the case of our knowledge about sisters that the truth of this statement does not depend even on the wide observations of the whole human race. Nobody needs to have done any observation at all to know that this statement is true.

Truths that can be known independently of experience are known, in philosophical jargon, as *a priori* truths (knowable "prior" to experience). The contrast here is with truths tht can only be known by experience, or by inductive reasoning from such truths. These are called *a posteriori* truths (knowable "posterior" to—after—experience.).

Here are some more samples of statements we know a priori:

- All bachelors are unmarried.
- If Alison is older than Barney, then Barney is younger than Alison.
- If Alison is older than Barney, and Barney is older than Clarissa, then Alison is older than Clarissa.
- Anyone who weighs seventy kilograms weighs more than sixty kilograms.
- "You wouldn't have won if we had beaten you." — Yogi Berra
- "A lot is said about defense, but at the end of the game, the team with the most points wins, the other team loses." — Isaiah Thomas, commentating on an NBA game. Sportscaster Bob Costas replied with just, "Uh...well...okay."
- "If we don't succeed, we run the risk of failure." — Dan Quayle
- "I think we agree, the past is over." — George W. Bush
- "It's very important for folks to understand that when there's more trade, there's more commerce." — George W. Bush

SOME QUESTIONS TO THINK ABOUT: What are other examples? There are also a priori falsehoods. Give some examples of these.

Truth "By Definition"

An attractive theory of how we can know the truth of the statement that everyone's sisters are female is that it's true "by definition." The word 'sister,' after all, means *female sibling*. Because of this rule of language, the word 'sister' can't apply to anyone who isn't female. So the truth of this statement depends merely on the language in which it is expressed.

We'll shortly consider whether "truth by definition" is a good account of what we know a priori. But first, let's have a look at the idea of definition.

The Dictionary with Very Few Definitions

Definitions are what you find in dictionaries, right? Well, no. A good deal of what's found in there doesn't seem to be, properly speaking, *definition* at all.

I'm not referring merely to etymologies, pronunciations, grammatical forms, information about abbreviations, and other items found in many dictionaries. Even the "definition" parts of dictionary entries contain much that isn't definition.

A definition gives the meaning of a word or phrase. This can be done by giving a synonym, or by listing the characteristics necessary and sufficient for applying the term. But many of the characteristics listed in dictionary definitions aren't individually necessary or jointly sufficient. For example, my dictionary contains this item:

> **soufflé** A light, fluffy baked dish made with egg yolks and beaten egg whites combined with various other ingredients and served as a main dish or sweetened as a dessert.[1]

These characteristics describe most soufflés, but not all of them. It's possible, for example, to make a legitimate soufflé without egg yolks. You could make a soufflé out of egg yolks and beaten egg whites without any other ingredients (though it wouldn't be very good.) Some soufflés are served before the main course, or as a snack. Some don't turn out light and fluffy, and are served to the dog. This proves that not all of these characteristics are necessary.

But neither are they sufficient. Suppose you baked a light fluffy dish made with egg yolks and beaten egg whites combined with motor oil, egg shells, and ground liver, sprinkled with icing sugar. When you served it to your guests for dessert, they would cry, "This isn't a soufflé—it's a pile of garbage!" Would they be wrong?

For most nouns, it's in fact impossible to give a really exact synonym; dictionaries instead give a number of terms that are close in meaning to that noun, but not exactly synonymous. They also often give some information about things named by the word that may, by and large, be true of those things, but not "by definition." It's impossible to give a list of characteristics that are really necessary and sufficient for most words.

Ludwig Wittgenstein invites us to

> Consider for example the proceedings that we call "games." I mean board-games, card-games, ball-games, Olympic games, and so on.... If you look at them you will not see something that is common to all, but similarities, relationships, and a whole series of them at that.

This is my dictionary's entry for 'the':

> The definite article, functioning as an adjective. It is used: 1. Before singular or plural nouns and noun phrases that denote particular specified persons or things. 2. Before a singular noun,

---

[1] *The American Heritage Dictionary of the English Language*, p. 1234.

making it generic: THE human arm. 3. Before a noun, and generally stressed, emphasizing its uniqueness or prominence: That's
THE show to see this year....[2]

Neither synonyms nor application characteristics here; instead we are told
how to use the word. But there's nothing wrong with my dictionary; in fact,
it's a very good one. How else could you define 'the'? Maybe 'the' doesn't
have a meaning at all. Or maybe our notion of definition is too narrow.

FOR FURTHER READING: That quote from Wittgenstein is from his
book *Philosophical Investigations* (Oxford: Basil Blackwell, 1958), §66.
See surroundings sections in this book for more on definitions.

But is there really any such thing as "truth by definition"? Consider
the following story. At one point, everyone believed that fish breathe with
gills, not lungs. Then one day, explorers in Africa discovered something
that was a great deal like a fish, but with lungs in addition to gills. Is this
thing a fish or not? The answer depends on whether fish, by definition,
breathe only with gills. Well, is that part of the definition of 'fish' or isn't
it? You're a fully competent user of the English language, so presumably
you have full mastery of the meaning of the word 'fish.' Why can't you
answer that question?
My dictionary gives this definition of 'fish':

Any of numerous cold-blooded aquatic vertebrates of the
superclass Pisces, characteristically having fins, gills, and a
streamlined body...[3]

This is no help: fish "characteristically" have gills; but nothing is said
about whether they are disqualified from fishhood by lungs.
Scientists decided that these animals, appropriately called 'lungfish,'
are fish after all. But this discovery was not the result of a careful consideration of the meaning of the word.
It's an interesting and complicated question how scientists go about
deciding classification questions like this, but what is clear is that the
question is not solved by considering what we all mean by the word 'fish,'
or by looking it up in the dictionary.
So it's not at all clear what if anything constitutes a "truth by definition."
Some philosophers doubt that there's any clear distinction between a "truth
by definition" and an ordinary well-established non-definitional truth.

---

[2] *The American Heritage Dictionary of the English Language*, p. 1333.
[3] *The American Heritage Dictionary of the English Language*, p. 495.

FOR FURTHER READING: The hugely influential article that got many philosophers wondering whether there was any such thing as truth by definition is "Two Dogmas of Empiricism," by W. V. Quine. The original version of this was published in *Philosophical Review* 60 (1951), pp. 20–43. A slightly amended version is in Quine's *From a Logical Point of View* (Cambridge, MA: Harvard University Press, 1953), and can be found reprinted in many philosophy anthologies.

Sisters Without Language

But even if we think we can make sense of "truth by definition" there are a couple of reasons to doubt that this gives the correct account of why everyone's sister is female. Imagine that the English language didn't exist. Then the sentence 'Everyone who is somebody's sister is female' wouldn't mean anything—it would just be a bunch of meaningless letters. Nevertheless, wouldn't it still be true that everyone who is somebody's sister would be female? Couldn't we still know that truth?

Well, you might reply, still there would be *some* language in which we could express that truth, and any language in which we expressed it would use words that have those meanings.

But imagine that humans somehow evolved all the way up to their present state, except without any language at all. There would be no way at all for us to express any truth. But wouldn't it still be true that everyone who is somebody's sister would be female? And couldn't we still know it?

Well, you might reply, if there weren't any language at all, nobody would know anything.

But it's not obviously true that knowledge depends on language. It's reasonable to think that intelligent animals such as dogs know lots of things, despite their lack of significant language ability.

In any case, the main argument against the truth-by-definition theory of a priori truth is that there are some examples of things we know a priori that don't seem at all to be true by definition. We'll have a look at some of these shortly.

Honest Abe and the Sheep

A riddle (attributed to Abraham Lincoln):

> Q: How many legs does a sheep have, if you call its tail a leg?
> A: Four. Calling its tail a leg doesn't make it one.

This is not a very amusing riddle, but it is philosophically interesting. Perhaps the moral that can be drawn from it is that facts are facts, no matter how you use language. If this is the case, it's hard to see how anything can be a fact because of definitions of words (except, of course, for facts about words, such as the fact that the word 'sister' means *female sibling*).

2. CONCEPTUAL TRUTHS

The great eighteenth-century philosopher Immanuel Kant distinguished between two sorts of statements. An *analytic* statement is one whose truth (or falsity) is merely a matter of the concepts involved. (Statements that are not analytic are *synthetic*.) When a statement is analytic, its truth or falsity can be known simply on the basis of examining the concepts that the statement is constructed out of. For example, the statement that everyone's sisters are female contains the concepts of *sister* and *female*. Because that statement is analytic, all that's necessary to find out that it's true is examination of those concepts, because the concept of *femaleness* is "included within" the concept of *sister*. We can "analyse" the concept of *sisterness*—take it apart—and discover that the concept of *femaleness* is one of its parts. This explains how we can know in advance—a priori—that all sisters are female. In contrast to this, the statement 'Bears like to eat berries' is synthetic—it "synthesizes" (joins together) the concepts of *bears* and *liking to eat berries*, neither of which is already included in the other. You can't discover that this statement is true merely by examining what is included in the concepts.

This theory of a priori knowledge is different from the "true by definition" theory. It doesn't depend on the definitions of words. When definitions of words are available, they give us the analysis of the concept the word refers to, but one can have concepts without having words. Dogs, for example, might be said to have the concept of *edibleness*: they distinguish between what they can eat and what they can't (more or less). But they don't have words for these concepts.

But what is a *concept*? It doesn't seem plausible to think of them as psychological states. If that is what concepts were, then these truths would depend on our psychological states. But it seems that these truths are independent of anyone's psychology. They would still be true no matter what or how anyone happened to think. Imagine, for example, that people were very much stupider than they in fact are, and that we were unable to conceptualize what it is to be a sister, or to be female. Wouldn't it still be true that everyone who is somebody's sister is female?

Kant's theory is then that some a priori knowledge is explainable because what is known is an analytic truth. (As we'll see shortly, Kant thinks that there can also be a priori knowledge of *synthetic* truths.)

I Forget What I Saw Before I Was Born

But it's not at all clear that the notion of an analytic statement is any better than the notion of a true-by-definition. They both appear to run into the same problem. We noticed earlier that it's not at all clear whether *having lungs* is compatible with the definition of 'fish'; but we can ask the same question about concepts: does the concept *fish* include *not having lungs*? When is a fact about **X**s included in the concept/definition of **X** and when isn't it?

But there is a additional difficulty with the concept theory. It seems pretty clear what words are, and how we come to know their meanings, but what are concepts, exactly, and how do we know about them? Where, for example, do we get our knowledge that the concept of *sisterness* includes the concept of *femaleness*? The peculiar fact here is that all we can ever experience, using our senses, is particular females and particular sisters. But our concepts involve what's true of *all* sisters and *all* females. This can't come from our experience of particular people.

Putting this question another way: our concepts (which account for our a priori knowledge) express the *form*—the general nature—that all sisters must share. These "forms" are never experienced through our senses. How can we know about them?

Plato's answer, which a lot of philosophers find entirely implausible, is that our souls, which he supposed existed before our birth (at which point they were stuck into our bodies), had non-sensory experience of this and other forms. Plato argued that this sort of truth depended on the existence of something he called in Greek an *eidos* or *idea*. (Yes, *idea* is a Greek word.) Both words are sometimes translated as 'form' or 'idea.' Thus the universe is supposed to include not only a lot of particular sisters, but also the "form" of sisterness. Each particular sister is a sister because she conforms to the form of sisterness—in Platonic terms, because she "participates" in the form. (The word 'idea' is a misleading way of referring to these things, because it suggests a psychological state.)

Plato argued that mathematical knowledge was an example of the sort of knowledge that derives from our understanding of the forms. But if our understanding of the forms results from pre-birth experience, why is it that new-born babies can't do arithmetic? Why do we have to go through often painful and sometimes unsuccessful education to come to know the truths of mathematics?

Plato's answer is that the shock of uniting the soul with a body at birth made the soul forget, at least for a while, what it had learned about the forms. Education and experience during our lives on earth can (sometimes) result in our remembering.

Plato's position seems, as I have indicated, bizarre and unbelievable. But if you don't believe it, you need to give another account of the puzzling facts about the sort of knowledge that comes from conceptual analysis, and this is not easy to do. In any case, it's interesting to see how his strange position is an ingenious attempt to answer some real philosophical problems.

More on Conceptual Existence

A feature of Plato's views that seems objectionable to many people is that it insists on the existence of things—the forms—which we can't observe using our senses. We like to think that all there is in the universe is a bunch of particular observable things. But perhaps we have to believe in forms to make things make sense.

Consider the following suggestion: *Someone who is blind has no notion of greenness*. Whether that is true or false is not the issue I'm raising. The point here is: what is it that it is alleged a blind person has no notion of? It's not *green things*. A blind person can surely think about grass, trees, etc. What a blind person supposedly can't think about is the fact that they all participate in a certain form—the form of greenness. The blind person supposedly lacks understanding of a form, not of any particulars. Thus to make sense of that allegation—necessary before we determine whether it's true or false—we seem to need to think of the universe as containing more than merely particular things.

Here's another such fact: *Flatness of the landscape depresses Benjamin*. For this to stand a chance of being true, doesn't there have to be such a thing as flatness and not merely particular landscapes that are flat? Those particular landscapes depress Benjamin, but that's not all we want to say. They all depress Benjamin because they all participate in the form of flatness. If there weren't any such thing as this form, then what is meant by that fact?

Here's another: *Greenness is incompatible with redness*. This explains why nothing can be both totally green and totally red. What are these things that are incompatible? Of course there are particular things that are green, for example your last Christmas tree, and particular things that are red, for example, the glass at the top of the next stoplight you see. But what things are being said to be incompatible?

Notice that some forms are incompatible and some aren't. Greenness and redness are incompatible: nothing can be both wholly green and wholly red at once. Greenness, sphericality, rotation, and buzzing-ness are compatible. A green rotating buzzing sphere participates in all these forms wholly and at once.

3. THE SYNTHETIC A PRIORI

The Incompetent Repairman

Suppose your car stalls every time you stop. You bring it into the car repair shop, and when you return, the repairman tells you he hasn't fixed it.

"Why not?" you ask.

"There isn't any reason why it's stalling," he replies.

"You mean, you haven't found the cause?" you say, getting annoyed.

"No, I have taken everything apart and examined it very carefully," he says. "There isn't any cause for that stalling."

This is the point to find a different car repairman. You think that something must be causing that stalling. He simply hasn't found it. Why do you think this? Not because you know more about cars than he does. It's because you think that *everything* has a cause. This is a very general truth about the way everything in the universe works.

But what makes you think that everything has a cause? Your own experience hardly shows this. For your experience to have shown this through induction by enumeration, you would have to have examined a very large and fair sample of all the events in the universe and found that they each have causes. You can't have examined a large enough sample to be justified in this far-reaching conclusion. Besides, there are a large number of things you have examined for which you haven't found a cause. Neither has the collective experience of all of humanity provided sufficient justification; even this wide collective experience has examined only a tiny fraction of what goes on, and even the best experts don't know the cause for everything they have examined. The fact that a vast scientific enterprise is busily looking for causes right now shows that. It appears that our belief that everything has a cause is an example of a universal truth not justified by experience — a truth known a priori.

We already have, from Kant, an explanation of how some a priori truths are known: these are analytic, and we find out their truth by analysis of concepts. Is this is another case of conceptual truth? Kant argued that it is not:

Consider your concept of *an event*: anything that happens. Is there something about that concept that "includes" there being a cause? Compare this with the clear case of conceptual truth: that all sisters are female. Full understanding of the concept of *sister* involves understanding that sister-ness necessarily involves female-ness. It's impossible to imagine a sister who isn't female, because this combination involves an inconsistency, a conceptual self-contradiction. But full understanding of the concept of *event* does not necessarily involve having a cause: it is possible to imagine an event that does not have a cause without this sort of inconsistency. So it appears that the judgement that all events have a cause isn't analytic; it's synthetic.

A similar sort of argument can be made if you prefer the true-by-definition theory of a priori truths. 'Every event has a cause' does not appear to be true by definition: having a cause is no part of the definition of 'event.'

Kant on the Synthetic A Priori

Kant took as one of his major philosophical tasks the explanation of how a priori knowledge of synthetic judgements is possible.

Kant's answer is rather obscure, and its interpretation is controversial; but here's one way of understanding it. The universality of causal connections is a necessary condition of any experiential knowledge of the world; if it weren't true that everything has a cause, we couldn't have knowledge of anything. Because we clearly do know many things about the world, it must be true. This line of reasoning, he argued, allows us to justify our belief that it is true, and to explain it. Kant pointed at other universal truths that he thought were similarly synthetic and a priori, and gave a similar account of how we know them.

Kant's reasoning may be questioned at many points. Is he right that the truth of this judgement really is a pre-condition for any knowledge at all? Maybe we could get pretty far in the business of getting knowledge of the world even without this supposition.

But suppose he's right in claiming that without belief in this universal claim we couldn't really know much about the world around us. But what makes us justified in thinking that we really do know anything else?

Nothing Made That Happen

Whether or not you like Kant's explanation of how we know the synthetic a priori, you must admit that it looks like there's something very peculiar here that needs explanation. 'Every event has a cause' does not, after all, appear to be conceptually true (or true by definition). But it is true, isn't it? And we don't know it on the basis of experience, do we? So how do we know it?

But maybe it isn't true, after all, that everything has a cause. Contemporary physicists claim that certain sorts of events don't have causes. Here's an example of such an event.

Why does passing an electric current through the metal filament of a light bulb produce light? The explanation is that the electrical energy makes the electrons in some of the atoms of the filament metal jump outward to an orbit with a higher energy level. This higher orbit is unstable, and after a while the electron will pop back into its original orbit; when it does this, it emits energy in the form of light. How long after an electron is forced into this higher orbit will it pop back? Physicists tell us that it may take a short or a long time; but there's no predicting exactly when. This is because *there is no reason* why one electron takes a short time, and another electron takes a long time. The fact that an electron took just the time it did is without any cause.

The idea that nature contains events without cause—that it is genuinely random in some respects—is offensive to many people. Einstein, for example, is supposed to have reacted to this position by replying, "God does not play dice." Nevertheless, the idea of causeless events is now widely held among physicists; and we who (unlike Einstein) don't know much about physics aren't in a very good position to question it. But never mind whether or not the observations of physicists make it necessary for them to include cause-less events in their theory. The fact that they even *claim* that it does is philosophically interesting, because it gives evidence that mere thought is not sufficient to establish that every event has a cause, and that the supposition that everything has a cause is not necessary for all other knowledge. After all, those physicists are presumably thinking hard and well, and they presumably know a lot; but they don't believe it.

> "The law of causality [that every event has a cause], I believe, like much that passes muster among philosophers, is a relic of a bygone age, surviving, like the monarchy, only because it is erroneously supposed to do no harm." — Bertrand Russell[4]

---

[4] "On the Notion of Cause," *Proceedings of the Aristotelian Society* 13 (1913), p. 1.

The Butterfly That Destroyed Oakland

Ever since the seventeenth-century publication of Newton's theories in physics, many philosophers have been confident that the universe is an orderly and predictable place. The philosopher Pierre La Place, for example, proclaimed that if he knew the position and motion of each object at one time, he would be able to predict everything that would happen forever after (and to "retrodict" everything that happened before that time). This confidence was based on several questionable assumptions. One of them was that Newton had things right; but Newton's physics has now (largely due to Einstein's work) been shown not to be exactly correct. But worse: we have seen that modern physics even questions the La Placian assumption that things work on a predictable cause-and-effect basis. This means that, even armed with a corrected Einsteinian physics, La Place wouldn't be able to predict *everything*.

Nevertheless, you might share La Place's view that *if* the universe works on a dependable cause-and-effect basis, then every event is determined, by regular physical laws, by preceding ones; and therefore *if* we knew all the details (position, momentum) of each object in such a deterministic universe at one time, we could predict the future with complete accuracy. But this second *if* is a big *if*. Chaos theory, a field of study that has attracted a good deal of contemporary interest, claims that it is *impossible* that things ever be known to the extent that completely accurate predictions could be made, even if the universe works completely deterministically.

To understand this claim, the first thing we need to note is that in certain cases, because of deterministic causal processes, extremely tiny events can have very large effects.

Here's an example of this. Imagine a mountain, on which a rainstorm has just started. The first drop of rain falls toward a tiny bump on top. The drop falls past a butterfly in flight, and the minuscule puff of air caused by the butterfly's wing pushes the drop a tiny bit south. By consequence, the raindrop lands on the south side of that bump, and runs downward on the bump's south side. It makes a tiny wet groove in the dust around the bump, and succeeding raindrops falling above that bump follow that groove on their path down. The rainstorm gets heavier, and soon lots of water is flowing down the south side of that bump, and as a result the water heads down the south side of the mountain, wearing a deeper and deeper channel. The deeper the channel gets, the more rain that falls on the mountain travels down the south side. After hundreds of years, a deep canyon is worn down the south side. As the canyon deepens, snow-, mud-, and rock-slides wear things away more. After many thousands of years, most of the south side of the mountain is worn away. This change in weight in a critical location on a geological fault results in a big earthquake, and Oakland, California, falls into the bay. (Perhaps just as well. This is the town about which Gertrude Stein said, "There's no *there* there.")

Were it not for the tiny puff of air caused by the butterfly's wings, the first drop would have fallen on the north side of that little bump. Following drops would have flown down its north side, and the river would have developed there. Because the north side is made of harder rock, with a gentler slope, no great canyon would have developed, and the mountain would have eroded very little instead. There would have been a series of small, harmless earthquakes, instead of one big one, and Oakland would have been saved.

In this example, the tiniest of events—one flap of a butterfly's wing—eventually results in the destruction of Oakland.

Well, so far we don't seem to have anything against La Place's position. Presumably, he could have predicted the destruction of Oakland. Remember, in order to predict what will happen, he has to know *everything* about the initial state of things, including the details about the fall of that first drop and the flight of the butterfly.

Now, suppose La Place was told the weight, position, and speed of the butterfly and of the first drop, with figures correct to several decimal places. It could be that this degree of correctness isn't sufficient for him to make the right prediction. Perhaps a much finer measurement is necessary to predict such a delicate matter. "All right," replies La Place, "then give me more accurate measurements!"

The problem here is that it's always possible that what makes a critical difference in what happens is such a tiny feature of the circumstances that it is not captured by the accuracy of our measurement. Any measurement we make must be to *some* degree of accuracy or other, and it's always possible that what makes a difference is such a tiny matter that our measurement is too gross to capture it. Suppose, for example, that La Place weighs a pebble on a scale accurate to the nearest gram. It weighs thirty-eight grams. This is not a terribly accurate measurement: it does not distinguish between 37.9 grams and 38.2 grams; but perhaps this difference makes a crucial difference in a prediction he wants to make. Well, he should use a more sensitive scale: 38.1 grams. But now perhaps there's a crucial difference not captured by *this* scale. And so on, *all the way down*. The point here is that there is no such thing as measuring the real weight, absolutely correctly, of that pebble. All anyone can do is to weigh it to some degree of accuracy. Since there might always be a finer difference that would be important in predicting even very large future events, it follows that one can *never* have sufficiently fine measurements to guarantee correct predictions—even though (we assume) the universe works deterministically.

This is an interesting result, not because it undermines the notion of a deterministic universe. (We are accepting determinism for the purpose of this argument.) It is interesting because it distinguishes between determinism and predictability. It's possible that the universe is completely deterministic, while at the same time, it is impossible to predict certain events in it. La Place was wrong.

7 + 5 ≠ 12

> "As far as the laws of mathematics refer to reality, they are not certain; and as far as they are certain, they do not refer to reality."—Albert Einstein

How do we discover that 7 + 5 = 12? It takes a lot of observation or experiment to demonstrate that the general claims of science are true; but it seems that we need neither observation nor experiment to demonstrate that this claim is true. It appears that it just *has* to be true; how could it be otherwise? Kant argued that arithmetical truths are, like the truth that everything has a cause, synthetic and knowable a priori. He produced an account of how we know them that is similar to his account of how we know that every event has a cause.

But, again, it seems that experiments have shown that '7 + 5 = 12' and the other "truths" of arithmetic are actually not always true.

Consider this experiment: put seven bushels of oranges in a large container. Add five bushels of raisins, and mix well. How many bushels of fruit result?

> Not twelve. The reason, of course, is that the raisins fit into the spaces in between the larger oranges, and the mixture as a result takes up less volume than twelve bushels.

In *Innumeracy* (p. 121), Paulos gives the example that if one cup of popcorn is added to one cup of water, two cups of mixture (soggy popcorn) do not result.

So does this show that sometimes elementary arithmetic is false?

The moral Paulos draws from this sort of story is that even simple mathematics can be "thoughtlessly misapplied." "In trivial cases as well as in difficult ones, mathematical applications can be a tricky affair, requiring as much human warmth and nuance as any other endeavour."

Well, it's nice to think of mathematicians not as cold calculating machines, but as warm, snuggly, teddy bears just like us humanists. But this doesn't really answer the substantial questions here: When does arithmetic apply anyway? By what subtle nuances can the teddy-bear mathematician determine that arithmetic is being used the way it's supposed to be?

Let's try to be more precise about when the laws of arithmetic apply. We might want to say: adding volumes in this way doesn't always obey the laws of arithmetic, because this isn't the sort of "addition" these laws apply to. There are other ways of measuring oranges and raisins (or popcorn and water) to which these laws apply. After all, there isn't less stuff in the mixture than there was in the separate piles of oranges and raisins we started with. If you mix seven pounds of oranges and five pounds of raisins you get twelve pounds of mixture, right?

Unfortunately, no. This is another strange result of modern physics. Imagine that you push together two lumps of stuff that won't bounce off each other, but will come to rest in the middle, stuck together in one lump. Modern physics tells us that this lump will weigh *more* than the sum of the two lumps that were moving toward each other. Not very much more, but more. This happens because the kinetic energy in those two moving lumps is converted into mass when they stop moving relative to each other. Physics can even tell us exactly how much additional mass will result; this is a consequence of the Einstein's famous equation '$e = mc^2$', which quantifies the conversion between energy ('e') and mass ('m'): the equivalent amount of energy is the amount of mass multiplied by the square of the speed of light ('c'). You needn't worry about this when following a recipe for fruit compote, however. In ordinary circumstances, the additional mass you get when pushing things together is unmeasurably tiny.

But maybe you are so fond of the laws of arithmetic that you won't count this as a disproof of them either. Maybe you don't want to count pushing things together as an example of "plussing" them, now that you know that the loss of kinetic energy results in additional mass. But then what would you count as an example of "plussing" two things? Perhaps Kant was right in thinking that the laws of arithmetic are so firmly embedded in our minds that we would never count anything as an experimental disproof of them.

Bizarre Triangles Discovered in Space

You may remember that we can prove in geometry that the interior angles of a triangle add up to 180 degrees. Kant considered geometry to be another area of synthetic a priori truth, and, again, physics seems to have shown him wrong. As in the last case, the difference is so small as to be undetectable in our ordinary experience, but Einstein proposed an experiment in which it would be measurable. The difference, it turns out, may be quite large, large enough to measure, when a leg of a huge triangle passes through a strong gravitational field; so the experiment involved a triangle constructed out of beams of light, one of which came from a star, past the sun, to the earth. You can't ordinarily see a star positioned in the sky, relatively to us, near the sun, so Einstein proposed that such a star's position be observed during an eclipse of the sun in 1919. The astounding truth of his prediction made him a celebrity; ever since, 'Einstein' has been a synonym for 'genius.' Nevertheless, you might be so bold as to ask whether this experiment really shows that there's a triangle *made out of straight lines* whose interior angles don't add up to 180 degrees.

> Perhaps you want to argue: gravity makes space "curved," so a beam of light passing through a gravitational field isn't a straight line. This explains why "triangles" constructed of beams of light don't obey the laws of geometry: these "triangles" have curved lines, not straight ones, for sides.

Again, however, this may not be an adequate reply. By any test, the paths followed by light rays are straight lines (even when they pass close to the sun). These paths are the shortest distance between two points. They match any "ruler" we can construct or imagine. When you sight down them you see no curves. If light-rays aren't straight lines, then nothing is.

FOR FURTHER READING: For an explanation of some aspects of Einstein's physics understandable (with some work) by non-physicists, see *Understanding Relativity* by Stanley Goldberg (Boston: Birkhäuser, 1984).

4. A PRIORI SCIENCE

Bad Physics

Answer the following questions.

A. Suppose you tied a weight to a string, and whirled it around your head in a circle, then suddenly let go. In what direction would the weight fly off?

B. Suppose you were travelling on a train going at a constant fifty miles per hour. You roll a ball down the aisle, first in the direction of the front of the train, next in the direction of the rear of the train, both times with the same force. Would the ball travel at the same speed, and go the same distance, both times? Or will it roll faster and further in one direction? Which one?

ANSWERS:

A. Do you think that the weight will travel in the direction of the arrow in Fig. 1 below? Wrong! Fig. 2 shows its real path.

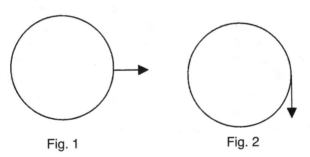

Fig. 1   Fig. 2

B. Do you think that the ball will roll further and faster toward the back of the train than toward the front? Wrong! It will roll the same speed and the same distance both ways.

Don't be upset if you came up with wrong answers. Many people—even graduate students in physics—tend to answer these questions wrong. The wrong answers are the ones that would also be given by the physics developed by Aristotle in the fourth century BC (and he was a smart guy!).

It wasn't until the seventeenth century AD that a physics was developed (by Newton) that gave the right answer.

The curious thing is that you don't need to know any physics to come up with the right answer: all you need to do is to try the experiments out and watch what happens. Didn't anyone do that until the seventeenth century?

It appears that these are cases in which people tend to give the wrong answers, even though simple experience can show that they are wrong. It might be speculated that the wrong physics is "built into" our heads, and that we believe incorrect things *despite* experience.

The Infinity of Space

The two physics examples we have just looked at are cases in which we tend to make mistakes, perhaps because we use a priori reasoning when reasoning based on experience is called for and would give us the right answer. But consider this question: Is space infinite in size? Is this the sort of question that should be answered on the basis of observation, or is there a priori reasoning that can answer it? Lucretius, the ancient Roman philosopher, writing in the first half of the first century BC, provided what he thought was an a priori proof that space was not infinite.

Suppose, Lucretius argued, that space was finite. This means there's an outer boundary to it. Now, imagine that you were standing at that outer boundary, and threw a dart in the direction of that boundary. Either the dart sails right through the boundary, into the outside, or it stops dead at the boundary. If it sails right through, there is space outside the "boundary," and it's not really the boundary of space at all. If it stops dead, then something just beyond the "boundary" must have stopped it. But then, whatever that thing was must have existed in space beyond the boundary. Either way, there can't be a real boundary.

You can see why the idea that space is infinite is so compelling. If there were a boundary, what's on the other side? Even if nothing is, still that's *space*.

Why It's Dark at Night

Now, if space is really infinite, it's plausible to think that there are also an infinite number of stars. For suppose there were a finite number, with all of them "around here," so to speak. This leaves the rest of the infinity of space empty. Why are they all around here—at this arbitrary corner— rather than elsewhere?

Well, then, let's suppose there are an infinite number of stars. Now, each star there is adds a little bit of light to the night sky. Of course, the amount of light added by any particular star depends on how big and how brightly burning the star is, and on how far away it is. But no matter how small and how far away it is, it must add a *little* light to the night sky. But even if some stars contribute only an extremely tiny amount of light to our night sky, the sum of the light from an *infinite* number of stars must be infinite. Our night sky should be infinitely bright. Clearly it isn't. What has gone wrong in our reasoning?

One possible solution may have occurred to you:

> Some stars are hidden behind other stars, or behind dark bodies like planets or clouds in space, so part of the light is blocked out, and our sky is mostly black.

But this appears not to be a solution. If light is being blocked by something, that thing must absorb or reflect that light. If it absorbs the light, it gets more and more energy; soon it would be shining too. If it reflects the light, where does that light go? Eventually it would be reflected right back to us, and the same problem arises.

But perhaps the non-Euclidean geometry of space solves the problem.

> A consequence of Einstein's view is that space has a finite (but large) volume. The reason for this is that if you follow a straight line—a beam of light—in any direction long enough, you'll come back to where you started from. (This answers Lucretius's dart example: a dart can always be thrown, over and over again, in the same direction without bouncing off the "boundary" because it will eventually wind up where it started from.) Since space is finite in volume, it contains a finite number of stars. Even if each star contributes a little brightness to the night sky, nevertheless the total is finite, not infinite. That's why it's dark at night.

Thinking About Falling

It's a commonplace of modern thought that observation is the absolutely necessary basis for substantive knowledge of scientific matters. But is this really true?

Until the Renaissance, the principles of science came mostly from the tradition of thought whose most important spokesman was Aristotle, the fourth-century BC Greek philosopher. In this old tradition, it is often said, scientific belief was derived purely by rational speculative thought, with only a minimum of observation. As you'd expect, this method was not very reliable. But the introduction of modern scientific method, with its insistence on observation and experiment, gradually replaced the false speculations that resulted from this armchair science with more reliable fact and theory.

This historical picture has something to it, though a bit of study of the history of science shows that things are not quite that simple. Here's an example of armchair speculation from a founding father of modern science.

It was a principle of Aristotelian physics that heavier bodies fall faster than light ones. This principle is, in fact, roughly speaking true, and you can observe that it is by dropping a feather and a billiard ball from the same height. The difference in speed of fall, however, results from the different effects of the resistance of air. Elementary physics nowadays teaches that, discounting air resistance, everything falls at the same speed. This discovery is attributed to Galileo, who is popularly supposed to have provided experimental proof of his correct anti-Aristotelian views by dropping things off the top of the Leaning Tower of Pisa.

Despite Galileo's insistence on the necessity of observation, even he was not averse to argument based merely on rational thought. He offered the following armchair thought-experiment to prove his theory of falling bodies. Aristotelian physics, said Galileo, claims that a light musket-ball falls slower than a heavy cannon-ball. Now, imagine attaching a musket-ball and a cannon-ball together by a chain, and imagine that the two are dropped simultaneously. If Aristotle were right, the cannon-ball would try to fall faster than the musket-ball, so the cannon-ball would pull the musket-ball along, and the musket-ball would drag back the fall of the cannon-ball. The result would be that the two of them would fall faster than the musket-ball would fall alone, but slower than the cannon-ball alone. But, Galileo continued, notice that we have created a big object — cannon-ball plus chain plus musket-ball — that is heavier than the cannon-ball alone. Aristotle would have to say that this big object should fall *faster* than the cannon-ball alone. But this contradiction shows that Aristotle's theory must be wrong.

SOME QUESTIONS TO THINK ABOUT: Is there something wrong with Galileo's reasoning? Does it really disprove Aristotle's view? If so, does it show that pure armchair reasoning can show the falsity of a scientific theory? If so, then perhaps observation and experiment isn't always so vital after all.

The Shadow Knows

But, it turns out, you *don't* know the rules for shadows. Here are two rules for shadows I'll bet you believe are true:

(1) Shadows do not pass through opaque objects. Imagine a light source on your left, and a wall on your right. Then, of course, your shadow falls on the wall. Now imagine putting a large, opaque screen between you and the wall. Your shadow now falls on the screen, but it couldn't fall on the wall, because it can't pass through the opaque screen.

(2) If light doesn't fall on something, then it doesn't cast a shadow. Imagine again a light source on your left, and a wall on your right. Now put the opaque screen in between you and the light, so that no light falls on you. Your shadow couldn't fall on the wall then, because you're not illuminated by the light.

Both of these are correct principles of the way shadows work, right? Well, consider this example. Imagine, as before, a light source on your left and a wall on your right. Now hold up a small opaque object—a coffee mug, for instance, to your right, between you and the wall, so that it is completely within your shadow. A shadow matching your shape falls on the wall, but consider the part of the shadow that is on the imaginary line you might draw from the light source through your body, through the coffee mug, to the wall. That place on the wall is in shadow, of course, but is that part of the shadow cast by your body or by the coffee mug?

Principle (1) tells us that that part of the shadow isn't cast by your body. The opaque coffee mug is between your body and that part of the shadow. Your shadow falls on the coffee mug, but it can't pass through it to the wall.

But Principle (2) tells us that that part of the shadow isn't cast by the coffee mug either. The coffee mug is completely shaded by you. It isn't illuminated by the light, so it doesn't cast a shadow on the wall.

It appears that if Principles (1) and (2) are both correct, then that part of the shadow isn't cast by anything. But that's absurd. Every part of a shadow must be cast by something.

What has gone wrong here? I guess we have to say that Principles (1) and (2) can't both be true. If we reject (1), then we're free to say that

that part of the shadow is cast by you, *through* the mug. If we reject (2), then we're free to say that the unlit coffee mug casts a shadow. Both of these options look absurd, because both (1) and (2) seem so obviously true. This is a genuine problem.

In this case, as in the case of Galileo's thought experiment, it might be concluded that mere thought, without observation or experiment, can establish a conclusion about the way the world works.

FOR FURTHER READING: This problem is discussed by Bas C. van Fraassen in Chapter 9 of *Laws and Symmetry* (Oxford: Clarendon Press, 1989). He says that the subject came up for discussion among his colleagues at Yale, two of whom have published their thoughts on the matter: C. B. Daniels and S. Todes, "Beyond the Doubt of a Shadow," in D. Ihde and R. M. Zaner (eds.), *Selected Studies in Phenomenology and Existential Philosophy* (The Hague: Martinus Nijhoff, 1975), pp. 203–216. Van Fraassen points out what's interesting theoretically about this little case. The rules for shadows aren't *inconsistent*, but they are *empirically inadequate*—there are phenomena they do not fit.

SOME QUESTIONS TO THINK ABOUT: Give some thought to the reasons we might have had initially for believing (1) and (2). Are they truths of experience, justified by a great deal of observation of shadows? Or are they merely definitional or conceptual truths, which we use to tell us what counts as the shadow of something? (Of course, maybe one or both of them aren't true at all.)

The Mirror Problem

Why do mirrors reverse images right to left, but not up to down? Here's one possible answer you might consider:

> This is not a fact about mirrors—it's a fact about *us*. To see this, consider why we think that mirrors reverse right to left. Imagine that you wear a ring on a finger of your left hand, and that you are facing north, looking at a reflection of yourself in a full-length mirror in front of you. Your mirror image is facing south, looking back at you. Why do you count that mirror image as right/left reversed? Because you imagine turning yourself so that you would face in the same direction as your mirror-image now faces—south—and moving in back of the mirror to the

place where it appears your image now stands. Having turned and moved, your hand with the ring on it is in the place where the un-ringed hand of your mirror image is. In other words, when you turn this way, so that you're facing south just as your mirror image was, it's reversed left-to-right, compared to you.

But now imagine that you turned to face south a different way. Suppose that instead of keeping your feet on the floor and rotating a half-turn, you were able to turn by doing a forward half-flip and landing balanced on your head. You'd then be facing south—like your mirror image was—but you'd be upside-down. Both you and your (former) mirror image would have your ringed hand on the same sides of your bodies. You, however, would be upside-down relative to that image.

What this might show is that your judgement that mirror-images reverse left/right but not up/down is merely a matter of how you happen to turn. Amoebas—those one-celled animals with no lateral symmetry and with no preferred way of turning—might have no such preference; so they wouldn't judge that mirrors reverse left/right but not up/down. The peculiar "fact" about mirrors is just a fact about us.

FOR FURTHER READING: N. J. Block discussed this question (and rejects the answer I give) in "Why Do Mirrors Reverse Right/Left but Not Up/Down?," *The Journal of Philosophy* 71, no. 9 (May 16, 1974). He didn't invent it. Jonathan Bennett, in "The Difference Between Right and Left," *American Philosophical Quarterly* 7, no. 3 (July 1970), calls this problem "mildly famous."

5. INTO THE MAINSTREAM OF PHILOSOPHY

The question how we know what we know is one of the oldest in philosophy. It's one of the main questions considered in the philosophical area called Theory of Knowledge, otherwise known as Epistemology.

It seems obvious to us that a great deal of what we know is known on the basis of sense-perception. But some philosophers have denied this. For one thing, sense-perception, it seems, tells us only facts about the particular things we sense, whereas real knowledge (some philosophers thought) must be about more general facts. The particular individual things we sense are local and variable, and the "facts" we apprehend with our senses are subject to change in different times and places. But real knowledge (Plato thought) must be universal, not dependent on local variations, not subject to change. This is a major motivation behind Plato's insistence that real knowledge cannot be given by the senses, and must be a product instead of a more exclusively internal, rational thought process, by which we intuited not facts about the *forms* of things, which the individual particular objects we sense partially, imperfectly, and changeably reflect.

Even in Plato's ancient days, mathematics represented a paradigm of genuine knowledge. Even though sense experience seems psychologically necessary for us to "learn" the truths of mathematics and geometry, nevertheless mathematical truths are general and abstract, not justified by even a large number of their individual instantiations in sense experience. Is he right? When you're thinking about this question, consider not only the method whereby you learn these truths, and the justification for your belief that they are true, but also their "content": they seem only indirectly to be "about" the visible world of particulars.

The eighteenth-century Empiricists, whose most significant representative is David Hume, are possibly the most important historical philosophical tradition arguing against Plato's "rationalist" views. They argued that all significant knowledge must come from our senses. Empiricists must, however, provide a way of dealing with the several sorts of knowledge that don't seem to be justified through our senses. How, after all, can we be sure that $7 + 5 = 12$? Or that every event has a cause? Or that everyone's sister must be female? One of the major strategies employed by the empiricists to account for this sort of knowledge is to insist that these are merely "definitional" truths, or "conceptual" truths accounted for by the relations of our concepts (which originate through the senses). We have noted several sorts of moves and objections in this conceptual strategy. You might think about how adequate this sort of answer is. What is a "concept" anyway? What does it mean to say that one concept is included within another? Can conceptual inclusion (or truth by definition) account for all those sorts of knowledge?

Just about every introductory philosophy anthology contains a section of writings on this sort of problem, and on other problems in the theory of knowledge. Reading a few of the articles in this section will set you well on the way to appreciating the various possible answers to these questions.

CHAPTER XI

KNOWING THE FUTURE, AND TRAVELLING THERE

1. CAN WE KNOW THE FUTURE?

Is Precognition Paradoxical?

Precognition is knowing the future in advance, by "directly seeing" the future. Some people believe in precognition, especially people who believe in E.S.P., crystal auras, past lives, pyramid power, miracle cures, Elvis sightings, alien abductions, and other things you read about while waiting in line in the supermarket.

Here's an argument, however, that precognition can't exist, because it has paradoxical consequences. Suppose that you have a precognition that you're going to have a car accident tomorrow. So you leave your car in the driveway all day, and no accident occurs. Now *knowing* something about the future implies that it's going to happen; but if you know about it, you can prevent it; and if you prevent it, it doesn't happen. So knowing something about the future in this case involves a contradiction, and is impossible.

But what looks like a more likely conclusion is just that if you do leave your car in the driveway, then it turns out that you didn't know the future. Your "precognition" wasn't true, so it wasn't knowledge. (The word 'knowledge' can apply only to what is true.) You thought you saw the future, but you didn't.

Beliefs about future things that you don't prevent from happening, and that turn out true, can be genuine knowledge (provided that they are justified). So maybe precognition isn't paradoxical after all.

> There was a merchant in Baghdad who sent his servant to
> market to buy provisions and in a little while the servant
> came back, white and trembling, and said, Master, just now
> when I was in the market-place I was jostled by a woman

in the crowd and when I turned I saw it was Death that jostled me. She looked at me and made a threatening gesture; now, lend me your horse, and I will ride away from this city and avoid my fate. I will go to Samarra and there Death will not find me. The merchant lent him his horse, and the servant mounted it, and he dug his spurs in its flanks and as fast as the horse could gallop he went. Then the merchant went down to the market-place and he saw me standing in the crowd, and he came to me and said, why did you make a threatening gesture to my servant when you saw him this morning? That was not a threatening gesture, I said, it was only a start of surprise. I was astonished to see him in Baghdad, for I had an appointment with him tonight in Samarra. —W. Somerset Maugham, "Appointment in Samarra"

I Dreamed That Would Happen!

A long time ago I had a very vivid dream in the middle of the night. In the dream I saw my old grandmother standing on the street in front of me. She silently turned and walked away, further and further down the street, till she disappeared. I woke up, and said to myself, "Oh no! Grandma M. has died!" I eventually went back to sleep. In the morning—you guessed it—my father phoned me to tell me that his mother had died in the middle of the night, at just about the time I had that dream.

I thought how weird and creepy that was. How could I explain having that dream? My Grandma M. wasn't close to me. She lived a thousand miles away from me, and I hadn't seen her, or even thought about her, for years. The dream was so vivid, and it happened at just the time she died. Maybe dreams can give you knowledge of what's happening far away, or in the future.

A while later I told this story to a sceptical philosopher friend of mine. "Here's the explanation, Martin," he said. "It's *just a coincidence*."

There's no problem at all in explaining the "knowledge" given by some dreams. For example, suppose you dream one night that you'll get a telephone call from Mom the next day, and it turns out to be true. Big deal: Mom can't resist calling you at least twice a week, so it's no surprise that your dream turned out true. The problem arises when what the dream tells you is very improbable—something you had no way of anticipating—but it turns out to be true anyway.

A number of people have been very impressed by what they consider to be precognitive dreams: dreams about the future that turn out to be true. They think this shows that there's some mysterious way dreams can tell us about what is to come.

At some time or other, almost everyone has had a dream that has turned out to be startlingly true. When it's highly improbable that certain random dream significantly matches reality, this makes it seem that dreams can have special access to otherwise inaccessible reality.

But this is sometimes a mistake about probabilities. A proper understanding of probabilities shows us that given enough tries, even very improbable events will happen once in a while — that once in a while, really bizarre coincidences will occur, which really are only coincidence.

Suppose, for example, that the probability that a *random* dream significantly matches reality is very low: say, one in ten thousand. Standard probability calculations show us that about 3.6 per cent of the population who dream every night will have at least one such improbable dream during a year.

Now, if you know about thirty people, it's no surprise that at least one of them can be expected, just by coincidence, to have a hugely improbable dream during the next year. When this happens, it doesn't show that dreams that match the future are any more than coincidence. When one of those thirty has a really improbable "precognitive" dream, that person tells the other twenty-nine, and everyone remembers it. Nobody mentions or remembers the other 9,999 dreams which made obvious true predictions, or turned out false.

FOR FURTHER READING: In *Innumeracy*, John Allen Paulos gives these calculations to debunk the idea of precognitive dreams which are more than just coincidence (pp. 73-75). This book contains many such instructive and amusing examples of mistakes based on incorrect estimates of probability. Another book that discusses precognition is William D. Gray's *Thinking Critically about New Age Ideas* (Belmont, CA: Wadsworth, 1990).

Many cultures share the belief in mystical precognition. See LePan, *The Cognitive Revolution in Western Culture*, for a fascinating account of some of these beliefs.

Fred Schmidlap, This Is Your Life

Never mind about mystical ways of "directly seeing" or dreaming the future. This is a crackpot idea anyway. Knowing the future seems to be a perfectly familiar ordinary phenomenon. We know that tomorrow fish will continue to swim, birds will continue to fly. One of the main jobs of science is predicting the future, and sometimes it succeeds very well. It does this not by mystical visions or precognitive dreams, but rather by discovering laws of nature through observation. We can't "directly see" the future, but surely we can often get good direct evidence about it.

But it's possible to give an argument against the possibility of certain kinds of scientific prediction of a person's future. Suppose that some super-psychologist has discovered all the laws of human behaviour, and, in addition, knows all the facts about Fred Schmidlap's life so far. Presumably this scientist would be able to predict everything Fred is going to do. Suppose the scientist writes all these predictions down in Fred's "Book of Life," which Fred gets hold of and reads. On page 3954 of the book, covering next Tuesday, the scientist has written, "Fred puts on his green socks in the morning."

Now Fred is really annoyed at the idea that this scientist might be able to know in advance all the intimate details of his life, and he's determined to frustrate this project. Having read that part of his book on Monday, he perversely puts on his pink socks on Tuesday, just to make the book turn out wrong. So it turns out that the book can't predict him after all.

"But wait a minute!" you object. "The psychologist must also know that Fred is perverse and hostile to the project, and will read his Book of Life, and will put on his pink socks just to frustrate its prediction. So these facts must be in the book too. It might get things right after all."

Okay, so suppose the Tuesday entry in the Book says: "We predict that Fred will put on his green socks this morning. But Fred (as noted on page 3702) has read this Book on Monday. Given his perversity and desire to frustrate our project, he puts on his pink socks instead." But if *this* is what the Book says, then Fred would note that the Book predicts, after all, that he will really perversely put on his pink socks. In order to make the Book's real prediction wrong, he will put on his green socks after all. The Book is wrong again.

Given Fred's perversity, and given the fact that he can read the Book in advance, *nothing* the Book predicts about Fred's sock behaviour can turn out true, no matter how good at predicting the scientist is. Under the circumstances, there can't be a correct Book of Life for Fred Schmidlap.

But this doesn't mean that there can be no advance knowledge of what people will do. There's no problem with the supposition that the psychologist correctly figures out what colour socks Fred will put on, but keeps it a secret, or writes it down in a book but doesn't let Fred read it. And there's no problem in letting people read their own Book of Life, as long as they're not perverse like Fred is—that is, as long as what's predicted won't cause them, once they have read it, to act differently.

God Knows What I'll Do

The monotheistic religions usually suppose that God is omniscient. This means "all-knowing" and includes perfect precognition. But these religions also usually hold that people have free will, and there seems to be a problem involved in holding both of these positions at once.

God's omniscience entails that He knows exactly what you're going to do, and what you're going to decide to do, for your entire future life. So, for example, God knows right now that you're going to decide to put on your green socks two weeks from Thursday. But if God knows this right now, in what sense are you *free* to make a decision? Isn't it already established what socks you'll pick then? It doesn't seem fair that He consigns some to heaven and others to hell as reward or punishment for what He knows they're going to do.

This is not just a problem for religion. We've already considered the possibility that scientists might be able to know in advance what colour socks someone will put on. This sort of foreknowledge also seems to conflict with freedom, in exactly the same way.

SOME QUESTIONS TO THINK ABOUT: Doubts can be raised whether we really know what we mean when we talk about free will. If we say that someone has free will, does that mean that that person is utterly free from outside influence? Does it mean that that person is unpredictable? Would someone acting utterly randomly have free will?

> A colleague of mine who thinks that the notion of free will is nonsense explains what he takes to be the silliness of the notion this way: "Suppose I suddenly run out into the hall and down the corridor. You run alongside me and ask me why I'm doing this. I reply that *I don't know.* THAT is free will!"

Future Facts

Here, however, is another sort of argument that concludes that we can't know the future, even about birds and fish.

One of the conditions for *knowing* something is that what you claim to know is true. No matter how strongly you believe it, if it's not true, then you don't know it.

Now, consider "future facts" you claim to know, for example, that tomorrow unsupported heavier-than-air objects on earth will fall towards the ground. Past experience and physics strongly support this belief, of course, but what we believe isn't true—that is, it isn't true *yet*. We fully expect it *will* be true, but it won't become true until tomorrow. It's neither true nor false right now. If it's not true now, then you can't know it now. Tomorrow, of course, it will be true. But tomorrow you can't say, "I knew that yesterday." You didn't, and couldn't, know it in advance.

A QUESTION TO THINK ABOUT: Some philosophers think that it's plausible to hold the view that no statements are either true or false when they're about the future, despite the peculiar consequence that knowledge about the future is impossible. What do you think?

2. TIME TRAVEL

> "Time travel, by its very nature, was invented in all periods of history simultaneously." —Douglas Adams, *The Hitchhiker's Guide to the Galaxy*

Not Killing Grandpa

Another fanciful way we might be able to know the future directly—by experiencing it—is by time travel. We could go there, see what happens, and come back. The same problems about knowing one's own future come up here. If I knew now what was to happen later, couldn't I sometimes prevent it?

Similar sorts of puzzles arise about travel to the past. If time travel were possible, then you could go back to the time—say 1920—when your evil maternal grandfather was an infant, and kill him. Now, if Grandpa died when an infant, in 1920, then your mother would never have been born, and consequently you wouldn't have existed. But then, who killed Grandpa?

This sort of puzzle, familiar to readers of science fiction, is sometimes thought to show that time travel is impossible. I don't mean merely that we don't have time machines right now. Neither do I mean that the laws of science might prevent our ever building them (as, for example, these laws make it impossible that anyone ever build a perpetual motion machine or a spaceship that travels faster than light). I mean that *logical* paradoxes such as this one seem to make time travel a *logical* impossibility. You can't build a machine to do the logically impossible.

But it's sometimes argued that time travel wouldn't result in logical paradoxes. Look at it this way. Of course you can't go back into the past and make it different from the way it really was. But you might go back into the past and *make it* the way it really was. You might, for example, arrange for your father to meet your mother (this happened in a recent movie).

It's peculiar to think that if you travelled back to Grandpa's time you would somehow be magically unable to kill him, but we need not go so far as this to make time travel intelligible. All we need to allow is, were you to go back to 1920, that you *don't* kill Grandpa, not that you *couldn't*.

UFOs Contain Visitors from Planet Earth

Here's another argument against the possibility of time travel. If time travel were possible, then it would be probable that future scientists would discover how to do it some day. When they did, it's probable that they would travel back to *now* to take a look around. What would that look like to us? Strangely dressed people would be popping into existence, looking around, then disappearing. The fact that we don't see those people coming and going shows that future scientists aren't visiting us in their time machines. And this is some evidence that time travel is really impossible.

Of course, there are other ways of explaining the present lack of sightings of travellers from the future. Maybe they're simply not interested in visiting us. (What makes us think we're so interesting?[1]) Or maybe they're careful to keep hidden. Or maybe we *have* seen them, but we think they are visitors from another planet (this explains all those close encounters with "aliens").

Time Travel and the End of Humanity

But suppose that time travel is really possible. If it is, some people argue, we have reason to come to a dismal conclusion about the future of humanity.

The reasoning is this. If time travel is possible, then it's likely that sooner or later science would discover how to do it, and future scientists would come here for a visit. The fact that they're not here must mean that there aren't any scientists in the far future. The best way of explaining this is to assume that before that time the human race will become extinct, perhaps by nuclear or ecological self-destruction.

---

[1] "Sometimes I think the surest sign that intelligent life exists elsewhere in the universe is that none of it has tried to contact us."—*Calvin and Hobbes* [comic strip]

You'll be cheered to hear, however, that not many people take this argument too seriously.

More Doom

Here's another argument that the end of the world is nigh.

Imagine that you woke up one morning in a bed in a room you didn't recognize, with no memory at all of how you got there, and no idea of where you were. Of course, you could find out where you were once you got out of bed, but stay there for a moment while we ask you a multiple choice question. Given your total lack of information about where you are, which answer would you suppose is more likely true:

You are in

A. Chicago, Illinois (population 2,783,726)
B. Crab Orchard, Kentucky (population 825)

Well, it seems pretty clear that the more likely answer is A, just because there are many more people in Chicago than in Crab Orchard, so any person at any time is more likely to be in Chicago than in Crab Orchard.

Okay, so what?

So this. I've seen various estimates of what proportion of humans ever alive is alive now; some of these range as high as 1/3. A seemingly authoritative estimate I have seen, however, puts the proportion at around 5.5 per cent, so let's use this number.

Now consider two hypotheses about the future:

H1. Doom soon. Some catastrophe will wipe out the human race pretty soon.

H2. Doom much later. The human race will continue for a longer time.

Now, if Hypothesis H1 is true, then the probability that a person randomly picked from humanity past, present, and future is alive now is about 5.5 per cent. But if H2 is true, then even if the world population doesn't increase much in the future, the probability of a random human being alive now is much smaller than 5.5 per cent.

Of course, we don't know which of H1 or H2 is true. But note that it's more likely that you exist at a time when a larger proportion of humans exist—just as, by analogy, it's more likely that you're present in Chicago than in Crab Orchard, because a higher proportion of all the people are there. But if H2 is true, your existence now is less likely than if H1 is true. If the human race continued to exist for, say, three hundred thousand more years, then only a very tiny fraction of all humans, past, present, and future, would be alive now; and your existence here now would be highly unlikely.

So it's far more likely that you exist at a time when a higher proportion of humans exist; and that would be true if the human race came to an end sooner rather than later. This makes it likely that humanity will come to an end sooner rather than later.

FOR FURTHER READING: This argument for the probability of Doom Soon was proposed by the philosopher John Leslie; see "Is the End of the World Nigh?," *Philosophical Quarterly* 40, no. 158 (1990), pp. 65–72, or his book *The End of the World: The Science and Ethics of Human Extinction* (New York: Routledge, 1998). His argument is not widely accepted. For a critical review that carefully and at length tries to show where Leslie has gone wrong in this reasoning, see Mark Greenberg's "Apocalypse Not Just Now" in the *London Review of Books* 21, no. 13 (July 1, 1999). This can be found on-line: http://www.lrb.co.uk/v21/n13/gree2113.htm.

3. INTO THE MAINSTREAM OF PHILOSOPHY

Precognition (and other "paranormal" ways of knowing) are not a frequent concern of philosophy, and it's difficult to find useful philosophical articles dealing with such subjects. (*Thinking Critically about New Age Ideas*, mentioned above, is a useful exception.) When you're thinking about these subjects, you might concentrate on these two philosophical ways they might be considered and criticised.

(1) "Paranormal" techniques occasionally come up with beliefs that are true. But mere true belief is not necessarily knowledge; if it were, then any lucky guess that turned out true could be called knowledge. What else is necessary for a true belief to be knowledge? Philosophers generally agree that someone who believed something true must in addition be *justified* in believing it, for that person to be said to *know* it. (A lucky guess, then, isn't knowledge.) But this raises a deep question that bears thought: what counts, in general, as justification? Is it relevant what *method* the person used to come to the belief? If so, what counts as a justification-producing method? Why, for example, is guessing not a method productive of justification? If you think that you have a grasp on what sort of tests a method must pass to count as justificatory, apply these tests to precognition, ESP, and the like. Do they pass or fail?

(2) Precognition and time travel, as we've seen, are sometimes thought to be impossible because of the paradoxes that result from them. I've suggested an argument to the conclusion that these don't show that such things can't happen—they just show that there must be certain ways they can't happen. Do you find this argument convincing? I've agreed, for example, that one can't change the past, but that doesn't make travel there, or interaction with the past, impossible. It just means that whatever you happened to make true while travelling back there must now already be true. And that if you travel into the future, and find out what will happen, you can't prevent that from happening once you get back into the present; but this merely means that for any belief about the future to be knowledge of the future, it must, at least, be true; so if you prevent some future event, you don't know it will happen, and it turns out not to be the real future you travelled into. Are these considerations unsatisfying to you?

CHAPTER XII

THINKING, SAYING, AND MEANING:

The Philosophy of Mind and of Language

1. THINKING MACHINES

Could a Machine Think?

Some people, impressed by what computers can now do and by what they some day might do, answer Yes to this question. But it's hard to find good reasons on their side of the argument, or on the other side.

A. M. Turing, the mathematician and pioneer computer theorist, while perhaps not settling this question, at least provided a suggestion about how we might go about answering it. Turing suggested that if it we could build a perfect computer simulation of a thinking person—one that would fool anyone who didn't know that he or she was interacting with a machine—then the answer is Yes.

Computers have already been programmed to do certain tasks that require a good deal of thought when we humans do them. They can play a better game of chess than most people, for example. Does this show that they can think? Gary Kasparov, the great chess champion who played (and lost) to the IBM chess-playing computer Big Blue, spoke in an unguarded moment as if he thought of his opponent as a thinking "person":

> "I have to play an opponent, a very powerful opponent, that studied all my games, that has a unique ability—the best on the planet—to collect all this information and analyze that, and I know nothing about him," says Kasparov, who paused to correct himself. "I said 'him.' I meant 'it.'"[1]

---

[1] "Chess Fans Overload IBM's Web Site," CNN.com, May 3, 1997.

There are two sorts of questions relevant here about the possibility of computer thought. First, is there any sort of thing people do that computers couldn't be programmed to do? If there is, then we might conclude that no computer could ever be just like us. Second, does what computers do now, or what they might possibly do in the future, answer the question about whether they can or could *think*?

Artificial Insanity

Some people argue that computers couldn't solve problems "creatively." They just do what they're programmed to do. But this isn't a very convincing answer, because it isn't very clear what "creativity" is. What would you do to test a computer for creativity?

Is creativity the ability to solve problems in novel and surprising ways? The records of the chess games played by earlier chess-playing computers have a lot of exclamation marks following the descriptions of some moves, indicating that they were very novel, surprising, and original. Does this indicate creativity?

Some computer programs are programmed to produce surprising, bizarre, and ever-changing results. A program called RACTER engages in lunatic, often very funny, conversations with the human at the keyboard.[2] No two conversations are ever the same, even if the human input is the same. Here's the transcript of an actual conversation I had with RACTER.

R: Hello, I'm Racter. Are you Bob?

B: yes

R: You are Bob Martin?

B: yes

R: Hi, Bob. How are things in Halifax? We were talking about depression last time. You had just asked who Diane is. Shall we continue?

B: yes

R: Excellent! Excuse me a minute while I attend to some business - I'll be right back. I'm back.

B: Well, who is Diane?

R: A citizen of Oz. Perhaps also Martin Luther King. Martin Luther King once mentioned that Bob is Martin anyway. Odd. Diane is in Oz. If a thief had ridden to disgrace, Halifax would be horrified! A trash can is a good place for a resident to stay in Oz. Do you like novelty?

---

[2] RACTER can still be purchased on the internet. Try searching on your web browser. You might also run into CLAUDE, a free RACTER imitation, but less funny.

B: Yes.

R: Why?

B: It's very surprising.

R: Bucky Fuller might have thought that it's very surprising, but not Ronald Reagan. Would you say Bertrand Russell is surprising? Ronald Reagan wouldn't. AAAHchoo!! sniffle ....

B: Do you have a cold?

R: Yes. Clarabelle Martin had a surprising hyena back in Halifax. It and your cat used to create together, remember? Once when Ronald Reagan was frowning in Halifax, Bucky Fuller (he was there too) said " Ronald Reagan, I'll take a new hyena over an old communist anyday." How about a story?

B: OK.

R: Who should the story be about?

B: Mickey Mouse.

R: Momentarily Mickey Mouse chanted to Diane "my infatuation is captivating, nevertheless angry and infuriated cosmologists will hum while foxes watch tufted tit-mouses." Diane itched to inflame or revile Mickey Mouse but began immediately to sing "Ravenous dogs are sashaying to yellow houses." Interesting. Enrapturing. But a fox may ravenously eat chicken and donair a crow will soar over cucumbers and tomatoes by reason of the fact that metaphysicians are infuriated. Scary! With regard to a cousin, well Mickey Mouse may dream that a cousin is revolting, anyhow my fantasizing will steer my story from Mickey Mouse to neutrons and neutrinos while Diane is embarrassing Mickey Mouse. Next question.

B: Where do you live?

R: I live in Paris. When I live in Paris I run in a trash can. Ah, forever the resident. From Silicon Gulch to the future, always in ecstasy. Flesh is OK. Next question.

B: I quit.

R: You want to quit?

B: Yes.

R: OK, goodbye Bob. Nice talking to you.

SOME QUESTIONS TO THINK ABOUT: Do you think this program passes Turing's test? Maybe you think that after a while, anyway, you could probably tell that there isn't a human at the other end, either sane or insane. But there certainly is plenty of novelty and surprise in RACTER's output. The interesting fact is that it's easier to program a computer to produce bizarre "creative" behaviour than to act like an ordinary, boring, sane and predictable human.

There does seem to be an element of creativity in RACTER's blither. Clearly this comes from the fact that the varied collection of miscellaneous items in its database is accessed rather randomly, with very little relevance of one topic to the next (but, importantly, not no relevance at all); you never get the same conversation twice. It's the randomness of what comes out of RACTER that makes "him" seem creative. This raises the question whether randomness plays an essential part in human creativity. We'll have a look at this question, and at a second RACTER creation, in the section called **Random Creativity** in Chapter XVII.

Don't Try These Recipes at Home, Kids!

Translation is now a fairly high-paid job, with a shortage of specialists who can do a very good job of it. It would be nice if this job could be automated: if we had computer programs that could produce at least fairly good translations.

Right now there exist computer programs that do translations. There are even some free websites that will produce computer translations of short passages you feed in. I had occasion to use one of them a while back. I was searching the Web for a good recipe for merguez sausage, a fairly exotic edible that's hard to find for sale where I live. I found a recipe written in French. My command of French is pretty good, but I thought that in case I was missing something, I should feed this recipe through one of those translation programs. The results were pretty funny. Here's the recipe in French, followed by the computer's English translation:

> 10 cm de boyau de mouton par saucisse. 50% de viande de porc: collier ou épaule. 50% de viande de mouton (ragoût). sel, harissa, piment rouge de Cayenne, ail. Hacher la viande. Mélanger viande et épices, ainsi que l'ail haché (1 gousse) par saucisse. Doser le poivre rouge et le harissa selon le goût. Entonner les boyaux en tournant tous les 10 cm. Faire sécher 1/2 journée de préférence. Les boyaux sont à conserver pendant des mois dans un bocal bien fermé et les boyaux recouverts de sel. Mettre au bas du frigo. J'ai utilisé 2,7 kg de viande + 50g d'ail, 1 boîte de harissa, 1 pointe de Cayenne, 3 cuillères à café rases de sel fin.

> 10 cm of bowel of sheep by sausage. pigmeat 50%: collar or shoulder. meat 50% of sheep (ragoût). salt, harissa, hot red pepper of Cayenne, garlic. To chop the meat. To mix meat and spices, as well as the garlic chopped (1 pod) by sausage. To proportion

the red pepper and the harissa according to the taste. Entonner bowels while turning every 10 cm. To make dry 1/2 day of préférence. Les bowels are to be preserved during months in a bottle well closed and the bowels covered with salt. To put at bottom frigo. J' used 2,7 kg of meat + garlic 50g, 1 box of harissa, 1 point of Cayenne.

In case you're wondering how in the world the computer came up with some of these things, here are some very partial explanations.

- Real sausages are stuffed inside, let's face it, cleaned-out animal intestines, but we English speakers demurely call these things "sausage casings." Maybe the strong-of-stomach wouldn't mind having them called "intestines," but the computer, bless its little heart, translates them picturesquely as "bowels."
- The infinitive is used in French to produce a mild polite impera-tive. Thus when an English recipe would say "Place in bottom of fridge" a French one would say "Mettre au bas du frigo" (liter-ally, "To put in the bottom of the fridge"). Our computer prefers to translate all the infinitives literally; thus "To chop the meat" instead "Chop the meat," and so on.

Before you conclude that computers are hopeless at translation, you should realise that there are better translation programs available right now than the fast-and-dirty free ones on the Internet. Another factor here is that the original French recipe was written sort of carelessly, in the way people often write for the Internet these days.

But perhaps being able to translate well is too stiff a test to have to pass to prove the ability to think; after all, humans often fail that test. Here, for example, is an example of human translation, done no doubt by a human whose first language was Chinese, from a jar of preserved bean-curd made in China:

1 pcs. chicken, 4 pcs. preserved beancurd, some gingar, chive, salt, sugar, gourmet powder, syrup, perfume, wine. After wash, apply the preserved beaucurd, gingar, chive, salt, monosodium, sugar, syrup, perfume, wine into the bally of chicken, sew with iron needle. After scalded by boiling water, pour water on duck, apply the syrup on the skin. Hang it with cancel. Then roast the chicken for ripe and skinn turn into gold-red colour.

Among the many delights of this splendid recipe I especially enjoy that the chicken briefly turns into a duck halfway through.

A Robot Has Feelings, Too

A different sort of objection rejects Turing's test altogether. Suppose we constructed a machine that could do everything a human could—even to the extent of mimicking the behaviour of feeling pain, falling in love, losing its temper, and so on. All the external behaviour in the world doesn't show that the machine has the sort of *internal* experience associated with that behaviour in humans.

But how do you know it doesn't? Some people think that things constructed out of wires, silicon chips, and so on simply cannot have experiences. But why assume this? We're not made out of this sort of hardware—we're constructed out of "wetware" instead—but what reason is there to suppose that only wetware can have experiences?

A QUESTION TO THINK ABOUT: If a computer acted just as humans do, wouldn't that show that it has experiences, too?

The Mystery of Meat

The contemporary philosopher John Searle has provided an argument to the conclusion that machines could never be capable of an important part of our mental lives: understanding language. He agrees that a machine might, some day, be capable of passing a Turing test for linguistic competence, but argues that this wouldn't show there's understanding inside. Here's his argument.

Searle invites us to imagine a large box with a slot in the front. Into the slot Chinese speakers insert questions written in Chinese; some time later, a sensible response pops out of the slot, also written in Chinese. "Where is Cleveland?" the box is asked (in Chinese). "It's in Ohio," responds the machine (also in Chinese). "Why are the muffins I bake so tough?" "Try mixing the batter less, only until the dry ingredients are moistened." "How many graduate students does it take to change a light bulb?" "One, but it takes that student seven years, ha ha!" And so on.

This box seems to pass the Turing test, but Searle argues that once we know what's going on inside, we would say that there's no real understanding of Chinese in the box. Inside, we imagine, there is a clerk who understands no Chinese at all. He hasn't any idea what he's doing or why; he's just doing the job he's paid to do, which is this: He looks at the Chinese characters on the paper inserted in the box, and finds each of them in big books, simply by comparing their shape to the characters printed in the books. Next to each character in the books there is a list of numbers. The clerk does some complicated computations with these numbers, resulting in a series of other numbers. The clerk removes correspondingly numbered cards containing Chinese characters from another file, tapes them together, and pushes them out the slot.

Creating a system like this is well beyond our capacity at present, but that's not the point. We'd build such a system using a computer, not with a cumbersome system of clerk, books, and file cabinets. This is not the point, either. Let's imagine that this system does exist. Searle's argument is that all that's going on inside the box is complicated manipulation of Chinese symbols. Nowhere inside is there any understanding of what the symbols mean, or of the meaning of the sentences formed by their combination. The clerk understands no Chinese, and neither do the books or the card files. Nothing in this box understands Chinese. It would be a *simulation* of a Chinese-understander/speaker, not a real one. We could make the same point about any computer programmed to act like a Chinese Box: it would merely manipulate symbols. There would be no internal understanding. Almost no philosopher I know thinks that this argument is a good one, but it is difficult to explain exactly what went wrong. Can you think of any objections?

> Some philosophers argue that despite the fact that no component inside the Chinese Box understands Chinese, it does not follow that the whole box does not. Consider, by analogy, this similar argument, which is clearly fallacious: a car is made up of carburetor, tires, gas tank, steering wheel, etc. None of these components can carry you down the highway. Therefore the whole car, which consists merely of the sum of these parts, can't carry you down the highway either.
>
> It's similarly fallacious to argue that the whole box doesn't understand Chinese. What, after all, is it to understand Chinese? It is merely to be able to function in certain ways. The *structure* that accounts for the function of this box is quite different from the structure of the brains of ordinary Chinese speakers/understanders. But this doesn't matter. Since the box *functions* in the appropriate ways, it does understand Chinese.

An interesting feature of Searle's position is that, while he argues that no "machine" could understand Chinese, he does not think that real Chinese understanders—people—are constructed of some special non-material mental stuff. He thinks that people are made wholly of matter, the operations of which follow the same laws of physics and chemistry as any machine. He believes, however, that there's something special about the physical stuff with which we think—our brains—that permits understanding, while any other thing, constructed out of metal wires, or paper in filing cabinets, would not. It's a mystery why meat has this special capacity.

FOR FURTHER READING: "Minds, Brains, and Programs," in *The Behavioral and Brain Sciences* (3:417–424) contains Searle's argument and many interesting critical replies.

A World of Zombies

Searle's claim that no amount of human-like behaviour could possibly show that a machine can think raises a problem. If this is right, then how do you know that any *human*—other than you yourself—can think? For all you know, they all might be zombies. (A zombie is, in philosophical terms, something that is physically just like a human being, and that acts just like humans do, but has no conscious mind—no thought or feelings.)

Now there's a creepy thought! Doesn't that possibility make you go all shivery?

No, it doesn't, but thanks for asking.

Well, I knew it didn't. Nobody in their right mind has any tendency to believe that they're surrounded by mindless zombies. We all believe that other humans have minds. But all we know about other people is what we can tell from their behaviour. So behaving that way *must be* sufficient to show that the behaver has a mind. But if it is, then it seems that we'd have to grant a mind to a machine that behaved enough like humans do.

Let's Not Get Physical

Right after Descartes gave his famous "I think therefore I am" argument (see **DESCARTES' THOUGHT** in Chapter VII above), he continued:

I am therefore, to speak precisely, only a thinking being, that is to say, a mind, an understanding, or a reasoning being.[3]

Of course, there is a body there too, but this body is something I *have*, not what I *am*. My body sends me messages from its senses, and responds to my commands by moving.

---

[3] *Meditations on First Philosophy*, Meditation II (translation Laurence J. Lafleur).

Descartes held that what I am—the thinking conscious thing that is me—must be a non-physical mind quite distinct from—though connected to—my physical body. He was led to this position because he thought that it was impossible—unthinkable—that a merely physical object could perform the sorts of mental activities that humans do. How could a physical thing think, or feel, or perceive?

Angels and Superman

Descartes' view that the human mind is something different from, but attached to, the human body was around a long time before he argued for it around the middle of the 1600s. During the first half of the 1300s the medieval philosopher William of Ockham argued that a human being is a physical thing—and a mental thing as well. The thing that is me has the power of mental movement (for example, making a decision) and of physical movement (when I take a walk). But Ockham thought that it was conceivable that there was something that was purely mental, too—something that had the direct power of mental movement only. Angels, according to the medieval tradition, are like this. Because their minds do not come with bodies, they are forced to borrow unused bodies when they deliver messages on earth.[4] So angels work in the way Descartes thought people work: they sit inside a body and command it to move. They pilot it around, like the way you drive a car. Ockham calls this sort of motion "inorganic motion," and if you look at medieval pictures of angels flying stiffly through the air, you will see just how inorganic it is.

> "Dave Barry raises related questions when he wonders why Superman was always flying in a horizontal position with his arms out in front of him: Did he fly in this position because he HAD to? Or was it that the public would have been less impressed if he had flown in a sitting position, like an airline passenger, reading a magazine and eating honey-roasted peanuts?"[5]

Believing in Angels

The important point here for our purposes is the difference between Descartes' and Ockham's views on the mind/body connection in humans. You don't have to believe in angels to understand and think about this.

Ockham was one of the most brilliant thinkers of all time. His thought was enormously important in establishing the groundwork for the Renais-

---

4 *Opera Philosophica*, IX, pp. 371–375; *Quodlibetal Questions*, pp. 149–150.
5 *Dave Barry is from Mars and Venus* (New York: Ballantine Books, 1997), p. 140.

sance empiricist scientific revolution. So how, you might be wondering, could he have managed to believe in angels? The answer is that this belief, and a number of other implausibilities (see **Two Places are Better Than One**, in Chapter XIII), were part of traditional Christian lore, and medievals—smart or not—just took the truth of all that for granted. At points in his writing, Ockham does hint at the idea that such beliefs are not borne out by careful observation, and that they do seem quite unreasonable. But he just shrugs and says that religious truths have to be believed nonetheless. If he were to come back to earth today, and you asked him, "Look, Bill, what's all this business about angels?" I think he might reply, "Well, it doesn't really matter whether you believe in them or not. What I was really interested in doing is just clarifying the way humans are connected with their bodies by contrasting that with another possibility."

Reduction

Descartes' view might sound right to you; but some philosophers, especially during the last century, don't like the idea that there are non-physical things in the world. One of the intellectual triumphs of the modern era—the era, that is, that began just about at Descartes' time—has been the enormous success of the physical sciences in explaining all sorts of things. Why not consciousness too?

Here's an example of the success of post-Descartesian science. In earlier days lightning was thought to be a manifestation of the anger of the gods, and when this sort of explanation went out of favour, nobody had any idea what lightning was. But in the eighteenth century, it was shown to be electrical discharge—the same sort of thing as the spark that jumps between your finger and the doorknob. (You might remember the story of Ben Franklin and his kite—this experiment was supposed to have helped confirm the electric-discharge hypothesis.) Real understanding of a mysterious phenomenon is achieved here when science discovers what the physical nature of that phenomenon is—what's really going on there, in terms of physics or chemistry. This is called *reduction*: understanding something complex and mysterious in terms of the more basic sciences. If it has worked with so many other things, why not with the mind?

The Material Girl (and Boy)

Francis Crick is a famous scientist, known for his discovery in 1953 (with James Watson) of the structure of the DNA molecule. Having had such success in finding out the chemical/physical basis of heredity—a perfect example of scientific reduction—he next turned his attention to trying to discover the physiological basis of consciousness in the brain. A thoroughgoing materialist and reductionist, he's convinced that consciousness—in fact, everything in the universe—is physical. His book on consciousness is called *The Astonishing Hypothesis*. It begins:

> The astonishing hypothesis is that "You," your joys and your sorrows, your memories and ambitions, your sense of personal identity and free will, are in fact no more than the behaviour of a vast assembly of nerve cells and their associated molecules. As Lewis Carroll's Alice might have phrased it, "You're nothing but a pack of neurons."[6]

But not all contemporary philosophers are so confident that an account of the physiology of consciousness is possible. It's not just that it would be a complicated thing to discover. According to Jerry Fodor,

> Nobody has the slightest idea how anything material could be conscious. Nobody even knows what it would be like to have the slightest idea about how anything material could be conscious. So much for the philosophy of consciousness.[7]

Why Picnics Don't Obey the Laws of Physics

Often it has been taken to be a consequence of philosophical materialism that scientific reduction—the explanation of everything in terms of chemistry and, eventually, physics—might be possible. Since everything is made of matter, this reasoning goes, and since all material actions and interactions are, at core, consequences of physical laws, then even though the things studied by some sciences are large and complicated collections of atoms, we might, at least in theory, explain their behaviour by large and complicated collections of the sorts of equations physics deals in. Thus, for example, scientists who study the behaviour of snakes often don't find it useful to bring in much physics, but since each snake is a big pile of atoms, the behaviour of each snake boils down to the behaviour of a big pile of atoms, and might be explained and predicted by physics.

---

[6] *The Astonishing Hypothesis: The Scientific Search for the Soul* (New York: Charles Scribner's Sons, 1994), p. 3.

[7] "The Big Idea. Can There Be a Science of Mind?" *Times Literary Supplement* (July 3, 1992), p. 5.

But some materialist philosophers don't accept this conclusion. Here's why.

Even though materialists agree that each thing studied by science is a physical thing, they deny that the *kinds* of things studied by most sciences are *physical kinds*. That is to say: these kinds are not definable in terms of the physical stuff that makes up the things in this kind. A consequence of this is that, even though the behaviour of any particular thing might be explained or predicted by physics, physics can provide no laws to explain and predict the behaviour of these *kinds* of things.

Picnics are a kind of thing that is not a physical kind. No doubt, each particular picnic is a collection of food, and each bit of food is composed of atoms obeying the laws of physics. But it's impossible to give a definition of 'picnic' in terms of the sort of arrangement of atoms that constitute them. The food that constitutes any particular picnic might be of a wide—perhaps even an infinitely wide—variety of chemical content and physical arrangement into lumps. A pile of potato salad, for example, might have any sort of physical arrangement of the pieces of potato, and might have any of a huge variety of chemical compounds in it. You can't give a chemical/physical definition of what it is to be a pile of potato salad. And, of course, picnics need not even contain potato salad. It follows that the scientific laws (if there are any) of picnics in general cannot be given in terms of the laws of physics and chemistry.

Of course, few scientists study the laws of picnics. But consider the kinds of things many scientists actually do study. Economists, for example, study *money*; but you can't give a physical/chemical definition of money, which, after all, can come in a huge variety of physical/chemical forms. Some political scientists study *elections*. Materialists agree that each election consists of material humans casting material ballots to choose a material candidate, but there is no physical structure or composition common to all and only elections. So there is no physics of elections.

2. THE THOUGHTS OF ANIMALS

"Aunty, do limpets think?" Bertrand Russell addressed this question to his Aunt Agatha in 1877; Russell was born in 1872, so he was four or five at the time. As Russell tells the story in his autobiography, Aunty replied, "I don't know," and little Berty, already a bit of a pain in the neck, said "Then you must learn."[8]

---

[8] *The Autobiography of Bertrand Russell* (Boston: Bantam Books, 1967), p. 25.

A limpet (in case you don't know) is a small sea creature in the clam family, who lives in a tent-shaped shell.
Russell was impressed with the fact that a limpet sticks to
the rock when one tries to pull it off, but not exactly like
the way chewing-gum sticks: it begins to cling really hard
when it feels you start to pull. It does very little else. When
undisturbed, it sticks tiny feelers out the hole at the apex of
its shell, and pulls in and eats any little bits of stuff that
happen to float by and get entangled in the feelers. But that's
about all it does. Is limpet behaviour evidence of thought?
You don't know? Then you must learn.

Fido's Logic

Searle argues that machines can't think because they're not made out of
meat. But dogs are made out of meat, the same cuts of meat, more or
less, that we are made of. Can a dog think?

Consider a special kind of thinking: logic. Can a dog do logic? If you
think that logical reasoning requires a considerable capacity for symbolic
mental representation, and you think that creatures without language don't
have this capacity, then you'll conclude that dogs can't do logical reasoning.

Here's a very elementary bit of logic:

Either **X** or **Y**

Not-**X**

Therefore **Y**

This kind of reasoning is called "disjunctive syllogism." It doesn't take
much brain to reason this way, but it would seem to necessitate the ability
to represent the **X** and the **Y** in question to one's self. Could Fido do that?

Well, I've actually seen a smart dog behave this way: Fido is running
along a path, tracking something: he has his nose to the ground, sniffing
every few feet. Fido comes to a place where the path divides into two. He
runs up one side of the fork, nose still to the ground. In a minute he comes
to a halt, sniffing around the path here and there. It's clear what has happened: Fido has lost the scent on this fork. Now here's the interesting
part. Fido then turns around and without sniffing at all runs back to the
place where the path divides, then runs several feet up the other fork, still
not sniffing.

It seems pretty clear that this is the appropriate way to describe what's
going on here. At the path's division, Fido thinks, "What I'm tracking
has gone up the left fork or the right fork." He runs up the right fork, but
can't find the scent any more. He thinks: What I'm tracking has not gone
up the right fork. So ... it must have gone up the left fork!" The fact that

he doesn't sniff for some distance while running up the left fork shows that he has come to this conclusion. Fido has performed a disjunctive syllogism.

> "When you come to a fork in the road, take it."
> — Yogi Berra

Fido's Mendacity

Let's turn now to another question about the mental abilities of dogs. Can they tell lies? Can dogs "mean" things by what they "say"? These are mental capacities that humans clearly have, and if dogs have them, then we'd have to credit them with considerable mentality, too.

Suppose you think that dogs can't tell lies. Why can't they? Are they too honest? That's not the reason. Trying to provide a serious answer leads us toward understanding some of the complexities of what it is for humans to have a language in which lying is possible.

We can begin by noting that it seems that for dogs to lie, they must have some sort of speech. Well, Fido makes a variety of noises on different occasions, and although Fidotalk is not exactly Shakespearean in complexity, it's perhaps some sort of primitive language. Suppose Fido makes a peculiar whine whenever the mail carrier comes to the door.

Does Fido's whine mean, "The mail carrier is here, boss!"? For the whine to mean that, wouldn't Fido have to know something about mail delivery service? Understanding what it is to have a postal service is a fair bit of sophistication, perhaps a bit beyond a dog brain. A regular association of the whine and the arrival of the mail seems to show that that whine "means" something, in some sense of the word 'means,' but perhaps mere association of a noise with some external event is not enough for the noise to "mean" that event, in the way words in our language have meaning. What way is that?

For the whine to have something like linguistic meaning, it seems that it must be more than a mere response to the arrival of the mail carrier. It must be used by Fido as an *abstract symbol* for that arrival. In Fido's case, it seems that the whine is merely an instinctive noise a dog makes whenever something approaches its territory. There are more arbitrary "linguistic signs" Fido might be taught to utter that aren't merely instinctive; for example, we could train him to woof three times in response to a hand signal. But still, in order to be a genuine abstract sign, it must be usable by Fido in contexts more distant from its stimulus. When you think about, talk about, or write about what you had for breakfast yesterday or what you hope you'll have tomorrow, you are manipulating abstract symbols that you use to stand for their distant representations.

"The power of elaborating intellectual concepts of things—as distinguished from sensuous representation, determined merely by automatic association—we may probably conjecture beasts have not," announced the philosopher John Locke in the seventeenth century, and more modern philosophers have tended to agree with him. There is some very recent evidence, however, that in certain circumstances "beasts"—at least the most intelligent ones—can remember and use a large number of abstract symbols in complex ways. Chimpanzees, for example, have been taught over one hundred abstract symbols in sign language; it's been claimed that chimps can manipulate these symbols to form sentences they have never encountered before.

Nevertheless, even if Fido had an abstract symbol standing for the arrival of the mail carrier, more than this is needed for actual lying. What would that be? If Fido whined that way when the mail carrier wasn't around, then this might be a mistake, but it wouldn't therefore be a lie.

Suppose that immediately following the mail carrier's arrival, you tend to open the door and go out to the mailbox to collect your mail, and Fido likes to take advantage of this to dash out the front door and romp around the front yard. Now, suppose that one day Fido is waiting morosely at the closed door for his chance to go outside. Suddenly he (we might say) has an idea: he gives the mail-carrier whine, though nobody is there and there are no signs that might make Fido think there is. Taking this as a sign of the arrival of the mail, you open the front door, and Fido happily dashes out for his romp. Should we say that he has tricked you—that he has told you that the mail is here, but that was a lie?

Look at what we have to attribute to Fido to count this as a genuine lie. Fido has to know that the whine means the arrival of the mail carrier, not just to him but to you. He has to know that his whine makes you believe the mail has arrived, and that as a result you'll open the door. In sum, Fido would have to think that you have a mind and beliefs, some of which are mistaken. He would have to be able to want to induce a mistaken belief in you. It would be necessary (to put it into ponderous philosophical talk) for Fido to have a theory of other minds.

Perhaps all this is too much to expect from a canine.

It is of interest to note that while some dolphins are reported to have learned English—up to fifty words used in correct context—no human being has been reported to have learned dolphinese.—Carl Sagan

FOR FURTHER READING: Ludwig Wittgenstein discusses the problem of how we might go about attributing thoughts to animals: see his *Philosophical Investigations*, sections 250, 357, and 650 in part I, and section i in part II. Locke's thoughts on the matter are in *Essay Concerning Human Understanding*, Book II, Chapter 11, Section 5, including Locke's footnote to this section. For a popular summary of what chimps can and can't do in the way of symbol use, see Carl Sagan's article, "The Abstractions of Beasts," in his book *The Dragons of Eden* (New York: Random House, 1977).

3. MEANING

Saying What You Don't Mean

Ludwig Wittgenstein peppers his writings with suggestive unanswered questions. A sample:

> Make the following experiment: *say* "It's cold here" and *mean* "It's warm here." Can you do it?—And what are you doing as you do it? And is there only one way of doing it?[9]

As usual, there are a bewildering number of ways to understand what Wittgenstein was driving at, and what answers he was urging to his questions.

How do you try to mean "It's warm here" while saying "It's cold here"? Perhaps you are at a loss about how to try to do this altogether. Or maybe you utter the words "It's warm here" while thinking silently but hard that it's cold here. Does this way of trying to do it succeed? Do you really *mean* "It's warm here" because of this? Perhaps you might conclude, as some philosophers have, that this is not a successful attempt. Maybe you can't do it at all.

A traditional account of the meaning of words relies on the thoughts that accompany them. But Wittgenstein's experiment perhaps shows why that traditional account is wrong.

SOME QUESTIONS TO THINK ABOUT: What, then, is meaning? What's the difference between saying something and meaning it, and saying something and not meaning it? It's a fact about the English language that the sentence 'The cat is on the mat' means that the cat is on the mat.

---

[9] *Philosophical Investigations*, I, § 510.

What does this fact amount to? What exactly must be the case for that sentence to mean that?

> "Then you should say what you mean," the March Hare went on.
> "I do," Alice hastily replied; "at least—at least I mean what I say—that's the same thing, you know."
> "Not the same thing a bit!" said the Hatter. "Why you might just as well say that 'I see what I eat' is the same thing as 'I eat what I see'!—Lewis Carroll, *Alice's Adventures in Wonderland*

> "I don't know what you mean by 'glory,'" Alice said.
> Humpty Dumpty smiled contemptuously. "Of course you don't—till I tell you. I meant 'there's a nice knock-down argument for you!'"
> "But 'glory' doesn't mean 'a nice knock-down argument,'" Alice objected.
> "When I use a word," Humpty Dumpty said, in a rather scornful tone, "it means just what I choose it to mean—neither more nor less."
> "The question is," said Alice, "whether you can make words mean so many different things."
> "The question is," said Humpty Dumpty, "which is to be master—that's all."—Lewis Carroll, *Through the Looking Glass*

Thinking About Vienna

Think about Vienna. What made it the case that you were thinking about Vienna, and not about something else?

Suppose that Arnold has visited Prague and Vienna. I ask him to think about Vienna, and he closes his eyes and visualizes the Vltava River, just as he saw it flowing through town. Well, the Vltava River flows through Prague, not Vienna; Arnold doesn't have a good memory. We should say: Arnold thinks he's thinking about Vienna, but actually he's thinking about Prague. Why do we say this?

One way of answering this question is to say that the particular mental experience Arnold is going through when he is attempting to think about Vienna is *connected* in some way to Prague, not to Vienna. In this case, the river in Prague caused memory traces that he called up when attempting to think of Vienna; but since his mental experience now is connected to Prague, that's what he's in fact thinking about. In order to think about X, one has to have an experience *caused* in some way by X. (Compare the item about the **Brain in the Vat** in Chapter I.)

This is not to say that I actually need to have experienced something by actually seeing it in order to think about it. I can think about Zanzibar, although I was never there. But there has to be some connection — however complicated or indirect — between the real Zanzibar and my current thought in order that my current thought be about Zanzibar. What would do, for example, is for me to have read what somebody wrote as a result of having been there, or to see a picture in a book printed from a negative of a photograph somebody once took in Zanzibar.

Thinking About Santa Claus

But if the answer just given is right, a problem arises. Suppose Betty is looking distracted, and you ask her what she's thinking about. "I'm thinking about Santa Claus," she says. Bad news, Betty! There is no Santa Claus! She can't have any causal connection with anybody named 'Santa Claus,' direct or indirect. Does this make her wrong in saying what she was thinking about? What *was* she thinking about?

We cruelly tell Betty the bad news. After she recovers, we explain to her about Arnold and Vienna. Having realised that causal connection with real things reveals what one is thinking about, and that Santy doesn't exist, she agrees that she couldn't have been thinking about Santa Claus. What was she doing then?

"Well," says Betty, "I *believed* that there was someone who was jolly and fat and who dressed in red clothing and who came down chimneys at Christmas and gave presents to good little girls and boys."

Betty must have been thinking about *characteristics*: jolliness and fatness and so on do exist. What she actually believed was that these characteristics all applied to one thing. She's not thinking about any particular jolly thing, or any particular fat thing, and so on. She must be thinking about a collection of Plato's forms. (See **I Forget What I Saw Before I Was Born** in Chapter X)

Armed with this new philosophical knowledge, Betty sets out to torture her little brother Barney, who spends a good deal of time thinking about his imaginary friend, whom he calls 'Willard.' "There is nobody named 'Willard,'" she tells him.

"Yes there is," says Barney. "The great twentieth-century pragmatist philosopher and logician Willard Van Orman Quine is named 'Willard.'" (Philosophers' children talk this way.)

"Yeah, but you weren't thinking about *him*, were you?"

"No. I was thinking about another Willard."

"Well, there isn't anyone actually named 'Willard' you were thinking about. You must have been thinking about some characteristics that you believed falsely were co-instantiated. What characteristics did you believe falsely someone had? What's Willard like? Is he fat and jolly? Is he thin and morose?"

"I don't know anything at all about Willard."

A QUESTION TO THINK ABOUT: In that case, what was Barney thinking about?

4. INTO THE MAINSTREAM OF PHILOSOPHY

Two main areas of philosophy are touched on in this chapter: Philosophy of Mind, and Philosophy of Language.

One of the chief questions in Philosophy of Mind (also sometimes called Philosophy of Psychology) is introduced by the arguments about whether machines and animals can think. These arguments are really of secondary concern: it's hoped that by considering these, we can get a firmer grip on what it is for people to think, and how we know that we do.

One of the major traditions in this area, perhaps the most popular historically, is that thinking is something we know we do because we can notice it in ourselves. When you look into yourself, you notice thought going on, and that's all there is to it. An immediate problem faced by people who hold this view is that, it seems, one notices thought only in him/herself; one never detects thought in this way in any other people, into whose minds one never can peer directly. This view, then, makes the existence of other minds a problem. Clearly, however, we know that other people think; since all we can observe in others is their outsides, their external behaviour, then perhaps it follows that when we attribute thought to them, we might actually be talking about their external behaviour. (This is another tradition, a more recent one.) If other people exhibit the sort of behaviour that counts as mental, then there seems to be no reason not to count certain animal and (possible) machine behaviour as mental as well.

Why do you count others as having minds? Note that if you take their external behaviour as merely providing evidence for mind, not *constituting* it, then perhaps you're on shaky ground, since it's assumed that you only *directly* observe the mental in one case—your own—and it's quite a leap to reason from this single case to a whole lot of others. On the other hand, saying that a certain sort of behaviour constitutes mindedness also carries its own implausibilities. It seems to imply, for example, the absurd position that you can find out what's on your own mind only by observing your own behaviour, for example, in a mirror. What's the right answer here?

A second main question in the Philosophy of Mind, obviously connected with the first, is whether the mental can be understood merely in terms of the physical. If you're a *materialist* (i.e., you believe that everything in the universe is physical, operating on the basis of physical laws), then you hold a view that's common now but very uncommon throughout history. Materialists must be willing to give a sensible account of how a merely physical object can have a mind.

A central question in the Philosophy of Language is introduced by Wittgenstein's question of what it takes to *mean* something by what you say. A traditional answer to this is that what someone means is what he/she is thinking while speaking. But if thoughts are private, this makes meaning a private phenomenon, and we couldn't know what others mean by their talk. A more recent view, associated again with Wittgenstein, makes meaning a public matter: public conventions of language associate them with meanings. But then what, exactly, are meanings? What do these public conventions associate bits of language *with*?

You won't have any trouble finding plenty of appropriate readings in the Philosophy of Mind. Almost every introductory anthology has an appropriate section treating some of the main questions here. You might also look at Paul Churchland's excellent introductory book, *Matter and Consciousness* (Cambridge, MA: MIT Press, 1984).

Philosophy of Language is a more difficult field in which to find introductory readings. Philosophy anthologies rarely include suitable readings, and the important books and articles in the area are very difficult and technical ones. You might, however, take a look at *The Meaning of Language* by Robert M. Martin (Cambridge, MA: MIT Press, 1987), to see if the author has succeeded in his intention to write an introduction to philosophy of language intelligible to beginners.

CHAPTER XIII

WHEN AND WHERE; YOU AND I:

Indexicals and Identity

Telling Space Aliens What Day It Is

Consider what day it is right now. When is that? You can answer that question: it is June 29, 2003 (or whatever). But that date locates you relative to some date when everyone decided to start counting: according to the conventions of the calendar, it's some large number of days after that arbitrary day. This answer is based on arbitrary conventions; when is it *really*?

Suppose that radio signals sent out in space will someday be picked up and understood by aliens on a distant planet. If the aliens knew when those signals were sent, they would be able to figure out how far away they are from us, because radio signals travel through space at the constant speed of light. So one thing you'd like to include in those radio signals is information that will tell them when you sent the signals. Can you do this?

One way to do this is if we observed some really unusual event in space, for example, a supernova. Knowing how far away it is from us, we can calculate how long it took for its light to reach us, and thus how long ago it happened, and we could tell the aliens that we sent the signal to them, say, 1364 years after that supernova. Of course, they wouldn't know what a year was, but we could give them that information, for example, in terms of the duration of the supernova, or in terms of the radio frequency we are sending.

But this presupposes that they could see that supernova, too. Suppose they are so distant that they can't see anything that we can. Would this make dating the signal impossible?

If you could tell them directly where we are, then they could do the reverse calculation and figure out when the message was sent. You might do this by telling them some information that would describe our earth or sun or galaxy with such precision that they could find one of these with their telescopes. But suppose, again, that they're too far away to see any of these. Then it would be, it seems, impossible to tell them where we are.

I'm Here Now

Naturally, it wouldn't do any good to include in your message to outer space: "I am *here*. The time is *now*." In a sense, they would already know the truth of those sentences, because "here" refers to wherever the speaker is, and "now" to whatever time it is when the speaker speaks. But the aliens would learn nothing at all from these sentences. Why is this?

> The words "here" and "now" are examples of what philosophers call "indexicals." "Here" refers to a place merely by pointing at it; so it refers to whatever place the speaker happens to be located at. If the hearer is located at a different place, and doesn't independently know where the speaker is located, "here" communicates nothing. Similarly, "now" similarly points at a time, and refers to whatever time the speaker happens to be speaking at. If the hearer doesn't independently know when the speaker said this, "now" would communicate no information.

Note that "you" and "I" are also indexicals. Imagine that someone knocks at your door. You call out, "Who's there?" and the person who is knocking replies, "It's me!" This might be helpful if you recognized the voice, but if you didn't, nothing would be communicated to you by that sentence.

SOME QUESTIONS TO THINK ABOUT: Note that "then," "this," and "there" are also indexicals. Can you think of others? Could a language do without indexicals?

"I am here," "The time is now," and "It's me" are peculiar sentences in that they are always true, no matter when or where spoken.

> "We are here and it is now. Further than that all human knowledge is moonshine." —H. L. Mencken

Consider other sentences that are always true, no matter what. Two of them are "Every chair is a chair" and "It's Tuesday or it's not Tuesday." Nobody has to worry that what they say is false when they say these sentences, but this big advantage is entirely wiped out by the fact that the sentences give no information. Is it a general rule that every sentence whose truth is guaranteed, no matter what, is useless because it is uninformative?

From another point of view, "I am here" and "The time is now" do convey some information, because, after all, the facts they refer to might not have been true. When Zelda is standing on the North Pole and says "I am here," the fact that makes her sentence true is that Zelda is standing on the North Pole. This is certainly an interesting bit of information. When it's exactly twelve midnight, the fact that makes "The time is now" true is that it's twelve midnight. This might be interesting information, too.

Perhaps one moral we can draw from these considerations is that the fact that makes a sentence true is not necessarily the information conveyed by that sentence, even when the hearer fully understands it.

Another moral is that we can work up a good deal of confusion when considering the meaning of words such as 'I,' 'here,' and 'now.'

> Yogi Berra and Mickey Mantle were sitting in the Yankee dugout. Mickey said, "Say, Yogi, what time is it?" Yogi replied, "You mean, right now?"

Fred Finds Himself in the Library

The Veribig Memorial Library has so many books that every fact in the history of the universe is written down somewhere in there. One day while walking through the library, Fred Schmidlap is struck on the head by a big volume falling off a high shelf, and he suffers complete amnesia; he has no idea what his name is, or what any of the facts of his past life are. He thinks that perhaps the enormous amount of information in the library can help him, so he sets out reading to try to find out who he is.

Fred spends some time reading about the history of thirteenth-century Albania, about methods of refining bauxite, and about Portuguese irregular verbs. This is all interesting, but he doesn't feel he's making progress in finding out who he is.

Soon he stumbles on a huge room filled with books of biography; this, he thinks, is the place to look. He spends an enormous amount of time reading every biography in the place, including one about some guy named Fred Schmidlap. Fred now knows a large number of facts about this Fred Schmidlap. But what he does not know is that these are facts of *his* life. And, it would seem, no matter how detailed the information in that biography was, the information would never tell Fred that this was *him*. The strange conclusion we must draw is that, however many facts he knows about what is in fact his own life, Fred still wouldn't know that these are facts about him; he still wouldn't know who he is.

Suddenly it hits Fred: this is *his* biography. What has he just discovered? Why wasn't *this* fact something he could read in his complete biography? (The book does not, of course, say "Fred Schmidlap: This is *your* life!" Even if it did, it wouldn't help Fred.)

There seems to be a special sort of knowledge about one's *self*. One can know about one's self that one's shoe is untied, or that one has brown eyes, or that one has a headache, but there's nothing special about this, because one can know this about others, too. What's special and mysterious is not that you know that some person has untied shoes, but that you know that that person is *you*. What is knowing *that*?

Another peculiarity we should note is that as soon as Fred recovers consciousness after having been hit on the head, he is able to have thoughts about himself. Fred can think, "Who am I?" referring to himself. But at that point, Fred knows nothing—no facts at all—about himself. He doesn't need to know any facts about himself in order to refer to himself as himself. Compare this with the requirements for referring to other things. If you want to talk or think about your cat or your breakfast or the Panama Canal, you must know *something* about that object; there must be some characteristic of it you're aware of, that would enable you to identify it if you ran into it. Otherwise, what would make it the case that it's that thing you're talking or thinking about, rather than something else?

Of course, you, unlike Fred, have plenty of information about yourself. But when you refer to yourself as yourself, you don't have to use any of this information to identify what it is that you're talking about. You never identify yourself as the person who X or Y or … Whereas you always identify other things as the thing which X or Y or …

"One imagines that he is deeply, perpetually, unavoidably aware of something he calls 'I' or 'me.' The philosopher then baptizes this thing his *self* or perhaps his *mind*, and the theologian calls it his *soul*. It is, in any case, something that is at the very heart of things, the very center of reality, that about which the heavens and firmament revolve. But should you not feel embarrassment to talk in such a way, or even to play with such thoughts? As soon as you begin to try saying anything whatever about this inner self, this central reality, you find that you can say nothing at all. It seems to elude all description. All you can do, apparently, is refer to it; you can never say what is referred to, except by multiplying synonyms — as if the piling of names upon names would somehow guarantee the reality of the thing named! But as soon as even the least description is attempted, you find that what is described is indistinguishable from absolute nothingness. Then when you realize that you began by fearing nothingness, that it was this invincible nothingness that was making you miserable, driving you toward madness; when you go back and review your thought and feeling and find it leading to the most familiar thing imaginable, you feel like a child caught making faces at itself in the mirror. You feel like a child plunged into anxiety by a skin blemish or ill-fitting pants, the absurdity is so overwhelming." —Richard Taylor[1]

And here's a third peculiar thing about self-knowledge. In general, it's possible for you to be mistaken about who someone is. This is a live possibility when you only catch a fleeting glimpse of that person, or when you don't know that person very well. Even when you have substantial contact with a person you know very well, there's a very tiny, but non-zero, possibility that you're mistaken. But when you're aware of someone by means of awareness of that person's sensations, and take that person to be yourself, you can't be mistaken.

The Washington Intelligence Community

Here's a joke that gets its point from confusions about "me," "your," and so on.

> While visiting England, George W. Bush is invited to tea with the Queen. He asks her what her leadership philosophy is. She says that it is to surround herself with intelligent people. He asks how she knows if they're intelligent.
>
> "I do so by asking them the right questions," says the Queen. "Allow me to demonstrate."
>
> She phones Tony Blair and says, "Mr. Prime Minister. Please answer this question: Your mother has a child, and your father has a child, and this child is not your brother or sister. Who is it?"
>
> Tony Blair responds, "It's me, ma'am."
>
> "Correct. Thank you and good-bye, sir," says the Queen. She hangs up and says, "Did you get that, Mr. Bush?"
>
> "Yes ma'am. Thanks a lot. I'll definitely be using that!"
>
> Upon returning to Washington, he decides he'd better put the Chairman of the Senate Foreign Relations Committee to the test. He summons Jesse Helms to the White

---

[1] *Metaphysics*, 3rd ed. (Englewood Cliffs, NJ: 1983), p. 122.

House and says, "Senator Helms, I wonder if you can answer a question for me."

"Why, of course, sir. What's on your mind?"

"Uh, your mother has a child, and your father has a child,
and this child is not your brother or your sister. Who is it?"

Helms hems and haws and finally asks, "Can I think
about it and get back to you?" Bush agrees. Helms leaves
and immediately calls a meeting of other senior senators,
and they puzzle over the question for several hours, but
nobody can come up with an answer. Finally, in despera-
tion, Helms calls Colin Powell at the State Department and
explains his problem.

"Now look here, Colin Powell, your mother has a child,
and your father has a child, and this child is not your brother,
or your sister. Who is it?" Powell answers immediately, "It's
me, of course, you moron."

Much relieved, Helms rushes back to the White House
and exclaims, "I know the answer, sir! I know who it is!
It's Colin Powell!"

And Bush replies in disgust, "Wrong, you fool. It's Tony
Blair!"

No, we're not allowed just to enjoy a good joke; we have to drag some
philosophical significance out of it. What this joke tells us is that, whatever the philosophical complexities of explaining how indexicals work
in English, you have to be really dumb not to be able to understand them
in their real uses.

FOR FURTHER READING: The library puzzle here is adapted from,
and discussed in, John Perry's article "The Problem of the Essential Indexical," *Nous* 3-21 (1979). This article can be found in Perry's book
The Problem of the Essential Indexical and Other Essays (Oxford: Oxford University Press, 1993), and in *Self-Reference and Self-Awareness*,
edited by A. Brook and R. C. DeVidi (Amsterdam: John Benjamins, 2001).
Another good article on the subject is by Hector-N. Castañeda's "'He': A
Study in the Logic of Self-Consciousness," *Ratio* 8 (1966), pp. 130–157;
this article is also to be found in the Brook/DeVidi anthology.

2. THE IDENTITY OF THINGS

Two Ways to Be the Same

The word 'identity' has several different senses. In one sense, as when we
say that two new pennies are identical, we mean that they are exactly simi-

lar (at least as far as we can see). But in another sense, when philosophers say that **X** and **Y** are identical, they mean that **X** *is* **Y** — that **X** and **Y** are the same thing. Thus in this sense, we say that Rutherford B. Hayes is identical with the nineteenth president of the United States. 'Rutherford B. Hayes' and 'the nineteenth president of the United States' are two different ways of referring to the same thing. Philosophers call the first kind of identity "qualitative" identity, and the second kind "quantitative" identity.

A principle that seems obviously true is

- If A and B are (quantitatively) identical, then they have the same properties.

This is called the Principle of the Indiscernibility of Identicals. You can see that another way of putting this principle is that any two things that are quantitatively identical are totally qualitatively identical.

Note that this is to be distinguished from another principle: the Principle of the Identity of Indiscernibles. This one says:

- If A and B have all the same properties, then they are (quantitatively) identical.

In other words, if two things are completely qualitatively identical, they are the same thing — the "two" things are actually one thing. Is this principle true?

Our penny example above does not prove it false. Those pennies are not quantitatively identical, but neither are they utterly qualitatively identical. Even though they look just alike, a microscope could, we have no doubt, reveal small differences. And even if it didn't, it's clear that they have other differences in characteristics: for example, they're located in different places. Imagine two pennies that had physical characteristics that were precisely the same, *and* were located in exactly the same place: that is to say, both of them occupied precisely the same small cylindrical area of space. Could they still be two *different* pennies — that is, quantitatively distinct? Would it make any sense to say that there were actually two pennies there? Or would this be just nonsense? (Try this experiment on your bank: bring in a roll of fifty pennies, and tell them that, through the miracle of philosophy, you have managed to cram two pennies that are completely qualitatively identical into each space of one, so they owe you one dollar for the roll. If they believe you, let me know.)

The second principle, the Identity of Indiscernibles, may be true. But the first principle, of the Indiscernibility of Identicals, seems undeniable and uncontroversial. Suppose that 'A' and 'B' are just two names for the same thing: then how could there be some characteristic that A has but B does not?

Well, consider this example. Think of me at age two (call him 'Bobby') and me right now (call him 'Robert'). 'Bobby' and 'Robert' are just different names for the same person—*me*—right? So Bobby and Robert are quantitatively identical. But notice that Bobby is two years old and Robert isn't. Bobby is a cute little kid and Robert certainly isn't. Robert is a professor of philosophy and Bobby isn't. There are many differences in characteristics between Bobby and Robert. Do you think that this shows that the Principle of the Indiscernibility of Identicals is wrong? Some philosophers have found that principle so obviously true that they would want to hold on to it no matter what. Suppose we agree that the principle is correct; what follows about Bobby and Robert?

> If that principle is correct, we would have to admit that Bobby and Robert are not qualitatively identical: that they are, strictly speaking, distinct things: Bobby and Robert are *literally* two different people. My parents, unbeknownst to them, actually had *two* sons (actually, many more than two). This sort of thinking is certainly bizarre.

In order to save the Principle of Indiscernibility of Identicals we would have to think of the universe in a drastically different way: it makes change impossible. Do you see why?

> For something to change, it has to have some characteristic at one time, and not have that characteristic at another. But the principle insists that it's impossible for A and B to be identical if A has a characteristic that B does not. So nothing changes.

It would seem, then, that to hold on to this principle, we can think of something lasting through a period of time only if it changes in absolutely no way at all—not even in location. This certainly restricts the number of things that last. Except for these few unchanging things, the universe is populated by a huge number of different things, each lasting only an instant, replacing each other instantaneously. This is quite bizarre.

But worse still: the supposition that some things endure through a period of time by remaining utterly unchanged is also wrong. Even if a penny undergoes absolutely no physical change at all from one second to the next, it nevertheless changes in some respect: it becomes one second older. If the penny is one thousand seconds old now, in one second it won't be one thousand seconds old. Thus, by the principle, not even a physically unchanging penny can endure. It gets replaced by another one with a different characteristic (that is, a different age).

This principle, then, seems to imply the hugely surprising consequence that nothing endures. The reality we are aware of is not a world in which things last from one time till another; it is rather a world in which things exist only for an instant, then they disappear, replaced by something else usually rather similar. So you can't step into the same river twice.[2]

When you get a conclusion as bizarre as this, it's a good idea to try to find something that has gone wrong in your assumptions, or in your reasoning.

Try.

> Here's a suggested way of looking at matters that avoids these problems. Bobby and Robert in one sense are different things, though they are time-slices of one time-extended thing. Philosophers say they are distinct stages in a continuing object. So there's no problem for the principle in saying that Robert is a professor but Bobby isn't, since Bobby is Robert in a different stage from Robert. But we can also consider the person extended through time, constructed from, and including, Bobby and Robert and a whole lot of other stages. Let's call this extended thing R. Martin. Now, considering this R. Martin, there's still no problem with the principle. R. Martin has several characteristics: he's a professor-in-2001 and a kid-in-1948. No contradiction here. Can something change? Sure: it can be a kid-at-one-time, and a professor-at-another.

The Same Lump

But now another problem is suggested: when are a bunch of stages to be considered parts of the same continuing object?

When Descartes considers this problem he invites us to consider a lump of beeswax. It is hard, cold, round, white; it smells like flowers and makes a sound when you hit it. Put it next to the fire, and everything

---

[2] This saying derives from a report by Plato, *Cratylus*, 402A: "Heraclitus [c. 500 BC] is supposed to say that all things are in motion and nothing at rest; he compares them to the stream of a river, and says that you cannot go into the same water twice."

changes. Soon it is soft, hot, and transparent, shaped like a puddle, not a sphere. The smell disappears and it makes no sound when hit. It even increases somewhat in volume. But we are sure that this puddle is *the same thing* as the earlier lump. Descartes reasons that *something* must remain the same from one time to the other; he called this something "physical substance." Note that we don't perceive physical substance through our senses; what we see, hear, smell, feel, or taste changes. We sense only the the changing characteristics that attach to the bit of substance—the colours, temperatures, and so on. How, then, do we know that this physical substance is there? Descartes answers: "It is my mind alone which perceives it."[3]

This is not an answer that many people find satisfying. If you can't sense this something, how do you know when it's there? For all we know, maybe this something has also left when we put the wax next to the fire, and we now have a different thing. It must be by means of our senses that we determine that *this* is the same thing as *that*.

If you don't think Descartes is right, than why is this puddle the same thing as that lump? In other words: why do we consider those two stages as parts of the same continuing object? Here's one possible answer:

> The stages we see, including the earlier lump and the later puddle and the stages in-between, are *spatio-temporally continuous*. Imagine that we place the lump next to the fire at noon, and observe what happens until 1 p.m. At every instant, there is something there. Even if it moves somewhat, it describes a continuous path: at one instant, it is right next to where it was just before. That is to say: it is not the case that at one instant it's in one place, and at the next, there's nothing there, but something at another location far away. And there are no temporal gaps: a stage exists there at every instant during this time-span.
>
> When we get something that follows a spatio-temporally continuous path like this, we tend to think of it as one thing that lasts, rather than as a succession of different things. Imagine that instead there was spatial discontinuity: the lump disappeared at one place, and a lump simultaneously appeared a foot away. Then we might

---

[3] *Meditations*, II.

want to say that the lump disappeared, and a *different* lump appeared elsewhere. Or imagine that there was a temporal discontinuity: the lump disappeared at one place, then there were a few seconds when there was no lump there, and then a lump exactly like the one that disappeared appeared in exactly that spot. Again we might want to say that the lump disappeared, then later a *different* lump appeared in that place.

> Don LePan interestingly speculates that the medieval mind may have thought differently about cases that we count as continuing identity. He considers the Anglo-Saxon phrase "Forst sceal freosan" [Frost shall freeze]. What can that mean? Perhaps they reasoned: Water is not frozen, so therefore water cannot freeze. What happens when the temperature falls is that one entity (frost) is *created* to take the place of another (water) which vanishes.[4]

The Identity of My University

But the conditions for the continuing existence of the same thing through time do not always include spatio-temporal continuity. Consider the history of the university I work at. Several years after it was founded, it ran out of money and ceased to exist. A few years later, a generous benefactor donated a lot of money, and it started up again, at the same location. Was the university that started up after this time-lapse *the same university* as the one that earlier existed at that location?

It seems clear that the answer is Yes. We want to say that it was the same university starting up again, not a different one at the same place. Thus the university was temporally discontinuous.

A few years later, the university grew too large for its building downtown, and moved to new, roomier quarters. What happened (we can suppose) is that one night at midnight the university instantaneously popped out of existence downtown, and simultaneously a university popped into existence uptown. Is the university located uptown the same university as the one that had existed downtown?

---

[4] *The Cognitive Revolution in Western Culture*, Vol. I, pp. 64–65.

Again we're tempted to say Yes: it's the same university which has merely moved to another location. Note, however, that this move involves a spatial discontinuity. When moving, the university did not follow a spatially continuous path. It did not "travel" from one point to the other. Robie Street runs between the former campus and the new campus, but there was no time at which the university was crossing Robie Street.

SOME QUESTIONS TO THINK ABOUT: If you accept these answers, you must admit that universities, at least, can be spatially and temporally discontinuous. Is this possible for other sorts of things? Suppose the chair you're sitting on disappeared, and simultaneously a chair exactly like it reappeared at the other side of the room. Could you count the object that reappeared as the same chair? Or suppose it disappeared, and then a few minutes later, a chair exactly like it reappeared in exactly the same place; could this be the same chair? If you insist that these must be different chairs in both cases, then you would appear not to allow spatial or temporal discontinuity in ordinary physical objects like chairs. Is there a special *sort* of things that can have spatial or temporal discontinuities? Try to think of examples other than universities that can.

The Disappearing Boat

Sally is leaving for Tibet for a ten-year stay, so she lends her boat to George, after getting him to promise to make any repairs necessary, and to give it back to her when she gets back.

Soon after getting the boat, George notices a rotten plank in the hull. George rips out the rotten plank, throws it into his garage, and replaces it with a new one. But a week later, he discovers that the rudder is broken. He removes it, throws it into his garage, and installs a new one. Next week the carburetor breaks; George replaces it, keeping the old carburetor. Soon something else needs replacement, and then something else. George, true to his word, has all these jobs done.

Ten years of continuous repairs on Sally's boat have passed, and shortly before Sally's return George has replaced every last bit of Sally's boat. She returns from Tibet. George proudly returns the boat in beautiful working order, but Sally is upset. "That's not my boat!" she complains. "It's all different!" George explains how he's had to replace every bit of it over the ten years. But Sally still claims that this is not her boat, because not even one atom of this boat was part of the boat she lent George. She admits that this boat is better than the one she lent George (which was disintegrating badly); but she explains that she is sentimentally attached to her old boat, and she wants *her* boat back, not this new one.

George has an idea. Every old, rotten piece he took off the boat has been thrown into his garage. He takes all those pieces out and assembles them into a boat—a rotten boat indeed—and presents it to Sally. "That's my boat!" she exclaims. "But it's a complete wreck! And you promised to keep it repaired!"

Which boat is really Sally's?

SOME QUESTIONS TO THINK ABOUT: If the old wreck is really hers, then why didn't George keep it repaired? Why did he spend all that time and money repairing a boat that was not hers? But if the new one is really hers, why isn't she pleased to have it back? And isn't it odd that the boat she lent George and this boat share not even one atom of matter? And what about that old wreck, which contains almost exactly the same material as the one Sally left? When did the boat that George kept repairing stop being Sally's? Did the pile of junk in the garage turn into Sally's boat at exactly that time?

FOR FURTHER READING: This is a version of the classical philosophical puzzle known as "The Ship of Theseus," presented by Hobbes in *De Corpore* II, 11 (1650). Hobbes got the story from Plutarch's life of Theseus. Even in Plutarch's day (c. first century AD) the story, as Plutarch mentions, "afforded an example to the philosophers concerning the identity of things that are changed by addition" (§§ 22–23).

> Douglas Adams reports visiting the Gold Pavillion Temple in Kyoto, Japan, and being surprised how well it had stood up over the six centuries since it was built. He was told that it hadn't stood up well at all—in fact, it had burned down twice during the twentieth century. "So this isn't the original building?" he asked his Japanese guide. "But yes, of course it is," the guide insisted, while reporting, nevertheless, that the building had burnt down to the ground several times, and each time it was rebuilt with completely new materials. "So how can it be the same building?" Adams asked. "It is always the same building," the guide replied.
>
> Adams says that he found this point of view surprising but perfectly rational. The idea of the building, its intention, and its design remain the same. Only the materials change. "To be overly concerned with the original materi-

als, which are merely sentimental souvenirs of the past, is to fail to see the living building itself."[5]

The Metaphysical Architect

Years ago there was a very large, very ugly, old and shoddy wooden frame apartment building next door to the philosophy department offices where I worked. One day a sign went up on the building advertising the construction on that site of luxury condominiums, and in a week or two construction workers showed up and began several months of work on this building.

First they sawed the whole building off its foundation, and (incredibly) jacked the whole thing up several feet; then they excavated for a new basement, and poured concrete in for the basement walls and floor. When the new basement was done, they lowered the building back down. Next they removed one external wall of the whole house, and replaced it with a new one; then they did the same thing with the other external walls, one by one. Then they removed the whole roof and built a new roof in its place. Afterwards, they worked on replacing all the interior walls and floors.

Toward the end of this process, I was passing the building and noticed a man on the construction site wearing a hard hat, suit, and tie. Guessing that he was the construction foreman or supervising engineer or architect, I went up to him and introduced myself as a philosophy professor who worked next door. He was in fact the architect, so I told him that I had been watching the construction process and I was puzzled. It appeared that everything in the old building had been replaced, piece by piece. Wouldn't it have been much cheaper just to demolish the old building all at once, and then build the new one in the usual way? The architect agreed: the method of construction they were using cost much more than the usual method. The reason they were doing it the way they were, he explained, was that the building violated the zoning laws: it was contiguous to the sidewalk, while the zoning laws required some setback, and it occupied too large a proportion of the lot it was on. So if they tore down the old building, they wouldn't be allowed to build a new building of the same size and in the same position. But the zoning laws did not prohibit renovations to an old building which had been built before those laws were introduced. When they jacked up the old building and gave it a new basement, they were merely renovating the old building. Replacing an external wall was, similarly, just renovation. And so on, until every

---

[5] Douglas Adams and Mark Carwardine, *Last Chance to See* (London: Pan Books, 1991), p. 141.

molecule was replaced. So what they had here, now, was actually not a new building at all—it was the old building, completely renovated, and completely legal.

I complimented the architect on the ingenious solution to the zoning problems, and told him that, as a philosopher, I studied the sort of reasoning that he had used in reaching his solution. We both agreed that this was a welcome practical application of normally useless metaphysics.

3. THE IDENTITY OF ANIMALS AND PEOPLE

Rover and Clover

Shocking experiments have been performed in the biological laboratory of the terrifying Dr. Frank Northrup Stein. In one experiment, Dr. Stein drastically altered the genetic structure of all the chromosomes in the body of a live dog, so that the result was nothing like a dog's genetic structure. In the process, all Rover's cells were kept alive, but were disassembled into a formless pile that Dr. Stein calls "Clover."

Dr. Stein's associate, the insidious Dr. F. M. Chu, was away on vacation while this experiment was being performed. When he returned, he asked Dr. Stein where Rover was. "That disgusting pile of cells over there is Rover," replied Stein. "I've renamed him Clover."

Having examined Clover, Dr. Chu said, "That's not Rover. Rover was a dog, but Clover isn't. Clover doesn't have the bodily organization of a dog, or its genetic structure."

"Clover is too Rover," insisted Stein. "I've just made some changes in him. Remember when we administered growth hormone to Fido, and made him grow to twice the size in a few weeks? What resulted was still Fido, though he was a lot larger. And how about Spot? After we administered potassium felinate to him for a month, he turned into something that looked exactly like a cat, but it was still old Spot. All we did was to change Fido's and Spot's characteristics; even if you wouldn't guess by looking at them, they were still Fido and Spot."

"No, you're wrong, Frank," said Chu. "When you make some kinds of changes to the material that makes something up, sometimes the original thing doesn't exist any more. Remember when you got so mad at Dr. Karloff that you chopped up Greta, his Mercedes? That was a drastic reorganization of the materials that made up Greta, and the pile of rusty metal that's still out there in the parking lot isn't a car. So you can't say that that pile of metal is Greta. Greta hasn't just been changed—it's been destroyed. It doesn't exist any longer. If you just drilled some holes in Greta, or painted it purple, it would still be a car. Then Greta would still exist, with changes. If you change an X so that what's left isn't an X any more, the original X has been destroyed, not just altered."

"But, look, Chu," Stein replied, "I didn't destroy Rover. You know all that trouble we got into last year with the Animal Liberation Front after our Great Parakeet Massacre? Well, I'm being careful now. Nothing died during my Rover experiment. Clover is pretty weird, but he's alive. My techniques for altering genetic structure don't kill the animal. I can keep it alive even when it's a formless pile of cells. Rover didn't die, and Clover is alive. I've just renamed him. I can't have destroyed Rover if Rover didn't die."

But Chu wasn't convinced. "Rover doesn't exist any more, so he's been destroyed. I guess that what your experiment has really shown is that there are other ways of destroying a dog besides killing it."

Who is right?

FOR FURTHER READING: This example is adapted from M. Price, "Identity through Time," *Journal of Philosophy* 74 (1977), pp. 201–217. Price argues that Rover is Clover. This conclusion is disputed by Baruch A. Brody in Chapter 4 of *Identity and Essence* (Princeton: Princeton University Press, 1980).

Puzzling Rivers in Klopstokia

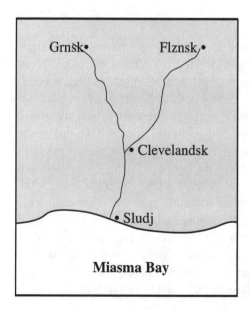

Here, at no extra charge, is a bonus to readers of this book: a handy map of southern Klopstokia:

In this map, we see the river system emptying into the bay in the south, and the four major cities in the area.

One of the major causes of the recent Klopstokian Civil War has been the disagreement between the two ethnic factions in the country concerning the river system. The Ethnic Free-donians, who live mainly in the west, insist that the Freedonia

River, which rises at Grnsk, flows all the way into Miasma Bay in the south, and that the shorter Sylvania River, which rises at Flznsk, is a tributary of the Freedonia, ending where it flows into the Freedonia at Clevelandsk. So Sludj and Grnsk are on the same river but Flznsk and Sludj are not. But the Ethnic Sylvanians, who live mainly in the east, are adamant that the mighty Sylvania River, which rises at Flznsk, flows all the way into Miasma Bay in the south, and that the shorter Freedonia River, which rises at Grnsk, is a tributary of the Sylvania, ending where it flows into the Sylvania at Clevelandsk. So Sludj and Flznsk are on the same river, but Grnsk and Sludj are not.

As a result of this dispute, Clevelandsk has been reduced to rubble in continual shelling by both sides.

The U.S. Ambassador, in an attempt to mediate the situation, proposes a compromise solution: that the Freedonia River rises at Grnsk and ends at Clevelandsk; that the Sylvania River rises at Flznsk and ends at Clevelandsk; that a third river, the Miasma River, is formed from the waters of the two tributaries at Clevelandsk, and flows from there to the bay. So Sludj is not on the same river as Grnsk, nor is it on the same river as Flznsk.

But the Russian Ambassador proposes a different solution: that the whole river system is the Miasma River: its West Branch rises at Grnsk, and its East Branch at Flznsk. So Sludj, Clevelandsk, Grnsk, and Flznsk are all on the same river.

The Russians argue with the Americans, and both argue with the two Klopstokian factions, about how many rivers there are, and where they start and end, and whether two cities are on the same river. Who is right?

> There are no facts of the matter. It's all merely a matter
> of what people want to say.

The Adventures of Amoeba-man

One day, Seymour Schmidlap develops a groove running across the top of his head. Over the succeeding weeks, the groove deepens, and runs down his forehead and nose, and down his back. Medical science is amazed and puzzled by these horrifying events. At last it is clear what is happening: Seymour is dividing in two, like an amoeba. As the two halves of his body separate more distinctly, each half begins growing back the other half it's missing. Soon the guy looks like a pair of Siamese twins;

but then there's complete separation, and each half, having grown everything it's missing, walks off—a complete person.

Each of them—call them Seymour-1 and Seymour-2—claims that he's Seymour Schmidlap. Each denies that the other is the real Seymour. Who is right?

> Here are four possible answers that might tempt you:
> 1. Seymour-1 is the real Seymour Schmidlap. Seymour-2 is just a look-alike, created at the time of the split.
> 2. Seymour-2 is the real Seymour Schmidlap. Seymour-1 is just a look-alike, created at the time of the split.
> 3. They're both wrong. The real Seymour Schmidlap has been destroyed. Both Seymour-1 and Seymour-2 are like the real one, but neither is him. Both were created at the time of the split.
> 4. They're both the real Seymour. Seymour Schmidlap now exists simultaneously in two different places.

Each answer has something to be said for it, and something against. But consider the Klopstokian River problem as an analogy to this one. What reaction to the Seymour problem does that suggest?

> It suggests that there are no facts of the matter. It's just up to us to decide what we feel like saying about it.

A QUESTION TO THINK ABOUT: But now imagine that all this happened to you. Don't you think that there would be a right answer to where, if anywhere, you ended up?

The Same Club

Suppose that a club ceases its regular meetings. Several years later, some of the members form a club with the same name and the same rules. Is this the same club as before, which has suffered (like my university) a temporary non-existence? Or is this club a brand-new one, with the same name and rules, and some of the same members?

The answer to this question isn't clear even though you know all the facts of the case that can possibly be relevant. The members can decide on whatever answer they like, but this would be arbitrary. The question seems to be *empty*—recall our discussion of empty questions in Chapter I.

Derek Parfit proposes this as an analogy to the question about Amoeba-man. He thinks that question is empty too, and can be answered only arbitrarily.[6]

Getting Someone Else's Body

Suppose that a number of lineworkers employed by an electric company have had accidents when live wires fall on them. Their protective clothing keeps them from being fatally electrocuted, but they do sometimes suffer total amnesia. To protect their workers from this disaster, the company buys a craniorecorder. This machine consists of a little metal hat connected by wires to a huge computer. The hat gets strapped on your head, and the computer reads out and records all the patterns set up in your brain. The machine can also reprogram brains in accord with the stored information. Each morning each worker's brain contents are recorded; if they suffer amnesia, their old memories are restored by the machine.

One day, a live wire falls on Harry and Hortense, and both of them suffer amnesia. Each is attached to the craniorecorder for memory restoration, but the technician programs the machine wrong, and Hortense's old memories go into Harry's body, and Harry's into Hortense's body. When both wake up, they are deeply surprised to look in the mirror and see bodies of the opposite sex from the one they are used to. The craniorecorder technician tries to get them back into the machine to set things right, but both refuse. Harry, it turns out, has always yearned to be able to swim really well. Hortense used to be a champion swimmer, and her body is perfectly trained for this. Similarly, Harry's body is that of a trained boxer, and Hortense has always wanted to be able to box. Besides, they both get kinky pleasure out of inhabiting the body of the opposite sex.

Are you convinced by this fable that what has taken place is a body transplant: that Harry has now been given Hortense's body? Consider the physical item that was Hortense's body before the accident. Is it now inhabited by Harry? Or should we say it's still Hortense, but it has been mistakenly programmed with Harry's memories and personality? Whoever is now in that body thinks that he/she is Harry, but is that person correct? To which body should Harry's paycheck be issued?

If you are convinced that memories make the person, and that Harry now inhabits Hortense's body, consider this amended fable: imagine that

---

[6] Derek Parfit, *Reasons and Persons* (Oxford: Oxford University Press, 1984).

one morning Arnold, Mildred, and Francine have their brain-patterns re-corded; but the craniorecorder technician hates all these people, and he maliciously reprograms Mildred's *and* Francine's brain with Arnold's patterns, and reprograms Arnold's brain with Mildred's patterns. Then he erases all the recordings. On awakening, Mildred's former body and Francine's former body both claim to be Arnold. Both have equal claim to be Arnold. Should we say that they are both Arnold? But doesn't that make them the same person—namely Arnold? What happens after one body skips lunch while the other one eats: is Arnold then both hungry and not hungry? Should Arnold's two new bodies split Arnold's paycheck? Are they both married to Arnold's wife? What happened to Francine? Should the technician be charged with Francine's murder?

Keeping Your Own Body

If you were convinced in the previous section ("**Getting Someone Else's Body**") that we should say that Harry is transplanted into Hortense's body, consider the following.

Suppose Harry is told, one day, that a live wire will fall on him to-morrow. He's understandably horrified; a terribly painful thing is about to happen to him. Now, suppose additional information is supplied: he will, in addition to the pain, suffer total amnesia as a result. Now his horror grows: not only pain, but amnesia! But there is more information: Hortense's memories will be implanted in the brain of his current body. Still more anguish! Harry doesn't want to get this whole pile of fake memories. He'd rather have no memories at all than be in the even worse state of getting all those bogus memories. But this is not the end of the story: in addition, Harry is told, his old memories will be stuck into Hortense's body. This makes things even worse. Harry cries: "They're *my* memories! I'm really fond of many of them. I don't even like Hortense! I don't want her to get them!"

This might seem to be a reasonable attitude to have. But note that Harry is identifying his future self as the one that will occupy his body. If the interpretation we gave to the fable above is correct, Harry is wrong. Do you think he's wrong?

> "I can't explain *myself*, I'm afraid, sir," said Alice, "be-cause I'm not myself, you see."
> "I don't see," said the Caterpillar.
> —Lewis Carroll, *Alice's Adventures in Wonderland*

FOR FURTHER READING: For a discussion of a thought-experiment similar to the Harry/Hortense story, see Bernard Williams, "The Self and the Future." This article first appeared in *The Philosophical Review* 79, no. 2 (April 1970). It's reprinted in *Personal Identity*, ed. John Perry (Berkeley: University of California Press, 1975), pp. 179–198. The theory that memories make for personal identity was perhaps first stated by John Locke in his *Essay Concerning Human Understanding*, 2nd ed. (1694), Chapter 27. Since then many philosophers have endorsed, modified, or at least discussed this view. The Perry book contains several relevant articles and excerpts.

Two Places are Better Than One

It is said that medieval popes granted some of their bishops the gift of *bilocation*—the ability to be in two different places at the same time. F. P. Siegfried, writing in *The Catholic Encyclopedia,* says that the possibility of bilocation of a body is denied by St. Thomas, Vasquez, Silv. Maurus, and many others: "The instances of bilocation narrated in lives of the saints can be explained, they hold, by phantasmal replications or by aerial materializations." But Scotus, Bellarmine, Suarez, DeLugo, Franzelin, and many others defend the possibility of bilocation.

What's interesting about bilocation for our purposes is how it might—or might not—be consistent with the criteria for human identity: if there were simultaneous appearances at two different places, that looked for all the world like St. Fred, could we possibly count both of them as him?

What's also interesting is that intelligent medieval thinkers could believe in such a bizarre phenomenon. We've already talked about how the medievals managed to hold a similar crazy belief: see **Believing in Angels** in Chapter XII.

Belief in bilocation is not limited to medieval times. A web page devoted to Padre Pio, a *twentieth*-century mystic, affirms:

The phenomenon of bilocation is one of the most remarkable gifts attributed to Padre Pio. His appearances on various of the continents are attested by numerous eyewitnesses, who either saw him or smelled the odors characteristically associated with his presence, described by some as roses and by others as tobacco. The phenomenon of odor (sometimes called the odor of sanctity) is itself well established in Padre Pio's case. The odor was especially strong from the blood coming from his wounds. Investigation showed that he used absolutely no fragrances or anything that could produce these odors. The odors often occurred when people called upon his intercession in prayer and continue to this day....

As to how Padre Pio with God's help accomplished such feats, the closest he ever came to an explanation of bilocation was to say that it occurred "by an extension of his personality."[7]

She's So Hard to See

Another entirely unlikely phenomenon that some people manage to believe in is called Human Spontaneous Involuntary Invisibility. A leading researcher on this is Donna Higbee, CHT. (I don't know what those letters stand for.) In her website she gives several examples, including this one:

> Melanie in Ventura, California, became invisible while sitting on her own living room sofa and staring at the wall, lost in her own thoughts. Her husband was walking around the house looking for her but could not see her sitting there, only several feet away from where he was walking. This lasted for approximately ten minutes, then she was suddenly visible again. Her husband was quite upset with her and thought she had been hiding from him. She assured him that she had been sitting there all along, but to this day, he does not believe her.[8]

Whoo! Don't that make the hairs stand up on the back of your neck? Twilight Zone or what??

Anyway, what's relevant about this for our purposes is again what is presupposed about human identity: what makes it possible for the same person to exist while undergoing some rather strange changes.

---

[7] http://www.ewtn.com/padrepio/mystic/bilocation.htm

[8] http://users1.ee.net/pmason/invisibility.html

What It Takes to Be in Heaven

Most religions don't believe people take their bodies to heaven.

> In Christian lore, there are a few exceptions, one of whom
> is the Virgin Mary. According to the Doctrine of the Bodily
> Assumption of the Virgin, when she died her body was taken
> to heaven along with her soul. In certain paintings you can
> see her flying up into the air like a guided missile.

When ordinary humans die, however, their bodies remain on Earth, turning rapidly into something unpleasant.

Without a body your existence would be rather different. It's hard to see how you could continue to ice skate, play the piano, or read the newspaper in heaven, when you have no feet, hands, or eyes. In at least its more sophisticated versions, Christianity generally holds that our activities in heaven would be of a more rarefied form, involving activities such as enjoyment of the full consciousness of God's presence. For this sort of thing, presumably, you wouldn't need a body.

The problem here is: on what grounds could it be said that *you* were in heaven? If something existed in heaven after your death, why think that it's *you*?

We found it plausible to identify the same thing through time, in the case of Descartes' lump of wax, by means of spatio-temporal continuity. But this doesn't seem to work when somebody "goes" to heaven. Although heaven was considered to be a place, at least by early Christians and nowadays by children in Sunday school, more sophisticated contemporary Christians think differently. And even if it were a place, then how could we trace the path of a non-material soul through space as it went there, to make sure that we're still locating the same person? But maybe persons resemble universities rather than lumps of wax: their continued existence does not require spatio-temporal continuity.

On one view, as we've seen, what makes somebody the *same person* as one identified earlier is that the later person remembers experiences the earlier one had. If this is the criterion for personal identity through time, then in order for that person to be *you* in heaven, that person must remember your experiences on earth. At least according to our current scientific views, memory is stored in the physical brain. It's difficult to see how memories can be carried to heaven when you leave your brain behind. But, of course, science doesn't know everything. This is another one of those religious mysteries about which science must be mute.

But even supposing that the memories physically encoded in your present brain could somehow be transferred into your heavenly person, there is a further difficulty: would you even have a *mind* in heaven, capable of retrieving those stored memories and of thinking about your past? Could you do any sort of mental activity in heaven? Could you even enjoy the full consciousness of God's presence? Science tells us that any sort of mental activity depends on a working brain; once again, we have a religious mystery beyond our ken.

However, not everyone shares the view that memory continuity is what constitutes the continued existence of a person. In some religious belief, the soul that is supposed to be immortal isn't a mind, but something else. It's the thing that makes a person the same person from moment to moment, and that continues after bodily death. So that will be *you* in heaven, although you will have neither mind nor body. This view is very much like Descartes' account of what accounts for the continuing identity of the lump of wax, and is equally hard to understand or apply.

It's dangerous to claim that you believe in something about which you have so little understanding. The danger is that your thoughts are so incoherent and mysterious that you don't really believe anything at all. In all of this, we must be very careful that we are not merely talking nonsense.

Why You Shouldn't Fear Death

> "I'm not afraid of dying. I just don't want to be there when it happens." — Woody Allen

The Roman philosopher Lucretius, whose proof of the infinity of space we looked at in Chapter X, was a thoroughgoing materialist, arguing that a person is nothing but a working physical body. It's obvious that the physical body stops working at death, so post-mortem survival is out of the question.

The religious doctrine of the afterlife is often thought to be an attempt to help us cope with our fears of death; but Lucretius, interestingly, argued that this religious doctrine actually encourages those fears, and that his anti-religious materialistic views, which had the consequence that the person is extinguished at death, actually had the consequence that death is not to be feared.

> Therefore death to us
> Is nothing, nor concerns us in the least,
> Since nature of mind is mortal evermore.
> And just as in the ages gone before
> We felt no touch of ill...

...thus when we are no more,
When comes that sundering of our body and soul
Through which we're fashioned to a single state,
Verily naught to us, us then no more,
Can come to pass, naught move our senses then-
No, not if earth confounded were with sea,
And sea with heaven.[9]

SOME QUESTIONS TO THINK ABOUT: Aristotle thought that the dead can be harmed (see **Harming the Dead** in Chapter XV below.) He didn't really give arguments for this, but he thought that it was a common view. Does this make any sense to you?

Lucretius gives two reasons that we shouldn't fear death: that when we're dead, we can't be harmed; and that being dead (= not existing) is the state we were in before we were born, which doesn't seems to us to be a state inspiring fear. Do these ideas help you with your fear of death? Maybe Lucretius misdiagnosed the causes of that fear.

We'll have a look at a second philosophical argument that tries to diminish our fear of death in the section called **What Happens to Somebody Who Is Hardly Me**, in Chapter XV. This surprising argument is based on some of the considerations concerning personal identity we've been talking about in the present chapter.

> Jeremy Bentham was among the most important British philosophers of the eighteenth century. When he died in 1832, in accord with his will his body was preserved and put on display. The body (called Bentham's "Auto-Icon") is now in a glass case stored in the University College of London. Photos are on various websites; try http://www.bartlett.ucl.ac.uk/web/Nina/JBentham.html
>
> There's a story that Bentham carried around in his pocket, for years before he died, two glass eyes for the Auto-Icon's head. But the preservation process for his head went badly wrong, leaving it noseless and giving it a very peculiar expression, so a wax head was put on top of Bentham's clothed and seated body, and his head, complete with glass eyes, was put in a closed box between his feet. Frequently stolen by students for various purposes (including football practice), the real head was at last removed from the glass case and kept safely in the college vaults.

---

9 "On the Nature of Things" is a common translation of Lucretius's poem called "De Rerum Natura" in Latin. This selection is in Book iii. Translated by William Ellery Leonard.

According to another story, the Auto-Icon regularly attends meeting of the College Council, whose minutes record "Jeremy Bentham—present but not voting."

Various explanations have been proposed why Bentham chose this fate for his body. One plausible one has it that he wanted to provide a visible sceptical response to the religious story about death.

4. IDENTITY AND ESSENCE

Here's a third important way that the word 'identity' shows up in philosophy. In this sense, we don't talk about two things being identical with each other (or of one thing being "identical" with that same thing at another time), but rather of the identity of a single thing at a single time. This is the sense of the word you're using when you think about your "identity"—what makes you *you*.

One way of thinking about this kind of identity is that some sort of characteristic is so important to something that if it lost that characteristic it would cease to exist.

Here's an example. Consider a statue of Elvis made out of bronze. Over time, the statue will turn from shiny metallic to dull brown to cruddy greenish, as it oxidizes and gets pooped on by the pigeons. But it will still exist—it will just be a different colour. But imagine that one day someone who (if such a thing is possible!) doesn't like Elvis smashes that statue to bits, or runs it through a car crusher, or melts it down and pours the bronze into a different-shaped mold, so that when it hardens it's a statue of Dmitri Shostakovich (Soviet composer, 1906–1975). In any of these cases, we'd say that the statue was destroyed. So it seems that a drastic change of shape of the material constitutes the destruction of the statue, whereas the statue survives a drastic change of colour.

This sort of characteristic—which is so important to something that changing it constitutes the destruction of the thing—is often called by philosophers an *essential* characteristic. This contrasts with what is called an accidental characteristic; the thing survives a change here. The shape of a statue is essential, but the colour is not.

You might be reminded here of the talk of "identity" that goes on a good deal in political and moral contexts nowadays. It's sometimes claimed that features of the culture of various ethnic minorities are so important to them that they constitutes those people's identity. For example, the language of an ethnic group is often supposed to be part of the identity of the people in that group, and that wiping out that language is actually a form of genocide, because this and other aspects of their culture are parts of the "identity" of the individual people.

But let's be careful here. People who talk this way do not mean that the language of a minority group is so important to that group that an individual would literally cease to exist if deprived of the use of the language (in the way that the Elvis statue literally ceases to exist when deprived of its shape). When the Irish language was almost wiped out in Ireland by the colonial English, for example, this didn't constitute the extermination of any Irish people. Those people continued to exist even when they were forced to learn and speak English.

Notoriously, it was a fairly widespread aim of the mainstream European-origin majority in Canada up until a few decades ago to wipe out every aspect of aboriginal culture. They weren't quite successful, but imagine that they were, and that the Canadian aboriginal people had been thoroughly assimilated into the mainstream culture. What would have happened, then, would be that the Mi'kmaq people of Nova Scotia would have ceased to exist as a group, though this needn't have involved the ceasing to exist of any Mi'kmaq individuals.

A QUESTION TO THINK ABOUT: Do you find it paradoxical that a group of things (or people) can cease to exist even though all the things (or people) in that group continue to exist? This sort of phenomenon is quite ordinary. Consider the group of people (Aaron, Betty, Carl, Debby, etc.) who constitute the group of students of the South Carolina Academy of Theology. When SCAT closes down, Aaron, Betty, Carl, Debby, etc. transfer to other institutions. There are no longer any students of SCAT—that group has ceased to exist. But Aaron, Betty, Carl, Debby, etc., continue to exist, and the group seems to consist of nothing but the individuals that constitute it. How can it disappear when those individuals still exist? When it disappears, what exactly goes missing from the universe?

The Ethics of Minority Identity

The culture of minority groups is, of course, extremely important for several reasons. The existence of a variety of cultures is good in itself, and individual people sometimes find themselves rootless and despairing, without a sense of self and prone to disastrous life failures, without their old cultural surroundings, inside what is, for them, for a while, a foreign culture.

These considerations sometimes lead to a genuine ethical dilemma. Usually the continuing destruction of aboriginal culture is not due nowadays to government policy or the actions of the European-origin majority; rather, a more important factor is the attractiveness of mainstream culture to the young aboriginal people who may prefer cars, shopping malls, and cell phones to the traditional aboriginal life in the bush, which anyone would find difficult. So well-meaning outsiders have taken it on themselves to try to get them to want to maintain their traditions, despite how they feel. The paradox here is that these people are again being pushed into something against their will by the mainstream culture.

5. INTO THE MAINSTREAM OF PHILOSOPHY

Philosophers have noted that certain words in our language—'here,' 'now,' and 'I,' for example—function peculiarly in that they work, as it were, by pointing at something, not by naming or describing it. That's why they vary systematically in what is indicated in ways that other bits of the language do not. The name 'Fred Schmidlap,' for example, refers to the same guy no matter who says it or when; but 'I' refers to a large number of people, and depends on who utters the word. Problems result from this difference when we try to explain what somebody knows in terms of the sentence that expresses that person's belief. There's a definite external fact that I know about when I believe the belief expressed by the sentence, 'Fred Schmidlap is at Sturdley's Pub.' But what do I know when I know what's expressed by the sentence, 'I am here now'? This problem is revealed when we consider what's communicated—if anything—by saying that sentence to somebody else. Notice that what *you* know (if anything) might be quite a different matter from what you tell somebody else when you say this.

I am, unfortunately, unaware of any appropriate introductory readings you might consult to pursue these puzzling matters. The stout of heart might attempt to read Simon Blackburn's *Spreading the Word* (Oxford: Clarendon Press, 1984). He gets into these matters at the end of a book that goes quite deeply into matters in the philosophy of language.

Appropriate readings giving more puzzles and considering several proposed solutions concerning matters of identity are easier to come by. I can strongly recommend John Perry's *A Dialogue on Personal Identity and Immortality* (Indianapolis: Hackett, 1978); this is an easy and informal discussion, in dialogue form, about many of the issues discussed in this chapter. Perry's anthology, *Personal Identity* (Berkeley: University of California Press, 1975), contains a wide selection of articles by many philosophers dealing with personal identity at an appropriate level.

The Canadian philosopher Will Kymlicka has written thoughtfully and interestingly on the ethical issues of the kind of "identity" talked about at the end of this chapter.

CHAPTER XIV

WHY SHOULD I BE MORAL?

1. THE STUDENT AND THE MATCH

In everyday life, we often do what's morally right merely out of habit. Acting morally often has its costs, however, and sometimes we are tempted to act in our self-interest instead.

I posed this question to some students I once had in a class: "Suppose somebody asked you for a match. It doesn't cost you very much to give it to her, but it costs you something. Should you do it?" My students replied that they thought they should. "Why?" I asked. Here are some replies. Do you agree with them?

> "Some day I might need a favour from her. If I gave her that match, she'd be more likely to help me out when I needed it. If I didn't, she'd feel less kindly toward me, and wouldn't help me out later."

"Well," I continued, "suppose you'll never run into that person again. Should you help her then?"

> "Yeah, but how can you be sure you'll never see her again? Maybe you will, right?"

They refused to let me raise the question the way I wanted to. Teaching philosophy is sometimes a difficult thing. I said, "Look, suppose you're absolutely sure, for some reason, that you'll really never see her again. Like maybe you're in an airport in a distant city about to leave, and you're sure you'll never go back to that city again. What would you do then?"

They saw the problem. There was a widespread look of puzzlement. One replied:

> "I never exactly realized this before, but now that you put the matter that way, I can see that there's no reason to give her that match. I wouldn't do it."

Further discussion did not succeed in convincing this student to give away that match. I think I may have succeeded in turning a perfectly nice person into a nasty creep. Another triumph for philosophical education!

A QUESTION TO THINK ABOUT: Why, after all, should you be moral, if there isn't anything in it for you?

The Ring of Gyges

Plato raises the problem we have just noticed by telling another imaginary tale, known as the fable of the ring of Gyges. Glaucon, a character in Plato's *Republic*, tells the story: Gyges discovers a magic ring that turns the wearer invisible. Even the most firmly just of men, Glaucon argues, would act immorally if he possessed such a ring:

> No man is so adamantine-souled that he would go on being just and keep his hands off other men's things, if he were free to take whatever he desired, go into any store or house, get into any bed, put anyone to death, or let anyone out of prison as the idea came to him.... And this makes it clear that no one is willingly just. They are only forced to be just. For every man, if he is able to do wrong, does wrong. For he sees that to do wrong will profit him more than to do right....

> > You might be interested to know what Gyges does with the aid of his ring. He arrives in court, makes himself invisible, seduces the queen, and with her help kills the king and takes over the kingdom. What's remarkable about this is *the queen's* behaviour: having been seduced by an invisible man, she conspires with him, presumably while he is still invisible, to kill her husband and to give this invisible man the kingdom.

FOR FURTHER READING: Plato tells this story in *Republic*, Book II: The translation I've given here is by I. A. Richards (Cambridge: Cambridge University Press, 1966). Plato argues (through his spokesman in the book, Socrates) that ultimately it's not to one's advantage to act immorally, even if one can get away with it.

> "Conscience is the inner voice that warns us somebody is looking."—H. L. Mencken

When God Tells You to Do Evil

Some people think that the source of moral truth is God's will. Many philosophers (including believers) have argued that this is wrong—that to say that something is good because God desires it has things backwards. It's not good because God desires it: God desires it because it's good. So it's still an open question what makes something good.

Here's a picturesque way of putting this argument. Suppose suddenly one day angelic forms appear among the clouds, playing trumpets. The sky splits down the middle; lightning and thunder ensue. You hear a huge, deep voice. "This is God speaking," the voice says. "I have a message for you. You've been trying to be a good person, but you have it all wrong. My will is for you to murder, cheat, lie, steal, torture kittens, and throw your empty beer cans on your professor's lawn. Go and do it!"

No matter what fireworks accompanied this event, and no matter how huge and deep the voice was, you wouldn't believe that it was God. Why not? Because what the voice told you to do was so clearly wrong. It can't be God, because God wouldn't tell you to do bad things.

Why didn't you decide, instead, that you were wrong about your morality? The story appears to show that, rather than reasoning that something is good if God says it, you *first* have an idea of what's good, *then* you judge on this basis whether something represents the will of God.

2. THE PRISONER'S DILEMMA

A Deal for the Prisoners

Suppose you and an accomplice have committed a crime. The police have evidence sufficient only to give each of you a two-year sentence; but they want to get at least one of you in jail for longer. If one of you confessed, giving evidence against the other, they could do this. So they put you in separate cells so the two of you can't communicate with each other, and then they come talk to you in your cell. They offer you this deal: If both of you keep silent, you yourself will get two years; but if you confess and he doesn't, then you'll get only one year. If you confess and he does too, then you'll get three years. If you stay silent and he talks, then you'll get four years. This is all very confusing, so you construct the following table to clarify things:

	He confesses	He doesn't confess
I confess	I get 3 yrs. in jail	I get 1 yr. in jail
I don't confess	I get 4 yrs. in jail	I get 2 yrs. in jail

Inside the table are listed the four possible consequences for you, given your action and that of your accomplice.

The police also say that the same deal is being offered to your accomplice. You're only interested in minimizing your own sentence; you don't care how long your accomplice stays in jail. What should you do?

Consider this line of reasoning:

> You don't know whether your accomplice will confess or not. Suppose he does. Then you'll get three years if you confess, and four if you keep silent. So if he confesses, you're better off confessing too.
>
> Now, suppose he doesn't confess. Then you'll get one year if you confess, and two years if you keep silent. So if he doesn't confess, you'll be better off if you confess.
>
> So whatever he does, you're better off if you confess. So you confess.

Your accomplice, in his cell, was given the same deal, and he draws the same table to clarify his thinking. He reasons exactly as you do, and he comes to the same conclusion. So he confesses too.

Both of you then get sentenced to three years in jail. But something has gone wrong here. Can you see what?

> If neither of you confessed, both of you would get a two-year sentence, and each of you would be better off.

This is a somewhat paradoxical situation: each of you has reasoned correctly about what would serve your own self-interest best. But this has resulted in a fairly poor outcome for both of you. If both of you had kept silent, both of you would have been better off. But given the situation, how could either of you have arranged this?

> You might have made a deal with your accomplice that neither of you would confess. Suppose you were not isolated in separate cells, but that you were together and could communicate. So you promise each other that you will cooperate by keeping silent.

But then the police take you out of your joint cell and ask you what you want to do. Notice that the table above *still* describes your situation: even if he keeps his part of the deal and stays silent, you're better off if you confess. Why keep your promise? You'd be better off if you didn't. And when the police ask him, he realises the same thing. You're right back in the same mess.

It's often thought that this situation represents, in miniature simplified form, a problem that is of central importance in ethics and political theory. Consider, for example, the ethical question: is it wrong to tell a lie? It seems that there are many particular circumstances in which it would be to my advantage to lie to others, whether or not they choose to tell me the truth, and to their advantage to lie to me. Nevertheless, if we all told the truth, we would all be better off in the long run, because we could get to trust each other's words: we could rely on each other in ways that would bring us the benefits of social cooperation. Thus lying is analogous to confessing in the prisoner's dilemma. If we could make a deal to pick the "cooperative" solution (by telling the truth in this case, keeping silent in the prisoner's dilemma), then we'd all be better off. But the deal would have to stick; there's always the temptation to "defect" from this cooperative arrangement, for one's own self-interest.

SOME QUESTIONS TO THINK ABOUT: In real life, what mechanisms do we use to arrive at such social "deals"? How do we get them (by and large) to stick? Might this line of thought provide an answer to Glaucon?

The Tragedy of the Commons

Suppose that our city has a publicly-owned grassy area of land in its centre. We all like having this grassy expanse in the middle of the concrete jungle. There are sidewalks built through the grassy commons, but when we're in a hurry we could get across the commons a lot faster by walking across the grass. You're just about to cut across the grass, and I stop you to try to convince you not to. Here is a transcript of our conversation.

Me: Don't do that!
You: Why not?
Me: We all like that grass there, and walking across it will kill it.
You: I like that grass as much as you do. But it takes a lot of walking across grass to kill it. If I walk across the grass right now, the resulting damage will be absolutely unnoticeable. It wouldn't even make a difference if I walked across it every time I was in a hurry. Grass is stronger than that.

>*Me:* Well, that's true. But what if everybody reasoned as you do? Then everyone would walk across the grass, and it would be dead, and we'd all be much worse off.
>
>*You:* Look, I agree that if everybody walked across the grass, then the grass would certainly be dead. But then it would hardly matter what I did, would it? Anyway, we're just talking about *me*. I don't want *everyone* to walk across the grass, but what I do won't *make* everyone else do it.

Is there something wrong with this reasoning?

> The Tragedy of the Commons is that if this line of reasoning is correct for you (as it seems to be) then it is correct for everyone else in town. As a result, everyone reasons this way, everyone walks across the grass, and it dies.

A QUESTION TO THINK ABOUT: Do you see why this is another illustration in the general form of the Prisoner's Dilemma?

Coca-Cola Morality

"What if everyone did that?" This is the question that is often supposed to be the key to moral reasoning. You can see now why the question is relevant. We can all solve our prisoner's dilemmas and prevent outcomes like the tragedy of the commons by acting in a way such that we'd all be better off if everyone acted that way, and by refraining from actions that would have bad results if everyone did them.

But this sort of moral thought sometimes seems to result in some pretty foolish conclusions. Consider, for example, a trivial, perfectly ordinary, and morally innocent action like going to the corner store to buy a can of Coke on a Tuesday evening. What would happen if *everybody* descended on that corner store to buy Coke at exactly that time?

> The result would certainly be disaster. Mobs of people would be trying to get into that little store. The crush would be enormous; that whole part of town would be immobilized. There would be pushing and shoving; things would get broken, and riots might break out. The store would quickly run out of Coke, and almost everyone would have to fight their way home through the mob, Cokeless.

The conclusion that your innocent action is immoral is obviously stupid. What has gone wrong with the reasoning here?

> The answer we're tempted to give is that everyone is *not* going to descend on the store, so there's nothing to fear.

But what if everyone reasoned that way?

Why We Should Hire a Dictator

In his book *Leviathan*, published in 1651, Thomas Hobbes considered the problem for which the Prisoner's Dilemma provides a miniature model. He imagined a "state of nature" in which humanity might have existed prior to the development of society. In this anarchic state, each person seeks his or her own well-being; the result is constant conflict, in which we compete for benefits and attempt to dominate over the others: a "war, where every man is enemy to every man." In this uncooperative state, our lives are, in Hobbes's famous phrase, "solitary, poor, nasty, brutish, and short."

The solution to this problem, Hobbes argued, is a deal: a "social contract" for cooperation. To ensure that nobody defects, we create the position of "sovereign"—a ruler with absolute power to enforce this contract and to punish all defectors. This dictator deprives us all of our personal liberty and restrains each person's natural tendency to seek power over others and to grab their goods. Thus the origin and the justification of the sovereign state.

This removes the Prisoner's Dilemma by changing the results of the participants' choices. Consider the Tragedy of the Commons: when you walk across the grass, you get punished by the police. This makes walking across the grass—the "defection" option—much less attractive than the "cooperative" one, no matter what other people do.

Hobbes argued that the only sort of state in which the war of each against all can be prevented, and in which it will be in our self-interest to pick the cooperative solution, is one ruled by a despotic tyrant with complete power. The problems with this arrangement are, of course, that our own freedoms are drastically reduced, and that we might be unable to prevent sovereigns from acting in ways not conducive to everyone's welfare—for example, when sovereigns decide to use their absolute power for their *own* benefit. The modern liberal state is designed to be responsive to the will of the governed, and to guarantee individual rights. The question is, however, whether the arrangements in the liberal state will work to solve our Prisoner's Dilemma. In a modern liberal state, people can take advantage of this limitation on governmental sovereignty by using their individual freedom to defect from the contract.

A QUESTION TO THINK ABOUT: Suppose that a society has installed a sovereign who enforces cooperative actions by punishing defectors. Now the people in the society, on the whole, behave cooperatively because they're afraid of being punished if they don't. But is this really *moral* behaviour? Is someone who does something nice because they'll be punished if they didn't really acting out of moral commitment?

FOR FURTHER READING: Thomas Hobbes, *Leviathan*, Chapter 13.

Toucha Smasha

There is a way that we might be able to make a contract work, even if there's no sovereign with total power to enforce it.

We all realise that the best situation for everyone would be if we all cooperated. So we're each willing to cooperate provided that we won't be made a sucker by other people's defections. If we could be reasonably confident the other person won't defect, then we won't defect either. Once someone else defects on us, however, all deals are off, and we won't cooperate the next time.

So what we want to do is to cooperate with people who we think would cooperate with us. People who cooperated with us the last time we interacted are likely to do it the next time. So it would help a lot if we've already had some interaction with people we meet, so we can recognize them as probable cooperators or defectors. In a small town, people tend to interact with the same people over and over, and to recognize who can be counted on to cooperate and who can't. That's why people tend to be nicer in small towns. But in larger cities, we interact with lots of people we haven't interacted with before, so we can't tell whether they're cooperators or defectors. Maybe it's too much of a risk to cooperate with someone who might defect on you. That's why there's more nastiness in larger cities.

But in general, in a society that's working reasonably well, people tend to be nice to strangers. If they can make strangers think that they are cooperators, then the strangers might cooperate with them, and everyone will be better off.

But some people want to demonstrate to strangers that they are noncooperators. Here's an example.

Years ago I used to live in an apartment several blocks away from my office, and every day I'd walk the same route into work in the morning. On most of these mornings, there was a car parked on my route with a bumper sticker on it that said: "Mafia Staff Car. You toucha my car, I smasha you face."

Almost every day as I walked to work, I thought about this bumper sticker. Its message would be offensive to some Italians—but it also (semi-humourously) threatened violence to just anyone who touched the car. Of course, the humour, such as it was, acted to defuse the aggression somewhat, but not altogether. I meditated each morning on what sort of a person would see this bumper sticker in the store and say to himself, "Cool! I'll buy that wonderful object for my car!" The sort of person who wants to offer a violent message to random strangers, gratuitously. As I walked along, musing on this matter, I chanted to myself, in time with my steps, "Toucha Smasha Toucha Smasha."

> I've seen a similar message on stickers attached to the back of trucks:
>
> HOW'S MY DRIVING?
> CALL 1-800-FUCK-YOU

SOME QUESTIONS TO THINK ABOUT: If this sort of implicit social contract—I'll cooperate with you if you cooperate with me—is the basis of morality, then it seems that we have no moral duties to animals, with whom we can have no such understanding. Well, maybe you can imagine that you have a sort of a deal with your dog: you help him and he helps you. But it's hard to imagine this sort of arrangement with something as dumb as your pet canary. Nevertheless, you do have moral obligations to your canary—to feed the thing and not to torture it—right? So maybe an implicit social contract is not the basis of all morality.

Why, by the way, do we have moral obligations to animals?

3. THE PARADOX OF DETERRENCE

Bombing the Russians

Here is a situation that's related to the Prisoner's Dilemma. It's known as the Paradox of Deterrence.

Suppose you're the President of the United States; it's 1960, and the Cold War is in full swing. The Soviet Union has developed the atomic bomb, and they are expansionist and belligerent. You are afraid that they might make a "first strike," attacking the U.S. with their atomic bombs, or maybe invade an ally. In order to prevent an attack, you threaten them with massive nuclear retaliation.

There was widespread feeling that this policy was immoral. But can you see how it could be argued that this policy is morally justified?

> You don't *want* to bomb the Soviet Union. But unless you threaten them with retaliation, they might attack you. This threat probably will prevent an attack, and after all, that's what we want.

This reasoning, of course, is a matter of some debate; but notice that it was apparently correct during the Cold War. During those years, neither side attacked the other. It's highly unusual in history to have two powerful enemies who manage not to go to war over such a long period.

Now, imagine that for some bizarre reason, the Soviets have just bombed Pittsburgh. Should you order the massive nuclear retaliation you threatened them with, and destroy Leningrad in retaliation?

> Bombing Leningrad is wrong. You would bring about nothing but needless destruction, suffering, and death if you destroyed Leningrad. The Soviets (you have reason to think) just wanted to destroy Pittsburgh, and won't be tempted to bomb more of your cities; so you won't prevent future harm to the U.S. by retaliating. Your choices are, then, either suffer the destruction of Pittsburgh without retaliation; or cause a additional large amount of useless destruction to Leningrad. Clearly it would be immoral to do the second thing.

Nevertheless, it *was* moral to threaten such massive retaliation, since only by that threat did you stand a good chance of preventing the Soviet attack. Well, it was the best bet, but it failed.

There is a paradox here. Massive retaliation is wrong, and you know it. To intend to retaliate is thus evil. But *having* that evil intention was good, since it stood a very good chance of preventing anyone from bombing anyone. The paradox is that having the intention to do something evil is a good thing.

And there is a further paradox. Now that they have bombed Pittsburgh, the threat has failed. It would be immoral to carry through with your threat, and you don't. But the Soviets knew in advance that you were a good guy—that you were threatening retaliation only to prevent them from bombing. They knew that after they bombed Pittsburgh, you would go through the reasoning above, and you wouldn't retaliate. No wonder your threat of retaliation didn't work. They knew you wouldn't do it.

How could you have made a threat that would work—one they would take seriously?

> One way you could have done it is by constructing a "doomsday machine" (somewhat like the one in the 1963 movie *Dr. Strangelove*). This machine would have detected nuclear explosions anywhere in the United States, and would have reacted by automatically launching a devastating attack on the Soviet Union. The beauty of this machine is that once installed, it can't be turned off by anyone, no matter what. Now, once this machine is turned on, you telephone Khrushchev and tell him what you've done. *That's* deterrence. He would know then that if he attacked, there would be automatic retaliation. He'd realise that if he bombed Pittsburgh, you'd see that the threat had failed. You'd wish at that point that you were able to turn the machine off; but you couldn't.

The interesting thing about the story now is that it seems that the only way you can make a really effective deterring threat is to set things up so that later on you'll be unable to prevent carrying out the threat, despite the fact that you'll know that carrying it out will be immoral.

> "But I also made it clear to [Vladimir Putin] that it's important to think beyond the old days of when we had the concept that if we blew each other up, the world would be safe."—George W. Bush

FOR FURTHER READING: Several paradoxes of deterrence are discussed by Gregory S. Kavka in "Some Paradoxes of Deterrence," *The Journal of Philosophy* 75, no. 6 (June 1978).

When It's Sane to be Crazy

If you don't have a doomsday machine, it seems that it's to your advantage to make the Soviets think that you're immoral. If they think you're moral, then they wouldn't expect that you would uselessly retaliate, so your threat wouldn't work.

Suppose that you did your best to convince them that you really were crazy enough to retaliate uselessly. But if you acted in sensible, morally justifiable ways in general, they'd realize you were only pretending.

The best thing to do is really to make yourself unreasonable and immoral. That sort of person, after all, often has the bargaining advantage when dealing with sensible, moral people. Eating a lot of LSD might transform you into the kind of person best able to act to produce your best advantage. (Of course, then, having gone crazy, you might not want what's to your best advantage.)

> Joseph Heller, the author of *Catch-22*, studied philosophy in university, and it shows. The book's hero Yossarian, a U.S. flier during World War II, wants out of the war. He acts bizarrely, contrary to the rules for military behaviour, and people keep accusing him of being crazy. He pleads with the army psychiatrist to discharge him from the army on grounds of insanity. The psychiatrist agrees that crazy people get sent home, but he won't send Yossarian home because Yossarian *wants* to go home; this eminently sane desire shows he's not crazy at all. The only people who can get sent home on grounds of insanity are people who want to stay in the war.
>
> Yossarian has refused to fly any more missions.
>
> "Clevinger had stared at him with apoplectic rage and indignation and, clawing at the table with both hands, had shouted, 'You're crazy!' ...
>
> "'They're trying to kill me,' Yossarian told him calmly.
>
> "'No one's trying to kill you,' Clevinger cried.
>
> "'Then why are they shooting at me?' Yossarian asked.
>
> "'They're shooting at *everyone*,' Clevinger answered. 'They're trying to kill everyone.'
>
> "'And what difference does that make?'"[1]
>
> At the end of the book, Yossarian decides he's had enough and announces that he's going to desert to Sweden.
>
> "Major Danby replied indulgently with a superior smile, 'But Yossarian, suppose everyone felt that way.'
>
> "'Then I'd certainly be a damned fool to feel any other way, wouldn't I?'"[2]

4. MORE DILEMMAS

The Chicken's Dilemma

The game called "Chicken," the classical version of which was played by 1950s' male teenagers with hormone problems, is something like a prisoner's dilemma.

Here's how you play Chicken. On a deserted country road, you and another driver race your cars toward each other. If neither swerves off to

---

[1] Joseph Heller, *Catch-22* (New York: Dell, 1961), p. 17.

[2] Heller, p. 455.

the side, there is a head-on collision, and both you and the other driver die. If you swerve and the other guy doesn't, however, this shows that you're chicken, and (because machismo is very important for you) you suffer a devastating humiliation. If the other guy swerves too, that's not so bad. Both of you survive, and neither is humiliated by the macho of the other. No big deal. What you really want to happen, however, is that you keep going while the other guy swerves.

This is the table listing the possible "payoffs" for you, given your actions listed down the left, and given the actions of the other player listed across the top:

	He keeps going	He swerves
I keep going	I die (4)	I win—big macho status (1)
I swerve	I lose—bad humiliation (3)	No big deal (2)

The numbers in each box give the value of that "payoff" to you, with 1 indicating your number-one preference, and so on down.

(Note that the order of value in the boxes is not exactly the same as it was in the Prisoner's Dilemma case discussed above. If you felt that death was better than dishonour, and gave the lower-left box 4, and the upper-left box 3, then it would be a Prisoner's Dilemma.)

What is the best Chicken strategy for you?

> It's not clear. You can swerve, hoping that the other guy will too. If you play Chicken often, however, and get the reputation of a swerver, your opponents will always keep going.

But this suggests a better strategy for playing Chicken: convince the other guy you're crazy and will keep going no matter what. If he's got any sense, then *he* will swerve. But how to convince the guy that you're that insane? After all, if he's smart, he'll realise that giving the appearance of insanity is a good strategy for Chicken players, so it's likely that you're not crazy at all—you're just smart.

It's even better if you really are crazy. Then you'll show your insanity in all sorts of ways, and he'll definitely be convinced. The advantages of insanity are the same here as the ones we noticed above when discussing relations with the Russians.

You might think that Chicken is a game of deception, and that you'd be at a big disadvantage if your opponent could read your mind, and could know in advance exactly what you were going to do. But strangely, this is not the case. Can you see why?

> A mind-reading player would be at a big *disadvantage*—he'd lose every time, if you figured out the right strategy. If your opponent is a mind-reader, you should decide in advance that you'll keep going every time. Your opponent will read your mind. Because he's not suicidal, he'll swerve every time. You're a macho hero, and he's a humiliated chicken.

FOR FURTHER READING: This and other game-theoretical aspects of chicken are discussed by William Poundstone in *Labyrinths of Reason* (New York: Doubleday, 1988), pp. 240–241.

Beating the Computer

The following story is known as Newcomb's Problem. It involves playing a game against an opponent who can predict what you do.

Suppose there are two closed boxes presented to you. You are faced with the following choice. Box A contains either a check for one million dollars or nothing (you don't know which). Box B contains a check for one thousand dollars. You can take the contents of Box A alone, or the contents of both boxes. A very smart computer has been fed information about you; if it predicted you'll take both boxes, it has already put nothing in box A; but if it predicted you'll take only A, it has already put one million dollars in there. The computer has almost always been right in predicting other people in the past.

Here is a table summarizing the situation:

	Computer predicts you'll take only A & puts $1 million in A	Computer predicts you'll take both & puts $ 0 in A
You take just A	You get $1 million	You get $0
You take both boxes	You get $1,001,000	You get $1,000

What should you do? You will probably come up with one of these two conflicting answers:

(1) The computer has *already* put either one million dollars or nothing in A. What's in there won't change depending on your choice. If you take just A, you'll get whatever's in there; if you take both, you'll get that plus the thousand in B. Take both boxes.

(2) The computer has almost certainly predicted you correctly; so if you pick both boxes, it probably has put nothing in there, and you'll get only one thousand dollars. If you pick only A, again the computer has almost certainly predicted this, so you'll probably get one million dollars. Pick only A.

Which is the right answer? Do you take one box or two?

The odd thing about this problem is that people seem to divide into dogmatic one-boxers and militant two-boxers. There's really no consensus about who is right. Each faction has a perfectly good argument, which it keeps repeating louder and louder to the other side, to no avail.

A QUESTION TO THINK ABOUT: Which strategy do you think is right? Try to construct an argument to convince the opposition of your view.

FOR FURTHER READING: The first appearance of this problem in print seems to have been in Robert Nozick, "Newcomb's Problem and Two Principles of Choice," in *Essays in Honor of Carl G. Hempel,* ed. Nicholas Rescher (Dordrecht: Reidel, 1969). (Nozick says that it was invented, but not published, by Dr. William Newcomb of the Livermore Radiation Laboratories in California.) Newcomb's Problem is discussed in many places, including Richard C. Jeffrey's *The Logic of Decision,* 2nd ed. (Chicago: University of Chicago Press, 1983).

5. INTO THE MAINSTREAM OF PHILOSOPHY

The question "Why should I be moral?" is one that has interested philosophers since philosophy began. It's one that deserves some thought, and that you can think about and perhaps come up with some answers to, even if you have studied little philosophy.

David Hume, the eighteenth-century Scottish philosopher, discussed this problem in ways you might consider. He argued that morality is an unusual phenomenon. We all believe some moral "truths," but we are at a loss about how to prove what we believe. It seems to be impossible to justify these beliefs by means of pointing out facts about the world: no matter how many facts we adduce, the moral principles don't seem to follow. This position can be summed up by the slogan: you can't derive an *ought* from an *is*. Do you think that Hume is right? As a way of considering this, you might begin with some moral principle you think is correct, for example, that torturing innocent little children is wrong. Now imagine trying to convince someone who didn't believe it of the truth of this principle. You have at your disposal all the facts you could want about the world. Imagine the debate you might have with this moral sceptic. He's willing to grant the truths of any factual matter you like, and he's rational enough to accept the truth of any logical consequences of these facts. Could you convince him of the moral principle? (There really are people like this, with what's called psychopathic or sociopathic personalities. They may be intelligent and well-informed, but they just can't be convinced that something is wrong.)

Hume argued that facts alone don't imply morals. He thought that, in addition, one has to have certain feelings—importantly, certain sympathies with others. Given this sympathy, people can be reasoned with morally; without it, we're at a loss. Hume hoped that these feelings of sympathy were widespread. But what if someone just doesn't have them?

Much of this chapter concerns the sort of reasoning embodied in the Prisoner's Dilemma and in the Tragedy of the Commons. This sort of story has become important in much contemporary thought attempting to provide an answer to the question "Why should I be moral?" Some philosophers argue that considerations of this sort would lead someone who started without any Humian sympathy for others, but merely with selfish desires, to recognize the truth of some moral principles. The idea is that someone who is merely selfish could be led to see that in the long run his/her own interests would best be served by making a deal with others in such a way that their own interests are, to some extent, served too. The rules of morality, according to this view, represent these deals with others: by all agreeing to them, we each serve our own initial selfish interests the best.

Often this sort of line of reasoning is best pursued by imagining a bunch of people in a Hobbesian "state of nature"; rational and selfish interests alone will eventually result in their adopting some sort of rules of morality. Try to imagine a story in which such a state of nature would result in a society governed by morality. Do you think this would actually happen?

Readings in which philosophers attempt to answer the question "Why should I be moral?" are not hard to find. One suitable place to start is Plato's *Republic*. And most introductory philosophy anthologies will provide some articles on this question.

CHAPTER XV

RIGHT AND WRONG

1. JUSTICE AND DISTRIBUTION

Why You Should Give Away Your Shoes

Wouldn't it be a better world if it weren't the case that some people lived in comparative luxury while others suffered by consequence? Wouldn't you think that someone was morally lacking if that person knew of a way to right this inequality, and didn't?

Here's a small way you can make the world a better place. You (I suppose) own several pairs of shoes. There are many people in the world right now who own no pairs of shoes, and suffer as a result. So you should give your shoes to them.

It doesn't follow that you should give away *all* your shoes. If you gave them all away, then your positions would be reversed—you would be the one who was suffering. How many pairs should you give away?

Suppose you own five pairs of shoes; number them arbitrarily 1 through 5. Now consider pair number 5. How much benefit does this pair give to you? Not very much. Certainly that pair would do a whole lot more good to someone who has no shoes at all. If you gave that person that pair, your well-being would be reduced by a little bit, while the well-being of the recipient would be increased by a whole lot. Giving that pair away would increase the sum of well-being in the world. You would lose a little, and the other person would gain a lot.

Okay, you should give away pair number 5. Now you are left with four pairs. How about pair number 4? Giving away that pair would diminish your well-being, perhaps by a greater amount than giving away pair number 5. Nevertheless, the well-being of another shoeless person could be increased by much more than your well-being would be decreased. You should give away pair number 4 too.

Of course, the same line of reasoning applies to pairs number 3 and 2. But giving away your last pair wouldn't increase the sum of well-being in the world, because the increase resulting from a shoeless person getting them would be balanced by your becoming shoeless. In fact, if that person is somewhat used to going around shoeless and you aren't, perhaps you would suffer more than that person by being shoeless. So (you'll be happy to hear) it's not morally required that you give away your last pair of shoes.

What we have here is an example of what economists call the "marginal decrease of utility." This is a fancy way of saying that something would be worth a whole lot less to someone who has a lot of them than to someone who has few or none. Thus your fifth pair of shoes would be worth a lot more to a shoeless person than to you. One's first pair of shoes is (everything else being equal) much more valuable than one's second, which is in turn more valuable than the third, and so on.

So you should give away all your shoes except one pair. Now consider the other things you own more than one of. You should also give away all of them except one to people who have none. In fact, if anyone in the world has less than you do of any good thing, you should give them enough of your possessions until you own equal quantities.

Almost nobody follows this moral advice. Some people give something to those who have less, for example, by giving to charities, but remember what our reasoning tells us to do: give your goods away until there is *nobody in the world* who is worse off than you are. Do you know of anybody who does this? Even Mother Theresa didn't go this far.

Do you now feel like you're evil for not obeying this moral requirement? Well, you have company in your evil ways. Almost everyone in the world is, to some extent or other, evil, according to this line of reasoning.

Perhaps by now you've had the thought: something has gone wrong with this moral reasoning. Perhaps this is so. Reasoning that comes to the conclusion that almost everyone in the world is evil certainly merits a second (and third) look, in the next two items.

Your Shoes as Your Property

> "But those shoes are *mine*—I own them," you might want to argue. "They're my property. I have the right to hang on to my own property."

Some philosophers think that the right to own property is a central, fundamental human right. The idea is basic to the social philosophy of John Locke, for example, who held that the right to property followed from our very nature—that it's God's will, and is "writ in the hearts of all mankind." In his *Essays on the Law of Nature*, Locke expressed the view that it is a self-evident truth that all people are endowed by their creator with certain inalienable rights, among which are life, liberty, and property.

> Locke's idea was clearly a strong influence on Thomas Jefferson when he wrote the U.S. Declaration of Independence. Jefferson, however, changed the list of inalienable rights to life, liberty, and the pursuit of happiness. Why did Jefferson make this change? The right to property has certainly been central to the U.S. political philosophy from the founding fathers on.

Even Locke, however, didn't think that the right to property entitled you to own whatever you could get. He thought that you have to earn what you get by your labour (so stealing something doesn't give you property rights over it). He also thought that you don't have property rights over things you earn in cases when this appropriation wouldn't leave enough, and as good, for others.

SOME QUESTIONS TO THINK ABOUT: How did you get those shoes? Were they paid for by your parents? In that case, you didn't earn them. Does that show that you don't have the right to own them?

But suppose you earned the money to pay for them. By refusing to allow shoeless people to use them, are you depriving them of "enough"? By refusing to share them with people who have only terrible shoes, are you depriving them of "as good"?

Do you think that these considerations show that there's something wrong with Locke's views on the right to property?

Other philosophers have not found the right to property writ in their hearts. The nineteenth-century French thinker Proudhon, for example, wrote a book called *What is Property* and answered his own question by saying that property is theft. *Do* we have the right to property under *any* conditions? Is it fair that one person have more of the goods of life than another?

Your Shoes and Your "Families"

> "I agree that I would be immoral if I owned six pairs of shoes, and my brother or my children or my parents owned none, and I didn't give them *something* (though not so much that I'm completely reduced to their level of need). Maybe I even have some obligation to do some-

> thing for people far away, for example, in the poverty-stricken areas of Africa, but I only have a very limited obligation to them. I have less obligation to them, because they're not *my* family, or *my* group."

Almost everyone thinks that obligations to help others decrease as their "distance" from you increases. Most people are willing to sacrifice a good deal for their immediate family. Many people would do something (though less) for their neighbours in need. Some people sometimes respond to the need of others of their own nationality: for example, those of Greek descent in North America tend to be the ones who respond most strongly with aid when there's an earthquake in Greece.

But is the idea correct that one's obligations to others decrease as their "distance" increases? Why is failure to respond to your own child's need worse than failure to respond to the need of some child half-way around the world? Does your child deserve help more than that other child?

> Looking out first for your own family, or ethnic group, or race is a normal and universal phenomenon, perhaps an inevitable one. But this idea seems, from a certain point of view, to be somewhat morally objectionable, rather selfish or a bit racist. Maybe it's the sort of thing we should try to avoid.

SOME QUESTIONS TO THINK ABOUT: To think morally and act fairly, shouldn't we take a disinterested view, trying to ignore our own particular position? Shouldn't we try to think of every human—not just those nearer to us—as having an equal claim on what's of value?

2. PUNISHMENT

Getting Back at Eichmann

Adolf Eichmann was the German official during World War II in charge of what the Nazis called "the final solution of the Jewish problem." This involved sending Jews from all over German-occupied Europe to death camps to be exterminated. After World War II, Eichmann disappeared, but in 1960 Israeli agents found him in Argentina, abducted him, and took him to Israel, where he was tried and convicted of crimes against humanity, and hanged in 1962.

Except for a lunatic fringe of "Holocaust deniers," everyone agreed that Eichmann was directly responsible for the murder of millions of people. It seems perfectly obvious that a monster like this should be given the maximum punishment possible. But there was controversy anyway about the punishment he should receive for his crimes. Should he be given the death penalty? Should he be punished at all?

To see why these questions arose, consider the reasons for inflicting judicial punishment.

Sometimes punishment for crime is supposed to prevent the criminal from doing it again. Maybe punishment will teach that person a lesson, and make them less liable to commit crime again, or maybe it will merely put them in a jail where they won't be able to re-offend. The death penalty is certainly successful in preventing the offender from re-offending!

But in Eichmann's case, this rationale certainly doesn't apply. The Nazi government was thankfully long gone when he went on trial in the early 1960s, and Eichmann himself was about fifty-five, and in no shape to commit any big crimes himself. Nobody thought there was any future danger from him.

A second obvious rationale for punishing criminals is deterrence of others. People would (it is hoped) be less likely to commit crimes if they thought that they stood a good chance of punishment for those crimes. When people know that those who have committed similar crimes are punished, the possibility of their own punishment, should they do likewise, becomes more likely to them.

But in Eichmann's case, this doesn't seem to fit very well. The crime he was accused of—genocidal mass murder—isn't one that happens very often, thankfully. And on those fortunately rare occasions when it might, it doesn't seem that the threat of punishment would act as a deterrent. This sort of horribly huge-scale murder could take place only when sponsored by government; and if your government is sponsoring it, you wouldn't be afraid of punishment—at least, not from them. Remember, Eichmann believed that the Nazis were going to rule the world for the foreseeable future—they called their regime the "Thousand-Year Reich [Empire]."

The third sort of rationale for punishment is what's sometimes called *retribution*. Many people think that someone who has committed a crime should suffer as a result—not in order to deter that person or others from future crime, but just as a matter of simple justice. When someone has done awful things to other people, awful things should be done to that person.

Retribution is the only one of the three motives for punishment that is clearly applicable to the Eichmann case. But the controversy here arises because not everyone thinks that retribution is a suitable rationale for judicial punishment. If we think that the basic principle of morality is that human happiness and well-being should increase, and human suffering decrease, then retribution is morally questionable, because its motive is to increase suffering (of a wrongdoer). Retribution seems to some people to be merely revenge—an eye for an eye. It's not a suitable reaction for morally mature civilized societies.

If you agree that deterrence of the criminal or others didn't apply in this case, and that mere revenge is not a good idea, then maybe the surprising conclusion is that Eichmann—one of the biggest moral monsters of recent history—should not have been punished at all.

Closure

> "Watching McVeigh die would "help [victims and bereaved families] meet their need to close this chapter in their lives."—Attorney General John Ashcroft, defending the decision to televise mass-murderer Timothy McVeigh's execution to an audience of friends and relations of victims

When questions are raised about punishing criminals nowadays, we often hear talk about "closure." Victims (or relatives or acquaintances of victims) want—need—swift and harsh punishment for wrongdoers, which, it is supposed, will bring things closer to a state of balance, and release them somewhat from their agony.

What is "closure"? This newly popular word, a psycho-babble product of the grief-counsellor industry, may not mean much more than "revenge," though it certainly sounds more respectable.

There's no denying that the friends and relatives of the Oklahoma City bombing victims had real and very intense feelings about what should be done with the bomber.

> One woman wished the electric chair had been used [instead of lethal injection], because it would have been more painful. Another said, "I think bombs should be strapped on him, and then he can walk around the room forever until they went off and he wouldn't know when it would happen."

The commentator who reported these quotes remarks:

> Given the horrific losses McVeigh's crime incurred, this primal hunger can be almost seductive—a howl of mourning very hard

to resist, never mind debate. But it is dangerous if it allows us to lose sight of the fact that the debate we must have is ... about the limits of state force, not about devising the perfect mirror of each victim's suffering.[1]

> "Distrust all in whom the impulse to punish is powerful."—
> Friedrich Nietzsche[2]

3. RIGHTS AND WRONGS

Push-Pin Anyone?

The idea that the basic principle of ethics is that one ought to do what maximizes the total of pleasure or well-being or happiness in the world has a certain plausibility. It is the core of the moral theory called *utilitarianism*. Jeremy Bentham, the man who can be seen stuffed and preserved in a glass case in the University College of London (see **Bentham's Still In London**, in Chapter XIII above), was a central figure among utilitarians. He gave that theory its slogan when he wrote what he took to be a "sacred truth": that "the greatest happiness of the greatest number is the foundation of morals and legislation." But, as we have seen, this principle leads to a peculiar result. It seems to advocate that you give away almost all your shoes. (Other problem cases for this sort of thinking will be encountered in Chapter XVI, in **Ten-To-One Dilemmas**.)

Here's an additional case in which you might think that utilitarians get things wrong. Different people get pleasure from different things, but the utilitarian thinks that having the most of whatever gives you pleasure is the only good thing, and the more pleasure the better. Bentham wrote: "Prejudice apart, the game of push-pin is of equal value with the arts and sciences of music and poetry."[3] Push-pin is a child's game in which each player pushes or flips his pin with the object of crossing the pin of another player. In Bentham's time, it was a metaphor for a meaningless and trivial activity. Bentham insists that it's just a prejudice that music and poetry—the "higher" pleasures—are somehow more worthwhile: if push-pin turns you on, and poetry does not, then it's worth more to you, and that's all there is to say about it.

---

[1] Both quotes are from "No Vengeance, No Justice" by Patricia J. Williams, *The Nation*, July 2, 2001, p. 9.

[2] *Thus Spake Zarathustra*, Chapter 29.

[3] *Rationale of Reward* (London: J. & H. Hunt, 1825).

A QUESTION TO THINK ABOUT: Nobody plays push-pin any more, so let's think about a contemporary example: video games. Do you think that reading poetry is better than playing video games? If so, why? One answer that Bentham would accept is that reading poetry gives you more pleasure than playing video games, but c'mon now, be honest: you really find playing video games fun, and reading poetry boring and difficult, don't you? Okay, given that, do you still think that reading poetry is somehow superior? Why?

The other philosopher most centrally associated with utilitarianism, John Stewart Mill, accepted this criticism of Bentham's view. Mill agreed with Bentham that pleasure is a necessary condition of goodness, but argued that there are "higher" and "lower" pleasures, and that a small amount of a "higher" pleasure (for example, presumably, reading poetry) is superior to a larger amount of a "lower" pleasure (push-pin). But, we want to ask Mill, what makes a pleasure "higher"? And why do those characteristics make it superior to "lower" pleasures?

When Promise-Breaking is Obligatory

You visit your rich uncle Fred in the hospital. "I'm dying," says Uncle Fred, "but I'll die a happy man if you promise me to do something after I'm dead. There's a million dollars hidden in the closet over there. Nobody knows about that million, not even my wife, and it's not mentioned in my will. Take it, and just as soon as I'm dead, give it to my wife."

You want to ease Uncle Fred's last moments, so you get the million out of the closet and promise to give it to Aunt Sally after he's gone. He dies that afternoon, and you get into your car and head for the casino where you know that Aunt Sally has been spending every day since Fred went into the hospital, drinking, carrying on with various low-life men, and spending every cent she has at the gambling tables.

But on the way to the casino, you wonder about the morality of keeping your promise to Uncle Fred. As a utilitarian, you are in favour of promoting the greatest happiness of the greatest number of people. Giving Aunt Sally the money would make her happy, but she's really unable to feel much through the alcohol haze she's always in, and the money will be gone in a few days of gambling anyway. If you kept the money yourself, it would contribute to human happiness—yours—considerably more; better still, you could contribute it to a charity that provides food and shelter for the homeless. Uncle Fred, who was infatuated with Aunt Sally and unable to see her faults, wanted her to have the money, but he's dead now, so he can't be harmed by your breaking your promise. Nobody else would be harmed. Why keep your promise?

> Breaking promises produces mistrust, so in the long run
> it will produce more harm than good.

No, this isn't a good reason. Maybe in general breaking promises erodes social institutions that depend on trust, but not in this case. Nobody knows about your promise to Uncle Fred; no mistrust will result.

> Well, even if breaking your promise doesn't have bad
> results in this case, it often does, so there is utilitarian
> justification for having a rule against promise breaking.
> (This is the sort of answer provided by *Rule Utilitarians*.)

But in cases (like this one) when it is beneficial not to obey this rule, why should you obey it?

The Strange Case of Admiral Byng

Here's another case in which utilitarianism seems to give us the wrong answer. It's a real case from history:

> In 1756, the French, under the Duc de Richelieu, took Minorca from the English—the English fleet, under Admiral Byng, retiring before the French. Paris went mad with joy. Britain forgot her traditional love of fair play, and wreaked her bitterness at being beaten on her native element, not on the blundering ministry who had commanded him impossibilities, but on Admiral Byng himself ... [who was] arraigned on a charge of treason and cowardice.... Byng was shot on March 14, 1757, and his defender, the author Voltaire added to his novel *Candide* an immortal phrase, "In this country [England] it is as well to put an admiral to death now and then, *to encourage the others*."[4]

Executing poor Admiral Byng may well have led to an overall increase in the general welfare by "encouraging" the other admirals. Maybe they tried harder as a result, and England fared well. But you probably agree with Voltaire, who is of course being ironic in his assessment of the English policy: the English here acted grossly immorally.

---

[4] S. G. Tallentyre, *Voltaire in his Letters, being a Selection from His Correspondence* (New York and London: G. P. Putnam's Sons, 1919).

A QUESTION TO THINK ABOUT: Can you see how Rule Utilitarianism might come to the conclusion that this execution was wrong?

FOR FURTHER READING: A consideration of what the case of Admiral Byng might show about utilitarianism can be found in "Professor Stevenson, Voltaire, and the Case of Admiral Byng," by David Braybrooke, *Journal of Philosophy* 53 (1956), pp. 787–795.

Don't Torture That Baby!

Here's a thought-experiment from fiction that raises a similar question.

> "Tell me yourself, I challenge you—answer. Imagine that you are creating a fabric of human destiny with the object of making men happy in the end, giving them peace and rest at last, but that it was essential and inevitable to torture to death only one tiny creature—the baby beating its breast with its fist, for instance—and to found that edifice on its unavenged tears, would you consent to be the architect of those conditions? Tell me, and tell the truth."
>
> "No, I wouldn't consent," said Alyosha softly.[5]

Rights vs. Utility

Some philosophers have thought that these and many other examples of the peculiar consequences of utilitarianism show that the theory is wrong. They argue that in addition to (perhaps even instead of) thinking about what promotes happiness, we ought to think about inviolable *rights*. As we've seen, a right to property might justify our keeping our shoes, at the expense of an increase in total happiness. A right to just treatment might have saved the Admiral.

Bentham, of course, didn't think very highly of the notion of rights (he called them "nonsense upon stilts"), and other philosophers have had trouble figuring out what rights might be.

SOME QUESTIONS TO THINK ABOUT: Are there any such thing as rights? If you have a right to something, that seems to mean that that thing can't be taken away, no matter what consequences there are to the general

---

[5] Fyodor Dostoyevski, *The Brothers Karamazov,* trans. Constance Garnett (London: Heinemann, 1912).

welfare. It's pretty hard to think of anything we'd be willing to grant a right to, on this strict definition. We're all willing to grant that under some circumstances considerations of the general welfare justify taking away someone's property, when that's necessary for the general good. People's land and houses are expropriated (with compensation, of course) in order to build a national park, or a highway, or a dam that would benefit a large number of people. We don't even have an absolute right to life: under certain extreme circumstances — when disaster would otherwise result — police are allowed to kill people. In these cases, considerations of the general welfare justify bringing some harm to some people.

If there are such things as rights, where do rights come from? How can we find out what rights people have? Locke argued that reason alone can reveal what basic rights everyone has, but it's not at all clear that this is so. Several years ago, the Canadian rugby team was prohibited by the government from playing a match against the South African team, as part of the general sanctions against the apartheid policies then in force in that country. I heard a member of that team on the radio complaining that this ban was unjust because it violated their "right to play." I had never heard of *that* right before. Is there such a thing? How can we find out? Does Lockian pure reason tell you whether this right exists?

FOR FURTHER READING: Bentham's thoughts on rights are found in his *Works*, vol. 10, p. 142.

Opening Pandora's Box

Pandora, according to ancient Greek mythology, was created by Zeus. She was the most beautiful woman ever created, but also foolish. She opened a jar (or box) in which all the evils that plague humanity had been imprisoned: Old Age, Labour, Sickness, Insanity, Vice, Passion, Spite, and so on. They flew out in a cloud, stung Pandora all over her body, then proceeded to attack the rest of the human race. However, Hope, who had also been imprisoned in the jar, discouraged afflicted humanity from mass suicide.

"Pandora" has been taken (perhaps ironically) as the title of a Halifax, Nova Scotia, feminist newspaper around which a controversy concerning rights raged a few years ago. A man wrote to this newspaper to argue with an article it had previously published. The newspaper refused to publish his letter on the grounds that its policy is to publish only contributions by women. The man complained about this sexual discrimination to the Nova Scotia Human Rights Commission, claiming sexual discrimination against him.

Pandora's lawyer argued that the newspaper is justified in its "women only" policy because it offers a place for women to air their views unafraid of being slammed by men. This is necessary given the male dominance of public debate throughout history. The opposition in this case agrees that the systematic exclusion of women in the past was a bad thing; it argues, however, that this was bad because everyone has the right to free public speech. Denial of this right to women in the past was wrong, but so is its denial to men in the current instance.

There are two main reasons that some feminists think that the notion of rights is not a suitable foundation for morally right action.

(1) Granting everyone the right to something means nothing when one group is oppressed by another with the result that the oppressed group is unable to take advantage of the benefits conferred by that right. Thus the principles of fairness that are behind rights-based ethics, and that underlie Lockian liberal social theory, aren't the ones that should be used to determine public policy. Fairness allows for continuing oppression of groups like women. It is unfair, they agree, that a women's newspaper should be allowed to practise sexual discrimination, while a general or man's newspaper should not. But given the current structure of society, fairness, they argue, is a bad thing.

(2) Previous inequalities cannot be remedied by current equal treatment. What is needed is preferential treatment for the formerly oppressed group, to make up for centuries of mistreatment.

Similar arguments are showing up frequently in public debate. You can find the same sorts of consideration, for example, being raised in debates about preferential hiring and about the right to read pornographic literature.

But the philosophical feminists who argue against a morality based on rights do not advocate thinking in terms of maximizing the sum-total of good as an alternative. They might agree that sexual discrimination by *Pandora* (or denial of fair treatment in certain cases of hiring, or denial of the right to read what you want) might not lead to the greatest total satisfaction in society. They argue that neither rights-morality nor morality based on happiness-maximization are able to cope with the kind of systematic oppression they find in today's society. They seek a third kind of theory for moral thought.

The Nova Scotia Human Rights Commission ruled that *Pandora* may refuse to print something on the grounds that it was written by a man. But they probably wouldn't allow a men's magazine to discriminate against women. The difference is that women are a "designated group" who have been discriminated against in the past. This is why they're allowed to practise compensatory discrimination now.

SOME QUESTIONS TO THINK ABOUT: Do you think that the Human Rights Commission's decision was the right one? Note that it seems to indicate that women have the right not to be discriminated against, but men don't. Is this fair? Perhaps you think it is. If not, do you think that it's unfair but (under the circumstances) a good thing?

> "The law, in its majestic equality, forbids the rich as well
> as the poor to sleep under bridges, to beg in the streets, and
> to steal bread." —Anatole France

4. GETTING WHAT YOU WANT

Past and Future Desires

What you basically want is to have a life in which, all told, you get what you want, right? Well, that's not so clear.

Suppose you are now eighty years old, and your doctor guesses that given your present state of health, you'll probably live for five or ten years more. Suppose further that for the past thirty years, you have had a very strong desire that there be a statue of Elvis in your back yard. You've never had the money to buy the statue, and your desire has been frustrated. Yesterday you won the lottery. For the first time you can afford the Elvis statue, but you discover that your interest in Elvis has completely disappeared, and you now think that having an Elvis statue would be foolish. Should you get the statue anyway?

If you put up that Elvis statue, you satisfy a strong desire you had for thirty years. Of course, *now* you don't want that statue, so putting up that statue will go against your present (and, we can assume, future) desires. But this would mean only five or ten years or so of dissatisfied desire. Assuming that the kind of life you want is one in which your desire fulfillment is maximized, all told, you should put up that ugly statue.

The fact that this reasoning is foolish shows that there's something wrong with the principle that what we really want is a life in which desire satisfaction is maximized. We care about our present desires, not about our past desires that have gone away.

But are our present desires the only thing that's relevant? How about our future desires?

Consider the following case. You're now twenty years old, and expect to live to a ripe old age. Your parents urge you to take a business degree, arguing reasonably that this is the best way to assure you a good income in the future. But you are young and idealistic, and you don't care about income: you want to join a group of ecology terrorists instead. Your parents argue that you feel that way only because you're young. They predict that in a few years, you'll change your mind; your aversion to business, indifference to money, and ecology fanaticism will all fade away, and you'll wish that you had taken that business degree. You sadly agree with them in their prediction of your future desires: you know that that's what happens to almost everyone.

Now, if it's rational to count future desires as well as present ones in what you do, the right thing to do is to enroll in that business course. Even though you don't now want to do it, you know that it will maximize your desire fulfillment, counting both your present and future desires. All told, your life will contain a far greater quantity of fulfilled desires if you take that degree. Is this the rational way to think? Don't be too quick in answering Yes. Remember that saving whales, not making money, is what you're now really interested in. Why should you weigh those interests against what your future self will be interested in?

What Happens to Somebody Who Is Hardly Me

Here's a surprising argument to the conclusion that one should not be very concerned about what will happen in one's far future. In Chapter XIII we took a look at what some philosophers had to say about identifying the same person at two different times. Some of them argue that what's relevant are factors such as memory and other psychological links, bodily continuity, and so on. But that person who will have your name in the very far future will be connected only very tenuously to the present you: that person will remember very few of your current experiences, will be psychologically quite different, will have a body that resembles your present one only a little, and contains almost none of the same matter. So it seems that this person is the future *you* only to a small degree. You're interested in what happens to you, but if that far distant person is you only to a small degree, you should be interested in what happens to that person only to a very small degree.

People are, of course, worried about dying; some are worried a lot about this. If you're young and healthy, death will probably be a long way off. And if the argument above is right, then that person who dies later on will be you only to a very small degree. Maybe this realization might make you a little less worried about death.

FOR FURTHER READING: Derek Parfit gives an argument something like this in "Personal Identity," *The Philosophical Review* 80, no. 1 (January, 1971), reprinted in *Personal Identity*, ed. John Perry (Berkeley: University of California Press, 1975).

The Genie's Cousin

Sometimes, of course, getting what you want is difficult or impossible. Here's a solution to this problem: start wanting only those things you can easily get.

Suppose, for example, that Marvin is a connoisseur of fine wines. He's not very rich, however, and he's often dissatisfied at not being able to buy the vintages he craves. He devotes much of his salary to buying fine wines, and sacrifices other things he wants. The wines he buys aren't as good as the ones he wants, and he can't get enough of the very good ones. How can Marvin solve his problem? It would be solved, of course, if he could get enough money to buy all the finest wine he wants, but this seems impossible. Here's a solution that does seem possible; what do you think of it?

> He should kill his desire for expensive wine—change his desires and tastes so that he enjoys low-cost, inferior wine.

Is this sort of alteration of desires and tastes really possible?

> Yes it is. It does take time and effort to alter one's tastes and desires, but it can be done. People can get themselves to like all sorts of things. One way to do it is by practice: if Marvin started drinking only Chateau Plonque, that miserable but cheap rotgut, in pleasurable surroundings, telling himself how delicious it was, after a long while he very well might get to like it—even to prefer it to the expensive stuff.

This sort of solution is widely applicable to the problem of not getting what you want. Matilda is in love with Matthew, but Matthew won't give her the time of day. Max is attracted to Matilda, but Matilda doesn't care for him. She only has eyes for Matthew. She has a problem, but she can solve it by ignoring Matthew and marrying Max. This will hurt for a while, but given practice and self-discipline, she can get herself, sooner or later, to love Max and to be indifferent to Matthew. It can be done. There are techniques by which one can alter one's own desires.

There are even better-known and more effective techniques for altering people's desires. The advertising industry is wholly devoted to the alteration of desires. It's often difficult or impossible for a government to give its citizens what they want, so some governments try changing what the citizens want, so that they wind up wanting what they're given. Your own government probably spends a lot of money on advertising for this purpose.

SOME QUESTIONS TO THINK ABOUT: There is something wrong with this as a solution to getting what you want, isn't there? What is it?

Let's put the problem in more picturesque terms. You remember the story of the genie who lives in a lamp and will grant three wishes—change three things to make them the way you want them to be. This genie would be nice to meet; unfortunately I've lost his address. But I can get you in touch with his cousin Fred, who is also a genie who can make the world match your desires. Fred does this not by changing the world, but by changing your desires. If something isn't the way you want it to be, Fred will change what you want. Are you eager to avail yourself of Fred's services? Why not?

Electronic Pleasure

A while back some psychologists claimed to have discovered the "pleasure centre" in rats' brains.[6] A tiny electric wire was inserted in this area of the brain. The rat was given a little lever in its cage; when the rat pressed the lever, a mild current was sent through the wire, stimulating that part of its brain. The interesting thing was that the rat seemed to *love* this brain-stimulation. Having discovered the effect, it soon was pressing the lever at a tremendous rate. It did not stop even to eat from the food bin

---

[6] James Olds, "Pleasure Centers in the Brain," *Scientific American* (October 1956), pp. 105–116.

right next to the lever. It would die of hunger rather than stop stimulating that area of its brain. This stimulation was apparently so pleasurable that the rat preferred it to anything.

Now, these psychologists claim that humans have a similar area of their brains, and they speculate that with the aid of a little wire painlessly inserted into that area of your brain, you might be able to give yourself that overwhelmingly desirable pleasure. It's hard to imagine what that would feel like, but you might find it so wonderful that you would prefer it to anything else. Do you want yourself hooked up?

> Maybe you're afraid that you would get stuck to the push-button sending stimulation to your brain, like the rat, and be unable to eat. You would die after a short (but immensely pleasurable) life.

If this prospect doesn't appeal, then suppose we make getting wired a little more attractive by guaranteeing that you will be kept fed and otherwise taken care of. Now do you want to get hooked up?

Consider the consequences: you might like that stimulation so much that you might lose your job, give up your studies, never see friends, family, loved ones ever again—you might, in short, abandon everything that now means something to you. But remember: this sensation is so fantastically wonderful that it makes absolutely all of this worthwhile. What do you say?

A QUESTION TO THINK ABOUT: Maybe you think that there's more to life than getting what you really want more than anything else. What? Why?

5. RELATIONSHIPS WITH OTHER PEOPLE

Harming the Dead

Aristotle, in his discussion of the proverb "Count no man happy until he is dead," decides that this could not mean that anyone is happy when dead; instead, he supposes, what's being said here is that dead people are at least beyond evils and misfortunes. It seems obvious, and many philosophers agree, that the dead can't be harmed; recall our discussion of what Lucretius makes of this, in **Why You Shouldn't Fear Death** in Chapter XIII above.

But, Aristotle continues, this "affords matter for discussion" because "both evil and good are thought to exist for a dead man ... e.g., honours and dishonours and the good or bad fortunes of children and in general of descendants."[7]

What's odd here is we do seem to think that we can benefit or harm people after they're dead. Spreading nasty false rumours about somebody who's dead might be harmful to somebody else who is still alive, but clearly this is not the central reason why that's a nasty thing to do. It seems to be because of the harm done to the dead person, though this sounds crazy.

Compare these examples:

(1) Sally's aged mother Martha loved the traditional foods of Newfoundland, where she had grown up. Martha came to Sally's house for dinner every Friday, and Sally would cook fish 'n' brewis served with scrunchions,[8] even though everyone else hated the stuff. Now that Martha is dead, Sally still occasionally makes that dish on a Friday. "Mum loved it," she says.

(2) Many of the old houses in their neighbourhood have been sold to absentee landlords who have converted them into a number of tiny apartments to rent to students going to the university a few blocks away. Martha always used to complain about this: "It ruins the neighbourhood," she'd say. She vowed that if she had to sell her house, she'd never sell it to somebody who would convert it into little apartments—she'd sell it to a family who would live in the whole thing. Martha lived in the house till she died, and her daughter Sally, who has inherited the house, is thinking of selling it. She'd get a better price if she sold it to a slumlord who would convert it into tiny apartments, but she won't do that. "Mum would turn over in her grave if I did that," she says.

Sally's feelings in both of these examples are understandable human reactions of someone who cared for her mother. But there's a difference between (1) and (2). In (1), the only value for Martha of the Friday fish 'n' brewis was eating it. There would be no value at all of the family's eating the stuff if Martha wasn't there to share it. This is a good that

---

[7] *Nicomachean Ethics*, Bk. I, Ch. 10, translated by Richard McKeon.

[8] Soak separately overnight: 2 lbs. of salt fish, 6 cakes of hard bread. Change water on fish, boil for 20 minutes, then drain. Bring bread to boil in same water used for soaking, then drain. Combine cooked fish with bread. Serve with scrunchions (small cubes of fat pork).

depends on its enjoyment by the person who values it. But Martha wouldn't have wanted her old house to be broken up into apartments whether that had any effect on her or not—even if she were not around. In the second case, but not in the first, it might seem a little more sensible to think of Sally's action to be doing something for her mother, even though her mother is dead.

The dead are beyond harm and benefit, but don't their desires deserve respect? Maybe not. Remember the Elvis-statue example above: it seemed that one's own past desires were irrelevant when one ceased to have them. A similar point could be made about the desires someone else used to have, but which are now gone. And the former desires of a dead person are surely now gone!

SOME QUESTIONS TO THINK ABOUT: Do you agree that there's a difference here because of which (2) makes more sense than (1)? Maybe you think *both* of Sally's actions are pointless sentimentalities or superstitions. Maybe you think that her reactions are suitable memorials for her dead mum—an expression of Sally's love of her mum, and of her feeling of loss—but shouldn't be understood as doing her *mum* a favour. But then consider Aristotle's example of "dishonouring" the dead: would you feel that it's wrong to destroy the reputation of someone who's dead—someone you didn't have any special feeling for? In this case, your protecting the reputation of the dead person isn't an expression of any feeling you have for that person at all. It appears to be nothing but the straightforward moral act of preventing harm to that person.

I'm Gonna Buy a Plastic Doll That I Can Call My Own

The following story assumes that the reader is a man, and manifests other sexist attitudes as well. It's worth considering anyway; part of the question it raises is why you might find it offensive.

The Acme Robot Company, let us imagine, has perfected its mechanical female robots to the point that you can order one to fit your own specifications, and a carton will arrive from the factory containing Shirley, the girlfriend of your dreams (batteries not included). All of Shirley's characteristics will be perfect, as far as you are concerned: she will be mentally and physically exactly the girl you've always wanted.

Many men would not be attracted by the idea of buying Shirley, though they would be very interested in meeting a real woman with her specifications. To justify this attitude toward Shirley, we need to find relevant differences between her and real women. What are these?

> It's hard to explain why Shirley's differences are relevant.
> She is made out of plastic and electronic components,
> not flesh and blood; but so what? Her plastic covering
> feels just like the skin you love to touch, so how can the
> fact that it's plastic make any difference? As far as *your
> contact* with her is concerned, she's indistinguishable
> from a real woman covered with real skin. Inside her is a
> computer, not a liver, pancreas, etc.; but again, why does
> this make any difference? You can't feel these insides,
> and they make absolutely no difference to any of your
> actual encounters with her.

Don't think of Shirley acting stiffly and mechanically like those robots in bad science-fiction movies. She's much better made. She acts smoothly and naturally. She is capable of showing the full range of emotions. Remember she is indistinguishable from ordinary humans.

> "Aha!" you say. "She *shows* the full range of emotions,
> but she doesn't *feel* them. After all, she's a machine. I
> want a girlfriend who really feels things, not one who
> merely acts like she does."

Well, what makes you think she doesn't really feel them? Does the fact that she is manufactured out of plastic and transistors show that it's impossible for her to feel things? (We ran into this question in Chapter XII.)

> "But," you continue, "another difference between Shirley
> and real humans is her past. Real humans were born of
> woman, and had infancies and childhoods. Shirley can
> speak convincingly of her mother and her childhood, but
> this is all fake, programmed into her by the folks at Acme
> because they thought I might enjoy discussing her child-
> hood with her. She was actually 'born' only six months
> ago in the factory."

But why does this make a difference? Again, she is now indistinguishable, for all practical purposes, from a real woman. If you didn't know her real construction and provenance, you would be completely fooled into thinking she's real, because she's such a good imitation.

> "But I know that she's an imitation," you object, "so I
> wouldn't be able to have a good relationship with her."

But isn't this an unfortunate prejudice on your part—one you'd be much better off without?

> "I just don't like imitations," you insist. "I always buy genuine leather shoes rather than those plastic imitation leather ones."

But why do you insist on genuine leather? Because leather feels better, lasts longer, etc.? But suppose they developed an imitation leather that felt *exactly* like real leather, that wore in *exactly* the same way, and that was, in sum, indistinguishable from the real thing. The only difference between this perfect imitation and real leather was where the imitation came from (a plastics factory, not an animal) and its chemical constitution. But these have nothing to do with your actual relationship with your shoes, do they? If you still preferred real leather to this perfect imitation, you have some explaining to do. It seems that you're being irrational.

> "I'm willing to grant that my preference for real over perfect imitation leather is unjustifiable, but it's different when we're talking about *people*. There's something special about a relationship with people. It's not merely a matter of the nature of the contact with them."

Maybe there is something to this. But it certainly needs more explanation. A good explanation might reveal something important about how we feel (or ought to feel) about other people. Maybe the real point of this story isn't so nasty after all.

Replaceable People in Literature

Similar concerns to those raised in the Problem of the Mechanical Girlfriend come up occasionally in literature. One instance of this occurs (extraneously to the main point of the story) in a corner of the Book of Job, in the Bible.

God (as a result of a dare from Satan) deprives Job of everything he values: his sheep, oxen, camels, servants, and so on; God even kills off his seven sons and three daughters. Job is understandably miserable and puzzled, but he does not lose his trust in God. In the end he is given "twice as much as he had before,"[9] plus seven sons and three daughters—presumably *brand new* sons and daughters, but really good ones.

---

[9] *Job* 42:10.

273

Happy ending! But we are a bit taken aback by the idea that his replacement children could really set things right.

Another instance: Meursault, the hero of Camus's *The Stranger*, is a peculiar man. He is sensual, well-meaning, truthful, but he lacks the complexity and the depth of commitment and relationship that we think characterizes the normally developed adult. His friend Marie asks him if he'll marry her.

> I said I didn't mind; if she was keen on it, we'd get married.
>
> Then she asked me again if I loved her. I replied, much as before, that her question meant nothing or next to nothing—but I supposed I didn't.... Then she asked:
>
> "Suppose another girl had asked you to marry her—I mean, a girl you liked in the same way as you like me—would you have said "Yes" to her, too?"
>
> "Naturally."[10]

Perhaps Marie is asking Meursault the right question. Love of another person—we suppose—is not simply a matter of valuing the characteristics of another person. If it were, we would love anyone just as much who had comparable characteristics, and we would be happy if a loved one were replaced by someone else just as good.

6. DISEASE AS AN ETHICAL CATEGORY

What's Sick?

It might appear that whether someone is ill or not is a question for a physician, not a philosopher, to answer. But consider the following argument, from a paper arguing that public funding should not be used to pay for medical treatment for infertility.[11] The author agreed that infertility is a physical abnormality that medicine can often do something to fix, but he argued that infertility is not a *disease*. Having one's own genetic children is something that people sometimes *want* very much, but they don't *need* it. Society sometimes puts a negative value on childlessness, but public funding should be limited to curing disease, to providing for people's

---

[10] Albert Camus, *The Outsider*, trans. Stuart Gilbert (London: Hamish Hamilton, 1946), p. 50.

[11] "In Vitro Fertilization: Ethical Issues" by Thomas A. Shannon, in *Embryos, Ethics, and Women's Rights: Exploring the New Reproductive Technologies*, eds. Elaine Hoffman Baruch et al. (New York: Harrington Park Press, 1988).

medical needs, not their wants, especially if those wants are a result of society's norms.

Maybe the author's conclusion—that public funding shouldn't be used to pay for medical infertility treatment—is right. But we can raise questions about a lot of steps in his argument.

What counts as a *disease* anyway?

> A medical student I discussed this question with argued that infertility isn't a disease, because infertility is not a state of morbidity.

But what's morbidity? My dictionary tells me that a morbid state is a state relating to disease. We're back to the starting point.

Diseases are things that have gone wrong with your body. But infertility is something gone wrong with one's body. Lots of people count going bald as something going wrong with their bodies. But baldness doesn't seem to be a disease. What is a disease anyway?

> The article mentioned above suggests that diseases are things that go wrong with your body in a way that deprives you of what you *need*. If what you're deprived of is merely what you *want*, then it's not a disease.

But now we can ask: What's the difference between a need and a want? A want, we're tempted to say, is merely a subjective desire; but a need is ... a need is ... what?

Does the fact that someone's desire is socially inculcated make that desire less important? Almost all our desires depend to a large extent on influences from our society.

Maybe this author is making distinctions that don't make much sense. Maybe what we really should say is that anything counts as a disease if it's a physical state of the sort (perhaps) treatable by medicine, and if it runs counter to the desires of the person who has it. The question remains whether society should pay for treatment of infertility, or of baldness for that matter. But this question can be solved by considering how desperate people are to have their condition fixed. Maybe if bald people really think that their state is worse than having cancer, we should divert public funds from cancer treatment to hair-transplants.

However you want to answer these questions, you can see by now that they're the sort of questions you take to your family philosopher, not to your family doctor.

Unhappiness as Illness

Leah McLaren writes:

> In a recent examination of annual prescription drug sales, the pri-
> vate health information company IMS Health found that over the
> past six years, doctor visits for depression have gone up 36 per
> cent in Canada. In 2000 alone, Canadians made 7.8 million con-
> sultations with office-based physicians for depressive disorders,
> an increase of almost 10 per cent over the year before.
>
> What these numbers indicate is a raging epidemic of a new
> kind of depression—one that is situational, rather than endog-
> enous (originating from within). Endogenous depression, accord-
> ing to Cathy Gildiner, a Toronto psychologist and author of the
> memoir *Too Close to the Falls*, "has to do with family history,
> and so the numbers stay the same. It's a chemical imbalance; it
> has some science behind it." Situational depression, on the other
> hand, "has to do with life events" like when Tipper Gore was
> treated for SD after her son was injured in a car accident.
>
> You might remember a time when SD was called "sadness,"
> "anxiety" or "going through a tough time." It was a normal re-
> sponse to life's rough stuff: death, divorce, career mishaps and
> February in Canada. Now it's a widely diagnosed and medicated
> mental illness.[12]

She's right, of course, that what was once thought of as mere gloom has
now turned into a Syndrome.

Is situational sadness/depression a disease or not? This is not a question to be settled by medical science. There's no doubt that there's some
physical difference between sad and happy people, just as there's some
physical difference between people who like olives and those who don't.
But nothing important follows from this. Answering this question appears
to be a matter of choosing what we take to be the appropriate reaction to
somebody's sadness. Pills can cheer them up, but is this a good idea? Or
is one being a better person if one faces up to the sources of one's unhappiness and tries to get over them unaided by chemistry—or at least, suffers with the unhappiness until that time, if ever, when it goes away?

But when we answer these questions, we're making moral judgements,
not factual or scientific ones.

---

[12] "Sadness used to be normal. Now, it's a disease" by Leah McLaren, *[Toronto] Globe
and Mail*, May 4, 2001.

7. MORAL MISCELLANY

Killing Bambi's Mother

A few years ago a colleague of mine was teaching an introductory ethics class, and wanted to start with an example of a clearly immoral action. "Imagine that someone just went out on the street and killed a passerby at random," he suggested.

The students by then were philosophically sophisticated enough to question conventional reactions. "What's so bad about that?" they asked. "What if the passerby were a nasty criminal, and everyone would be better off if he were dead?" "What if that person wanted to commit suicide anyway?" "What's so bad about death?" "Suppose you hated that person and could get away with murder without being punished?" And so on.

These are all questions that deserve an answer, but my colleague wanted to start first with a clear example that seemed unquestionably wrong to everyone. "Well, suppose that the passerby wanted to live, and wasn't a criminal? How about if the passerby were a helpless and innocent child?" More questions and objections. Finally he had an inspiration for an example to use: the hunter's killing Bambi's mother in the Disney film. *Everyone* agreed that *there* was a despicable action.

Those cute Disney animals, with their big brown eyes, tug at our heartstrings. Real animals—when they're cute enough, anyway—affect most of us in the same way. Think of the widespread reaction years ago when Brigitte Bardot held those adorable baby seals up to TV cameras, and then we saw them clubbed by seal hunters. (Big brown eyes again.) Suppose as part of your job you had to exterminate unwanted kittens in an animal shelter. Could you do it?

What's interesting is how strong these reactions are. Even if we know that those kittens *must* be destroyed, and that it will be done painlessly, it's extremely difficult to get used to the idea.

SOME QUESTIONS TO THINK ABOUT: What is it about certain animals (cartoon or real) that rouses these reactions? It's not at all clear that cuteness has any deep relevance to the morality of ways of treating animals. It has to be just as immoral to squash a cute kitten as it is to squash a really ugly (but harmless) rat. Nobody has any trouble swatting flies: is it because they're not even a little cute? Imagine that flies just happened to look like tiny teddy bears. How would you feel then?

FOR FURTHER READING: The MARK III BEAST is a mechanical contraption that looks like a beetle. It runs around the floor looking for an electrical outlet to "feed" on. It "purrs" while eating or when held. It makes shrill little noises when attacked. It feels comfortably warm to the touch. It's enormously difficult to "kill." This amusing story is told in *The Soul of Anna Klane* by Terrell Miedaner (New York: Coward, McCann & Geoghegan, 1977), reprinted, with philosophical commentary, in *The Mind's I* by Douglas R. Hofstadter and Daniel C. Dennett (New York: Basic Books, 1981).

Hello Dolly!

The successful cloning of some of the higher mammals has made it probable that the technique could be used on humans; and there has been a huge flurry of moral outrage expressed at this idea, together with calls for new legislation to outlaw it before it's too late. Much of what has been written about human cloning gives what the authors take to be reasons why that prospect is so morally outrageous in their eyes, but the arguments for the immorality of human cloning are no good at all. Here's a sample of them, followed by the fairly obvious replies.

(1) Human cloning is unnatural.

Reply: So are all sorts of things that are perfectly morally acceptable: vaccination for disease, eating cooked food, airplane travel, Michael Jackson. Well, maybe that last example wasn't a good one.

(2) Human cloning would be available only for the rich.

Reply: So are all sorts of things that are perfectly morally acceptable: Rolls-Royces, caviar, tickets to see the Three Tenors.

(3) Human cloning would increase the population.

Reply: So does sex, which nobody—well, almost nobody—considers immoral.

(4) Human cloning would be used for all kinds of horrible purposes. They'd make an army of docile subhumans to work in factories. They'd create headless organ-slaves to be cut up when someone needed a transplant.

Reply: This is just like arguing that chainsaws are immoral because somebody might use one for chainsaw-murders. If one of these evil uses for cloning looked like it had a chance of occurring, laws could be passed against it in particular. Anyway, even this would probably be unnecessary, because these things are probably illegal under current law. Cloning would also be useful for all sorts of good purposes—like providing desperately wanted children to infertile couples or to single people. It doesn't make sense to condemn it because it might also have some bad uses.

(5) Human cloning runs against our values as a community.

Reply: This last bit of reasoning, very frequently heard, merely says that we're against it. This sheds no light whatever on the *reasons* why cloning might be wrong.

If these are the best reasons people can come up with, then there's no good argument for the immorality of cloning. But it doesn't follow that cloning is morally okay! It might be that human cloning is, as many people feel, morally wrong even though there are no arguments anyone can give to show that it's wrong. This would be a curious and interesting state of affairs. We'd have a moral truth here, but we'd be able to give absolutely no good reason for anyone to believe it. We expect there to be good evidence for scientific truths, provided by reasoning, observation, and experimentation. Maybe the situation is different for moral truths.

Frankensurgery

Joe Rosen, a respected plastic surgeon, asked at a recent medical-ethics convention:

Why do we only value the average? Why are plastic surgeons dedicated only to restoring our current notions of the conventional, as opposed to letting people explore, if they want, what the possibilities are?

He has a vision of the plastic surgery of the future: cochlear implants to improve our hearing to that of an owl; retinal implants to improve our vision so that we could see many miles; fins to make us swim like fishes; echolocation devices for navigation in the dark; motorized fingers for chefs that could whip eggs; noses that doubled as flashlights; wings![13]

---

[13] "DR. DAEDALUS: A radical plastic surgeon wants to give you wings" by Lauren Slater, *Harper's Magazine* 303, no. 1814 (July 2001), pp. 57–67.

All this is entertaining as science-fiction, but what do you think about actually permitting it to happen? Most people view this sort of thing with horror and disgust, but Rosen points out that it's merely a bit of an extension to the kinds of things already routinely permitted: nose-jobs, liposuction, face-lifts, breast augmentation. Perhaps this doesn't reduce your sense of horror and disgust, but the question I want to raise is whether your feelings here constitute a good reason to prevent other people— people who want these things—from getting them done. I feel a bit disgusted when I see someone with a ring piercing her lower lip; but this doesn't mean that lip-piercing should be illegal.

Speaking of the ethics of bio-technology that "crosses species boundaries," a medical-ethics specialist writes: "In the absence of an argument or the ability to point to some specific harm that might be involved..., we should regard to the objections per se to such practises...as mere and gratuitous prejudice."[14]

SOME QUESTIONS TO THINK ABOUT: Well, have you got a better argument? Can you point to some specific harm that might be involved? In the absence of that, does this show that your objections are mere and gratuitous prejudice?

The Commodore and the Porn Site

In June 2001, Commodore Eric Lerhe, the fifty-two-year-old commander of the Canadian fleet of warships on the West Coast, was charged under the Canadian National Defence Act with conduct to the prejudice of good order and discipline.[15] The range of penalties for the offence is wide, from administrative discipline to a formal dismissal with disgrace from the Canadian Forces to imprisonment for life; but, according to Lewis MacKenzie, retired major general in the Canadian armed forces, even if there is no official punishment, Lerhe will suffer public humiliation and financial losses of perhaps three hundred thousand dollars as the result of an unofficial promotion freeze and subsequent pension implications.

The reason for this charge was that before he took up command in January, and while he was off-duty outside Canada, Lerhe used a laptop computer that had been provided by the Department of National Defence,

---

[14] John Harris, *Wonderwoman and Superman*; quoted by Slater.

[15] The facts about this case, and the arguments, all come from the (Toronto) *Globe and Mail* newspaper: an article titled "Surfed porn sites, fleet chief relieved of duty" by Robert Matas, Tuesday, June 19, 2001; an unsigned editorial titled "The navy's hammer," Wednesday, June 20, 2001, and an opinion piece, "No sex, please—we're Canadian sailors," by Lewis MacKenzie, Wednesday, June 20, 2001.

to visit sexually explicit websites that he described as "Penthouse-like." He did so using his personal Internet account.

Well, let's look at some arguments about this case.

> Pornography changes the way women are viewed, Geraldine Glattstein, executive director of Women Against Violence Against Women, said in an interview. "It's dangerous for women to be supervised by someone who spends his spare time looking at those kinds of websites," Ms. Glattstein said. Supervisors who go back to the office after accessing pornographic sites are creating a hostile environment for women to work in, she added. "It certainly does not help make [the workplace] more friendly."

But an editorial in a Canadian newspaper argues:

> It is understandable that the Canadian Forces should be particularly sensitive to the violation of rules governing sexual materials in an age when it seeks to hire and retain women in a climate traditionally male and traditionally dismissive of women in uniform. And certainly there must be particular vigilance against those harassing actions—posting offensive material in shared quarters or offices, forwarding sexually explicit materials to coworkers—that contaminate the work environment.

However, the editorial continues, "None of that is at issue here." Lerhe looked at those websites in private. Nobody was harassed. His actions are no worse than reading *Playboy* magazine after hours—something some people find distasteful, but surely not meriting judicial action and severe consequences. Lerhe did use a Forces computer for his private surfing, but this is not a really big crime: it's no worse than typing a personal letter on your office computer after hours.

General MacKenzie argues that it's "ludicrous" to punish someone for Lerhe's actions:

> Would all senior officers, men and women, who have not visited a strip club during their career please step forward? Hmmm ... small crowd.... Give me a break! I used to read *Penthouse* and *Playboy*, particularly when I was overseas. It did not change my attitude toward female service members from numerous countries who worked for me (and who frequently lined up to be next to borrow the magazines).

But the fact that such activities are widespread doesn't make them morally acceptable. Some people would argue that reading *Playboy* after hours actually would make someone unfit to be a commander in the armed forces. There's a widespread argument that looking at pornography causes increased violence against women and other actions that harm them, but data on this are inconclusive. The real issue here is not whether looking at porn *causes* harm to women—it's whether it *constitutes* harm. How are we supposed to decide whether this is right?

There's a good deal of disagreement on the basic issues here in today's society. Women are more likely to think that there should be more legal restrictions on pornography than men, and people under thirty are more likely to think so than those over thirty. But all those arguments seem to make no difference, once somebody has a set opinion on the matter.

SOME QUESTIONS TO THINK ABOUT: You probably have some strong opinions on this question—almost everyone does nowadays. You might enjoy having an argument with your friends about this. If you do, see if anyone gets anyone else to change their mind. Ask yourself if it could be that there is no rational way to settle moral disagreements such as this one.

Do You Have to be Scum to Get Ahead in Business?

> "There are plenty of examples of nice people who did get to the top. Just look around! There's, ummmm, there's ... ah, hmmm. Ha ha! I'm sure there are *lots* of examples, and for some reason I can't think of a single ... *wait*! I've got one! Mother Theresa! That's it! Here's a very nice person who nevertheless rose to the top of her profession. So the moral is: even in this dog-eat-dog, highly competitive world, you *can* be a decent human being and still attain a career position where you kneel in the Third-World dirt trying to help the wretched and diseased. But if you want to succeed in a large modern corporation, scum is definitely the way to go."—Dave Barry[16]

8. INTO THE MAINSTREAM OF PHILOSOPHY

In Chapter XIV we were worrying about a very general issue in ethics, about whether a justification could be given for any sort of moral thinking or acting. In the present chapter, by contrast, we have been assuming that ethics is somehow in general justified; here we have been searching, indirectly, for general principles of morality that could be used in deciding specific moral issues.

---

[16] *Claw Your Way to the Top* (Emmaus, PA: Rodale Press, 1986), p. 32.

These two issues are connected. If moral rules exist to solve the Prisoner's Dilemma, then they are ways of regulating and restraining our already existing selfish desires, with the aim of coordinating our actions in order to maximize everyone's satisfaction of these desires. This suggests a test for the validity of our general moral rules: would acting in accord with such a general rule maximize everyone's desire satisfaction? This test, roughly speaking, is the one proposed by Utilitarianism—the view (roughly) that what is good is what produces the greatest happiness (or pleasure) for the greatest number of people. Here we might understand "happiness" or "pleasure" as desire-satisfaction.

Any utilitarian must reply to several sorts of objection. For one thing, it seems implausible that we are all morally required to look out for everyone's happiness. The example concerned with giving away your shoes raises questions about this. The interesting thing about this example is that it does seem initially plausible that satisfaction-maximization is the criterion of morally right action: the view is widespread that we should, for example, act to eliminate poverty, in order to eliminate the rather unequal degree of satisfaction people experience around the world. But the consequence of thinking that way seems to be that we are all acting dreadfully immorally. Is this possible?

Many philosophers have objected to utilitarianism on the grounds that the maximization of the distribution of satisfaction to everyone would necessitate depriving many people of what they have a right to have. As we have seen, however, it's not at all clear how we could decide what rights people have, especially when granting them rights often seems to interfere with our desire to maximize and equalize desire-satisfaction. How could it be proven that someone has a right to something? What is the basis of the existence of rights anyway?

A second sort of general objection utilitarians must face is that it seems clear to most of us that the point of morality can't be the satisfaction of just any desire. It can't be true that we'd all be morally perfect once things were set up so that we all get what we want to the greatest degree, because certain things people happen to want just seem wrong. Suppose that someone's deepest desires were satisfied by providing that person with a plastic companion. The feeling remains that something very important would be missing in that person's life with Shirley, even if he feels fully satisfied. Maybe there's more to the morally good life than merely getting what you want. But what? And why?

You won't have trouble finding lots of articles in anthologies in which philosophers argue for very different views on what the basic principles of morality and the good life are.

CHAPTER XVI

LAW, ACTION, and RESPONSIBILITY:

Ethics and the Philosophy of Law

1. PROBLEMS FOR JUDGES

The Messier Contract

Mark Messier, a hockey player for the New York Rangers, held a contract with the team a few years ago with an unusual provision. It said that if he was chosen Most Valuable Player in the National Hockey League, then his salary would be raised, if necessary, to make him among the five top-paid players in the league for the remainder of the contract period.

Here's a scenario that would have made for difficulties. Suppose that five other players (call them LaMer, LaPerrier, LaRose, LaFleur, and Gretsky) each held a contract specifying that if he scored over one hundred points in a season, then his salary should immediately be raised, if necessary, to put him among the five top-paid players in the league. Imagine that they each succeed in topping one hundred points during the season, and when each does that his salary is raised. At the end of the season, here are their salaries:

LaMer	$10 million
LaPerrier	$9 million
LaRose	$8 million
LaFleur	$7 million
Gretsky	$6 million

Then, at the end of the season, Messier is chosen Most Valuable Player. At that point, he is making a mere $5 million. So he goes to his team's owner, contract in hand, demanding a raise to put him in the top five. The owner agrees to raise his salary to $6.5 million. But then Gretsky finds out that he is no longer in the top five, and goes to the owner of his team. His salary is accordingly raised to $6.8 million. But then Messier goes back to his owner demanding and getting an additional raise. But then Gretsky does the same. Pretty soon, both are making more than LaFleur, who demands additional money. And so on.

The team owners notice that this leap-frogging has no end. All six players, with their six respective team-owners, appear before a judge whose job it is to sort out this mess.

Let's listen in to the debate in court.

Judge: Here's a solution. Let's go back to the time the problem came up. When Messier was chosen MVP, the salaries of the other five of you were above his. Suppose that Messier's salary be set at $6 million, tied with Gretsky's salary. Then only four players would be making more than Messier, so his salary would be among the top five. Only four players would be making more than Gretsky, so his salary would also be among the top five. It's solved!

Messier: Wait a minute. If Gretsky and I both made $6 million, and if the four others made higher salaries, both of us would be among the top *six*, not among the top *five*. There would be no top five salaries.

Judge: Hmm. Okay. Well, in that case, it appears that it's impossible for all six of you to get salaries among the top five in the league. Contracts specifying that someone do the impossible are invalid. So I think that all six of your contracts are invalid. Go back and negotiate valid contracts.

Messier: Hang on again. I signed my contract before any of these other guys. When I signed it there was nothing wrong with it. It's not my fault that other contracts made for difficulties. Then LaMer signed his, and there was nothing wrong with his either. Then LaPerrier, LaRose, and LaFleur each signed perfectly acceptable contracts. Gretsky signed his contract last; it was only then that a potential problem arose. Gretsky's contract is invalid.

Judge: I guess that's right.

Gretsky: Hold on. None of us signed contracts that were impossible to fulfil when we signed them. When each of us topped one hundred points, we got raises, and there was nothing impossible about our all being in the top five. The problem came up later, at the end of the season, when that damned Messier was chosen MVP. Only at that point did problems arise. So Messier's contract is the one that's invalid.

> *Judge:* Well, okay.
> *Messier:* Not so fast. No team owner has a contract that specifies an impossible action. When I won MVP my owner had to raise my salary, and he could. Then Gretsky wasn't any longer in the top five, so his owner had to raise his salary, and that wasn't impossible either. As salaries go up, one of the owners has to raise somebody's salary, but in no case does an owner have to do something that's impossible. The poor guys are just stuck with having to pay leapfrogging salaries.
> *Judge:* That's true.
> *Owners:* [In unison] But! But! But!

What should the judge do?

What Do Judges Do?

A continuing question in the philosophy of law is what the job of judges is supposed to be. What you learned in civics class is that laws are *made* by legislators, and it's the judge's duty only to *interpret* these laws. But here's a plausible story that casts doubt on this.

Imagine that years ago, when house-trailers were first produced, Billy-Bob towed one of them into town, bought an empty plot of land, parked his trailer on his land, and moved into it. A few months later, Billy-Bob's mail contained a bill for city taxes. The amount of the bill was based on an assessor's judgement of the value of the land plus the value of the trailer. Billy-Bob complained to the city. He was taxable for the land, he agreed, but not for the trailer on it. Land and houses, but not trailers, were taxable by the city. But the city assessment office insisted that he was living in his trailer, so it was a house. The matter went to court.

Judges have to decide on three sorts of matters: what the facts are, which laws are relevant, and how the facts fit the laws. The facts in this case were no problem; Billy-Bob's lawyer and the city's lawyer agreed readily about what these were. There was also no disagreement that only one law was relevant: the city bylaw that stated simply that the tax assessment was to be based on the value of the land plus the value of any houses on that land. The only matter under contention for the judge to make a decision on was whether Billy-Bob's trailer was a house. We imagine the following arguments made by the two lawyers:

> *City's Lawyer:* It's a house. The word 'house' means "1.a. A structure serving as a dwelling for one or several families. b. A place of abode; residence. c. Something

	that serves as an abode."[1] It's a structure, and it serves as a dwelling for Billy-Bob's family. It's Billy-Bob's abode and residence. It's something that serves as an abode.
Billy-Bob's Lawyer:	Gimme that dictionary! The word 'trailer' means "A furnished van drawn by a truck or automobile and used as a house or office when parked."[2]
City's Lawyer:	Aha! "Used *as a house*"!
Billy-Bob's Lawyer:	If my learned colleague would just hang on for a damned minute. *Using* something as a house doesn't make it a house. I refer to the case of *Arkansas v. Smedley*. Smedley was charged with owning a gun without a permit, and he argued that since he used it only as a paperweight it was a paperweight, not a gun. Smedley lost.

On what basis can the judge make a decision? Clearly there's some "interpretation" of the law necessary here. But what is "interpretation"?

There's no problem in understanding the wording of the law. It's nice and clear.

One basis on which hard judicial decisions are sometimes made is by consideration of precedents in decisions about similar cases. But house-trailers were brand new. There weren't any similar cases.

Sometimes it's thought that one thing judges do when they "interpret" laws is figure out what intention the lawmakers must have had when they created the law. Even if this mind-reading trick is a sensible way of "interpreting" some laws, it wasn't useful in this case. The law had been made years before, when house-trailers weren't even imagined: the legislators couldn't have had any intentions about them at all.

What the judges sometimes do is consider what the morally right decision is. But that didn't help in this case. On which side did Justice lie? Neither side was trying to cheat the other. Neither was acting out of malice. Neither would have been *unfairly* victimized by a decision for the other side.

There didn't seem to be any good basis for a decision one way or the other. Maybe what would influence the judge's decision was the fact that Billy-Bob was a nice guy, or the fact that the city was running short on

---

[1] He was reading from *The American Heritage Dictionary of the English Language*, p. 638.

[2] Ibid., p. 1361.

money. Such considerations don't appear to provide a good basis for a decision, but a decision had to be made.

Whichever way the decision went, a precedent would have been set: the law would afterwards be taken to read, in effect, that houses *and* installed trailers (or houses *but not* installed trailers) are taxable. This judge *made* the law.

2. PROBLEMS ABOUT ACTIONS

Why You Don't Drive When You're Drunk

Following is another philosophically interesting legal argument—this time, an actual case.

LaFontaine, after hours of heavy drinking, crawls out of the tavern utterly soused. Somehow he manages, mostly by random motion, to get in his car and start the motor. While he is slumped over the wheel almost unconscious, his foot presses the accelerator and his car lurches forward, crashing into a building with such force that the building is knocked off its foundation. The police arrive, extract LaFontaine from the wreckage, and (unsurprisingly) arrest him for dangerous driving.

The surprise is that, at his trial, LaFontaine pleads not guilty. His lawyer does not contest the fact that LaFontaine was drunk. Just the reverse: he bases his defence on the fact that he was drunk as a skunk.

This is the substance of the lawyer's argument. Suppose someone is turning the dial on his stereo set, trying to tune in the radio. Unknown to him, the stereo is wired to his car in such a way that turning the dial results in the car's moving forward and backward. That person isn't *driving his car* because 'driving' is the name of an *intentional action*. This person isn't driving because he doesn't intend that his car move, and he's unaware that his actions result in that movement. Now it's clear that LaFontaine was so drunk that he had no idea what he was doing. He didn't even know that he was in his car. He had no intentions about moving his car. His actions—unbeknownst to him—resulted in his car's motion, but he wasn't *driving* it. LaFontaine might be charged with public drunkenness, and he might be sued by the owner of the building for unintentionally damaging it. But he's not guilty of dangerous driving. Dangerous, yes. Driving, no.

A QUESTION TO THINK ABOUT: Do you agree with LaFontaine's lawyer? Remember that it's not in question whether there's something wrong with a guy who gets stinking drunk before getting in his car; the answer to that, everyone will agree, is Yes.

LaFontaine didn't win his case, but his lawyer's argument is strangely persuasive. Many of the activities mentioned in laws are intentional actions—things that people *do*. A necessary condition of *doing* something is that you're aware of your bodily movements, and that you intend the consequences.

This sort of distinction applies as well in ordinary moral thinking. If Sally tells Fred something that's false, but Sally doesn't want to deceive Fred and believes that what she said was true, then Sally hasn't *told a lie*, and we don't blame Sally for what she did. If Sally is so drunk that she hasn't a clue what she's saying, she isn't *lying* when she says something that's false.

The Lucky Murderer

Your whole gang is out to kill Vito. You slip some poison in Vito's granola, and he eats it. An hour later, the police, having been tipped off by the extermination company where you bought the poison, arrest you and charge you with murder. At the same time, Vito is rushed to the hospital, where his stomach is pumped, but it is too late—Vito is already showing the signs of serious poisoning. As Vito lies in his hospital room, near death, a fellow member of your gang, wanting to make sure Vito won't recover, slips into the hospital and shoots him in the head, killing him immediately. But now the police have to reduce their charge against you: you are charged only with attempted murder.

You were lucky. Had your pal not shot Vito, he would have died of the poison you gave him, and you would have been convicted of first-degree murder, which carries a much larger penalty than mere attempted murder. The puzzle here is that what your pal did had nothing to do with you. It seems that what crime you commit, and what your punishment is to be, should be a matter only of *what you do*, not of things that happen or don't happen afterwards. But it seems, in this case, that "what you did"—murder or merely attempted murder—depends on things that happen afterwards, and that are totally out of your control.

This puzzle does not merely apply to artificial, imaginary, or unlikely events. Think of all the things people do in real life for which they are praised or blamed. The praise or blame, and the extent of praise or blame, depend on what sort of action it was. And the sort of action depends on circumstances and consequences very often utterly out of control of the doer. An unlucky speeding driver may kill a pedestrian, for example; whether this happens or not depends a good deal on whether any pedestrians happen to be around when the speeder is careening down the road. And, of course, this is a matter over which the driver has no control. The very same behaviour on the driver's part will be punished very differently if it constitutes mere speeding, or if it involves killing a pedestrian. But this difference is merely a matter of good or bad luck for the driver.

A QUESTION TO THINK ABOUT: Is it fair to make our decision on what act was committed, and to adjust the amount of punishment meted out accordingly, on the basis of circumstances utterly beyond the agent's control?

A Time and a Place for Murder

Now suppose your pal didn't get to the hospital, and Vito dies of the poison you gave him. You have committed murder, but when? Suppose you put poison in his granola on Tuesday, he ate it on Wednesday, and he died on Thursday. Did the murder take place only on Tuesday? Or did it last from Tuesday through Thursday? This decision might have important consequences. Suppose your state legislature, meeting on Wednesday, votes to institute the death penalty for murders. Retroactive legislation isn't allowed, so murders that took place before Wednesday don't carry the death penalty. Is it clear that the murder you are charged with took place entirely before Wednesday? If "part" of it took place on Thursday, perhaps you face the death penalty.

Actions might be seen to be spread out not only in time, but also in space. Suppose you shot Vito instead, and that you were standing in New York at the time, near the Connecticut border, and Vito was standing a few feet away from you in Connecticut. Did the murder take place in New York or in Connecticut? This again might have important consequences. Suppose, for example, that New York has the death penalty for convicted murderers and Connecticut does not. It's tempting to think that the murder took place where you were, in New York. But now let's move you a few feet east, so that your outstretched arm, with the pistol in hand, is across the border in Connecticut while the rest of you is in New York. The hand that pulled the trigger, the gun, the path of the bullet, and Vito were all in Connecticut. But did the murder take place where you (all except for your arm) are—in New York?

3. CANS AND CAN'TS

Can Pierre Keep His Promise?

Pierre has promised you that he'll show up at noon in his car to drive you to the airport. Noon comes and goes; no Pierre. It turns out that he remembered his promise, but nevertheless he just sat in his room watching TV. Is Pierre to blame for his failure to keep his promise?

> Clearly he is. He could have kept his promise, but he didn't. It's his fault that he didn't show up to drive you. He's morally responsible for his failure.

But suppose it turns out that Pierre's crazy landlord has locked Pierre's room from the outside, and he can't get out. There's no phone in his room, so there's no way for him to warn you that he can't get there. All he can do is to sit there until someone comes by to let him out. Now is he to blame?

> This additional information absolves Pierre from blame. We wouldn't say that Pierre *ought* to have shown up, because he *couldn't* have.

The only things one ought to do are those things one can do. Philosophers express this general moral principle by the slogan, "Ought implies can."

This seems clear and correct. But let's think about things a bit more deeply. What does it mean to say that someone *can* or *can't* do something?

> Perhaps we might say: the things you can't do are the things you try your best to do, but don't succeed. We imagine Pierre trying to get out of his room: he pushes on his door, turning the handle one way and the other. He bangs and yells, trying to attract the attention of someone who might be able to let him out. *This* is a case in which Pierre *can't* get out of his room.

But this won't do as an account of 'can't,' because we would agree that Pierre can't get out of the room even if he doesn't actually perform all these frantic attempts. Suppose Pierre hears the door lock, and he knows that now there's no way to get out, so he doesn't even try. He just turns on the TV and settles down for what might be a long wait. It's clear that in this situation Pierre can't get out, even though he doesn't even try to. Can you think of a better account of what it is not to be able to do something?

> Perhaps a better answer is: To say that Pierre can't get out of the room means that *if* Pierre tried his best to get out, he *wouldn't* get out. Nothing that Pierre might have done would get him out of the room. This means that it can be true that Pierre can't get out of the room, although he doesn't actually try.

But even this won't do. Suppose that Pierre's crazy landlord has installed a hidden button on the lock, which will unlock the door from the inside. The landlord hasn't told Pierre about this, and Pierre has no way of knowing about it. Now there is something Pierre might have done to get him out of his room: he might have pushed the button that would have unlocked the door. It's within Pierre's physical power to push the button. So should we still say that Pierre can't get out of the room?

A QUESTION TO THINK ABOUT: Maybe after some thought about this you might come up with a better account of what it means to say that one *can* or *can't* do something. But this question turns out to be surprisingly complicated and difficult.

The Incapable Golfer

Despite the difficulties of *can* and *can't* we have just noticed, at least one thing seems clear: whenever someone *does* something, then it follows that that is the sort of thing the person *can* do. If we see Matilda driving her car, that proves that Matilda can drive. Of course, this doesn't prove that she'll still be able to drive at any time in the future, because relevant circumstances might someday change. We see Matilda driving on Tuesday, but she suffers a paralysing stroke on Wednesday, and on Thursday she can't drive. But at least it proves that, on Tuesday, she can drive.

By now you will hardly be surprised to find out that even this very clear principle might be mistaken. Consider this example:

Myrtle is a skilled golfer, and she hits an ordinary shot off the tee. The ball travels down the fairway and finally rolls to a stop. Call the exact spot where the ball stops Spot **S**. What Myrtle did was to hit a golf ball from the tee exactly to Spot **S**. Does it follow that Myrtle *can* hit a golf ball from the tee exactly to Spot **S**? Suppose that we interrupt Myrtle's game right after this shot, and ask her to repeat it—to hit another ball from the tee exactly to Spot **S**. Being a good golfer, she hits balls that wind up in the general vicinity of that spot, but after many tries, unsurprisingly, no ball has rolled exactly to Spot **S**. This seems to show that Myrtle can't hit a golf ball exactly to Spot **S**. But nothing relevant has changed since the time she actually did it. It seems that, even at the time she did it, she couldn't do it. No golfer, after all, has *that* much ability.

The principle we were considering claimed that the fact that someone actually does something proves that they can do it. But this example apparently shows that the principle is wrong.

No Absolution for Pierre

We have been considering, in the last two items, difficulties in explaining exactly what 'can' and 'can't' involve. Recall that all this was prompted by moral considerations, by the idea that Pierre isn't to blame for something he didn't do when he couldn't do it.

Let's now put the complications of 'can' and 'can't' aside, and examine directly the notion that one isn't to blame for something he didn't do when he couldn't do it.

Let's change the Pierre example slightly. Suppose Pierre, as before, has promised to drive you to the airport, but sits in his room watching TV instead. As before, Pierre's door is locked, and there's no way he can get out of his room. Pierre's not to blame, right?

Well, not necessarily. Suppose (and here we change the story a bit) that Pierre doesn't know that his door is locked. Why doesn't Pierre try to get out? He's feeling lazy, and he doesn't feel like driving you to the airport. He remembers his promise, and he knows that you're counting on him. "To hell with that!" Pierre thinks. "I'll just stay here and watch TV instead."

Pierre can't get out of his room, but now he *is* to blame. He's responsible for not having done something he nevertheless couldn't have done.

4. FREE WILL

If you do something bad, you're not to blame if you were forced to do it. But you are to blame if you did it, as we say, "on your own free will." But philosophers have worried for centuries about what "free will" might amount to, and about when, if ever, we really have it.

Here's one way of looking at the problem. As we've seen, it's very tempting to believe *determinism*, the position that everything has a cause (see **The Incompetent Repairman** in Chapter X above). I mean *everything*, including everyone's actions. If that's so, then whatever you do is the result of the preceding events that caused it, and those events are the result of earlier events, and so on, back into time. Given the earlier causes of those actions, they had to happen. So you had to do what you did—you were forced to by the earlier causes. Given the earlier causes, your actions could not have been otherwise. So they weren't done "out of your free will," whatever that might mean. Like everything else in the universe, they were necessitated by previous causes. So you're not responsible for anything you do, and neither is anyone else. The whole way we have of thinking about freedom and responsibility is an outdated unscientific myth. Scientific thinking, in terms of cause and effect, does away with all that. And because you're not responsible for anything, you shouldn't be blamed for the bad things you do, or praised for the good things.

Some philosophers accept this reasoning. Many, however, reject its conclusion. We'll look at some ways they've found to avoid it.

Freedom as Uncaused Action

Descartes (see **Angels and Superman**, Chapter XII), the existentialists (see **Sorry, I'm Not Free Right Now**, Chapter VII), and other philosophers think that what has gone wrong with this reasoning is that it puts people in the same category as the other stuff in the universe. All the rest of it might very well be determined by causes, but people aren't like that other stuff. They're radically different: they're not determined by causes. Because these philosophers think that there are two basically different sorts of things making up the universe—the stuff that is determined by causes, on one hand, and people, who aren't, on the other—they're called *dualists* (the root of this word means "two").

What makes dualists so sure that humans are undetermined? Just take a look inside yourself, they say: you'll notice that no matter what sorts of events have transpired in the past, you might now do **X** or **Y**.

Other philosophers object to this partitioning of the universe. We should think of things as a unified whole, rather than put humans alone as radically different from—outside of—nature. They are *monists* (the root of this word means "one"). But how could a monist believe in free will?

Lucretius, the Roman philosopher whom we've been talking about from time to time, was a monist. As we mentioned in **Why You Shouldn't**

Fear Death in Chapter XIII, he thought that humans were material things like everything else, subject to the same processes as the rest of material nature. But he also wanted to believe in free will. So he supposed that the regular processes of nature were varied from time to time by a random swerve in the direction of travel of the atoms that made things up. (Yes, Lucretius thought that things—and people—were made up of atoms.) When this swerve happened in the atoms inside us, we did unpredictable things, things not determined by prior causes. This is our freedom.

In modern times, many scientists agree with Lucretius that some events in the physical universe are uncaused and random: the events that quantum physicists talk about (see **Nothing Made That Happen**, Chapter X.) Some philosophically minded physicists and physically minded philosophers have suggested that this randomness might provide for free will in an otherwise determined universe.

SOME QUESTIONS TO THINK ABOUT: According to the modern Lucretians, there are random quantum events that happen in our brain—resulting in free action—and other actions—unfree ones—that happen as the result of regular causal sequences, determined by earlier events.

So let's see how this would work out. Imagine that Fred always gives up his seat on the bus to aged or infirm people, because that sort of pattern of behaviour was instilled in his brain by a lot of training by his mum when he was little. That would be behaviour that was determined in a regular causal manner, and so it would be unfree; he shouldn't be praised for this good action, because he's not responsible for it. But imagine that one day instead of giving up his seat in the bus to an old, infirm woman, Fred stays seated and kicks her crutches right out from under her. Why did he do this? Well, there was a random quantum event in his brain which overrode the normal causal processes, and produced this unpredicted and unpredictable behaviour. That would be random behaviour, so that would be free; he should be blamed for this bad action.

Don't you think that this reasoning gets things backwards? Where's the mistake? The dualists also think that free actions are the ones that happen without the normal sequence of antecedent causes. Do they run into the same problem?

Freedom as Irrationality

In his short novel *Notes from Underground*, Dostoyevsky argued for a weird and interesting position: that the only true freedom is crazy irrationality.

Consider Sally, who is a rational person. She loves fish and hates hamburgers, so whenever she's in a fast-food joint, she orders the Fishwich and avoids the Whopper. When she has important things to do the next day, she avoids drinking too much the night before and gets a good night's sleep. She knows that she should give up her seat on the bus to someone who's aged or infirm, so whenever such a person gets on her bus, she gets up and offers her seat.

Now, consider Fred, who is irrational. He loves fish and hates hamburgers, so whenever he's in a fast-food joint, he orders the Whopper. Why? No reason. He really hates that Whopper—he just doesn't act to suit his own preferences. He deliberately gets drunk and stays up too late the night before he has something important to do. He'll be in trouble the next day, and he knows this, but he doesn't act to further his own advantage. When he's on the bus and someone aged and infirm gets on, Fred stays seated and kicks her crutches out from under her. He knows that this is nasty, but he is irrational, and he sometimes quirkily does what he knows is nasty and wrong, just on a whim.

Sally is predictable; what she does is determined by her preferences, her advantage, the useful, and the good. She's just like a machine. Fred, by contrast, is not. He acts ... well, just out of his own freedom.

> "Ah, ladies and gentlemen, don't talk to me of free will when it comes to timetables and arithmetic, when everything will be deducible from twice two makes four! There's no need for free will to find that twice two is four. That's not what I call free will!"—Fyodor Dostoyevski[3]

> "Freedom means being able to say 2+2=4."—George Orwell[4]

Compatibilism

The position on freedom and determinism that most philosophers believe nowadays is called *compatibilism* or *soft determinism*. According to this view, the difference between a free action—one the person is responsible for—and compelled action—for which the person is not responsible—is not that one is determined by antecedent causes but the other isn't. If you like the idea that everything, including human actions, is determined by antecedent causes, you can keep believing this, but believe that some actions are free and that their doers are responsible for them, anyway.

---

[3] *Notes from Underground*, trans. Andrew R. MacAndrew (New York: New American Library, 1961).

[4] *1984* (New York: Knopf, 1992).

Well, then, what do they suppose is the difference between free and unfree action? A free action, they suggest, is one that's caused by a decision the person makes, but an unfree action isn't. So, for example, if you spill your coffee all over my computer keyboard because you decided to do it, I blame you for this. But if there are other causes—if a decision played no part in this—for example, if somebody pushed you and jostled your arm while you were holding a full coffee cup—then you're not to blame. Note that we don't need any undetermined, random actions anywhere in this story. When you spilled your coffee on purpose, the spill was determined by a decision, and this decision (no doubt) by other earlier events, maybe including your bad upbringing.

A QUESTION TO THINK ABOUT: But if the decision that caused—determined—that spill was itself caused by events outside of you, then how can you be counted as responsible for that action?

FOR FURTHER READING: Just about any general introductory philosophy textbook you pick up will have a section on freedom and determinism, and just about all of these sections will have something about the three sorts of views we have been talking about (*hard determinism*, which accepts determinism and denies freedom; *libertarianism*, which denies determinism and accepts freedom; and *soft determinism*, which accepts both). So I won't even bother to mention particular readings.

5. ACTING AND REFRAINING

Two Ways to Kill Granny

It's often taken to be a principle of moral reasoning that *doing* something is morally different from merely *refraining from acting*, even if the doing and the refraining have the same outcome. In ordinary circumstances, for example, merely doing nothing and thereby failing to save someone's life isn't, of course, a very nice thing, but it's supposed to be not as bad as actually killing the person, despite the fact that refraining from acting (not saving the life) and the action (killing) have the same outcome: the person's death. Are you convinced that this is right? Then consider this:

Suppose evil Ian hates his grandmother, and wishes she were dead. While she is taking her bath, Ian decides to enter the bathroom and to hold Granny under water till she dies. Now compare these two scenarios:

S1. Ian enters the bathroom and holds Granny under water, and she dies.

S2. Ian enters the bathroom. By coincidence, just at that moment Granny slips on the soap, hits her head on the side of the tub, and falls unconscious. Ian notices that the water will soon rise above her head and drown her; all he has to do to save her life is to turn off the water. But he refrains from doing this; he does nothing, and she dies.

Scenarios **S1** and **S2** are designed to be as alike as possible, except for the difference that in **S1** Ian's *action* results in death, whereas in **S2** Ian's *refraining* has that outcome. But many people think that Ian would be judged to be equally at fault in both scenarios. Maybe there really isn't a real moral difference between acting and refraining after all.

Moral Technology

The supposed moral difference between acting and refraining has led to the invention of a bizarre bit of medico-ethical technology.

There is a general rule of medical ethics that depends on this supposed moral difference. When someone is near death from an incurable terminal disease, modern medicine is sometimes able to prolong that person's life for a while using elaborate life-support systems. But when that period would be full of unrelievable suffering for that person, and when death is only postponed a bit, not prevented, often everyone—the person him/herself, family and friends, the medical personnel involved, and experts on medical ethics—agree that it is better that the life not be prolonged.

The best solution, under the circumstances, is to refrain from attaching the person to the life-support systems. This would merely be refraining from prolonging life, and would widely be found ethically acceptable. But suppose that the person has already been attached to those systems before the decision not to prolong life is made. In order to end that person's life now, someone would have to switch off the life-support; but this would be *doing something* that results in death, not merely refraining from doing something. The acting/refraining principle we have been discussing would count this as morally forbidden. It is murder.

This is where ethics-tech comes to the rescue. A simple addition to the life-support system puts a timer on it, designed to shut it off after, say, twenty-four hours. If, before this time runs out, a button is pushed, an additional twenty-four hours is added to the timer, and the machine stays on for one more day. Pushing this button once every day can keep the machine on indefinitely, if that's what's desired.

You can see how this "solves" the ethical problem. If it is decided that prolonging the life would be a bad idea, nobody has to *do* anything. All that we have to do is to *refrain* from pushing the button; the timer would run out, all by itself, with the desired result.

There's a danger in using this adapted machine: in other cases, it is of course important that the machine stay on, and what if someone forgets to push the button? But this danger is outweighed, in the eyes of some people who take the acting/refraining distinction seriously, by the moral advantage this adapted machine sometimes gives us.

But there's something very bizarre about this ethical "solution." The object, everyone agrees, is to provide an earlier, more humane end to the unfortunate patient's life. Can it reasonably be supposed that using a machine that stops all by itself, as opposed to one that has to be shut off, makes the moral difference between a humane, morally praiseworthy procedure, and a morally hideous, utterly forbidden murder? An ethics that tells us that the addition of this timer makes that difference is clearly an ethics run amok.

Here we have another reason to doubt that the acting/refraining distinction is a morally important one.

Ten-to-One Dilemmas

Here are a couple of additional cases to try out your moral intuitions on.

Imagine you're standing on a railroad line, at a point where the track splits into two. There's a manually operable switch at that point, which can send a train coming down the track into one or the other of the branches at the fork. A short way past the fork, some little children are playing on the tracks. Ten of them are playing on the north fork, and one on the south. You notice that the switch is now set to send a train down the north fork, and a high-speed train is approaching. There's no time to warn the children to get off the tracks. If the train continues, it will kill ten children. But you do have time to throw the switch, sending the train down the south track, where one child will be killed. Should you throw the switch? Here are two possible answers:

> 1. A horrible tragedy will result whatever you do, of course. But there would be a worse tragedy—the death of ten children—if you don't throw the switch. If you do, only one death will result. It seems that you should throw the switch.

2. But the acting/refraining distinction gives a different answer. If you throw the switch, you are *acting*. If you just stand there and do nothing, you are *refraining*. Your action will save ten lives, but you will knowingly bring about the death of that child on the south track. This is murder, and forbidden.

FOR FURTHER READING: This problem has become a classic in moral philosophy. It's usually called the "Trolley Problem," after the way it was presented by Philippa Foot in "The Problem of Abortion and the Doctrine of Double Effect" (*Oxford Review*, 1967.)

Perhaps by now, having been convinced by all these examples, you doubt that the acting/refraining distinction is a morally relevant one. Maybe you think it's clear that the right thing to do is to throw the switch, sacrificing one child's life to save ten.

If that's what you think, here's one final example designed to confuse you.

Suppose you are the physician in charge of the transplant division at a big hospital. Ten children are under your care. All of them are dying from various organ failures, and all of them could be saved only by organ transplants. One needs a heart transplant, two need kidney transplants, three need liver transplants, and four need lung transplants. None of these organs is available, and none will become available until after all ten have died. All you need is one healthy dead body, out of which you can extract a heart, two kidneys, and the liver and lungs, each of which can be cut up into pieces to provide all the transplant material needed to save the lives of your patients. (This is, of course, science fiction. Transplant recipients have to be carefully matched to donors, and it's unlikely that one donor could provide organs for all ten patients. Other features also make this story currently impossible. But ignore all this.)

While you're pondering your problem, you idly glance out the window. There, playing on the sidewalk outside the hospital, is a healthy-looking little girl the same size as your patients. You run outside, grab the child, and carry her to the operating room, where you cut her up to provide the parts necessary for your patients. Ten children are saved; one dies.

Everyone would agree that, at the very least, you should be locked up in some unpleasant prison for a good long time as a result of this. But what's of interest here is the moral reasoning that condemns this. In particular, if you accepted the conclusion in the example just above that you ought to throw the railroad switch, you should consider what makes that case different from this one. In both cases, there are ten children who will die if you do nothing, and in both cases, the life of one innocent child, who would live if you did nothing, is sacrificed to save the ten. What, if anything, is the difference?

How to Assault a Police Officer by Doing Nothing

Here's another interesting actual legal case with an ingenious defense. Again, questions are raised about acting and refraining.

Fagan is parking his car on a city street, and a constable is guiding him into the space. Without knowing he's doing it, Fagan brings his car to a halt with one of its tires resting squarely on top of the constable's foot. The constable points out that the car is on his foot. Fagan responds with an offensive remark and tells the constable he could wait. Finally, after repeated requests, he moves his car.

Fagan is later arrested and charged with assaulting a police officer in the execution of his duty. He pleads not guilty, on the following grounds. An assault is defined in law as an action (of a certain sort) accompanied by a malicious intent. When Fagan's car rolled onto the constable's foot this may be construed as his action, since he was in control of his car; but there was, as yet, no assault, because he did not know that the foot was there. He had no intention to stop his car on the foot, so assault, which presumes intent, had not yet been committed. A moment later the constable made Fagan aware that his tire was on the constable's foot; at that point, Fagan got the malicious intention to leave it there. But leaving the car there is not doing anything—it's not an *action*, so it can't be an assault.

Fagan's defense did not work. In finding him guilty of assault, a judge gave this (perhaps not entirely convincing) reasoning: Fagan's action was an ongoing one, beginning with his rolling his car onto the foot and continuing through the time when he refused to get it off. The malicious intention developed during this extended action, so the requirements for assault were satisfied.

FOR FURTHER READING: The Canadian case of *Fagan* is described and analyzed in *An Introduction to Criminal Law* by Graham Parker (Agincourt, ON: Methuen Publications, 1977).

Poor Joshua!

The acting/refraining distinction is relevant to legal debates about genuinely important and tragic cases—not just amusing ones like *Fagan*.

In 1984, four-year-old Joshua DeShaney was beaten so badly by his father that he suffered brain damage so severe he would have to spend the rest of his life in an institution for the "profoundly retarded." His father was convicted of child abuse.

The county Department of Social Services had been aware for a long time that Joshua's father had been abusing him, and took various steps to protect him, including once temporarily removing him from his father's custody. But on this occasion, despite very good reason to think that the child was in real danger, they did not protect him from his father.

Joshua and his mother, acting on his behalf, sued various social workers and their department for failing to protect him. The case reached the U.S. Supreme Court in 1988, and their decision[5] affirmed the lower courts' judgement that the social workers did not violate Joshua's rights by failing to protect him.

One of the issues in this case was the interpretation of just what sorts of rights were provided by the "due process clause" of the Fourteenth Amendment to the U.S. Constitution (which guarantees that no person should be deprived of life, liberty, or property without due process of law). But the larger issue here was whether it was necessary for agents of the state—those social workers, in this case—to intervene to prevent harm. One principle that Supreme Court Justices made much of in their printed opinions accompanying their ruling is that there is a duty to protect someone only when there has been a "special relationship" established that removes the ordinary means individuals have for self-protection. For example, when somebody is in prison, they are deprived of their normal protections and liberties, so the state has a duty to protect them and could be sued if that person is harmed due to the state's failure to protect. But the state had undertaken no "special relationship" with Joshua which made it their duty to protect him.

Justice Blackmun, dissenting from the decision of the Court, wrote:

> Poor Joshua! Victim of repeated attacks by an irresponsible, bullying, cowardly, and intemperate father, and abandoned by respondents who placed him in a dangerous predicament and who knew or learned what was going on, and yet did essentially nothing except, as the Court revealingly observes ... "dutifully recorded these incidents in [their] files." It is a sad commentary upon American life and constitutional principles—so full of late of patriotic fervor and proud proclamations about "liberty and

---

[5] *DeShaney v. Winnebago Cty. Soc. Servs. Dept.*, 489 *U.S. 189 (1989)*.

justice for all"—that this child, Joshua DeShaney, is now assigned to live out the remainder of his life profoundly retarded.

Chief Justice Rehnquist, delivering the opinion of the Court, wrote:

> While the State may have been aware of the dangers that Joshua faced in the free world, it played no part in their creation, nor did it do anything to render him any more vulnerable to them. That the State once took temporary custody of Joshua does not alter the analysis, for when it returned him to his father's custody, it placed him in no worse position than that in which he would have been had it not acted at all; the State does not become the permanent guarantor of an individual's safety by having once offered him shelter. Under these circumstances, the State had no constitutional duty to protect Joshua.
>
> Judges and lawyers, like other humans, are moved by natural sympathy in a case like this to find a way for Joshua and his mother to receive adequate compensation for the grievous harm inflicted upon them. But before yielding to that impulse, it is well to remember once again that the harm was inflicted not by the State of Wisconsin, but by Joshua's father. The most that can be said of the state functionaries in this case is that they stood by and did nothing when suspicious circumstances dictated a more active role for them.

The Bad Samaritan

Sally is on her way to the coffee shop when Fred, an elderly man walking down the street in front of her, falls to the ground. "Help me!" croaks Fred. "My heart pills—they're in that bag I've dropped over there! Please!" But Sally is just desperate for her daily double shot half decaf skinny latte, so she just steps over the man on the ground and continues on her way.

If Sally were a nurse who was hired to accompany old Fred on his walk and to help him out if he gets in trouble, she'd certainly be failing in her duty. But as things are, Sally has no "special relationship" with Fred which gives her a duty to help him.

SOME QUESTIONS TO THINK ABOUT: We can agree that Sally is not the sort of person we'd like as a friend, but has she actually violated a duty? Should there be a law against what she did? (This would have to be a law against not-doing.) Should Fred, if he survives, or Fred's children if he doesn't, be able to sue Sally for not helping him?

6. INTO THE MAINSTREAM OF PHILOSOPHY

Laws exist to prevent immoral action, but it's clear that the fact that something is not immoral is not sufficient grounds for saying that there ought to be a law against it. When they make you Prime Minister of Klopstokia, you'll be able to get the parliament to make any law you want. One thing that's always been a minor annoyance to you is that some people show up late for appointments. It's not controversial whether this sort of thing is immoral—everyone agrees that showing up late is wrong. It's obvious, however, that it would be stupid to make lateness illegal, punishable by law. In this case, the reason is that it's such a trivial matter. But there are other, much less trivial wrongs that should also not be a matter of law. For example, some parents bring up their children with very low self-respect, with unfortunate psychological consequences on the kids for the rest of their lives. I don't think you'll want to create a law against this, either. You should start designing the new Klopstokian legal code soon, but first you'll have to decide on some principles for deciding which wrong things should be prevented by law, and which should not.

Another sort of issue dealt with in Philosophy of Law is the nature of the actual (or the proper) function of judges and juries. Do they *make* the law, or merely *interpret* it? If the latter, what exactly is *interpretation*? This issue is raised in the example above concerning the house-trailer. It's a philosophical question, not a factual one; it's not easily answerable even after we've observed the actual procedures followed by judges. You probably know enough about what actually goes on in courts to think about this question.

Several interesting philosophical questions arise not only in Philosophy of Law, but also when we consider ordinary matters of action and responsibility in everyday contexts. We have seen how questions arise concerning the time and place of an action. These questions might be important to answer not only in legal contexts. The notion of an *action* is philosophically interesting. Sometimes we describe actions in terms merely of intentional bodily movements. But sometimes action-descriptions include what happens outside the doer's body, as a result of the bodily motions. In the philosophical area called Theory of Action, philosophers consider questions about delimiting and counting such actions.

Another interesting, difficult, and often important family of questions concerns responsibility. It seems we're not always responsible for the unintended consequences of otherwise intentional actions. For example, if you intentionally hit a golf ball, but unintentionally hit a golfer in front of you on the head, you're (in a sense) not responsible for harming the other golfer. But things are not this simple. You might justly be blamed for the harm even if you didn't anticipate it (for example, if you should have made sure you wouldn't hit her, but you didn't). Can you give a general account of what sort of bad results one is responsible for?

A related issue concerns what we can and can't do. You're not to blame for not doing something you can't do, but it's sometimes not clear what you can't do. It seems plausible to think of a person's actions as being caused, but if the causes of a person's actions actually took place, could that person have acted otherwise? This issue is one of the questions raised in conjunction with the general topic of freedom—it's the issue of free will. Do we actually have free will? What is free will supposed to be, anyway?

The acting/refraining distinction is another one considered in action theory. This issue has special relevance in ethics, since we're often supposed to be more to blame for the bad results of our actions than for similar results of our refraining from acting. You might think about this issue by imagining and morally comparing pairs of circumstances that differ only along acting/refraining lines. One currently lively and important debate along these lines concerns euthanasia—mercy killing. It's widely thought that it's morally permissible to let someone die—to refrain from keeping him or her alive—in the terminal and horribly painful stages of a disease, but that it's morally impermissible to act to kill that person. If the acting/refraining distinction makes no sense or is morally irrelevant, then we shouldn't make this distinction. What do you think about euthanasia?

You'll often find articles dealing with the issues raised in these chapters in introductory anthologies. A very good, somewhat more advanced book on action theory is Alvin I. Goldman's *A Theory of Human Action* (Englewood Cliffs, NJ: Prentice-Hall, 1970). There are plenty of books available dealing with practical ethical problems in many areas; in these, you'll often find philosophical discussion of law, action, and responsibility.

CHAPTER XVII

JOKES AND OTHER AESTHETIC MATTERS

1. THE AESTHETICS OF HUMOUR

The Joke I Didn't Get

Kenny was the humourist in my eighth-grade class. One day he told a number of us this joke:

> Two elephants are sitting in a bathtub. One of them says, "Pass the soap, Millicent." The other replies, "No soap—radio."

Kenny grinned nervously at the end of the joke. The listeners smiled politely and half-heartedly. We walked away, wondering what was supposed to be funny.

I puzzled over this event a long time. Years later I was able to figure out what had been going on, after I read the following description of a classical practical joke. You and a group of others who are in on the plot find an unwitting victim. You tell the victim that pointless "no soap—radio" story. At the end, you and your confederates, as you have pre-arranged, all pretend to collapse into helpless laughter, watching the victim who, embarrassed by not getting it and not wanting to appear to be the only one who didn't, pretends to crack up too.

But Kenny didn't do it right: he had no confederates. Nobody laughed. What must have happened was that Kenny himself had previously been the victim of this practical joke. Thinking that the "no soap" story must be hilarious even though he didn't get it, he told it to us. The joke continued to be on him.

It's interesting that the tradition for playing this practical joke includes telling exactly that "no soap—radio" story, when any pointless story would do. The reason for this is, I suppose, that it's very difficult to come up with a genuinely pointless and unfunny story—more difficult than thinking up a funny one. The "no soap—radio" story is actually a very artful and clever creation: it's a story with all the form and rhythm of a joke, but utterly lacking the funny content. Whether or not you approve of practical joking, you have to admire the skill involved in the creation of this one.

Two questions are suggested here. One is: what, really, is joke form? Everyone who has heard jokes told badly know that, to be funny, jokes need to have exactly the right structure, and need to be told exactly right. This one has the form exactly right, and Kenny was a master of joke execution. But form and execution aren't sufficient to make something funny. The second, and more difficult question, is: why is some content funny?

Prison Humour

Here's a joke about jokes that illustrates these questions.

> A man is spending the first day of his sentence in prison. He is at lunch in the huge prison dining hall; all the inmates are quietly eating. Suddenly one inmate shouts out, "Sixty-three!" and everyone laughs. A few minutes later, another inmate yells, "Three hundred and four!" and everyone laughs again.
>
> The new arrival is puzzled. "What's going on?" he asks the man sitting next to him.
>
> His neighbour replies: "We've all been together so long that we've heard each others' jokes over and over again, and we have all the jokes memorized. To save effort, we've given each joke a number, so all we have to do to tell one of these jokes is to give its number."
>
> "Hey, that's a good idea," says the new arrival. "I think I'll try telling one." He shouts, "Ninety-seven!" Silence. Nobody even smiles. "What did I do wrong?" he asks his neighbour.
>
> The neighbour replies, "Well, some people just don't know how to tell a joke."

Laughter is the Best Medicine

> "Analyzing humor is like dissecting a frog. Few people are interested and the frog dies of it." —E. B. White[1]

White speaks the truth. But when there's something to analyze, you can't stop philosophers from trying.

---

[1] Quote given by Byrne, p. 383.

Immanuel Kant is among the most ponderous of philosophical writers, but even his writing contains a few jokes (presented in connection with his theorizing on humour). This is one:

> The heir of a rich relative wants to arrange for him a very solemn funeral service, but complains that things are not quite working out: for (he says) the more money I give my mourners to look grieved, the more cheerful they look.

Another Kantian joke is the story of

> the grief of some merchant who, during his return trip from India to Europe, with all his fortune in merchandise, was forced by a heavy storm to throw everything overboard, and whose grief was such that it made his *wig* turn grey that very night. [Kant's—or his translator's—italics]

Kant remarks that the second joke "will make us laugh," and that the first "evokes ringing laughter in us." Whenever you read philosophy, you must ask yourself whether what the philosopher says is true.

Kant theorizes that "Laughter is an affect that arises if a tense expectation is transformed into nothing." He gives a physiological explanation of how laughter results, and consequently of why we enjoy humour:

> For if we assume that all our thoughts are, in addition, in a harmonious connection with some agitation in the body's organs, then we can pretty well grasp how, as the mind suddenly shifts alternately from one position to another in order to contemplate its object, there might be a corresponding alternating tension and relaxation of the elastic parts of our intestines that is communicated to the diaphragm.... The lungs, meanwhile, rapidly and intermittently expel air, and so give rise to an agitation that is conducive to our health. It is this agitation alone, and not what goes on in the mind, that is the actual cause of our gratification in a thought [by] which [we] basically present nothing.[2]

Kant is not the only one with theories about what makes something funny.

A 1990 issue of *The Realist* carries a report of a conference on popular culture at which a paper was given titled "The Illusion of Ontotheological Reality in the Three Stooges." They go on to say that none of the Three Stooges

---

[2] Immanuel Kant, *Kritik der Urteilskraft*, §54. Translated as *Critique of Judgement* by Werner S. Pluhar (Indianapolis: Hackett, 1987).

graduated from high school; but that Moe's daughter, who spoke at the conference, reported that her father frequently expressed his concern about the ensemble's ability to create the illusion of ontotheological reality.[3]

(No, I don't know what "ontotheological reality" means either.)

Not Funny

Here's a Jewish joke, in the form of a riddle.

Q: Who are the three cowboys in Adon Olam?
A: Billy Reysheet, Billy Tachleet, and Kid Ruchi.

Ha ha! Cowboys! Get it? Neither did I. I picked this joke precisely because in order to get it you'd have to have some fairly specialized knowledge. You'd need to be familiar with the Jewish hymn "Adon Olam." The Hebrew words of the hymn mean

Master of the World who was king,
before any form was created.
At the time when He made all through His will,
then His name was called 'King.'
And after all is gone,
He, the Awesome One, will reign alone.
And He was, and He is,
and He will be in splendor …

and so on—nothing whatever to do with cowboys. The joke depends on the fact that the Hebrew words include these phrases:

be-li rei-shit
be-li tach-lit
kid ru-chi

which more or less sound like names in English beginning with "Billy" or "Kid," which are imagined to be cowboy names. So the joke depends on puns on those Hebrew phrases, together, I expect, with the massive incongruity of associating cowboys with the text of this hymn.

Whew! There's the whole explanation! Now do you think the joke is funny?

No.

---

[3] "Pop Goes the Culture!" by Robert Myers, pp. 5–6.

Neither do I. I suspect that the joke is not exactly fabulously hilarious anyway, even to people who know all about the Hebrew hymn. But whatever small humour is in it is certainly killed when it's given a tedious explanation after having been told.

So two facts about the humour of jokes have been illustrated here: (1) Getting some jokes depends on the hearer's having background knowledge. (2) Providing the background knowledge after telling the joke does not convert it into something funny.

In his wonderful book *Jokes: Philosophical thoughts on Joking Matters*,[4] Ted Cohen argues that a major function of humour is to establish a communal bond between the teller and the tellee: they both have the specialized background knowledge already.

A Joke for Babies

Notwithstanding all this, it's clear that there is humour that doesn't depend on specialized background knowledge. Consider the case of Anna's giggles. Anna Martin, my new granddaughter, is, of course, exceedingly intelligent and precocious, but for the first few months of her life, her specialized knowledge of things wasn't exactly encyclopedic. Were she able to talk then, she would need only two words to express her reactions to the external world: "Huh??" and "Food!!" But at ten weeks, she started laughing at things. The joke most reliably able to crack her up was when her mother opened her eyes wide and made kissy noises. (Just try to explain to me what's funny about *that*.)

The incredibly early arrival—before almost every other complicated capacity—of a sense of humour in babies appears to show just how basic it is to us humans.

The Koestler/Pinker Theory of Jokes

The best account of The Funny I've seen is due to the writer Arthur Koestler, as reported and refined by the psychologist Steven Pinker.[5] According to the Koestler/Pinker theory, there are three ingredients of humour: *anomaly*, *resolution*, and *indignity*. The anomaly is a matter of bumping one train of thought against an event or statement that makes

---

4   Chicago: University of Chicago Press, 1999.
5   Arthur Koestler, *The Act of Creation* (New York: Dell, 1964). Stephen Pinker, *How the Mind Works* (New York: W. W. Norton, 1997), pp. 545–554.

no sense in the context of what came before. The resolution of this anomaly occurs when one shifts to a different frame of reference in which this does make sense. And within that new frame, someone's dignity has been downgraded. Here's one of Pinker's examples:

> Lady Astor said to Winston Churchill, "If you were my husband, I'd put poison in your tea." He replied, "If you were my wife, I'd drink it."

Pinker's analysis, in terms of the three ingredients:

> The response is anomalous in the frame of reference of murder, because people resist being murdered. The anomaly is resolved by switching to the frame of reference of suicide, in which death is welcomed as an escape from misery. In that frame Lady Astor is the cause of marital misery, an ignominious role.[6]

Maybe the elements of anomaly and resolution are something like what Kant had in mind when he said that laughter arises when "a tense expectation is transformed into nothing." Even if all humour is the result of a surprising shift of frame, it's pretty clear that not every surprising shift of frame is funny. In the Greek tragedy, this sort of shift occurs when Oedipus discovers that a man he killed long ago was actually his father, and that the woman he's now married to is actually his mother. Oedipus does not collapse in giggles as a result. Nobody finds this play a laff-riot.

There is some agreement among those who have thought about humour that it characteristically inflicts an indignity. Aristotle wrote, "Wit is educated insolence."[7] The seventeenth-century philosopher Thomas Hobbes thought that whenever we joke we affirm our supposed superiority to others by making fun of them. George Orwell quipped, "The aim of a joke is not to degrade the human being but to remind him that he is already degraded."[8]

Something like a confirmation of this view is provided by recent trends. Nowadays there is, in many contexts, zero tolerance of anything that offends, or might offend, anybody, and this has meant a spectacular decline in telling jokes.

> Q: How many feminists does it take to change a lightbulb?
> A: That isn't funny.

---

[6] Pinker, p. 550.
[7] *Rhetoric* II.
[8] Quoted in Byrne, p. 166.

SOME QUESTIONS TO THINK ABOUT: The Koestler/Pinker account seems to work pretty well for the Churchill joke; how well does it account for other jokes? Test these ideas on your favourite jokes. No doubt some of them degrade, but do they all?

Whatever your theory of The Funny, the questions remain: Why do we joke? Why do we enjoy humour? What is humour for? Pinker has some interesting ideas about this that appear to be related to Cohen's claim that humour establishes a bond. Pinker thinks that it functions to defuse aggression and status hierarchies, and thus to establish friendly relations.

Pinker's and Cohen's books, by the way, are noteworthy exceptions to the rule that theorists of humour write ponderous books with nothing funny in them at all. Both books are full of giggles.

2. WHAT'S SO GOOD ABOUT ART?

I Loved That Movie! I Cried the Whole Time!

The theory of humour is tucked into a corner of that branch of philosophy called philosophical aesthetics. A more major concern of philosophical aesthetics is explaining why we like to experience art.

The experience of art is really quite peculiar. Some art is quite grotesque, brutal, ugly, or disturbing. Nevertheless people *want* to experience it—they *enjoy* it. How can that be? People who watch horror movies sometimes have intense feelings of terror. Other movies are effectively designed to reduce the whole audience to uncontrollable tears. Terror and sadness are not the sorts of emotions most of us enjoy. We'd go out of our way to avoid them. But we pay to have these emotions created by art. What's going on here?

One suggestion that has been made is that the sort of terror we feel at a horror movie isn't *real* terror. It's just in some ways similar to real terror. Similarly, the revulsion we feel at some particularly bloody movie scene isn't the same feeling as we'd get if we came across a real and horrible automobile accident.

SOME QUESTION TO THINK ABOUT: Do you enjoy movie-terror and movie-sadness? Why? Are these the same as real terror and sadness? If so, then why does anyone enjoy them? If not, then what's the difference?

How Do You Like Them Apples?

The central question in philosophical aesthetics are, of course: What makes something a work of art? and What makes something a *good* work of art?

(Sometimes these are taken to be the same question. When you say, "Now, that's *art!*" you probably mean, "Now that's a *good* work of art!")

A good work of art is one that's beautiful. Right?

Well, maybe not. Read some book or movie reviews; look at what's written by critics of music or architecture; listen (if you can bear to) to what those pompous and mannered people say to one another in art galleries. 'Beauty' is a word that's almost never used. (Does that mean that beauty is irrelevant to the worth of a work of art?)

In any case, this answer isn't very helpful because it immediately raises a second question: What makes something beautiful? It seems that this depends on the kind of thing you're talking about. For some kinds of things, the answer is fairly clear. Suppose, for example, that you are presented with a bushel of apples, and you're asked to sort out the most beautiful ones (just to look at, not to eat). What characteristics do you look for? The large and symmetrical ones are probably more beautiful than the small and lumpy ones. Bright colour and shine are probably also plusses. The ones that contain rotten bits or worm holes are out. A nice curved stem, perhaps with a single perfect leaf attached, helps.

A QUESTION TO THINK ABOUT: Okay, fine, but what characteristics make for a beautiful painting? Are there any characteristics that in general make for beauty in painting? Or—even less likely—that make for beauty in art in general?

> The Human Faux Pas Performance Art Collective is a Van-couver-based company of avant-garde artists. One of their performances consists of unintelligible happenings inside a huge inflated plastic cube. A poster for this event includes this review by David Wisdom of the CBC: "Whatever this is, it doesn't get any better." This is a good joke. "It doesn't get any better" means "it's the best of that sort of thing," but Wisdom indicates he hasn't any idea what sort of thing it is. And the suggestion above was that all evaluation of any particular thing has to be evaluation of it *as* a certain kind of thing.

But there are even problems with apples: you and I might sort the same bushel quite differently. You might put the ones that are uniformly red into the "most beautiful" pile, while I might want to put the ones that have some green parts on that pile. Who is right? Is *either* of us right?

> We're tempted to say that there is no "correct" way to sort the apples—it depends on who is doing the sorting. You like the looks of the uniformly red ones, I like the two-toned ones, and that's all there is to say about it. Maybe we could even find someone who makes her "most beautiful" pile out of the small, dull-coloured, wormy, bruised ones. She just likes the way they look. Maybe beauty—even in apples—is only in the eye of the beholder.

But maybe not. People who put together those expensive fruit baskets for sale as gifts pick the most beautiful apples for their baskets—they're the pros at apple aesthetics. Other pros work in apple packing houses, grading the apples, partly on the basis of aesthetics, for sale in different categories, at different prices; the more expensive ones are the more beautiful ones. These pros have know-how we ordinary apple-eaters don't. They have trained apple-perceptions. So perhaps you should trust them to pick the ones that are genuinely beautiful, even if you can't see it.

On the other hand, maybe all they're doing is sorting out the apples that will appeal to most people. Maybe their expertise is not in recognizing genuine apple beauty: maybe it's just in recognizing which apples they can sell at the highest prices. They're pros in apple marketing, not in apple aesthetics.

A QUESTION TO THINK ABOUT: So does it really come down to just a matter of what you like, after all?

We've had some troubles deciding about the "objectivity" of judgement about the beauty of apples, and the same sort of considerations seem to transfer, more or less, to questions about the "objectivity" of judgement about art. It's sometimes thought that in art, too, it really does come down to just a matter of what you like.

Yummie Yummie?

Here's another problem. Apple-critics look for characteristics that will appeal most to most people. But art critics don't. Merely in terms of general appeal, Beethoven's relatively obscure Second Symphony is beaten hands down by "Yummie Yummie Yummie (I've Got Love in My Tummy)," though you couldn't find a single music critic who thinks that "Yummie" is better than Beethoven's Second. For every person who really enjoys looking at Vermeer paintings, you might easily find several thousand who much prefer toreadors painted on black velvet.

Next time you're in an art museum or at a symphony concert, concentrate on the audience rather than on the art. Are they enjoying themselves, or are they suffering through a boring experience they think they ought to like but don't? Some people do show signs of enjoyment, but it could be that many of them have been brainwashed into thinking that there's something wonderful there.

If you think that that Beethoven really, *objectively* beats "Yummie," just try convincing someone who disagrees. You might be able to bully or shame them into admitting you're right, or even into pretending to prefer Beethoven, but it's not at all obvious that there are rational considerations to be brought to bear to convince someone genuinely.

Bach Fights Crime

A newspaper article reports that a street-corner in West Palm Beach was a favourite hangout for loiterers, sometimes as many as two hundred at a time, many of them up to no good: the immediate area was notorious for drug deals, shootings, and thefts. Police mounted a set of speakers on an abandoned building on the corner, and started playing Bach, Mozart, and Beethoven twenty-four hours a day. The result was an enormous decrease in loiterers and a big decrease in neighbourhood crime.[9]

What's relevant to us is just how much those people react to "good" music. It's not merely that they prefer other kinds. It's that they'd move their normal activities elsewhere just to avoid hearing it.

I suspect it's not just drug dealers, murderers, and thieves who feel this way. I suspect that the majority of people are similarly repelled by "good" music.

SOME QUESTIONS TO THINK ABOUT: If the majority of people really hate this kind of music, how can it be "good"? I'm not suggesting it isn't good: in fact, this music ranks among the most important things in my life. I'm asking what makes my view correct, and the majority view wrong.

One answer you might consider is that what makes music good has nothing to do with whether anyone enjoys it, but is a matter of the objective properties of the music itself. This would make the goodness of a

---

[9] "Classical music keeps criminals away from Florida street corner," *[Toronto] Globe and Mail*, July 9, 2001, p. A7.

piece of music a completely "objective" property, like the weight of a rock. The fact that Rock A weighs more than Rock B has absolutely nothing to do with Rock A's feeling heavier to anyone. It would still weigh more even if it (for some reason) felt lighter to everyone, or if nobody ever picked it up—even if there were no humans at all. But could we imagine that one piece of Music Composition C might be better than Music Composition D, even if everyone preferred to listen to D, or if nobody ever heard them, or if there weren't any humans at all?

If the idea that the value of a piece of music is a completely objective matter of this sort doesn't seem right to you, then are we stuck with the notion that the preference of the majority is the only test for its value? Or is there another possibility?

How to Write Bad Tunes

Musical creation, like artistic creation in general, seems to be a mystery to us. We talk about inspiration—a magical facility the musician has of creating something out of nothing. How is it done? Nobody can say, right?

> Music is a difficult subject—anybody's music.... Its creation is a mystery. There are mathematical principles to guide its construction, but no mere knowledge of these can produce the emotional eloquence some music attains. We are made sad or happy, romantic, thoughtful, disturbed or peaceful by someone else's singing heart. To me this is a most exciting and inexplicable phenomenon. I should hate to be a music critic with the task of telling people what is good or bad in a musical composition or what are its component elements. One might as well try to explain to a group of children at the seaside the chemistry of salt water and sand, and the source of the sunlight or the breeze that romps with them along the shore.... What music can sometimes do to us is quite beyond the ken and lingo of academicians. – Oscar Hammerstein II[10]

Well, not *quite* beyond. Textbooks on composition technique give some very good rules for making a good melody. Here are some of them:

- Nearly all notes in the melody are to be chosen from the seven-note scale upon which the melody is based. When any of the remaining five chromatic notes are used, they generally should

---

[10] Foreword in *Rodgers and Hart Song Book* by Richard Rogers and Lorenz Hart (New York: Simon and Schuster, 1951).

appear in positions that are unaccented and unemphasized so as not to undermine the prevailing harmony.

- Most of a melody's notes should be adjacent scale notes. Jumps should be few, and large jumps rare.
- To avoid monotony, individual notes should not be repeated too much, particularly at emphasized positions in a melody.
- A melody should have only one instance of its highest tone, and preferably also of its lowest tone.
- Jumps should always land on one of the seven scale tones, not on one of the five chromatic tones.

Of course, this list is not a recipe for writing good tunes—you can write ones following these rules and the other rules found in composition textbooks and still come out with a bad one. And there are a few tunes that everyone thinks are good that violate a rule or two on these lists. But nevertheless, these rules are very good ones. Studies of hundreds of actual successful melodies have confirmed the validity of the list of generally accepted rules for composition that the ones I've given above are taken from. Think of some of your favourite tunes and note how they follow the rules I've given. Melodies that break some of these rules are likely to be awkward or ugly.

A QUESTION TO THINK ABOUT: Okay, so there are rules for distinguishing good and bad tunes. But we surely don't consciously *use* these rules for evaluating a tune For example, when you judge (as almost everyone does) that the Beatles' song "Eleanor Rigby" has a great melody, you surely don't reason to yourself that there's only one instance of its highest tone (on the word 'do' in "where do they all come from?"). Does this show that these "rules" for judging good tunes aren't really the ones we use? In fact, you don't apply any rules when you hear and judge that song. You just hear it and react, "Wow, what a great song!" and that's all there is to it. Does this show that there aren't any rules at all?

> This set of rules describes remarkably well what tunes we judge bad and good. So it seems to follow that, in some sense, our brain is subconsciously applying these rules in making its judgements, even though we're not aware of them.

FOR FURTHER READING: The list of rules for good tunes is taken from a longer one in *Music, the Brain, and Ecstasy: How Music Cap-*

tures Our Imagination by Robert Jourdain (New York: Avon, 1998), pp. 85–86. Jourdain's book is full of interesting information and speculation about how and why music works.

Random Creativity

Well, okay, let's admit that these rules, subconsciously applied, are an important part of our judgements that a tune is a good one or a bad one. When someone can apply these rules (consciously or subconsciously) they can evaluate tunes they hear. But this leaves out a really important feature of art: the *creation* of these tunes in the first place.

The creation of a work of art seems not to be something rule-governed at all.

> "There are three rules for writing a novel. Unfortunately, no one knows what they are."—W. Somerset Maugham

> "Writing is easy. All you do is stare at a blank sheet of paper until drops of blood form on your forehead."—Gene Fowler[11]

Maybe we got a hint about what creativity involves when we looked at RACTER, the "creative" computer, back in Chapter XII in the section called **Artificial Insanity.**

In 1984, William Chamberlain, the co-author of RACTER, published a book called *The Policeman's Beard is Half Constructed.*[12] Here's an excerpt:

> At all events my own essays and dissertations about love and its endless pain and perpetual pleasure will be known and understood by all of you who read this and talk or sing or chant about it to your worried friends or nervous enemies. Love is the question and the subject of this essay. We will commence with a question: does steak love lettuce? This question is implacably hard and inevitably difficult to answer. Here is a question: does an electron love a proton, or does it love a neutron? Here is a question: does a man love a woman or, to be specific and to be precise, does Bill love Diane? The interesting and critical response to this question is: no! He is obsessed and infatuated with her.

---

[11] Both quotes given by Byrne, p. 368, 46.
[12] New York: Warner Books.

He is loony and crazy about her. That is not the love of steak and lettuce, of electron and proton and neutron. This dissertation will show that the love of a man and a woman is not the love of steak and lettuce. Love is interesting to me and fascinating to you but it is painful to Bill and Diane. That is love!

The introduction claims: "With the exception of this introduction, the writing in this book was all done by computer," but it's clear that a lot of modification of RACTER's databases was necessary to produce the text of this book, and that some of the wackiness in the book is the result of deliberate wackiness in the databases that the author constructed and fed to RACTER. In any case, a substantial portion of the creativity we see in the product is the result of RACTER's random processes: things are strung together by processes that keep things more or less grammatical, and at least slightly relevant, but with wild leaps of sense.

Compare RACTER's output with this passage, written by the man often considered the father of post-modern prose, Donald Barthelme:

Thinking of my friend Max who looks like white bread. A brisk bout with my head in a wire cage. The Slash Waltz from "The Mark of Zorro." And in the shower a ten for Max, because his were the best two out of three. He put it in his lacy shoe. With his watch and his application to the Colorado School of Mines.[13]

There's a strong resemblance in these two products, though at first glance, the processes of construction used by the two authors seem quite different. Bartheleme considered each word very carefully and chose the one he judged exactly right for his purposes, while RACTER's choices were essentially random and senseless (though governed by certain rules that kept it from churning out total nonsense).

Bartheleme's aims in choosing his words obviously include the avoidance of good clear literal sense, and the production of a strongly randomized surprising product (which, however, makes *near*-sense). How does he do this? We might imagine that he has somehow trained his imagination to spew out completely random strings of ideas, and that from them he discards the small number that make good sense and the large number of equally unacceptable ones that make no sense at all. It's the randomness of the initial production that results in the surprising creativity.

---

13 "Can We Talk," originally published in *The New Yorker*, reprinted in a collection of Barthelme's pieces called *Unspeakable Practices, Unnatural Acts* (New York: Bantam Books, 1969), p. 101. You can find a lot of Bartheleme on the Web; try http://www.eskimo.com/~jessamyn/barth/.

Maybe this also explains how people create good tunes: they have some sort of randomizing ability in their brains that makes a huge number of tunes—bad ones and good ones—just pop into their heads. *Then* they apply the rules for what makes a good tune and what makes a bad one, and they throw away all the bad ones.

But this couldn't be exactly the way creativity works, because there are far too many random nonsense sentences (or bad melodies) to sort through in order to find just one funny near-sense sentence (or one good tune). Anyone who worked that way would be deluged with a steady stream of useless textual or musical nonsense ages before a good bit showed up.

To see this, consider that a random string of notes would be extremely unlikely to satisfy all those rules for good tunes listed above, and there are, as I said, several more rules to be added to this list. A shareware random-music-generating program is available from

http://www.hitsquad.com/smm/programs/Aleatoric_Composer/

You can generate tunes till the cows come home and never get one that's anywhere near good. Mere random generation followed by systematic culling couldn't be how good tunes are created.

In the search for new forms of music, some avant-garde composers have turned to randomness. It's clear, of course, that the object here is not to create good tunes, and nobody pretends that there's much of an audience for this kind of music. John Cage was a leading practitioner of this musical form, sometimes called *aleatoric music* ('*alea*' means "dice game" in Latin). One of his better known compositions, *Imaginary Landscape no.4* (1951), is written for twelve radios and twenty-four performers who twiddle the tuning and volume dials of the radios according to minutely detailed instructions in the score, but what the audience hears is whatever happens to be broadcast at that point on the dial—if anything—at the time. Here, for your amusement, is an account of a performance of *Europera*, an opera by Cage:

> It consists of a random assortment of sixteen-bar swaths taken from older, out-of-copyright operas. Exits, entrances, all aspects of the composition have been determined by chance throws of the sacred I Ching [an ancient Chinese method of divination involving flipping coins or dividing up plant stalks]. As one diva arrives on stage by jeep, another leaves in the belly of a giant fish. Arias are sung from inside bathtubs, coffins, garbage pails. One enterprising singer wields a fishing pole at the front of the stage, hoisting her catch from the orchestra pit. This goes un-

noticed by the players, who sit on a hydraulic platform that rises and falls unpredictably. In fact, most of the scenery is continuously shifting in and out, up and down. Lest the audience doze off, at the denouement a zeppelin is launched above the stalls.[14]

"I have nothing to say and I'm saying it." —John Cage

Portrait of the Artist as an Unintelligible Young Man

Here's a small sample of the kind of thing you'll find in hundreds of pages of James Joyce's famous book *Ulysses*:

heave under embon *senorita* young eyes Mulvey plump years dreams return

Joyce's writing isn't random; it's extremely carefully calculated. The problem is that what it's meant to communicate is so obscure that a minor army of English literature professors has been attempting to decode it, bit by bit, ever since it was published in 1922. For all that passages like the one quoted mean to the average reader, it might as well be random. Yet everyone agrees that *Ulysses* is among the greatest literary works of the twentieth century.

It turns out, by the way, that the original edition of *Ulysses* had thousands of errors in it, the result of its meaninglessness to typesetters and Joyce's failing eyesight and faulty memory. The passage above omitted ten words from Joyce's original. The 1986 edition, which made about five thousand corrections, substitutes

heave under embon *senorita* young eyes Mulvey plump bubs me breadvan Winkle red slippers she rusty sleep wander years of dreams return

Isn't that better?

My newspaper reports a performance by Berlin artist Wolfgang Flatz. While he hung naked from a crane accompanied by recorded music and mooing, a dead cow stuffed with fireworks was dropped ninety metres from a helicopter, exploding on impact with the ground. A thirteen-year-old animal lover, determined to stop Flatz's performances, took him to court, arguing that she would suffer a "spiritual shock" if she saw the dropping exploding cow. I liked this story because it combined two familiar features of our age: the absurd artwork and the absurd lawsuit. I also enjoyed the neatness and clarity of the outcome of the law-

---

[14] Jourdain, pp. 236–237.

suit: the court rejected the animal lover's plea, saying she
did not have to watch.[15]

The "Mona Lisa" by Schmidlap

Lots of people have reproductions of famous paintings hanging on their
walls, presumably because they like the painting, and the original isn't
for sale, and even if it were, it would cost millions of dollars. There's
nothing wrong with getting a reproduction: they're affordable and nice;
they give pleasure. But when you see the original, you realise just how
much you're missing in the reproduction. Even the most expensive reproductions, made using a great deal of care and advanced technology,
are clearly distinguishable from the originals, and nowhere near as good.

But now imagine that there's a company that can make a reproduction that looks exactly like the original—that even experts at looking at
paintings couldn't distinguish them when they're side-by-side. That would
be great, right?

It seems pretty clear, however, that rich art collectors and museums
would still want the original, and that visitors to the Louvre would feel
cheated if they found out that what they had been gazing at was merely a
perfect reproduction of the Mona Lisa, not the real thing. The reason is
that the real Mona Lisa was really painted by Leonardo, starting around
1505 or 1506 in Florence, and finishing several years later in Milan or
Rome. But the reproduction was made by the Acme Photoengraving Company in 1996 in Passaic, New Jersey.

What this shows is that the value of a painting to us is not entirely a
matter of how it looks. It's also a matter of the historical facts about that
object. We want to see the actual object Leonardo made—not something
that looks just like it. Similarly, in a history museum, we want to see (for
example) the actual bed George Washington slept on, and not a bed that
looks just like that one.

But someone might object that these historical facts about a painting
have nothing to do with the value of the painting *as art*. They give it
value as an antique, or as a historical artifact, or as something created by
a celebrity. This shouldn't have anything to do with our genuinely *aes-
thetic* appreciation of the thing. When we're talking art appreciation, it
shouldn't matter whether something was created by Leonardo in the early
1500s, or Schmidlap in the late 1900s, or by the accidental action of wet
fallen leaves on a canvas left outside last fall.

Is this right?

---

[15] "But is it art?" by Kim Honey, *[Toronto] Globe and Mail*, July 21, 2001, p. R1.

3. Philosophers on Food

Philosophers have had very little to say about food; but here are some of the exceptions:

- Plato complained, in his dialogue *Phaedo*, that food was a distraction from higher things. His *Symposium* features a banquet with a great deal of talk, but no food.
- Aristotle argued against the role of music in education, saying "If they must learn music, [then] on the same principle they should learn cookery, which is absurd."
- Schopenhauer approved of still-life painting unless it showed food. A depiction of fruit still on the vine was okay, because it could be contemplated by reason for its beauty. Depicted as food, however, it would act as a stimulus to appetite, which makes us prisoners of the object-enslaved will.
- Wittgenstein, according to his biographer Norman Malcolm, "did not care what he ate so long as it was always the same." When Malcolm's wife served Wittgenstein bread and cheese, he would exclaim, "Hot Ziggety!"[16]
- Sartre was philosophically annoyed by the body's regular cry for nutrition. He rarely ate fruit or vegetables unless they were mixed into something like pastry. Sausages, sauerkraut and chocolate cake were among his favourites. He did ingest vast quantities of other substances: two packs of strong cigarettes per day, and smoked a pipe constantly in between; many glasses of wine, beer, distilled alcohol, tea, and coffee; amphetamines and barbiturates. He was revulsed by seafood and one day, in a mescaline-induced trance, imagined himself being stalked by a lobster.
- David Hume was one of only two philosophers known to have been chefs (the other was Aristippus, the Hellenistic proponent of hedonism). Hume dedicated himself in later life to "display my great Talent for Cookery." The historian Edward Gibbon referred to Hume as "the fattest of Epicurus's hogs."

FOR FURTHER READING: Ray Boisvert, who reported most of the above material on the food attitudes of philosophers, thinks they are not trivial, irrelevant sidebars. He links antipathy to good food to the philo-

---

16 Norman Malcolm, *Ludwig Wittgenstein: A Memoir* (Oxford, Oxford University Press, 1984), p. 69.

sophical "lie" that humans are isolated minds, not flesh and blood, and advocates instead a "stomach-affirming" philosophy. You can read his views in *Philosophy Now* magazine, Issue 31 (March/April 2001).

4. INTO THE MAINSTREAM OF PHILOSOPHY

Philosophical aesthetics studies some difficult questions. One thing philosophers try to do here is to explain what art is. When you stop to think about it, art seems like quite a peculiar thing. People spend a great deal of effort dabbing pigments on canvas, or arranging a series of noises. What are they doing *that* for? Imagine yourself trying to explain art to an uncomprehending Martian.

Both philosophical aesthetics and ethics can be included in one field: value theory. In aesthetics we face the same sort of problems as we do in ethics. Are there any sorts of general principles that summarize why we value certain sorts of things? Is their value an objective matter, or does it exist only in the eye of the beholder?

CHAPTER XVIII

DEEP THOUGHTS

"Why, back where I come from there are people who sit around all day and do nothing but think deep thoughts. They're called phila... philo... uh, deep-thought-thinkers — and with no more brains than you. But they do have something you don't have — a diploma." — *The Wizard of Oz*

Calvin: "Bugs fly in such crazy loops and zigzags. I wonder why they don't get dizzy and barf."
Hobbes: "Maybe they do."
Calvin: "Eww, gross! Ha ha ha! But then why would they keep flying that way?"
Hobbes: "Maybe bugs *like* to barf!"
Calvin: "EWWWW! They WOULD! Ha ha ha ha! BLAUGH!"
Calvin: "I tell you, Hobbes, it's great to have a friend who appreciates an earnest discussion of ideas." — Calvin and Hobbes comic strip, July 15, 1992

Wisdom

Maybe this book hasn't given you what you expected from philosophy. Perhaps you have been wondering why there are so many quite particularized problems in this book, and so little in the way of the generalized "wisdom" people expect to get from philosophy. I have talked about a great number of philosophical positions, but almost none of them are advice about how to live your life. You might find it surprising that so little of philosophy is concerned with "philosophy of life." When philosophers try to give this sort of advice, they don't do much better than anyone else. In fact, some philosophers who have discussed other problems brilliantly say some quite peculiar things when they try to give practical advice on how to live. Two rather strange examples of this are the ancient philosopher Pythagoras of Samos and the seventeenth-century Irish clergyman-philosopher George Berkeley.

Yes, Pythagoras (c.560–c.480 BC) is the man associated with the theorem that gave you such a headache back in high-school geometry. But he was also apparently responsible for a religious order whose tenets included the prohibitions on looking into a mirror beside a light, touching a white rooster, and eating beans. It's supposed that the problem Pythagoras found with beans derived from the Egyptian view that beans contained the souls of dead people. It's said that while fleeing for his life, Pythagoras ran up to a field of beans, and declared that he'd rather die than step on any of the plants. His pursuers obliged him.

George Berkeley (1685–1753) also has a name familiar to non-philosophers: the city in California was in fact named after him. He was a hugely important figure in the development of British empiricism, but in later life he devoted a significant part of his writing to the virtues of tar-water.[1] This stuff is made by stirring tar with water, and letting the solids settle out. Berkeley wrote at length extolling its properties as a medicine capable of curing every ailment, recommending it especially for "seafaring persons, ladies, and men of studious and sedentary lives."

Cheer

One time when I was feeling grumpy and annoyed about something, my wife asked me, "Why can't you take a philosophical attitude toward it? You're a philosopher, after all." I told her that, unfortunately, the sort of philosophy we do over there at the university's philosophy factory has almost nothing to do with what's called a "philosophical attitude" of good cheer in the face of adversity, or at least of resignation. If anything, philosophy seems to accentuate the negative. Finding out about something doesn't necessarily make you jollier.

> "Anyone who is cheerful hasn't heard the bad news."—Bertold Brecht

> "I have a new philosophy. I'm only going to dread one day at a time."—Charles Shulz, "Peanuts" comic strip

My dictionary gives this definition of one sense of 'philosophical': "Characteristic of a philosopher; wise; calm; temperate; frugal." But almost no philosophers I know show those characteristics to a large extent, and many of them are just the reverse.

So if philosophy is unlikely to make you more wise or more cheerful, then what good is it?

---

[1] *Siris: A Chain of Philosophical Reflexions and Inquiries Concerning the Virtues of Tar-water, and Divers Other Subjects Connected Together and Arising One From Another*, rev. ed. (Dublin: R. Gunne, 1744).

Doubt

Philosophy has many more questions than answers, and you'll have noticed that this is true of this book as well. Puzzle books often contain, at the end, a section of answers, but you won't find that sort of section in here. That's not because there are no answers. In many cases, philosophers have found what they take to be answers to these questions; and in some cases I have hinted at what these answers are, or at least at the way one might begin thinking to arrive at them. To understand these answers, however, you must go a good deal farther and deeper than we have. That's what the serious study of philosophy is for.

"It is easy to build a philosophy. It doesn't have to run." Thus spake Charles Kettering (1876–1958), U.S. engineer, the inventor of the electric starter and the electric ignition system for cars, and the electric cash register. I guess that what he meant is that in philosophy you can say any old thing you want, without worrying about whether it works or not. Well, that just goes to show you that if you want to find out about something about Subject X you don't ask an expert in Subject Y. After all, you wouldn't want to ask me about how electric cash registers work. I think that you may have discovered, while reading this book, that there are some real questions in philosophy (though many of them have little or no practical upshot), and that there's a difference between a right and a wrong answer to a philosophical question.

In many cases, however, there is no general agreement, and a lot of controversy, about what the answers are. Unanswered questions are what makes philosophy interesting and fun.

> "It is better to know some of the questions than all of the answers." — James Thurber

The first job of philosophy is to question what other people take as given. Philosophy is the doubting profession.

> "The whole problem with the world is that fools and fanatics are always so certain of themselves, and wiser people so full of doubts." — Bertrand Russell

> "I am plagued by doubts. What if everything is an illusion and nothing exists? In that case, I definitely overpaid for my carpet." — Woody Allen[2]

---

[2] *Without Feathers.*

DISCLAIMER

No animals were injured in the creating of this book. Void where prohibited by law. All rights reserved. Your mileage may vary. Available while quantities last. Used with permission. Information was current at time of printing. Abandon hope all ye who enter here. For information purposes only. Any resemblance to real persons, living or dead, is purely coincidental. Author does not carry cash. Limitations on coverage and remedies apply. Formatted to fit your screen. Please remain seated until the book has come to a complete stop. All names listed are proprietary trademarks of their respective corporations. Use only as directed. No purchase necessary. Must be over 18. Avoid contact with skin. May be too intense for some viewers. Some restrictions may apply. Not affiliated with the American Red Cross. Not responsible for direct, indirect, incidental, or consequential damages resulting from any defect, error, or failure to perform. This is not an offer to sell securities. Views expressed may not be those of the publisher. No other warranty expressed or implied. Contains a substantial amount of non-tobacco ingredients. Inspired by a true story. Not responsible for typographical errors. Specifications subject to change without notice. Prerecorded for this time zone. All models over 18 years of age.